Ottoman Land Reform in the Province of Baghdad

The Ottoman Empire and Its Heritage

POLITICS, SOCIETY AND ECONOMY

VOLUME 66

The titles published in this series are listed at *brill.com/oeh*

Ottoman Land Reform in the Province of Baghdad

By

Keiko Kiyotaki

BRILL

LEIDEN | BOSTON

Cover illustration: Kerim, A. (1923). *Where the Dates Are Packed for Export.* Courtesy of Special Collections, Fine Arts Library, Harvard University.

Library of Congress Cataloging-in-Publication Data

Names: Kiyotaki, Keiko, editor.
Title: Ottoman land reform in the province of Baghdad / by Keiko Kiyotaki.
Description: Leiden ; Boston : Brill, [2019] | Series: The Ottoman Empire and its heritage : politics, society and economy, ISSN 1380-6076 ; volume 66 | Includes bibliographical references and index.
Identifiers: LCCN 2019006191 (print) | LCCN 2019011674 (ebook) | ISBN 9789004384347 (E-book) | ISBN 9789004366596 (hardback : alk. paper)
Subjects: LCSH: Land reform—Iraq—Baghdad (Province)—History. | Taxes, Farming of—Iraq—Baghdad (Province)—History. | Land tenure—Iraq—Baghdad (Province)—History. | Iraq—History—1534–1921. | Turkey—History—Ottoman Empire, 1288–1918. | Baghdad (Iraq : Province)—Relations—Turkey. | Turkey—Relations—Iraq—Baghdad (Province)
Classification: LCC HD1333.I7 (ebook) | LCC HD1333.I7 .K59 2019 (print) | DDC 333.3/156747—dc23
LC record available at https://lccn.loc.gov/2019006191

Typeface for the Latin, Greek, and Cyrillic scripts: "Brill". See and download: brill.com/brill-typeface.

ISSN 1380-6076
ISBN 978-90-04-36659-6 (hardback)
ISBN 978-90-04-38434-7 (e-book)

This book is printed on acid-free paper and produced in a sustainable manner.

Printed by Printforce, the Netherlands

Dedicated to
the Memory of
Professor Kemal H. Karpat
(1923–2019)
My teacher and advisor

Contents

Acknowledgements

My interest in Ottoman Iraqi history was aroused when Professor Kemal H. Karpat, in his seminar class in 1989, assigned me to present "The Ottoman Land Code of 1858 and Its Impacts on Anatolia, Syria, and Iraq." It was challenging, but he encouraged me by saying that the land problem is the fundamental issue to understand the history of Middle Eastern countries. While working on this paper, I came across the works of Doreen Warriner, Saleh Haider, and Albertine Jwaideh, and came to know the worth of Ottoman archival documents. Ever since, this topic has underlain my studies, whose result I presented in my Ph.D. dissertation. Later, when I gave him a part of the manuscript, he suggested the new title of "Ottoman Land Reform in the Province of Baghdad." Then, I extended this theme into modern Iraqi land problems, as Prof. Karpat advised in the beginning, including the issues of tax farming, Ottoman state finance, and land policies during the periods of Sultan Abdülhamid II, the Young Turks, and the British mandate. Fulfilling his assignment, I now appreciate Prof. Karpat and his advice with my sincere gratitude.

During my research at the Ottoman Archives (Başbakanlık Osmanlı Arşivi), I always occupied the desk behind where the late Professor Halil Sahillioğlu had been working. One day, I came across the survey report of governor Namık Pasha in 1866 on crop sharing and *uqr* in the province of Baghdad. I rushed to Prof. Sahillioğlu, asking the meaning of this survey and *uqr*. Examining the document carefully, he told me, "Keiko, this is a very important document. Work hard on it!" It took a year for me to read the survey report, but by the end, I realized its real value. Prof. Sahillioğlu always encouraged and supported me at the archives. I still keep on my desk the signed reprint of his article, "Osmanlı Döneminde Irak'ın İdarî Taksimatı," that he gave me. I regretfully did not have an opportunity to thank him properly, but I can now finally show him the outcome of my study.

Through the process of publication, Professor Suraiya Faroqhi helped me to improve my introduction. I thank her and other referees on their valuable comments. I also extend my thanks to Dr Deniz Balgamiş, Ms Paula Benkart, Mr Daniel Sentance for his excellent copy-editing, and particularly, Ms Franca de Kort of Brill who encouraged and patiently waited for my slow progress.

This book could not have been accomplished without research at the Ottoman Archives. I am grateful to the staff for research permit and assistance.

Finally, I would like to thank my husband and teacher in economics, Nobuhiro Kiyotaki, for his comments while advising his own students.

Illustrations

Figures

Maps

Tables

Introduction

In 1534, Sultan Süleyman the Magnificent conquered Baghdad (*Bağdat*) from the Safavids. After a short second period of Safavid rule, lasting from 1623 to 1638, Sultan Murad IV (1623–40) reconquered the province. Thereafter, Baghdad remained in Ottoman hands until the British occupation of 1914–18. Once the Peace of Amasya (1555), and the later Treaty of Zohab (1639), had determined the domains of the Ottoman and Safavid realms, the Ottoman central government regarded Baghdad as a border province, whose military corps (*ocak*) had considerable political flexibility and whose revenues served largely for defensive purposes. The central control of the government was, moreover, limited by difficulties of communication from the early 1600s. The Tigris River, on whose banks the city was located, was unsuitable for river transport because the level of water in the river was frequently too low for ships to navigate and spring flooding often hindered the passage of boats. The tribes living near the river imposed high tolls on the boats and attacked passing caravans, a situation that impeded trade with the central provinces and made even the transportation of state revenue risky. Although the rule of the sovereign was distracted by the distance and by the disobedient tribes, it did not impede the position of Baghdad, which remained a major province of the Ottomans under an empowered governor, regular army, and retained ruling organization.[1]

In terms of religious adherence, too, the province of Baghdad was a contested terrain. The Ottomans defined themselves as defenders of Sunni right belief vis-à-vis the Shiite Safavids, and therefore regarded the existence of a sizeable Shiite population in Iraq as a thorny political problem. The Shiite sites of pilgrimage, the graves of Imam Ali (*Imâm ʿAlî*) and his son Imam Husain b. Ali (*Imâm Hüseyin*) were located in Najaf and Karbala respectively, reaching from Baghdad on major roads through Hilla in the province. Respected also by the Sunnis, Karbala had become the major district town, ensuring public order and safety for the numerous pilgrims and preventing the propagation of endemic diseases.[2] In the late 1700s and early 1800s, moreover, Baghdad became the defensive front against the aggression of the Wahhabis. The

1 Stephen Hemsley Longrigg, *Four Centuries of Modern Iraq* (Oxford: Clarendon Press, 1925), pp. 21–95; Cengiz Orhonlu, "Dicle ve Fırat Nehirlerinde Nakliyat," in Orhonlu, *Osmanlı İmparatorluğunda Şehircilik ve Ulaşım Üzerine Araştırmalar*, ed. Salih Özbaran (Izmir: Ege Üniversitesi Edebiyat Fakültesi Yayınları, 1984), pp. 116–39.

2 Anja Pistor-Hatam, "Pilger, Pest und Cholera: Die Wallfahrt zu den Heiligen Stätten im Irak Als Gesundheitspolitisches Problem im 19. Jahrhundert," *Die Welt des Islams* 31, no. 2 (1991), 228–45.

 | DOI:10.1163/9789004384347_002

Wahhabis promoted their own brand of Sunni right belief, completely rejecting reverence for graves and the building of mausoleums, practices that had become traditional in the Ottoman world. This doctrinal stance justified the plundering of the mausoleums of Imam Ali and Imam Husain b. Ali, where devotees had deposited many precious gifts over the centuries.[3] For ten years, Baghdad suffered from swift raids and plundering, until in 1798 the governor in Baghdad and his janissaries, mercenaries, and artillery, accompanied by the Ugail, Ubaid, Shammar, and other tribes, finally drove them out. The Wahhabis returned to Basra in 1802, but they could never reach Karbala and retreated in 1810. Thus, among other issues, retaining control over the province of Baghdad involved defending sacred towns and handling the religious diversity and conflict that heavily burdened the provincial government.[4]

With respect to the neighbouring provinces, the districts of Sincar, Ana, Hit, Mosul, and Hadise became part of the Ottoman realm during the reign of Sultan Selim I (1512–20). As detailed above, Baghdad was conquered in 1534, by Sultan Süleyman the Magnificent (1520–66). In fact, between 1563 and 1574 (covering the late period of his reign and the reign of Sultan Selim II, 1566–74), four provinces, namely Shahrizor (Şehrizol), Baghdad, Basra, and Ahsa, were established in Iraq. During the war with Persia (1538–1618), the administration organized Mosul (*Musul*), Pelengân, and Mihrivân as a province, although Pelengân and Mihrivân were removed in the latter half of the sixteenth century. The treatises (*risâle*) of Ayn-i Ali Efendi (1609) and Sofyalı Ali Çavuş (1653) show that the region now had five provinces: Mosul, Shahrizor, Baghdad, Basra, and Ahsa. In 1670, Ahsa fell into the hands of the Bani Khalid tribe, thus ending Ottoman rule. In Baghdad, there were nineteen districts, seven of which were assigned as fiefs to military men (*timar* and *zeamet*). Otherwise, Baghdad and Basra were so-called *sâlyâne* provinces, in which the governor collected revenues for remittance to the Porte at predetermined sums.[5]

In administrative terms for most of the Ottoman period, Iraq (*Arâzi-i Irak*) consisted of the provinces of Baghdad, Basra, Mosul, and Shahrizor. Baghdad

---

3 Suraiya Faroqhi, *Pilgrims and Sultans: The Hajj under the Ottomans, 1517–1683* (London: I.B. Tauris, 1994), pp. 135–39.

4 Longrigg, *Four Centuries of Modern Iraq*, pp. 212–17, 229–31.

5 According to Ali Çavuş, in Mosul there were five districts, of which two were reserved for the expenses of military troops as *yurtluk* and *ocaklık* and three contained fiefs (490 *zeamet* and 2,000 *timar* including tribal *timar*). In Shahrizor, six districts were in the hands of fief-holders (500 *zeamet* and 3,000 *timar*), and thirteen districts financed bodies of troops, once again as *yurtluk* and *ocaklık*. In Baghdad, the administration assigned 980 fiefs, but the number of tribal *timars* amounted to about 4,500. Halil Sahillioğlu, “Osmanlı Döneminde Irak'ın İdarî Taksimatı,” *Belleten* 54, no. 211 (1990), pp. 1233–57.

was the largest province in size and population, containing many self-proclaimed autonomous domains, which the central government tolerated – a full-scale conquest would have been far too expensive. Tribal confederations apart, there were former fiefs (*timar* and *zeamet*) that had devolved into the properties of their holders. In addition, district governors, military commanders, and local magnates controlled significant estates, while certain tax farms had become inheritable properties, known as lifetime tax farms (*malikâne*).

On the provincial level, certain personages, often tax farmers or representatives of absentee governors, managed to raise themselves over the ordinary provincial notables by building households consisting of armed free and slave retainers, often manumitting the latter after a period of service. With this power behind them, these power-holders curtailed the role of the military corps that had played a central role in the Arab provinces during the 1600s. As observed in eighteenth-century Egypt, politically active households had come to dominate the scene, an empire-wide trend that happened in Baghdad. Such groups might even form around an officer residing in military barracks, put differently within a formally constituted *ocak*.[6] In 1704, Ottoman governor of Baghdad Hasan Pasha (*Paşa*) established a powerful household featuring large numbers of Georgian military slaves, known as *köle* or *kölemen*, perhaps following seventeenth-century Persian rulers, who had used slave soldiers from Georgia in an attempt to balance the power of the so-called Qizilbash, tribesmen who formed the core fighting force of the Safavids.[7]

In Baghdad, governors deriving their power from their households controlled the province until 1831, when Sultan Mahmud II (1808–39) overturned Davud Pasha (1817–31), the last personage with a sizeable *kölemen* household. As observed in other parts of the empire, violent repression accompanied the fall of the Baghdad *kölemen* regime and prominent families. Certain families held on to at least a fraction of their property, and some of their members and descendants staffed the higher echelons of the late Ottoman bureaucracy.[8] The challenge of the nineteenth century began with the proclamation of

6 Jane Hathaway, *The Politics of Households in Ottoman Egypt: The Rise of the Qazdağlıs* (Cambridge: Cambridge University Press, 1997), pp. 20–21.

7 Longrigg, *Four Centuries of Modern Iraq*, pp. 123–31; Andrew Newman, *Safavid Iran: Rebirth of a Persian Empire* (London: I.B. Tauris, 2006), pp. 52–53.

8 Governor Ali Rıza Pasha even married the daughter of another prominent figure of the pre-1831 regime. As for Davud Pasha, who continued to enjoy significant support in Baghdad, the Ottoman central administration, after a short period of banishment, re-employed him in the Balkans and Anatolia, where he served as governor of Bosnia and *mutasarrıf* of Ankara, before ending his life as the *şeyhülharem* in Medina. For the history of the *mamlûk* period in Baghdad, see Sâbit (Süleyman Fâik), *Bağdad'da Kölemen Hükûmetinin Teşekkül ile İnkırâzına dâir Risâledir* (Istanbul, 1292 AH [1875]); Longrigg, *Four Centuries of Modern Iraq*, pp. 163–276;

Tanzimat in 1839. In Baghdad, the Ottoman government put off its implementation until 1844. It brought in new objectives of improved communication, centralized province, and applicable arrangement for provincial administration. Increasing agricultural production and tax revenues gained some more importance than before for achieving the objectives, which this book aims to examine in detail.

1 The Challenge of the Ottoman Governors in Baghdad in the Nineteenth Century

After the reconquest of Baghdad by the Ottoman army in 1831, the officially appointed governor administered Baghdad as a revenue-bearing province, revitalizing agriculture, refurbishing the port of Basra for international trade, and safeguarding the outlet route to the Gulf. The Ottoman central government needed urgently to increase revenues for the modernization of the army and, later, for the construction of communication lines and the modernization of infrastructure and urban sanitation facilities.[9] The government was also heavily burdened by interest payments for domestic and international borrowing. The province of Baghdad, governed by the Ottoman governor, who concurrently served as the commander-in-chief of the Sixth Army, remitted a portion of state revenues to the Imperial Treasury besides financing the administrative and military expenditures in the province. These financial pressures drove the governor increasingly to integrate the province under the sultan's sovereignty and increase agricultural production and tax revenues.

However, reforms to improve agricultural output needed the cooperation and participation of the local people, especially the urban notables and tribal sheikhs. The Ottoman governors and their staff convinced the notables that the Tanzimat reforms were in their best interests and encouraged them to invest their capital in agriculture. Administrative reorganization and improved

---

Mehdi J.H. al-Bustani, "Bağdad'daki Kölemen Hâkimiyetinin Te'sisi ve Kaldırılması ile Ali Rıza Paşa'nın Vâliliği (1749–1842)," Ph.D. diss., Istanbul University, 1979, pp. 6–184; Thomas Lier, *Haushalte und Haushaltpolitik in Bagdad*, 1704–1831 (Würzburg: Ergon Verlag, 2004), pp. 119–213. Reintegrating former rebels in this fashion had been standard practice even in the years around 1600, when former commanders of rebellious mercenaries received high positions near the Ottoman-Habsburg frontier. Karen Barkey, *Bandits and Bureaucrats: The Ottoman Route to State Centralization* (Ithaca: Cornell University Press, 1994), pp. 24–48, 163–228.

9 Stanford J. Shaw and Ezel Kural Shaw, *History of the Ottoman Empire and Modern Turkey*, ii: *Reform, Revolution, and Republic: The Rise of Modern Turkey, 1808–1975* (Cambridge: Cambridge University Press, 1977), pp. 91–105.

infrastructure underlay the expansion of local markets and trade, which in turn stimulated people's interest in agriculture. The tribal sheikhs also began to benefit from this expanding commerce and trade, and so began to accept the governor's authority. In response, the governor incorporated the tribal sheikhs into the Ottoman government system as administrators and officials, and their domains as districts and sub-districts. Turning the tribal sheikh into the power-holder in administration, the governor entrusted the sheikh to maintain safety in his domain, although he occasionally needed military forces to subdue the sheikhs who continued to refuse cooperation.

In this improvement of tribal administration, tax farming was a useful means of revenue collecting and encouraged local notables and tribal sheikhs to involve themselves in agriculture. Although large areas of productive land needed irrigation and were located in tribal domains, agriculture had great potential for development owing to reliable water resources from rivers and canals. It already had become the dominant income-generating activity, providing since the early Ottoman period a livelihood for many people, although that livelihood was often insecure. Capable tax farmers and landholders profited from the cultivation of dates and grain crops, sold domestically or else exported. Merchants and tribal sheikhs benefitted as well, by expanding agricultural production and trading of its products. The potential for agricultural growth was high, owing to rich water resources supplied by the Euphrates and Tigris Rivers, large areas of arable land, and significant populations of Arab peasant tribesmen. The governor of Baghdad therefore launched irrigation and land reclamation projects on a wide scale, and reformed the administration of the tribal domains. In some cases, under a more centralized authority, he attempted to reconfigure tax farming and land tenure as well, in conformity with local custom and tribal tradition as effective measures for improving agricultural production.

Concerning land tenure, during the Tanzimat, the possession right over state land and its transfer to the private individual were legitimized by *tapu* title. The governor, now used to agricultural policy measures, attempted to introduce it as an incentive for prospective investors in cultivating abandoned lands. The land reform, as discussed in this book, progressed rapidly after the enactment of the Land Code of 1858, by which local notables and tribal sheikhs now gained the right to possess land by *tapu* (title deed). Legally speaking, this arrangement was leasehold, and came close to, but was not identical with, the private property right, as the state retained ownership and was able to take back lands that had been left uncultivated for a number of years.[10] Tax farmers

10 Shaw and Kural Shaw, *History*, ii, pp. 114–15.

collected the tax in such reclaimed land, while the landholder received his share from the land produce, according to the local custom of crop sharing.

At the end of World War I and after the dissolution of the Ottoman Empire, the British began governing Iraq under the mandate of the newly formed League of Nations (1914–32). The British mandate government continued to rely on a system of land tenure built on tax farming and crop sharing, finding little reason to change these arrangements, no matter that officials had initially regarded the Ottoman system as obsolete. The Tanzimat reforms thus continued to affect both settled people and tribal society. However, towards the end of the British mandate and after Iraqi independence, the government replaced the Ottoman-style tithe by a land tax. A new land tenure arrangement called *lazma* (title deed conferring a right of possession on state land) rapidly prevailed, and the custom of crop sharing faded, mostly eliminating the communal land use of peasant tribesmen under the management of their local sheikhs (*serkâr*). These changes disrupted cooperative effort toward farming and other agricultural activities of peasant tribesmen and their sheikhs that had been traditional in the region. The result was their rapid impoverishment as landless tenant peasants.

The modernization that began with the Ottoman governors' challenge of increasing agricultural production and tax revenues widened the sphere of tax farming, which had been regarded solely as a means of revenue collecting, and the function of private landholding. It had lasting consequences, traceable even after the Ottoman rule through the British mandate period, and therefore suggests the necessity of studying the reasons and applicability of its principle to modern land reform. Ottoman documents suggest that the Tanzimat reforms resulted in this long-term progress of agriculture and a concomitant change in tribal society. The Ottoman governors in office during the middle decades of the nineteenth century made use of established practices and local custom to promote agricultural activities, with the aim of raising both production and tax revenues. While in the nineteenth and early twentieth centuries, the backwardness of Ottoman rule was frequently featured, a close investigation of archival sources shows that, on the contrary, the governors of Baghdad succeeded in promoting the growth of agricultural output and tax revenues under their constraints.

This book aims to present the accomplishment of the Ottoman governors in Baghdad by a detailed examination of tax farming, *tapu* landholding, and crop sharing during the Tanzimat period, 1839–76, and the modification of these practices during the Hamidian period and the rule of the Committee for Union and Progress (1876–1914), followed by the British occupation and mandate period (1914–32). The book focuses on tax farming as related to agricultural production and crop sharing, and the landholding system in its entirety.[11]

The book begins in 1831, when the victorious commander-in-chief of the Ottoman army Ali Rıza Pasha (Ali Rıza Paşa al-Lâz, gov. 1831–42), confiscated the private properties of the rebellious officials and notables of the previous regime, declared them to be state land, and administered them accordingly. From 1831 to the tenure of Governor Midhat Pasha (1868–72), the Ottoman government viewed tax farming and land tenure as inseparable issues. As noted, these two institutions were the main means of raising state revenues, which increasingly fell short of expenditure. In addition, since a large proportion of the inhabitants of Baghdad province adhered to tribal units, tax farming provided a means of administering these populations. Perhaps even more important, tax farmers made profits, which if everything developed according to plan, they might invest in land improvements and thus sustain agricultural development. The Ottoman years following Midhat Pasha's tenure (1872–1914) and the British period (1914–32) witnessed significant social change as well, and we therefore continue the analysis of institutional arrangements after the end of World War I and terminate our discussion with the end of the Mandate period in 1932.[12] For understanding the local practices, we briefly review the

---

11 For a general history, see Longrigg, *Four Centuries of Modern Iraq*; Longrigg, *Iraq, 1900–1950: A Political, Social, and Economic History* (London: Oxford University Press, 1953); Habib K. Chiha, *La province de Baghdad: Son passé, son présent, son avenir* (Cairo: Al-Maarif, 1908); ʿAbbās al-ʿAzzāwī, *Tāʾrīkh al-ʿIrāq baina Iḥtilālain* (Baghdad: Maṭbaʿat Baghdād, 1935–56), vols. 7–8.

12 Studies of Iraqi history in the Ottoman period have proliferated in recent years. For example, Tom Nieuwenhuis, *Politics and Society in Early Modern Iraq* (The Hague: M. Nijhoff, 1981); Yitzhak Nakash, *The Shiʿis of Iraq* (Princeton, NJ: Princeton University Press, 1994); Dina Rizk Khoury, *State and Provincial Society in the Ottoman Empire: Mosul, 1540–1834* (Cambridge: Cambridge University Press, 1997); Hala M. Fattah, *The Politics of Regional Trade in Iraq, Arabia and the Gulf, 1745–1900* (Albany: State University of New York Press, 1997); Meir Litvak, *Shiʿi Scholars of Nineteenth-Century Iraq* (Cambridge: Cambridge University Press, 1998); Sarah D. Shields, *Mosul before Iraq: Like Bees Making Five-Sided Cells* (Albany: State University of New York Press, 2000); Thabit A.J. Abdullah, *Merchants, Mamluks, and Murder: The Political Economy of Trade in Eighteenth-Century Basra* (Albany: State University of New York Press, 2001); Lier, *Haushalte und Haushaltpolitik*; Gökhan Çetinsaya, *The Ottoman Administration of Iraq, 1890–1908* (London: Routledge, 2006); Sinan Marufoğlu, *Osmanlı Döneminde Kuzey Irak* (Istanbul: Eren Yayıncılık, 1998); Kerem Kayi, *Bagdad, 1831–1869: Untersuchungen zur Entwicklung einer osmanischen Provinzhauptstadt im 19. Jahrhundert* (Frankfurt am Main: Peter Lang, 2007); Ebubekir Ceylan, *The Ottoman Origins of Modern Iraq: Political Reform, Modernization and Development in the Nineteenth-Century Middle East* (London: I.B. Tauris, 2011); Christoph

works on Ottoman tax farming that historians have undertaken during the last forty years.

2 Research on Tax Farming and Land Tenure under Ottoman and British Rule

In use for many centuries, Ottoman tax farming has been a topic of study from the 1970s onwards. Scholarly interest began with Mehmet Genç's pioneering article on lifetime tax farming (*malikâne*). This work has laid out the details of how officials in the service of the Ottoman central administration chose the candidates eligible for bidding, determined the tax prepayment (*muaccele*) required, and collected data from which today's historians can understand the prosperity or decay of the economic activities generating the taxes at issue.[13] This pioneering study initiated a wide range of research into tax farming. Highlighting the social aspects of this practice, Suraiya Faroqhi's book (1984) on Anatolian urban life in the 1500s and early 1600s intuitively suggests the emergence of tax farmers as a privileged class, although at the time studied, there was still no *malikâne*. While perhaps of modest backgrounds, tax farmers collected a variety of taxes from peasants and townspeople, thereby acting as temporary office holders of the sultan.[14]

In a major study of pre-Tanzimat tax collection, published in 1996, Linda Darling analyzed the mechanics of bidding for tax farms and the bureaucratic supervision of tax farmers during the sixteenth and seventeenth centuries, again before the holders of *malikânes* appeared on the scene.[15] With a focus on sociopolitical struggles, Murat Çizakça has shown that in the seventeenth century, Ottoman military men pushed out the Jewish tax farmers who had played a certain role during the 1500s, thus beginning the process that, after 1695, resulted in the restriction of lifetime tax farms to established figures.[16]

Herzog, *Osmanische Herrschaft und Modernisierung im Irak: Die Provinz Bagdad, 1817–1917* (Bamberg: University of Bamberg Press, 2012).

13 Mehmet Genç, "Osmanlı Maliyesinde Malikâne Sistemi," in Osman Okyar and Ünal Nalbantuoğlu, eds., *Türkiye İktisat Semineri* (Ankara: Hacettepe Üniversitesi, 1975), pp. 231–96.

14 Suraiya Faroqhi, *Towns and Townsmen of Ottoman Anatolia: Trade, Crafts and Food Production in an Urban Setting, 1520–1650* (Cambridge: Cambridge University Press, 1984).

15 Linda T. Darling, *Revenue-Raising and Legitimacy: Tax Collection and Finance Administration in the Ottoman Empire, 1560–1660* (New York: E.J. Brill, 1996).

16 Murat Çizakça, "The Economy," in *The Cambridge History of Turkey*, ii: *The Ottoman Empire as a World Power, 1453– 1603*, ed. Suraiya Faroqhi and Kate Fleet (Cambridge: Cambridge University Press, 2013), pp. 270–71.

While lifetime tax farms certainly aided decentralization, Ariel Salzmann has pointed out that at the same time, they made central and provincial elites stakeholders of the Ottoman polity, as their tax farms would have been meaningless without a sultan to legitimize them.[17] This capacity for integrating potentially disruptive upper echelons may well have been one of the reasons why the Ottoman Empire survived the crises of the late seventeenth and late eighteenth centuries.

From a different perspective, focusing on institutional aspects, in 1986 Yavuz Cezar published a detailed study on the financial administration that the Ottoman government instituted in the late 1700s and early 1800s, well before the Tanzimat. The new arrangements included the sale of small shares in tax farms that permitted the central government to mobilize the savings of modest property holders without the status or resources to bid for *malikânes*.[18] Besides it, Metin Coşgel, Timur Kuran, and Şevket Pamuk have looked at sixteenth- and seventeenth-century taxation data to answer questions asked by economic historians worldwide, especially those oriented towards institutional economics.[19] These scholars have provided a framework for analyzing tax farming as an institution and the effects of changes in its application on the economy. Their works are especially relevant for interpreting the arrangement in the nineteenth century, as the authors tend to adopt a long view and modern analytical models.[20]

Research of tax farming in its various shapes allows us to envisage the Baghdad governors' tax policies under the Tanzimat and their probable

---

17 Ariel Salzmann, "An Ancien Régime Revisited: 'Privatization' and Political Economy in the Eighteenth-Century Ottoman Empire," *Politics & Society* 21, no. 4 (1993), pp. 393–423; Salzmann, *Tocqueville in the Ottoman Empire: Rival Paths to the Modern State* (Leiden: Brill, 2004).

18 Yavuz Cezar, *Osmanlı Maliyesinde Bunalım ve Değişim Dönemi: XVII. yy dan Tanzimat'a Mali Tarih* (Istanbul: Alan Yayıncılık, 1986).

19 Metin M. Coşgel and Thomas J. Miceli, "Risk, Transaction Costs, and Tax Assignment: Government Finance in the Ottoman Empire," *Journal of Economic History* 65, no. 3 (2005), pp. 806–21; Timur Kuran, "Separation of Powers and the Medieval Roots of Institutional Divergence between Europe and the Islamic Middle East," in Masahiko Aoki, Timur Kuran, and Gérard Roland, eds., *Institutions and Comparative Economic Development* (New York: Palgrave Macmillan, 2012), pp. 99–115; Şevket Pamuk, "Institutional Change and the Longevity of the Ottoman Empire, 1500–1800," *Journal of Interdisciplinary History* 35, no. 2 (2004), pp. 225–47; Pamuk, "The Evolution of Financial Institutions in the Ottoman Empire, 1600–1914," *Financial History Review* 11, no. 1 (2004), pp. 7–32.

20 Stanford J. Shaw, "The Nineteenth-Century Ottoman Tax Reforms and Revenue System," *International Journal of Middle East Studies* 6, no. 4 (1975), pp. 421–59; Pamuk, "Evolution of Financial Institutions"; Nadir Özbek, *İmparatorluğun Bedeli: Osmanlı'da Vergi, Siyaset ve Toplumsal Adalet (1839–1908)* (Istanbul: Boğaziçi Üniversitesi Yayınevi, 2015).

outcomes. In many places, tax farmers remained integral to rural and tribal societies, and the reforms had little immediate impact on their practices. However, we still do not fully understand the complexity of tax farming, shaped as it was by local custom and tribal tradition. Tax farming, in close association with crop sharing, evidently was crucial in provincial administration, land use, and tribal policies. Given their contribution to agricultural progress, we need to view tax farming reforms in a broad perspective. My interpretation focuses on the close association of tax farming with the local customs of crop sharing and tribal tradition, emphasizing the impact of these factors on productive activities.

The reform of land tenure has attracted more researchers than tax farming has done, because the Land Code of 1858 instituted landholding by *tapu*, which, as we have seen, gave the possession right that approximated full private property. The Code has been studied mainly by jurists; historical studies have been fewer, among which those of Ömer Lütfi Barkan and Kemal Karpat are notable.[21] Ömer Lütfi Barkan's publication appeared already in 1940, although the author revised it for later publication. At the time of writing, access to the Ottoman archives was very difficult, and the author thus limited his work to a close reading of the law, keeping in mind earlier edicts concerning Ottoman provincial taxation (*kanûn-nâme*), on which he was an acknowledged expert. Barkan emphasized that the Ottoman system of landholding (*mîrî toprak sistemi*), despite its apparent uniformity, had many local and provincial variations and, moreover, the state land system had largely collapsed well before the new law came into effect.[22] Writing in the 1960s, Kemal Karpat analyzed the disintegration of the state land system already observed by Barkan, and noted that the Code's enactment was a major factor allowing the prevalence of *tapu* land. In enacting the Land Code of 1858, the government aimed to promote the efficient cultivation of state land, to end the prevailing confusion concerning different land laws of local validity, and to implement a new land regime compatible with the requirements of a market economy. The Code was thus a milestone in the transformation of Ottoman society, resulting in the rise of an agrarian middle class that included agriculture-oriented entrepreneurs and tribal sheikhs who made their wealth from landed properties.[23]

---

21 Ömer L. Barkan, "Türk Toprak Hukuku Tarihinde Tanzimat ve 1274 (1858) Tarihli Arazi Kanunnamesi," *Türkiye'de Toprak Meselesi* (Istanbul: Gözlem Yayınları, 1980), pp. 291–375; Kemal H. Karpat, "Land Regime, Social Structure and Modernization in the Ottoman Empire," in William R. Polk and Richard L. Chambers, eds., *Beginnings of Modernization in the Middle East* (Chicago: University of Chicago Press, 1968), pp. 69–90.

22 Barkan, "Türk Toprak Hukuku Tarihinde Tanzimat," p. 371.

23 In the larger sociopolitical context of the property right, Huri İslamoğlu-İnan considered the Code as the changing relationship between the state and society. Huri İslamoğlu-İnan,

While the bibliography on Ottoman tax farming is still limited, the formalization of *tapu* in the province of Baghdad has attracted many more researchers because primary sources are easily available. British officials working during the mandate period authored numerous administrative reports on Ottoman land tenure. Generally, the British civil administration that took over the province in 1916–17 did not value or even notice the progressive changes in agriculture, the economy, and land use during the Tanzimat period (1839–76). One British official, Stephen Hemsley Longrigg, author of *Four Centuries of Modern Iraq* (1925), considered Ottoman officials ignorant and their rule backward, barring all pathways to progress.[24] He was particularly critical of Ottoman tax systems and, while inspector-general of the powerful Department of Treasury in 1927, endorsed a major tax reform, abolishing the tithe and instituting a land tax. British and Iraqi officials wishing to abolish the tithe and tax farming agreed with Longrigg's proposal, but a minority opposed the demand for rapid change, recognizing the rationality of the Ottoman land and tax systems. These officials expressed their deep concern about the consequences of hasty reforms that would become evident after years or even decades. Voluminous British official writings thus document the hesitations of different public administrators, whose close analysis may help us appreciate the invisible merits of Ottoman and local practices.

After the end of the British mandate, historians studying Iraqi rural history focused not so much on land tenure as on the disintegration of tribal society, which by then had given rise to large landownership. Doreen Warriner's pioneering book, *Land and Poverty in the Middle East* (1948), which, incidentally, motivated me to undertake this book, suggested that the formation of large landownership and the consequent tenancy problem of Iraqi peasants needed to be a priority of our research agenda.[25] Subsequent studies by Albertine Jwaideh, based on Ottoman documents, and by Saleh Haidar, whose published article cites consular reports as well as the writings of Mandate officials, recognized the significance of *tapu* in tribal society and the rise of tribal sheikhs as large landowners. Later on, Hanna Batatu acknowledged the large

---

"Property as a Contested Domain: A Reevaluation of the Ottoman Land Code of 1858," in Roger Owen, ed., *New Perspectives on Property and Land in the Middle East* (Cambridge, MA: Harvard University Press, 2000), pp. 3–61.

24 Longrigg, *Four Centuries of Modern Iraq*, pp. 320–24.

25 Doreen Warriner, *Land and Poverty in the Middle East* (London: Royal Institute of International Affairs, 1948), pp. 99–119; Warriner, *Land Reform and Development in the Middle East* (London: Oxford University Press, 1962), pp. 113–83.

landowners as a social class and more thoroughly studied their emergence in Iraqi society.[26]

Concerning the economy, Muhammad Salman Hasan contends that increased foreign demand for wool, dates, wheat, barley, and other produce pushed up production for export and helped impel the change from tribal landownership to private landholding by *tapu*. In order for exports to increase, however, agricultural production had to expand faster than domestic demand. While Hasan explains that improved soil fertility, flood control, and quality of seed – as well as an increase in labour supply due to the settlement of nomads – bolstered production, he pays little attention to the Ottoman institutions that had driven agricultural and economic developments from the Tanzimat period onwards.[27]

While research on land tenure in Iraq has greatly progressed owing to the efforts of several generations of historians, we still know very little about how indigenous custom affected the practice of land tenure.[28] Apart from the formal Ottoman practice that British officials surveyed, Gertrude Bell, the oriental secretary to the civil commissioner and subsequently to High Commissioner Sir Percy Cox, witnessed during her time in office, diverse and conflicting

26 Albertine Jwaideh, "Midhat Pasha and the Land System of Lower Iraq," *St. Antony's Papers*, no. 16, Middle Eastern Affairs (Oxford: Oxford University Press, 1963), pp. 106–36; Jwaideh, "The Saniyya Lands of Sultan Abdul Hamid II in Iraq," in George Makdisi, ed., *Arabic and Islamic Studies in Honor of Hamilton A.R. Gibb* (Leiden: E.J. Brill, 1965), pp. 326–36; Jwaideh, "Aspects of Land Tenure and Social Change in Lower Iraq during the Late Ottoman Times," in Tarif Khalidi, ed., *Land Tenure and Social Transformation in the Middle East* (Beirut: American University of Beirut, 1984), pp. 333–56; Saleh Haider, "Land Problems of Iraq," in Charles Issawi, ed., *The Economic History of the Middle East, 1800–1914* (Chicago: University of Chicago Press, 1966), pp. 164–78; Haider, "Land Problems of Iraq," Ph.D. diss., The London School of Economics and Political Science, 1942; Hanna Batatu, *The Old Social Classes and the Revolutionary Movements of Iraq* (Princeton, NJ: Princeton University Press, 1978), pp. 5–361.

27 Muhammad Salman Hasan, "The Role of Foreign Trade in the Economic Development of Iraq, 1864–1964: A Study in the Growth of a Dependent Economy," in M.A. Cook, ed., *Studies in the Economic History of the Middle East* (London: Oxford University Press, 1970), pp. 346–72.

28 Rony Gabbay, *Communism and Agrarian Reform in Iraq* (London: Croom Helm, 1978), pp. 19–41; Haim Gerber, *The Social Origins of the Modern Middle East* (Boulder, CO: L. Rienner, 1987), pp. 91–93; Samira Haj, *The Making of Iraq, 1900–1963* (Albany: State University of New York Press, 1997), pp. 27–31, 41–49; Charles Tripp, *A History of Iraq* (Cambridge: Cambridge University Press, 2000), pp. 51–52; Toby Dodge, *Inventing Iraq: The Failure of Nation-building and a History Denied* (New York: Columbia University Press, 2003), pp. 101–29; Marion Farouk-Sluglett and Peter Sluglett, "The Transformation of Land Tenure and Rural Social Structure in Central and Southern Iraq, c. 1870–1958," *International Journal of Middle East Studies* 15, no. 4 (1983), pp. 491–505.

claims to land. In Bell's perspective, these conflicts resulted from the customary practice of crop sharing and from tribal traditions that the Ottoman government had allowed to continue without interference.[29] In order to understand these conflicting interests, we must be aware of the indigenous origin of the interests in agriculture that tax farming and land tenure had affected. This book attempts to understand what Gertrude Bell witnessed with respect to agricultural crop sharing, by scrutinizing an Ottoman survey record in 1866 during the tenure of Governor Namık Pasha (1851–52, 1861–68).[30] To show how nineteenth-century Ottoman reform worked itself out, in the following section I take a closer look at tax farming with crop sharing, *tapu* landholding, and the contribution of these practices to agricultural progress under the Ottomans and their successors.

3 Tax Farming, Crop Sharing, and Landholding

Tax farming and land tenure, the main concerns of this book, shared some remarkable features dating from the very early period of Ottoman rule. *Sâlyâne* payments soon disappeared, replaced by tax farming or the arrangement known as *malikâne-dîvânî*, in which revenues were divided between the state and the landowner, or else the state and a *vakıf*.[31] The financial administration had reduced the size of certain fiefs, or else confiscated the relevant revenue sources to lease them out as tax farms. Tax farmers obtained their rights to revenue originally by auction, grant, or inheritance, paying a prearranged deposit and holding their tax farms for a fixed number of years. In many cases, however,

29 Iraq, Civil Commissioner, *Review of the Civil Administration of Mesopotamia* (London: HMSO, 1920), p. 90.

30 The impact of the Ottoman Land Code is observed in Iraqi land tenure, under which *tapu* land constituted 38.8 per cent and *lazma* land 32.9 per cent of the total cultivated area in 1958, and even 13.2 per cent and 16.4 per cent respectively, in 1974, after the agrarian reforms of 1958 and 1970. Republic of Iraq, Ministry of Economics, Principal Bureau of Statistics, *Statistical Abstract 1950* (Baghdad, 1952), pp. 108–13; ʿAbdul Wahhāb Maṭar al-Dāhirī, *Iqtiṣadiyāt al-Iṣlāḥ al-Zirāʿī* (Baghdad: Maṭbaʿat al-ʿĀnī, 1976), pp. 175, 394–95.

31 Ömer L. Barkan, "Türk-İslâm Toprak Hukuku Tatbikatının Osmanlı İmparatorluğu'nda Aldığı Şekiller: Malikâne-divânî Sistemi," *Türkiye'de Toprak Meselesi* (Istanbul: Gözlem Yayınları, 1940), pp. 151–208; Huri İslamoğlu-İnan, *State and Peasant in the Ottoman Empire* (Leiden: E.J. Brill, 1994), pp. 56–77; Margaret L. Venzke, "Aleppo's *Mālikāne-Dīvānī* System," *Journal of the American Oriental Society* 106, no. 3 (1986), pp. 451–69; Venzke, "Special Use of the Tithe as a Revenue-raising Measure in the Sixteenth-Century *Sanjaq* of Aleppo," *Journal of the Economic and Social History of the Orient* 29, no. 3 (1986), pp. 239–334.

practice on the ground had changed considerably.[32] In irrigated areas, the agricultural lands cultivated by a village or a row of fields along an irrigation canal formed a unit of tax collection (*mukâtaa*) assigned as a lifetime tax farm (*malikâne*), often accompanied by tax privileges.

The Ottoman government had instituted lifetime tax farming for broader application in 1695, in an attempt to raise funds for the ongoing war against the Habsburgs and their allies. According to the newly promulgated rules, members of the governing elite with the necessary means could buy a tax farm by remitting a sizeable prepayment (*muaccele*), guaranteed by a solvent money changer (*sarrâf*). For the remainder of their lives, these tax farmers paid a fixed annual sum and, later, they could even ensure that their revenue collection rights were inherited by their children. Applied across the eighteenth-century Ottoman Empire, this arrangement promoted provincial decentralization, while consolidating the sultans' office holders. Ordinary taxpayers could bid for short-term tax farms (*iltizam*) if they had the requisite funds, but the *malikâne*s were off limits and provided the bulk of the revenue collected.[33]

Concerning land tenure, before the Tanzimat, the provincial government in Baghdad had little power to enforce the principles governing the holding of Ottoman state land. Private land (*mülk*), classified as *harâç-* or *öşür*-paying in accordance with the tax rate applicable on these properties, was a holdover from the pre-Ottoman period. Such lands, containing orchards, vegetable gardens, and grain fields, were often placed under the control of religious endowments (*vakıf*). The remaining cultivated land largely belonged to the state (*mîrî*), whose officials had assigned these lands as *timar* or *çiftlik* (farmsteads). Although officially abolished in 1831, certain fiefs (*timar*) existed well into the 1850s in the northern districts of the province of Baghdad. Tax farmers commonly held lands as inheritable tax farms or *malikâne*s, while tribesmen occupied large tracts of territory as their tribal domains. On state-owned lands, forests, pastures, threshing grounds, and uncultivated fields featured as public land, reserved for common use; mountains, deserts, rocky grasslands, and marshes counted as wasteland.

Formally, most of the agriculturally usable land was the property of the sultan. Provincial land laws (*kanûn-nâme*) termed this Ottoman version of eminent domain, *rakaba*. Ottoman law also recognized a right of possession, which implied the use and cultivation of the land (*tasarruf*). In addition to the prescriptive right of possession called *hakk-ı karâr*, peasants received the *tasarruf* of their fields as an inheritable right upon the payment of a due known as

32 For the province of Mosul, see Khoury, *State and Provincial Society*, pp. 75–108.

33 Genç, "Osmanlı Maliyesinde Malikâne Sistemi," pp. 236–49.

icâre-i muaccele (immediately payable rent).[34] In practice, however, the clear distinction between ownership and possession that had prevailed in the early centuries of the *timar* system had become blurred by the manipulation of the possession right on the part of the Ottoman administration.

The differences between *mîrî* and private land became further blurred if dignitaries acquired fields, houses, trees, watermills, and other appurtenances of the land as a *çiftlik*. These landholdings were likely to emerge on grazing lands, in abandoned fields, or around watermills.[35] If state land became a *vakıf* or *çiftlik*, the government would struggle to collect the fees payable upon land transfer, to say nothing of the taxes due from the resulting produce. To further complicate the situation, the revenues from some state lands served to pay local soldiers (*ocaklık* and *yurtlık*), or the locals used them as common pasture land (*kışlak* and *yaylak*). Officials leased the remaining state lands to peasant cultivators or farmed them out to tax farmers and other tax-collecting agents. Fief holders were responsible for tax collection and administration in the lands assigned to them; tax farmers and tax-collecting agents carried out the same duties in their tax farms.

In the eighteenth century, the governors of Baghdad became holders of lifetime tax farms as well. Their treasury paid imperial and local troops, and due to their growing military power and wealth, their appointments tended to be longer. As noted, Hasan Pasha (1704–23) was the first in a series of governors who recruited slave soldiers (*mamlûks*), a practice that lasted until 1831. Governors continued to amass wealth from agricultural dues and landed properties, even after Sultan Mahmud II, in his drive to recentralize, had destroyed Davud Pasha's household-based power.

During the Tanzimat period, the office of the grand vizier, known to outsiders as the Sublime Porte, became the locus of power. As increasing the tax revenue became the ultimate target of provincial governors in Baghdad and elsewhere, these office holders soon resorted to tax farming, the historically accepted Ottoman solution for many problems linked to the distribution of incomes, tax collection, rural administration, farm management, and even work in the fields. Tax farming also provided the incomes of district administrators, military officers, merchants, tribal sheikhs, and urban notables, who won their tax-farming rights at public auction or purchased them in other

---

34 Bernard Lewis, "Ottoman Land Tenure and Taxation in Syria," *Studia Islamica* 50 (1979), pp. 109–24.

35 Halil İnalcık, "The Emergence of Big Farms, Çiftliks: State, Landlords, and Tenants," in Çağlar Keyder and Faruk Tabak, eds., *Landholding and Commercial Agriculture in the Middle East* (Albany: State University of New York Press, 1991), pp. 17–34.

ways. Eventually, however, the central government forbade its officials from bidding for such contracts. Some tax farmers resold the rights that they had acquired, while others had agents collect the tax in the fields. Whatever collection routine the tax farmer might prefer, however, the profits, prestige, official title, and employment, in addition to the penalties incurred by payment default, sustained the active involvement of tax farmers in the management of their holdings. Because the system entailed a partial prepayment of the money determined at public auction, the tax farmer, who, in line with the custom of crop sharing, usually received a share due to his role as production manager and seed owner, stood to benefit from any production increase.

Although tax farming thus promoted increased production, it had significant drawbacks. It was easy for tax farmers to line their own pockets, and oppression of the peasants by these men led to uprisings of the tribes, to which the rural population mostly belonged. Above all, reliance on crop sharing complicated tax farming procedures and increased the amount of uncultivated land, as tax farmers not only allocated more investment to their better fields but also sometimes abandoned their less productive lands altogether.

Nevertheless, crop sharing, locally called *müzâraʿa*, was widely used for farm management and to some extent compensated for the deficiencies of tax farming. Although its origin is unclear, by the Tanzimat period, *müzâraʿa* broadly prevailed in all cultivated areas. In grain fields under irrigation, it determined the crop distribution at harvest time among the peasants or tribesmen (labour), the government (tax), the seed owner (profit), other service providers (fees), and the landowner, if any (rent). In this system, the tax farmer was the central figure. Because he collected the government's share and received a commission, his share could be the largest of all, even though an increase in total production benefitted the other participants as well. In short, the tax farmer's role in agriculture provided a fixed revenue and a tax prepayment for the government, employment for the rural populations, a police service in the rural areas, and a tool for extending political administration into tribal domains.

As noted above, however, tax farming and crop sharing occasionally rested on a complicated traditional system of land tenure. Owners of broad acres of uncultivated land that had originally been in private hands claimed their share, called *uqr*, once production had resumed, as Islamic law entitled them to do. Because these landowners collected a percentage of the profits without contributing to production, their privilege diminished the tax farmer's incentive to commit to long-term improvement projects such as irrigation, land reclamation, and housing for peasants. Yet as long as agricultural production took place within a set of arrangements dominated by tax farming, productivity depended on investment by the tax farmer. It consequently became necessary for the government to reform the system of land tenure, in order to raise more revenue than tax farming could supply.

To support the revitalization of previously abandoned grain fields, the government offered tax farmers various kinds of financial support and bonuses. Nevertheless, the produce of the reclaimed lands still was subject to crop sharing at the customary rate, which as noted, diminished the return on the tax farmer's investment. Moreover, the likelihood that any profits from the crop would go to the landowner as *uqr* discouraged the tax farmer from participating in production as the seed provider. Moreover, his profit – that is, his share of the crop less the cost of tax prepayment and seeds – would become more vulnerable to fluctuations in the harvest. Although such vulnerability discouraged some people from becoming tax farmers, under improving domestic market and trade, many of them continued their agricultural activities for increasing production.

As summarized above, my examination of tax farming, focusing on the reform and its implementation, will make explicit the multiple functions of tax farming, which, when exercised in a manner compatible with local custom and tribal tradition, benefitted the government, the settled population, and tribal society. Particularly, crop sharing made possible the transition from lifetime to short-term tax farming without major disruption, and furthermore improved agricultural production. However, the use of uncultivated land did not progress as fast as the governors had expected, because of complicated landholding arrangements and a lack of sufficient financial support for irrigation and land reclamation. To explain this situation in detail, I examine the land reform in the province of Baghdad, at the time when the government enacted the Ottoman Land Code of 1858.

4 Ottoman Land Reform in the Province of Baghdad

The second part of my book examines the formalization of *tapu* landholding that the Tanzimat governors achieved, applying the new Land Code to state land and uncultivated private land, while retaining tax farming and crop sharing in practice. In the province of Baghdad, the unique combination of *tapu* landholding with tax farming, crop sharing, and the continuation of *uqr* was the main reason for the successful application of the Land Code of 1858. The Code proved to be far more useful than expected because it made allowance for the dominance of irrigation agriculture, the existence of large tribal domains, and the power of tribal sheikhs engaged in agriculture. The effective resolution of land issues promoted considerable agricultural improvement in the province.

After Ali Rıza Pasha's reoccupation of Baghdad in 1831, during the reign of Sultan Mahmud II, large areas of state land previously in private hands reverted to the state. Sometimes, the default of heirs permitted confiscation; in other cases, the measure was a punishment, directed against those landholders who had rebelled against the sultan or signed the Charter of Alliance (*Sened-i İttifak*) in 1808.[36] Moreover, because of the abolishment of fiefs, followed by heavy taxation on the part of tax farmers, endless wars, and a variety of natural disasters, many peasants were unable to cultivate the land and so abandoned it. In order to raise revenue from vacant lands, the government aimed at leasing them to the peasant, farming them out to the tax farmer, or transferring possession by sale to a person who could cultivate the fields and pay the requisite tax. In many cases, however, the government did not receive the full revenue due from these transactions, because of deductions granted to the tax farmer, or maladministration and corruption on the part of officials and tax farmers. More seriously, the purchaser often turned the land into a religious endowment (*vakıf*) or retained it as his private (*temlîk*) property. In such cases, the government lost control over the land despite owning the requisite *rakaba*, so could neither collect the transaction fees nor charge the regular taxes.[37]

After the promulgation of the Tanzimat edict in 1839, the government embarked on a series of legislative measures, centralizing the bureaucracy in order to control the operation of tax farming and the transfer of state land under proper registration. With respect to the transfer of vacant, uncultivated state land, the government attempted to survey, register, and issue title deeds in accordance with the new land legislation.[38] The legal changes of this period

---

36 Ali Yaycıoğlu, *Partners of the Empire: Crisis of the Ottoman Order in the Age of Revolutions* (Stanford, CA: Stanford University Press, 2016), pp. 203–26.

37 Barkan, "Türk Toprak Hukuku Tarihinde Tanzimat," pp. 291–375.

38 A document relevant to Sâkız Cezîresi (Chios Island) in 1843 (1259 AH) clarifies the policies of the government with respect to vacant land. To assess the acreage of these lands, the government attempted to undertake a census, while defining what made a given piece of land legally vacant. This procedure reasserted the right of ownership (*rakaba*) accruing to the sultan. However, a person who proved his possession through receipts of prior tax payment or other official documents retained his land, if he claimed his rights within two years.

For every piece of land documented, the survey recorded the acreage, the boundaries, and the name and title(s) of the possessor, the expected amount of produce and the number of sheep, cows, and other livestock. Memoranda (*ilmühaber*) conveyed this information to the relevant officials, who had it copied into the property record book (*emlak-ı* introduced a concept of ownership and a private right of possession with respect to state lands, with a system of registration to guarantee the rights of the purchaser. In the province of Baghdad, the law of 1858 thus stimulated private interest in land acquisition.

Even earlier, during the governorship of Reşit Pasha (1851–56), the importance of agriculture as a source of provincial revenues increased dramatically, and the modernized type of landholding allowed the public sale of vacant lands to private persons. The authorities expected the purchaser to carry out irrigation and land reclamation on that land and take responsibility for farming it according to local practice, but the new participant could obtain financial support, such as grants-in-aid that partly covered the cost of cleaning irrigation canals and constructing houses for the peasant tribesmen cultivating the field. The profit from the investment was large, for the purchaser received higher-than-average net returns from his investment in seed. The reform proved especially popular where irrigation was less costly, and in the Diyala River basin, settled peasants soon cultivated many fields using seed furnished by a new landholder. Where the cost of irrigation was high or the tax farmer was of political consequence, however, the transfer of vacant land proved difficult. In those cases, because of the large government share, possible investors likely considered the net profit too small, so that the transfer of land had become increasingly commercialized, and they needed to consider carefully the risks and profits of investment.

Since 1831, political centralization had netted the Ottoman government a considerable amount of taxable resources. By 1861, however, with peace and order re-established, that revenue ceased to grow. Although officials pinned their hopes on increasing revenue from trade, deficient port facilities and insufficient supply of exportable materials limited the amount of revenue collectable from this source. To increase trade, agriculture had to yield larger surpluses, ideally by increasing the productivity of cultivated land and

---

kayd). The person claiming possession paid a fee for registration, including the cost of paper and the dues collected by the scribes. Upon registration, the claimant received *tapu* title. He was exempt from any other fees previously demanded by the officers of the Islamic court. The *nâzir-i mukâtaât* (superintendent of state estates) in Istanbul supervised the process of registration.

At the end of the two-year registration period, land without an owner, inheritor, or legitimate claimant entered the record as vacant land. These procedures, known as the preparation of the so-called *temettuât defterleri*, took place in large sections of Anatolia and the Balkans during the 1840s, but not in the Arab provinces. Turkey, Prime Ministry General Directorate of State Archives, Directorate of Ottoman Archives (Başbakanlık Devlet Arşivleri Genel Müdürlüğü, Osmanlı Arşivi Daire Başkanlığı [BOA]), Buyruldu ve İlmühaber Defterleri 3, pp. 79–81, 19 Muharrem 1259 AH.

expanding the use of marginal lands. To initiate that development, the government needed to survey the local custom of crop sharing and *uqr* landholding.

Following the enactment of the Reform Edict (*Islahât Fermânı*) in 1861 by Sultan Abdülaziz (1861–76), Governor Namık Pasha (1851–52, 1861–68) almost succeeded in giving a new significance to the province of Baghdad, far from Istanbul on the remote south-eastern borders of the empire. The governor was fully cognizant of agriculture's potential. He made more efficient use of private property rights in promoting cultivation, through widespread seizures of uncultivated private land and the transfer of possession rights to individuals capable of generating a satisfactory output. Having closely observed experimental farms in England during his service as ambassador to Great Britain, Namık Pasha focused on the degradation of cultivable land, particularly of fields privately owned, and on the custom of extracting, in conformity with Islamic law, the share of an absentee landlord (*uqr*). He carefully drew up a regulation that restricted the right of *uqr* to a maximum of one-twentieth of the total produce, thereby increasing the shares of the tax farmer, peasants, and service providers, and eventually decreasing the costs of landholding and production. As noted, the governor gained a reputation for appropriating uncultivated private fields, transforming them into state land, and then conveying them to new landholders who would cultivate them.[39]

Making the right of the new landholders legitimate and operative, Governor Midhat Pasha (1869–72) continued and expanded the application of this breakthrough measure, which triggered the evolution of a private property right in land and increased agricultural production and tax revenues. Having achieved political centralization early on, he made rapid progress in land registration by establishing local offices for registry. While the sale of uncultivated land increased dramatically, the governor implemented land registration by *tapu* in agricultural areas and thus expanded private investment in land. In order to eliminate disputes, Midhat Pasha at the same time enacted a new regulation on the privilege of preference (*rüçhan*) and pre-emption (*şufʿa*) concerning the lands transferred to their new holders. As interest in landholding visibly increased, legally documented transfers promoted the expansion of agricultural lands registered as *tapu* holdings, which then became a major category of land tenure.

Amid changing international conditions after 1873, when Europe experienced an economic slowdown, Sultan Abdülhamid II (1876–1909) banned the sale of land in 1881 and began acquiring it for himself in order to collect the owner's share for his privy account. Officials managed the process of leasing,

---

39 BOA, İrâdeler (İ). Meclis-i Vâlâ 24610, 24 Şevval 1282 AH.

tax farming, and crop sharing on this crown land, called *saniyya*. Now that agriculture had become a premier project, the sultan benefitted greatly from large-scale production and increased export, thus pushing up overall agricultural production. After Abdülhamid's loss of power in 1908–09, the Young Turk government took over his lands and their management, now known as *mudawwala*, without damage to their productivity. When German interest in the province grew as a result of the Baghdad Railway project, local expectations for agriculture rose further, increasing land values. At the same time, the improved water and canal works of the Young Turks and the installation of irrigation pumps along the rivers and canals expanded the area cultivated and cultivable.[40] As Kamil Mahdi points out, with the state as a key factor in stimulating agriculture, the late Ottoman era was a period of "expansion of traditional low yield and utilization of idle resources."[41] Even though growth was slow, it initiated a crack in tribal solidarity, resulting in the breakdown and subsequent incorporation of large tribal confederations into the framework of the provincial administration.

In consequence, Namık Pasha deserves credit for applying the Land Code to agricultural state land; Midhat Pasha, for institutionalizing *tapu*. My study of their records, moreover, asserts that Namık Pasha's policy of retaining the *uqr* share on state land was crucially important to Ottoman land reform as realized in the province of Baghdad. The governor legally took over uncultivated private (*mülk*) land as vacant (*mahlûl*), declared it state (*miri*) land, and then sold it as *tapu* landholding, allowing the original owner to claim a limited share in the crops. In this way, the purchaser of the land could reclaim it for cultivation, an activity that the original owner had failed to carry out. Thus both the landholder and the original landowner gained revenue shares from the previously uncultivated land. Midhat Pasha's establishment of local land registries protected the rights of the purchaser as the legally recognized landholder, a measure that increased the attractiveness of landholding by *tapu*. The combination of tax farming, *tapu*, and crop sharing, including *uqr*, was a watershed sign of modernizing reform in the province of Baghdad, the main topic of the present book.

Extending the survey period from the Tanzimat to the rule of the Committee for Union and Progress, I examine the reasons why *tapu* landholding became so popular, even though Sultan Abdülhamid II halted the process for almost three decades. Relying on the custom of crop sharing, *saniyya* officials made

40 Çetinsaya, *Ottoman Administration of Iraq*, pp. 38–39.

41 Kamil A. Mahdi, *State and Agriculture in Iraq: Modern Development, Stagnation and the Impact of Oil* (Reading, UK: Ithaca Press, 2000), pp. 67–91.

available significant revenues gained by way of leasing, tax farming, and direct collecting. Overall production increases continued, from which the sultan himself was the largest gainer. Trade and commerce increased as well, leading to rises in land values and realizing *tapu* landholding as a secured asset after his reign. Given this continuous reliance of the Ottoman rulers on indigenous customs, we need to ask what the long-term consequences of this policy may have been and, for this purpose, to take a closer look at tribal society.

5 Tribal Society in Change

To understand the profound changes in tribal society during the Tanzimat, late Ottoman, and mandate periods, we need to focus on the key role of tribal sheikhs in state affairs. In the Ottoman province of Baghdad, outside the major cities and towns most inhabitants were tribesmen belonging to large tribal confederations. The paramount tribal sheikh enjoyed a degree of autonomy in his tribal domain, but this autonomy collapsed rapidly after the defeat of the last local governor, Davud Pasha, in 1831. During the Tanzimat period, the authority commanding the provincial governor shifted from the sultan to the Sublime Porte, elevating the governor's political power to a height unanticipated by most people.

The central government reorganized the tribal domains into districts and sub-districts, in which the governor's authority was delegated to a district governor and tax farmer, who was at the same time the paramount tribal sheikh. For the tribesmen, their sheikh's authority was no longer informal. Rather, the new principles of the Ottoman regime made this personage into a highly official figure. For the now-bureaucratized tribal sheikhs, their priority was to acquire enduring incomes by invigorating agriculture and pursuing the commercial opportunities opened up by telegraphic communication, steamship navigation on the Tigris River, and improved transportation. Engaging in foreign trade, certain tribal sheikhs could benefit from modernized facilities and began to participate regularly in the grain trade. In so doing, they participated in the market for agricultural produce.[42]

42 By the 1870s, the total capacity of the steamships active in Ottoman waters had reached 1,000 tons. Donald Quataert, *The Ottoman Empire, 1700–1922* (Cambridge: Cambridge University Press, 2000), p. 118.

The influence of the tribal sheikhs in agriculture, irrigation, water control, and other activities increased along with the progress of the Tanzimat.[43] Commanding large numbers of tribesmen, these sheikhs could mobilize labour both for their work and also to maintain their sociopolitical status, which grew as they secured a footing in state affairs and profited from the public funds spent on the development of agriculture. The profits, commissions, and fees the sheikhs and their tribesmen could derive from modernization and agricultural progress encouraged them to become involved in tax farming, crop sharing, landholding, and other agricultural activities.

After 1876, Sultan Abdülhamid II made himself the largest landholder by purchasing state land. Concomitantly, he isolated the paramount sheikhs of large tribal confederations from state affairs and limited their privileges by establishing the *saniyya* administration. As a result, certain lesser sheikhs and sheikhs of peasant tribesmen (*serkâr*) working as taxpaying cultivators on agricultural land, including the sultan's *saniyya*, played active roles in production, although they could not obtain any *tapu* titles. In 1908, when the Young Turk government took over the *saniyya* land and its administration, the new regime lifted the previous sultan's prohibition of the sale of land by *tapu*. Owing to increased land values, however, only the paramount sheikhs of tribal confederations and the sheikhs of large tribes could afford to purchase land, apart from non-tribal wealthy notables and merchants. Thus the major tribal sheikhs re-emerged as large landholders. As they played an active role in state-sponsored irrigation and flood control projects as well, in addition to the construction of railway networks, these personages regained much of the power they had attained during the Tanzimat period and partially lost under the regime of Abdülhamid II. The burgeoning grain trade further strengthened their position.

6 Modification of the Tax and Land Systems during the British Mandate Period

My survey on tax farming and land tenure extends to the British mandate period. Its aim is to compare British practices with those of their Ottoman predecessors and determine the long-term consequences of Ottoman and British policies. According to current historiography, large tribal sheikhs and landholders further increased their wealth when the area was under British control,

43 Şevket Pamuk, *The Ottoman Empire and European Capitalism, 1820–1913* (Cambridge: Cambridge University Press, 1987), pp. 86–87.

while after independence, small tribal sheikhs and peasant tribesmen became impoverished. Numerous works have documented this crucial change in tribal society, but few authors have included the Ottoman institutional perspective.

Under the British occupation and mandate government (1914–32), tax farming and *tapu* continued without substantial change. Although agriculture lost its position as the main revenue source to oil and trade, it remained an important economic sector, and both tax farming and an ownership-like right of possession played vital roles in maintaining production in private hands. Peter Sluglett, in his authoritative work *Britain in Iraq, 1914–1932*, observes that "revenue was inextricably linked with tenure, and here the British authority also aimed to leave things more or less as they found them."[44] While the British civil administration had the power to legislate and enforce changes, the political officers, after grass-roots surveys on administration, agriculture, and land tenure, considered the Ottoman system politically effective and therefore preserved it. Yet numerous disputes over land and revenues did occur, and the tribal system changed profoundly under pre-existing agrarian conditions and new political ethics. According to the oriental secretary to the civil commissioner, Gertrude Bell, in her *Review of the Civil Administration of Mesopotamia*, "any administration which succeeds them must bring to the task, if it is to be accomplished, singular integrity and diligence, combined with a just comprehension of the conflicting claims of different classes of populations."[45]

After reading Bell's report, and particularly her perceptive suggestion that *tapu* land tenure was the main cause of divergent interests among the people of the region, British political officers, especially Sir Ernest Dowson, found that considerable numbers of *tapu* landholdings had been registered in Ottoman times, indicating the long-term gravity of conflicts over land.[46] For promotion of land registration on the cultivated land by the use of pumps or in newly reclaimed areas, the British mandate government thus formed a new tenure, called *lazma*, following almost the same principles as the Ottoman *tapu*.

The changes in land tenure, alongside the worldwide depression of the 1930s, which severely troubled agriculture, seriously affected tribal society. However, the consequences differed from what we have observed in the Ottoman period, when demand for agricultural products had been mostly high. Issues that had arisen during the brief Young Turk period, such as the

---

44 Peter Sluglett, *Britain in Iraq, 1914–1932* (London: Ithaca Press, 1976), p. 239.

45 Iraq, Civil Commissioner, *Review of the Civil Administration of Mesopotamia*, p. 90.

46 Great Britain, The Directorate General of Public Security, Baghdad, *Reports of Administration of the Various Divisions and Districts of Mesopotamia for the Years 1917–21* (Baghdad, n.d.); Sir Ernest Dowson, *An Inquiry into Land Tenure and Related Questions* (Letchworth, UK: Garden City Press, 1931), p. 18.

settlement of land disputes, land registration, the installation of irrigation pumps, and the expansion of cultivated land, continued to be of significance to the British administration as well. Towards the end of its tenure, the mandate government struggled with worsening conditions of commerce and trade. Although the area of land irrigated by pumps expanded rapidly, it failed to bring production increases as expected. Instead, numerous land disputes continued between pump owners and the tribal sheikhs having prescriptive rights over the reclaimed land.

Under these conditions, the government enacted the Lazma Law of 1932, by which persons having the prescriptive right to land were granted the right of possession, called *lazma*, similar to *tapu*. Although the arrangement of *lazma* resembled the Ottoman *tapu*, it rapidly prevailed in the irrigated areas, particularly after the Land Settlement Law of 1932 became effective and enabled the progress of the settlement of land disputes and land registration. As a consequence, the right to landholding was secured, and marketable assets were often transferred from the cultivating peasant to another person as moneylender, merchant, and urban residents. The Law Governing the Rights and Duties of Cultivators (1933) put the peasants at more decisive disadvantages, as it defined the new concept and rights of farm owners and the duties of the peasants as an agricultural debt. The new land legislation to the favour of the landholders, pump owners, and farm owners, which were beyond the scope of the Ottoman laws, caused greater changes in tribal society. The sheikhs of large tribal groups, once they managed to receive title to the land, grew prosperous; minor sheikhs close to the peasant tribesmen (*serkâr*), and the peasant tribesmen themselves, became landless cultivators and, under worsening conditions of commerce and trade, impoverished tenants of the large landholders.

As the principles of Ottoman land reform were discernible in the interwar period, we need to demonstrate the unintended consequences of the reform for the peasant tribesmen and their sheikhs by studying the Ottoman and mandate periods together. The institutional arrangements involving the triad of tax farming, *tapu*, and crop sharing had been compatible with the traditional custom of agricultural production continued through the early mandate period. From 1927 until Iraqi independence in 1932, during which time the British began to reduce the administrative burden, land policies became more market oriented, representing the interests of pump owners and townspeople, who by then had become landholders or farm owners as defined by law. Most of them were absentee landholders who relied on peasant tribesmen as tenant farmers. The policy changes during the late British mandate period critically disrupted the delicate balance in the Ottoman practice of tax farming, *tapu* landholding, and crop sharing, in which large and small tribal sheikhs played a critical role, leading to increased numbers of troubled peasant tribesmen and stagnating agricultural production. They suggest that understanding the compatibility of formal institutions and local custom that the Ottoman land reform in the province of Baghdad ensured is important for designing better policy for agricultural development.

7 Scope of the Book and Sources

To present the land reform policies of the Ottoman government and the governors who implemented them, I examine tax farming and land tenure in chronological order, placing due emphasis on the role of indigenous customs. Accordingly, the book covers three periods: 1831–61, 1861–76, and 1876–1932. Chapters 1–3 discuss the first period, examining Ottoman provincial administration, agricultural conditions, tax farming, and the custom of crop sharing. In this section, I stress the dominance of tax farming. The characteristic of the second period is the institutionalization of *tapu*. In Chapter 4, I present land problems and Ottoman land policies around the time when the Land Code became operative. Chapter 5 deals with Namık Pasha and Midhat Pasha's land reforms and their long-term effects, while Chapter 6 surveys the modifications of these reforms during the eras of Sultan Abüdlhamid II and the Young Turks. Changes in agriculture and land policies during the British occupation and mandate period are the topic of Chapter 7. Lastly, Chapter 8 evaluates the Ottoman legacy, especially changes in taxation and land tenure and the harmful results of the latter on peasant tribesmen and tribal sheikhs.

For the years 1831–1908, the main primary sources are archival, especially the correspondence between the Sublime Porte (Ottoman central government) and the provincial governors, which dealt mostly with tax records, laws, and regulations. Usually, provincial correspondence went to the prime minister's office, whose officials forwarded these letters, as appropriate, to the ministries of domestic affairs, foreign affairs, finance, or trade and agriculture, or to religious foundations. For further deliberation, the relevant officials sent each ministry's decision to the Supreme Council of Judicial Ordinance (Meclis-i Vâlâ-yı Ahkâm-ı Adliye), established in 1838 as the chief body responsible for legislation, or else to a special committee (*meclis-i mahsûs-ı vükelâ*). The prime minister's office prepared a summary of the deliberations and provisional resolutions, and sent it to the sultan for his final decision. The relevant document then returned to the prime minister's office, which finally issued the sultan's order to the Baghdad provincial government. This correspondence on land and tax issues is very useful for the present research, as it includes letters and memoranda from the governors and other officials, in addition to the reports of the administrative council and various commissions of the Porte, the drafts of orders issued by the grand vizier, and finally the sultan's command. Thus, this correspondence contains a coherent narrative of developments relating to land and agriculture as experienced in the province of Baghdad.[47] For the British period (1914–32), the administrative reports of the British Civil Administration and the High Commissioner's office are the main sources, some of which have recently been compiled and published.

Regarding Ottoman Turkish words, I use English translations where appropriate, but I have transliterated those terms that defy clear translation, according to modern Turkish orthography. The governors' names appear in their modern Turkish guise, and I have transliterated the proper names of no longer existent Iraqi towns, villages, canals, and tribes according to Mehmed Hurşid Pasha's *Seyâhatnâme-i Hudûd*.[48] For names that do not appear in Hurşid Pasha's text or in any other documents, I have transliterated the relevant terms according to the text in which I have found them, employing the norms for transliterating Ottoman Turkish.

---

47 Their correspondence includes the letters (*tahrîr; sükka*) and memoranda (*lâyiha*) of the governors and other officials, the reports (*mazbata*) of the administrative council and various commissions of the central government, the drafts of orders (*tezkire*) made by the Grand Vezirate, and the sultan's command. These documents are in the collections known as *İrâdeler* and *Mektûbî Kalemi*. Some records, such as *Ayniyât Defterleri, Buyruldu ve İlmühaber Defterleri, Mühimme Defterleri,* and *Mektezâ Defterleri*, complement this correspondence. The tax records examined are from the catalogues known as *Mukâta'a Defteri, Baş Muhâsebe Defteri,* and *Maliye Nezâreti Defterleri.*

Useful works of reference on the Ottoman archives include: Ali Akyıldız, *Tanzimat Dönemi Osmanlı Merkez Teşkilatında Reform (1836–1856)* (Istanbul: Eren Yaıncılık, 1993); Mübahat S. Kütükoğlu, *Osmanlı Belgelerinin Dili (Diplomatik)* (Istanbul: Kubbealtı Akademisi Kültür ve San'at Vakfı, 1994); Mehmet Seyitdanlıoğlu, *Tanzimat Devrinde Meclis-i Vâlâ (1838–1868)* (Ankara: Türk Tarih Kurumu Baımevi, 1994); T.C. Başbakanlık Devlet Arşivleri Genel Müdürlüğü, *Başbakanlık Osmanlı Arşivi Rehberi* (Ankara: Başbakanlık Devlet Arşivleri Genel Müdürlüğü, 2010).

48 Mehmet Hurşid Pasha, the commander-in-chief of the Sixth Army from 1846 to 1858, surveyed the region from 1846 to 1848. His report was soon published: Mehmed Hurşid Pasha, *Seyâhatnâme-i Hudûd* (Istanbul: Takvimhâne-i Âmire, 1277 AH [1860]), transliterated by Alâattin Eser, *Seyâhatnâme-i Hudûd* (Istanbul: Simurg Kitapcılık ve Yayıncılık, 1997).

CHAPTER 1

The Province of Baghdad

Before the Tanzimat reforms were implemented in the province of Baghdad, internal authority belonged to the Ottoman governor and equally to the paramount sheikhs of large tribal confederations. Baghdad had not yet established itself as the solid provincial capital – its population was still small, and it was often isolated after recurrent flooding of the Tigris River. Outside the city dwelled tribesmen under their sheikh's commanding power. This situation changed to the advantage of the governor during the period from the first governor, Ali Rıza Pasha (1831–42), to the enactment of the Reform Edict of 1861. During this period, the paramount sheikhs rapidly lost their autonomy, and their tribal domains effectively became Ottoman administrative units – districts (*kazâ*) and sub-districts (*kâimmakâmlık*). Appointed as the district governor or the chief administrator of the sub-district, the tribal sheikh captured official political status beyond the chieftainship. The empowered tribal sheikh, moreover, gained a different source of wealth, as he was officially recognized as the tax farmer of his tribal domain. For the governor, implementing the Ottoman administrative system and tax farming in the tribal domains created the new government authority that continued throughout the Ottoman regime. This chapter examines the relationship between the Ottoman administration and the tribal domains, focusing on how the tribal sheikhs became the pillar of the provincial government in Baghdad and the extent to which tax farming facilitated the penetration of the Ottoman administration into the tribal domains during the first half of the Tanzimat.

1 The Province of Baghdad and the Tribal Domains

The city of Baghdad, capital of the province of Baghdad, was located on the south-eastern frontier of the Ottoman empire at a distance from Istanbul (*İstanbul*) that required travel of about 431 hours by a land route through Üsküdar, Amasya, Tokat, Sivas, Diyarbakir, Mardin, and Mosul. The journey could be shortened by taking a ship from Üsküdar to Trabzon, on the Black Sea, and then travelling by land from Trabzon through Erzurum, Van, and Mosul to Baghdad. The city was situated on both the eastern and western banks of the Tigris River. The main part, called Rusafa, developed on the eastern bank, surrounded by walls with gates in the north-west, north-east, south-east, and south. The north-west gate allowed access to the government complex (*saray*), which accommodated public offices and the residences of the governor and the governor's retinue. Mosques, schools, guest houses, inns, and the residences of high officials and notable Sunni Muslims were built near the *saray*, showing the strong tie between the Ottoman governor and local upper-class residents.[1]

The residents on the east bank were Sunni Muslims; on the west bank, besides a few Sunni Muslims, were the Shiite Muslims, who resided near the Kadhimiya mosque. The non-Muslim communities (*millets*) – the Roman Catholic, Armenian, and Greek Orthodox Christians and the Jews – lived on the east bank, away from the government house. They were divided into quarters separated from one another by a small alley with a few entrances to each quarter. The Jewish quarter, called al-Thawra, was located to the east of the government compound and markets. To its south was the Christian quarter, called Suq al-Ghazal. The governor maintained a close relationship with a representative of each community to deal with tax collection, police and judicial activities, and daily civil affairs. In addition, this representative received a seat on the administrative council comprising high civil officials, military commanders, Muslim clergymen, and merchants. Community leaders cooperated with the governor on financial help, military conscription, and tax payments and, in return, received various privileges for protection of their own wealth and security.[2]

1 For contemporary maps of Baghdad, see Muṣṭafá Jawād, Aḥmad Sūsah, Muḥammad Makīyah, and Maʿrūf Nājī, *Baghdād* (Baghdad: Niqābat al-Muhandisīn al-ʿIrāqīyah, 1969), p. 118; James Wyld, *Map of the Ottoman Dominions in Asia: with the Adjacent Frontiers of the Russian and Persian Empires* [Map], 100 miles=2.2 inches (London, 1835). For the journey from Istanbul to Baghdad, see Justin McCarthy, *The Ottoman Turks: An Introductory History to 1923* (London: Longman, 1997), p. 219; Ebubekir Ceylan, *The Ottoman Origins of Modern Iraq: Political Reform, Modernization and Development in the Nineteenth-Century Middle East* (London: I.B. Tauris, 2011), p. 27. For "hour" as a unit of measurement between places, see Ariel Salzmann, *Tocqueville in the Ottoman Empire: Rival Paths to the Modern State* (Leiden: Brill, 2004), p. 48 n. 53.

2 Kerem Kayi, *Bagdad, 1831–1869: Untersuchungen zur Entwicklung einer osmanischen Provinzhauptstadt im 19. Jahrhundert* (Frankfurt am Main: Peter Lang, 2007), pp. 77–100, 221–22. Reports of political resident in Baghdad, Lieutenant Colonel Robert Taylor (1828–43) also offer glimpses into the city life of Baghdad. For example, the National Archives of the UK (TNA): FO 195/113, No. 26, 16 Apr. 1832; No. 56, 27 July 1832; No. 65, 29 July 1833; No. 67, 5 Sept. 1833. Among numerous sources, Jean Baptiste Rousseau, *Description du Pachalik de Bagdad* (Paris: Treuttel et Würtz, 1809), pp. 1–122; L'abbé É. de Vaumas, "Introduction Géographique à l'Étude de Baġdād," *Arabica* 9 (October 1962), p. 244; Kahtan A.J. al-Madfai, "Baghdad," in Morroe Berger, ed., *The New Metropolis in the Arab World* (New Delhi: Allied Publishers, 1963), p. 44; ʿAbd al-Karīm al-ʿAllāf, *Baghdād al-Qadīma* (Baghdad: Maṭbaʿat al-Maʿarif, 1960), pp. 146–48; ʿAbd al-ʿAzīz Sulaymān al-Nawwār, *Taʾrīkh al-ʿIrāq al-Ḥadīth min Nihāyat Ḥukm Dāwūd Bāshā ila Nihāyat Ḥukm Midḥat Bāshā* (Cairo: Dār al-Kātib al-ʿArabī, 1968), pp. 380–87;

The population of the city was estimated at about sixty thousand by British traveller James Buckingham, who stayed in Baghdad from July to September 1816, and it steadily increased to eighty thousand between 1854 and 1862, with gradual improvements in peace and order. There were over a hundred mosques, of which about thirty were large Friday mosques; the rest were smaller. The public inns (caravanserai) numbered as many as thirty, among which the Khan Orthma (the present Khan Murjan) was the largest. Numerous bazaars contained some 1,200 shops along long, straight, and relatively wide streets.[3] Another commercial area, located in Karkh, on the west bank, had been constructed by Governor Süleyman Pasha (1780–1802). Major roads radiated out of the city in three directions: to Basra through Hilla in the south, to Mosul and Khanaqin through Baʿqūba in the north-east, and to Mandali through Kut al-Amara (Wasit) in the south-east.[4]

Traffic on the route to Basra was heaviest, as Basra was situated at the outlet to the Gulf.[5] Early in the eighteenth century, it intensified in strategic importance for defence against the Wahhabis, a religious movement started by Sheikh Muhammad b. Abd al-Wahhāb (1703–92) in al-Uyaynah. The Wahhabis drove numerous Arab tribes out of Nejd into Basra and beyond, and they had attacked Basra by 1786. In 1793 the Wahhabis occupied al-Hasa (Lahsa), despite a counter-attack by Muntafiq and Khazaʿil tribal forces and, in 1801, they marched to Karbala and captured the town. Süleyman Pasha petitioned the Ottoman and Persian governments in vain for military help to protect Karbala, fortify Najaf and Zubayr, and recover al-Hasa, and after making joint forces, he finally ousted the intruders. Since then the strategic importance of Basra has never ceased.[6] In 1832, Governor Ali Rıza Pasha integrated Basra into his province of Baghdad as the district to which he appointed the district governor from among his retinue, seeking to restore Ottoman authority following the

---

John Gulick, "Baghdad: Portrait of a City in Physical and Cultural Change," *Journal of the American Institute of Planners* 33, no. 4 (1967), pp. 246–55.

3 Bab al-Azaji, Maʿmuniya, Suq al-Thalatha, and Nahr al-Mualla were lively, prosperous marketplaces that raised the purchasing power of city residents, according to James S. Buckingham, *Travels in Mesopotamia* (London: H. Colburn, 1827), pp. 372–79.

4 There was a considerable difference in the altitude of the land. According to modern surveys, the average elevation in Baghdad is 33–34 m. The highest area is in the central part of the city, approximately 37 m above sea level; the lowest, at 32 m, is in southern Baghdad. The lower areas consequently suffered from inundation by the Tigris River. See William C. Fox, "Baghdad: A City in Transition," *The East Lake Geographer* 5 (1969), p. 9.

5 The "Gulf" in this book refers to the gulf bordered by today's Iran, the United Arab Emirates, Saudi Arabia, Kuwait, and Iraq.

6 Stephen Hemsley Longrigg, *Four Centuries of Modern Iraq* (Oxford: Clarendon Press, 1925), pp. 212–17.

devastation from the domestic battles. Eventually Basra began to flourish as a port town after grain exports increased in the 1840s, becoming the second largest city with an observed population of fifty thousand by 1854–62.[7]

A mile south of Basra, on the left bank of the Haffar Canal, was the disputed fortress town of Muhammara, constructed by Mirdaw and his son Yusuf by order of the Kaab sheikh Ghayth in 1812. The brother of Yusuf, Jabir succeeded its governorship in 1819–20. Opposite Muhammara was another fortress town, Kut al-Sheikh, where the next heir to the paramount chief of the Kaab, Shamir, the younger brother of Sheikh Ghayth, was stationed, until his moving to Fallahiya as the paramount sheikh in 1832 or 1833. Jabir had caused such incessant unrest in Muhammara, aiming at independence from Sheikh Shamir, that in 1837 Ali Rıza Pasha marched against him to protect Basra from the Kaab disturbance. He levelled the walls of Muhammara and appointed his favourite, Abd al-Razzaq, as the paramount chief of the Kaab, based on the old allegiance of the Kaab to the sultan's authority. Although Sheikh Shamir fled to Kuwait, and Jabir to Bushire, Abd al-Razzaq failed to keep the Kaab in peace and order. After two months of stay, Ali Rıza Pasha returned to Baghdad, and both Sheikh Shamir and Jabir also returned from evacuation. Displacing Abd al-Razzaq, Sheikh Shamir signed an agreement with Ali Rıza Pasha that established himself as the paramount chief of the Kaab, and pledged his allegiance to the district governor in Basra. However, as Muhammara developed as a port town, it attracted Persian interest and came under their influence.[8]

Mosul, located 56 hours (400 km) north of Baghdad, was a separate province until the mid-1860s. It served as a commercial centre of transit trade and a military base for peacekeeping in the north-west region of Baghdad province and the southern parts of Kurdistan. The political jurisdiction of Mosul extended over the districts of Amadiya and D'hok, where the emirate of the Bahdinan had been located, and an area called al-Jazira, previously the site of the Bohtan emirate of the Bedirhans. Ince Bayraktar Mehmet Pasha, who replaced Yahya Pasha of the Jalili family as the governor (1835–43), greatly advanced integration of these emirates into Mosul province and stationed permanently a regiment of the Iraq and Arabia Army (later, the Sixth Army)

7 TNA: FO 78/870, No. 3, Baghdad, 17 Nov. 1851; FO 78/1711, Turkey: Euphrates Valley, 1854–62, "European Interests in Railways in the Valley of the Euphrates," by Count Edward de Warren, 15 Mar. 1857, pp. 16–17. For broad population movements in this period, see Kemal H. Karpat, *Ottoman Population, 1830–1914* (Madison: The University of Wisconsin Press, 1985), pp. 60–77.

8 TNA: FO/204, No. 9, 1 July 1843; FO 195/237, 15 May 1844; Tom Nieuwenhuis, *Politics and Society in Early Modern Iraq* (The Hague: Martinus Nijhoff, 1982), pp. 136–37; Willem Floor, "The Rise and Fall of the Banū Ka'b: A Border State in Southern Kuzestan," *Iran: Journal of the British Institute of Persian Studies* 44 (2006), pp. 288–307.

for operations in these areas. The governor of Mosul, appointed by the Porte, carried out administrative duties and military operations independently of the Baghdad governor, who was involved in the political affairs of Mosul only when cooperation was necessary to deal with the Shammar Jarba tribe and boundary disputes with Persia.[9]

The boundaries and make-up of the province of Mosul fluctuated over time. Its north-eastern portion formerly belonged to the emirate of Soran, of which Rawanduz was the central town. The area to the south-east of the province of Mosul had formed a separate province, Shahrizor (Kirkuk), which was integrated into Baghdad in 1833 upon the disturbance of the Soran. After formally organizing Rawanduz as a district of Baghdad in 1835, the Baghdad governor appointed its governors and himself commanded the military force in the region, because of its strategic importance as a border with Persia. Shahrizor became a separate province again in 1842 due to political instability after the departure of Ali Rıza Pasha, but it returned to Baghdad province as a district in 1850. Under the influence of the Hamawand (*Hemavend*) tribe in Shahrizor, the Jaf tribe in Köysanjaq, and the Baban (*Bâbân*) family in Sulaymaniya, this area had been a strategic buffer zone between the Ottoman and Persian states where military clashes and tribal disturbances never ceased.[10]

The Baghdad governor had been directly involved in the Ottoman-Persian conflicts. When Sultan Mahmud II declared war on Persia in 1820, he appointed the governor of Erzurum, Hüsrev Pasha, and that of Baghdad, Davud Pasha, as commanders-in-chief on the northern and southern fronts respectively. More aggressive in the north, the Persian army captured Bayezit in 1821 and advanced to Bitlis, Erzurum, and Diyarbakir, until cholera broke out. In the Mandali district, where disputes were local and mostly over taxation on land and water use, the governments of Baghdad and Kermanshah settled them peacefully in 1824. They agreed on a fee of 300 toman a year to be paid by landowners in the Mandali district for using water from streams on the border, on top of the taxes they paid to the government of Kermanshah and to the Persian tribe of the Khalhur in the high mountain areas. After the peace treaty was concluded at

9 Ceylan, *Ottoman Origins of Modern Iraq*, pp. 45–53; Christoph Herzog, *Osmanische Herrschaft und Modernisierung im Irak: Die Provinz Bagad, 1817–1917* (Bamberg: University of Bamberg Press, 2012), pp. 228–34.

10 Mosul was governed by Bayraktar Mehmet Pasha as a province composed of the districts of Aqra, Amadiya, D'hok, and Sinjar. Dina Rizk Khoury, *State and Provincial Society in the Ottoman Empire: Mosul, 1540–1834* (Cambridge: Cambridge University Press, 1997), pp. 25–26.

the Congress of Erzurum in 1828, there were few clashes, except for boundary disputes in Zahab and Muhammara.[11]

Outside the provincial capital of Baghdad, district towns were established as subunits of the province. These included Sulaymaniya, Erbil, Köysanjaq, Harir, and later Shahrizor in the north; Khorasan, Khalis, and Khanaqin in the north-east; Dulaim (Ana) in the north-west; Hilla, Diwaniya, and Karbala in the central region; and Mandali in the south-east. The district governor was usually a lieutenant of the garrison troops in the town or an appointee from among the civil officials. The district was further divided into sub-districts, called *kazâ*, under a judge of the Islamic court, and *nâhiye*, administered by the district governor's deputy.[12] Numerous villages along the roads connecting the district towns provided marketplaces, postal stations, travel inns, and community centres for residents of the rural hinterlands occupied by tribesmen.

The tribal areas were characterized by different types of agricultural holding. Peasant tribesmen might be settled in villages or semi-settled as peasant cultivators, or they might be migrants working as day labourers or tribal nomads. Some small tribal groups lived in the suburbs of Baghdad, free of the large tribal confederations. These tribes had been divided into three groups – the tribes of followers, the Turanian tribes, and the tribes under patrol guards – and registered as such by Ali Rıza Pasha for taxation. The tax revenues, in turn, were assigned to the officials in charge of their administration and the police guards stationed in the fortress. The tax-paying tribes could be found in Baghdad, Khalis, Khanaqin, Khorasan, Mahrut, Baladruz, and Shahriban along the Diyala River; along the Dujail Canal and Saqlawiya Canal in Aqr Quf; in Abu Ghraib, Radwaniya, Jurf al-Sakhar, and Iskandariya along the Middle Euphrates River; in Samarra, Taji, Rashidiya, Rahmaniya, Imam Musa, and south-east of Baghdad along the Tigris River; and in Mandali, Badr, and Jisan.[13] Agriculture proliferated on their land to meet the rising demands of residents in Baghdad.

Beyond the vicinity of Baghdad, outside the district towns, were the tribal domains of the Arabs in the central and southern regions and of the Kurds in northern areas. The Arab tribesmen were classified as peasant tribes, tribes of marshland, sheep-breeding tribes, and camel- and horse-breeding tribes.

---

11 TNA: FO 195/318, No. 33, 20 June 1848; Longrigg, *Four Centuries of Modern Iraq*, pp. 242–47. According to Bustani, toman (tümen altını) was equal to 105 kuruş, and küçük tümen was 82 kuruş. Mehdi J.H. al-Bustani, "Bağdad'daki Kölemen Hâkimiyetinin Te'sisi ve Kaldırılması ile Ali Rıza Paşa'nın Vâliliği (1749–1842)," Ph.D. diss., Istanbul University, 1979, p. 348.

12 For a list of districts and sub-districts, see Kayi, *Bagdad, 1831–1869*, pp. 114–17.

13 Mehmed Hurşid Paşa, *Seyâhatnâme-i Hudûd* (Istanbul: Takvimhâne-i Âmire, 1277 AH [1860]), pp. 185–94, 210–11.

Each clan within these tribes was a quasi-independent tribal group belonging to a larger tribal confederation. The paramount sheikh of the confederation usually was elected from among the sheikhs of the leading clans of the camel- and horse-breeding tribes and officially acknowledged by the government in Baghdad or in Basra with fixed tributes for his chieftainship. Such confederations were numerous, including the Shammar Jarba on the west side of the Tigris River, the Tay and the Ubaid on the east side of the Tigris, the Dulaim on the Upper Euphrates, the Aniza between the two rivers, the Khazaʿil and the Zubaid on the Middle Euphrates, the Muntafiq on the Lower Euphrates, the Shammar Togha on the Middle Tigris, the Bani Lam on the Lower Tigris, and the Kaab in the west of the Shatt al-Arab. The Aniza, the Shammar Jarba, and the Tay were not involved in agriculture to any substantial extent. The Ubaid, originally pastoral nomads, had begun to settle in Falluja, Tikrit, and Mosul after the truce between the government and the Shammar Jarba in 1817.[14] The others were seldom settled, but they adhered to tribal tradition.

In addition, smaller tribal groups were semi-settled yet virtually free from the command of the paramount sheikh of the large confederations. On the Middle Euphrates, from Radwaniya to Abu Ghraib, for example, the lands along the river belonged to the Zubʿa. The tribesmen of the Zubʿa had been scattered in Abu Ghraib and Hor Aqr Quf, and some of them had been transferred to Baʿqūba as peasants on reclaimed land. Below Abu Ghraib, in the Hilla district, was the domain of the half-peasant and half-nomad Albu Sultan, whose territory stretched as far toward the desert as the water ran in winter. In summer they settled in date groves as temporary workers. Other tribes in Diwaniya and Hilla, as far down as Shamiya and Dughara, also were half-peasant and half-nomad, but the longer the distance from the district centre of Hilla, the more nomadic and armed were the tribesmen. Because their sheikhs were at liberty to police their tribesmen and collected levies for their own and the tribe's revenue, they fiercely resisted the government's intervention into tribal affairs.[15]

The uprisings of the self-ruling tribal sheikhs tended to be abortive hit-and-run raids within their domains. Afterwards, the defeated sheikh was forced to arrange tax payment to the state, but he then was officially acknowledged by the government as the paramount sheikh of the tribe, received governmental subsidies such as grains and foodstuff, and was honoured with the robe of investiture. As the sheikh's external political power shrunk, he thus gained internal power within the tribe and economic wealth as the paramount sheikh. This change became even more significant when the appointment of the Arab

14 Nieuwenhuis, *Politics and Society in Early Modern Iraq*, pp. 127–28.

15 TNA: FO 195/752, No. 16, 22 Apr. 1863; No. 20, 8 May 1863.

tribal sheikh as the tax farmer or district official ceased to be a nominal honour and acquired the true responsibilities of tax payment and administration in the early Tanzimat period.

In the absence of Ottoman authority before 1831, the province of Baghdad had been divided vaguely into urban residential areas, agricultural areas in which tax farming was implemented, and the domains of the large tribal confederations. The local *mamlûk* (military slave) regime could fairly govern the city, the towns, and their surroundings, but not the areas beyond them, where tribesmen had been equipped with weapons. After the Tanzimat, their centralizing process began habitually through incessant battles and compromise between the Ottoman governor and tribal sheikhs.

Upon the reconquest of Baghdad, Governor Ali Rıza Pasha (1831–42) first gained the obeisance of the urban notables in the city and then of the nearby tribesmen, empowering him to carry out the routines of government and bring up bills for local application. Subsequent governors – Mehmet Necip Pasha (1842–49), Abdülkerim Nadir (Abdi) Pasha (1849–50), Vecihi Pasha (1850–51), Mehmet Namık Pasha (1851–52 and 1861–68), Mehmet Reşit Pasha (1852–57), Ömer Lütfi Pasha (1857–59), and Mustafa Nuri Pasha (1859–61) – continued the discipline of Ali Rıza Pasha and solidly established Ottoman suzerainty over the province. They were followed by Ahmet Tevfik Pasha (1861), Mehmet Namık Pasha (1861–68), Takiyüddin Pasha (1868–69), and Midhat Pasha (1869–72). Already renowned figures before assignment, a few were subsequently promoted to higher positions in the Sublime Porte, including Abdülkerim Nadir (Abdi) Pasha (Abdi Pasha in the following) to commander-in-chief of the Ottoman army, Namık Pasha to commander-in-chief of the artillery, and Midhat Pasha to prime minister. All except the Croatian Ömer Pasha were Turks and came into office with large retinues of their own, and all but Vecihi Pasha concurrently served as commander-in-chief of the Iraq and Arabia Army (Sixth Army after 1847), therefore sometimes being branded as dictatorial governors. Their terms of office were brief, as was usual for governors, but in contrast to previous periods, the governors now had established disciplines of centralization to follow.[16] Their tribal policies and new reforms in this period precluded deeper changes in the relationship between the government and the tribes and, subsequently, within tribal society. Their history

16 Studies on other provinces under Ottoman rule after the Tanzimat are proliferating. Khaled Fahmy, *All the Pasha's Men: Mehmed Ali, His Army and the Making of Modern Egypt* (Cambridge: Cambridge University Press, 1997); Johann Bussow, *Hamidian Palestine: Politics and Society in the District of Jerusalem, 1872–1908* (Leiden: Brill, 2011); Thomas Kuehn, *Empire, Islam, and Politics of Difference: Ottoman Rule in Yemen, 1849–1919* (Leiden: Brill, 2011).

until Mustafa Nuri Pasha in 1861, briefed below, presents how their centralizing policy affected the tribal sheikh and tribesmen in the province, suggesting the deep changes that followed.

2 The Governorships of Ali Rıza and Necip Pashas, 1831–1849

Ali Rıza Pasha's regime retained some characteristics of the *paşalık* (Pasha's province) with little change from the previous era.[17] After disbanding the *mamlûk* troops and janissaries and winning the support of notables in the city, he initiated an endless battle against the rebellious tribesmen. The source of his authority was the Iraq and Arabia Army of the Ottoman New Army, which was disciplined and equipped with modern weapons. The artillery regiment and two battalions of the cavalry and infantry regiments were stationed in Baghdad for military campaigns against the Arab tribesmen, as well as for the defence of the city. A northern battalion of the infantry regiment, in Mosul, could be called on if needed. Cavalrymen and infantry soldiers, recruited from among the irregular troops of the tribesmen, were supplemented by the armed forces of the friendly tribal sheikhs and a regiment of troops from Diyarbakir. For these extra expenses, Ali Rıza Pasha obtained 50,000 kuruş from the Imperial Treasury after repeated petitions to the Porte.[18]

17 Born in Trabzon, Ali Rıza Pasha had served as the district governor in Manisa, the customs official in Izmir, and the district governor in Menemen in the Izmir province. In 1828–29, he was promoted to deputy governor of Aleppo and, in the following year, to governor of Aleppo. He then was appointed commander-in-chief of the expedition against Governor Davud Pasha in Baghdad and, after defeating him in 1831, was appointed Baghdad governor. Al-Bustani, "Bağdad'daki Kölemen Hâkimiyetinin Te'sisi," p. 168.

18 The troops were organized according to the Ottoman system. The regiments of infantry and artillery were composed of the First Alây, the Second Alây, the Mosul Alây, and the Topçu Alây, and the regiments of cavalry were composed of the Ali Rıza Pasha Alây, Salim Pasha Alây, and İsmail Hakkı Pasha Alây. Under a commander-in-chief, each Alây (troop) comprised a lieutenant general, major, adjutant, centurion, lieutenant, sergeant, cadet-sergeant, cadet-centurion, corporal, and soldiers, with a staff of imam, standard-bearer, payroll scribe, and scribe. Ten foot soldiers composed a squad under the leadership of a corporal; two squads were led by the sergeant, and four squads by the lieutenant. The unit of eight squads, called a century, was commanded by the centurion. Eight centuries made up a battalion, which was commanded by the major. One to three battalions were organized into a regiment under the command of the colonel. A cavalry regiment contained three battalions, an infantry regiment three battalions, and an artillery regiment one battalion. BOA, İ. Mesâil-i Mühimme 2038, 4 Cemaziyelâhir 1260; Necati Tacan, "Tanzimat ve Ordu," in Turkey, Ministry of Education, Tanzimat (Istanbul: Maarif Matbaası, 1940), i, pp. 3–7.

Supported by the strongest military forces in the region, Ali Rıza Pasha inaugurated civil administration. The chief officials in his government were the deputy governor, the chief treasurer, the head secretary, and the head of the customs house in Baghdad. The head secretary supervised the various kinds of scribes who performed administrative routines. All official correspondence with the Sublime Porte went through his office, and he was responsible for organizing the administrative council composed of high government and military officials, ulema, merchants, and representatives of the Christian and Jewish millets. Only administrative matters involving religious issues were left to the ulema. The chief judge (*kadı*) was appointed by the *Şeyhülislam* in Istanbul and seldom stayed longer than a year or two. The *müftü*, *Şafî müftü*, and *nakîb al-aşraf* were judges of the highest rank in Baghdad, assisted by scribes, *kapıcı*, *mühürdâr*, *Arap kâtibi*, and *Fâris kâtibi*. Most judicial matters actually were handled by the vice-judge (*nâib*) appointed from the local ulema.[19]

The chief treasurer was appointed by the Imperial Treasury in Istanbul from among its officials and was directly responsible to it. He oversaw the financial matters of taxation, bookkeeping, and regular reporting to the capital, but he always colluded with the governor, who forced him to overlook any corruption. Both military and public expenses were funded by tax revenues and proceeds from the chief treasurer's auction of properties and tax farms confiscated from the military officials, administrators, and notables who had supported the previous government. Under the influence of Ali Rıza Pasha, however, the powerless chief treasurer transferred the tax farms to relatives of the governor and his retinue, high-ranking officials, and notables in Baghdad without the required payment or the issue of authorization. Because of such corruption and maladministration, that chief treasurer was replaced in 1837 by a new treasurer from the Imperial Treasury. The rights to tax farming that the discharged treasurer had illegally transferred were cancelled, auctioned again, and properly recorded by the new treasurer in the official account books.[20] The details of the new auction were reported to the Imperial Treasury, and the letter of authorization was issued only after receipt of the report and required payment. But the centralized bribe remained an informal way of maintaining political control over the people. Consequently, tax farms were still often

---

19 The administrative council (*meclis-i idâre* or *meclis-i kebîr*) was officially renamed *meclis-i şurayı* in 1841. After Ali Rıza Pasha's resignation, the council was held twice a week. BOA, İ. Mesâil-i Mühimme 2044, 19 Receb 1262; İ. Dahiliye 2133, 21 Receb 1257; Nieuwenhuis, *Politics and Society*, pp. 26–29; Ceylan, *Ottoman Origins of Modern Iraq*, pp. 110–15.

20 The revenues were recorded in the entries of *malikâne kalemi* and *başmuhâsebe kalemi*. The deposit and fees paid by the tax farmer were recorded in *resm-i kasr-ı yedi* and *harâç-ı aklam*.

granted to those who bribed the governor, the treasurer, and members of the administrative council, and the amount of the tax itself was discounted or evaded, decreasing the revenue for the treasury.

Probably due to their short distance from Baghdad, a number of tribal sheikhs in the Hilla district on the Middle Euphrates River accepted the governor's authority by way of tax farming. Each was appointed as tax farmer of his tribal land, contingent on being acknowledged as the tribal sheikh by the government. Most such tax farms awarded to sheikhs were exempt from paying tax in return for the sheikh's service to the government. In the Hilla district, Ali Rıza Pasha deliberately manipulated the application of tax farming according to the balance of power among the tribes and within the tribal confederation, and his seizure of tribal tax farms proved effective in bringing change to the area. After bitter battles, uncooperative tribal sheikhs were forced to accept the label of tax farmer. When there was a change in governor, however, the sheikhs tended to revert to violence if the tax price was punitive. Outside Hilla, in the tribal domain, the government collected the tax from the tribal sheikh as state money at the amount set when he was acknowledged as the paramount sheikh of the tribal confederation.

In 1839, the Tanzimat edict was officially declared in Baghdad, drastically curtailing Ali Rıza Pasha's political authority, although the principle of the edict was little understood by the local people. One of its direct effects was the growing influence of the administrative council over civil administration under supervision of the Porte. According to an order of the sultan in 1841, the council was authorized to discuss issues independently of the governor, and the head secretary reported its discussions and decisions monthly to the Porte for the approval of the sultan. Ali Rıza Pasha was said to have become so frustrated by this constraint on the authority he had enjoyed for eleven years that he repeatedly petitioned for transfer out of Baghdad. He was eventually appointed governor of Aleppo in 1842. During his term in Baghdad, he borrowed nearly five million kuruş from local individuals to cope with a deficit resulting from a skip (*sıvış*) year in the fiscal calendar, and he left Baghdad before he could repay it.[21] Although he took the elite troops of his regiment with him to Aleppo, numerous foot soldiers deserted at his departure, weakening the military forces considerably and demonstrating that the Ottoman

21 In principle, the tax farmer paid his taxes in March and August, according to the solar calendar, but the revenues were spent according to the lunar calendar and for shorter, quarterly intervals. Halil Sahillioğlu, "Sıvış Year Crises in the Ottoman Empire," in M.A. Cook, ed., *Studies in the Economic History of the Middle East* (London: Oxford University Press, 1970), pp. 230–52.

regime in Baghdad was yet fragile. On the other hand, as pointed out by Mehdi I.H. al-Bustani, Ali Rıza Pasha deserves recognition for maintaining peace and order for the nearly twelve years after his reconquest of Baghdad. The Ottoman regime he established continued to expand and stabilized under the next governor, Necip Pasha (1842–49).[22]

Necip Pasha preserved a spirit of the pasha's province as he had no experience as a governor or an official.[23] He began, as had his predecessor, with a weakened military force and a vision of a centralized province inclusive of tribal domains. According to British Consul in Baghdad Henry Creswicke Rawlinson, Necip Pasha's priorities were the complete subjugation of the tribes to Ottoman authority; showing a bold front to Persia, for which he had intolerant hatred; agricultural development focusing on flood control, irrigation, and land reclamation; and the extension of tax farming more widely and efficiently for revenue collection. By implementing them, he attained greatness in the eyes of the local people and provided a blueprint that subsequent governors more or less followed.[24]

Rawlinson further noted that Necip Pasha's resolve to challenge Persian aggression was not groundless, since defiant Persians and rebellious tribes had caused formidable trouble to the government. Karbala, for example, had been ruled by a party of up to 2,500 reckless Persian criminal refugees, deserters from the army, and outlaws. Three-quarters of Karbala's eighty thousand residents were Persians, who did not recognize any authority. Although they frequently entered the Ottoman army during recruitment drives, neither the Persian consul nor the Baghdad government could exercise political power over them.

In 1842, apprehending that the Persian rebels in Karbala were divided and weakened, Necip Pasha planned a decisive attack against them. In order to mobilize troops from the north, he requested the Porte to separate the district of Shahrizor from the province of Baghdad and temporarily reorganize it as a province. Then, he stationed in Karbala a massive force that reportedly numbered five or six thousand men. A dreadful battle brought the rioters under the complete control of a new chief judge and governor, through arbitration with the Persians in the town, and the appointment of Karbala's governor by Baghdad became customary thereafter.[25]

22 Al-Bustani, "Bağdad'daki Kölemen Hâkimiyetinin Te'sisi ve Kaldırılması," p. 168.

23 Reportedly the governor purchased the post for an annual revenue of 50,000 kese (25 million kuruş). TNA: FO 195/334, No. 7, 11 Mar. 1850. On the governorship of Necip Pasha in Baghdad, see Herzog, *Osmanische Herrschaft*, pp. 91–104.

24 TNA: FO 195/334, No. 18, 23 May 1849.

25 By 1844, the number of pilgrims returned to the previous average of 50,000, yielding a profit of at least 150,000 pounds sterling yearly. Juan R.I. Cole and Moojan Momen, "Mafia,

Another disputed area was Muhammara, in which the sheikh Jabir had rebuilt the fort after its attack by Ali Rıza Pasha in 1837. Because Muhammara had begun to prosper as a port town since then, the Ottoman navy placed warships on the Haffar Canal to prevent boats laden with Indian goods bound for Muhammara from passing through the Shatt al-Arab. The boats now either sailed up Banisher instead of the Shatt al-Arab, or, if there was flooding, they landed their cargo on the island of Abadan, a few miles below the mouth of the Haffar Canal, and carried their goods across by land. The rapid expansion of the port of Muhammara also drew the interest of the Persian government, and in 1843, after a series of battles, the sheikhs Hachim and Jabir were captured by the Persian authority in Dizful which, unlike Necip Pasha, did perceive the future strategic and commercial importance of Muhammara. In 1845, after agreeing to an annual payment of 70,000 keran (3,500 pounds) to the Persian governor of Dizful, the captured sheikhs were released and returned to Fallahiya and Muhammara respectively. Later in the same year, however, Jabir, alerted to a threat from the powerful Persian troops, evacuated the town with a large portion of his tribe, crossed the Euphrates River, and joined the Muntafiq Arabs on the right bank of the river. A Persian garrison was established in Muhammara without delay after Jabir's retreat. Necip Pasha had failed to counterattack the Persian troops in support of Jabir because the ongoing domestic war in the Lower Euphrates region left him with insufficient forces to do so. In 1847, the two governments agreed to remove Ottoman guardianship from the Haffar Canal but confirmed the authority of Basra over shipping on the Shatt al-Arab.[26]

Although he lost control over Muhammara, Necip Pasha secured peace and order in the agricultural areas on the Middle Euphrates River by pacifying Karbala. Besides appointing the district governor for administration, he established an amiable relationship with the powerful sheikh of the Muntafiq

---

Mob and Shiism in Iraq: The Rebellion of Ottoman Karbala, 1824–1843," *Past and Present* 112, no. 1 (1986), pp. 112–43.

26 In 1846, Muhammara and its dependencies north of the Haffar Canal were occupied by Hamed Ibn Sandal for a tributary payment of 33,000 keran. The southern fortress of Muhammara and the island of Abadan were taken by Salman Ibn Ghadban for 30,000 keran. Fallahiya, along with the lands of Jerrahi to the plain of Ruiminz and Karun as far as Ahwaz, continued under the authority of Sheikh Faris for 38,000 keran. The dependency of Fallahiya, including Guban and the lands between that place and the Bamishere (Mesene) Canal, bounded on the north by the Fallahiya Canal, and on the south by the sea, were administered by petty chiefs under Sheikh Faris in exchange for 29,000 keran and yielded a total revenue of 130,000 keran to the Persian government. TNA: FO 195/237, No. 1, 6 Jan. 1844; FO 195/237, No. 9, 4 Feb. 1846.

tribe, who yielded to him voluntarily.[27] This peaceful relationship then proved a great help to the governor in mobilizing tribesmen for military campaigns, as well as for agricultural and irrigation projects. He gave the tax farm on the Hindiya Canal to his son Ahmet Pasha and that for the tribal district of Hilla and the Nahr Shah Canal to the paramount sheikh of the Zubaid tribe, Wadee, a warlord over the Albu Sultan, Madan, and other small peasant tribes in the Hilla district.[28] When the tribesmen in Hindiya defiantly refused to pay taxes, the governor won the support of the paramount sheikh of the Khaza'il tribe; took over the strongest tribal fortress in the area, Qal'a Hammar; and stationed Ottoman troops there permanently. Extending his expedition on the right bank of the Euphrates River, he destroyed the other tribal fortresses, settled peasant tribesmen, and constructed observation posts in their settled locations.

Necip Pasha, moreover, established a district government in Diwaniya and appointed the military commander as the district governor, with responsibility for tax collecting in this pacified area. In support of the district governor, he constructed a new fortress and stationed there irregular troops composed of the pro-government tribesmen of the Ugail (*Ukayl*) to protect the cultivating peasant tribesmen in the area. Reinforcing the military force, he embarked on military operations against the Khaza'il in Shamiya, the Madan in Dughara, and the Ufak in Ufak, where the local government had hardly trooped.

Establishing peace and order in the Middle Euphrates region, Necip Pasha endeavoured to promote agriculture, over which he publicly asserted his interests. Among the projects for water control, irrigation, and land reclamation he implemented were repairing the Hindiya Barrage in Musaib to control flooding from the Euphrates, cleaning the Abbasiya Canal, and a number of irrigation projects in Hindiya, Abu Ghraib, Mahmudiya, Radwaniya, and Iskandariya.[29] While mobilizing large numbers of tribesmen to work on these improvements, he enhanced his prestige among the tribes. The consequent increase in both tax revenues and his personal income easily covered the initial cost of paying off Ali Rıza Pasha's debt and reinforcing his troops.

---

27 For reform in this period, see BOA, İ. Mesâil-i Mühimme 2054, 6 Muharrem 1263; TNA: FO 195/334, No. 7, 11 Mar. 1850. For the governor's tribal policies, see Ceylan, *Ottoman Origins of Modern Iraq*, pp. 137–41.

28 For a Scottish traveller's visit in Sheikh Wadee's tent in 1835, see James Baillie Fraser, *Travels in Koordistan, Mesopotamia, & C.* (London: Richard Bentley, 1840), ii, 45–48.

29 Rhoads Murphy, "The Ottoman Centuries in Iraq: Legacy or Aftermath? A Survey Study of Mesopotamian Hydrology and Ottoman Irrigation Projects," *Journal of Turkish Studies* 11 (1987), pp. 17–29; Ahmed Sousa, *Irrigation in Iraq: Its History and Development* (Baghdad: New Publishers, 1945), pp. 22–36.

Necip Pasha clearly preferred the old style of quasi-independent *paşalık* to the principle of the Tanzimat movement. British Consul Henry Creswicke Rawlinson's handwritten diary during an excursion from Baghdad to Persia in 1847 hints at the pasha's recognition of reality in the rural area. His conversation with a *zabit* (village official) in Kızlarbat (Qizlarbat) is noted in his shorthand writing:

> Kizil Rubat [Kızlarbat] is this year in Necip Pasha's own hands. The *zabit* is one of the Baghdad officers whom I know intimately. He says the harvest is not so bad as the farmers wish to make out. He will realize this year for the portion more than usual amount of the farm and he adds that he thinks the assessment will go far to assess the contracts, which under ordinary circumstances unfavorable to government. Enquired about thieves and he said the country was quite clear of them. In fact he acted at wherever here find the road disturbed depend upon that the robbers are in league with the *zabit* and this strongly suspect to be true. He complaint however sadly of *Tanzimat* all very well he said for a civilized country like Rumelia and Anatolia but for these Kurds and Arabs the wallet and tent are the only things to keep them in order.[30]

In Shahriban, Baladruz, and Mandali, where he stayed overnight during the excursion, Rawlinson also observed the significant role of the *zabit*, who resided in a rural area and established himself as a local magnate. He carried out tax farming, supervised agricultural production, maintained canals, and performed the administrative duties of maintaining safety and dealing with plunder by nearby tribes. Especially the *zabit* in Kızlarbat (Qizlarbat) was a notable official as he was descended from an old Baghdad family serving as the agent for tax farms held by the treasurer of province (*defterdar*). His opinion that the Tanzimat was ill-suited for pastoral society, as recorded by Rawlinson, is suggestive of the local governor's harmonizing attitude towards local customs and tribal traditions.

Necip Pasha, while intimately acquainted with local society, mishandled his relations with the Porte, which had been gaining control over provincial

30 Henry Creswicke Rawlinson kept writing this diary in a tent at halting places, even arriving after two-hour's hot wind at night or departing at two o'clock in the morning. Royal Geographical Society Archives, H.C. Rawlinson Collection, no. 10 [Excursion from Baghdad? 1850]. Rawlinson left Baghdad on 29 June 1847 and started his return to Baghdad on 25 September 1847.

affairs by enacting new regulations.[31] He often neglected his duty to report revenues to the Imperial Treasury and appointed the *defterdar* himself. He demanded bribes openly, threatening to remove tax exemptions long held by tribal sheikhs, ulema, and notables. The costs of his improvement of projects were added to the taxes, which he collected in a new, more oppressive manner. When he increased the amount of the tax at the renewal of Sheikh Wadee's tax farming privilege, the peasant tribesmen rose up against both the tax farmers and the government, and the uprising soon spread due to the discord between Necip Pasha and the commander-in-chief of the Sixth Army, Abdi Pasha. The two had repeatedly confronted each other over the bribes and oppressive tax farming on peasant tribesmen, and Abdi Pasha had frequently lobbied the Porte for Necip Pasha's removal and for implementation of the Tanzimat. The animosity between them now escalated into an open conflict throughout the Middle Euphrates, a conflict that became one of the worst uprisings of the nineteenth century. The Porte finally cancelled Necip Pasha's appointment as governor and replaced him with the so-called man of Tanzimat, Abdi Pasha, in 1849.

After his removal, Necip Pasha was criticized for the wealth he had amassed in Baghdad and was officially prosecuted by an investigative committee for extortion and bribery. Nevertheless, his achievements were not negligible. He evidently understood the basic principles of local administration, an understanding that had escaped Ali Rıza Pasha. Besides dramatically increasing the total amount of agricultural revenue paid to the government, he excavated a number of small canals for irrigation, built and repaired various public edifices, publicized the need to develop agriculture and increase foreign exports, and was openly concerned for the interests and welfare of the people under his control. Although many of his plans were never undertaken, for lack of public funds, they provided a blueprint for the agricultural projects and tribal policies of subsequent provincial governors following a period of tribal uprising in the region.

---

31 For regulations affecting the provincial administration in Baghdad in this period, see Ceylan, *Ottoman Origins of Modern Iraq*, pp. 113–22; Stanford J. Shaw, "The Origins of Representative Government in the Ottoman Empire: The Provincial Representative Councils, 1839–1876," in Bayley R. Winder, ed., *Near Eastern Round Table, 1967–1968* (New York: Near East Center and the Center for International Studies, New York University, 1969), pp. 76–78; Stanford J. Shaw and Ezel Kural Shaw, *History of the Ottoman Empire and Modern Turkey*, ii: *Reform, Revolution, and Republic: The Rise of Modern Turkey, 1808–1975* (Cambridge: Cambridge University Press, 1977), pp. 84–89.

3 The Arab Tribal Uprising of 1849–1852 and the Policies of Reşit Pasha, 1852–1857

The tribal disturbance in the Arab domains that broke out near the end of Necip Pasha's term withstood the efforts of five governors to suppress it. As a capable career officer, Abdi Pasha, Necip Pasha's successor, was expected to restore peace, but his upright personality left him unable to make a political compromise with the Arab tribesmen and unwilling to manipulate the practice of tax farming for political purposes. The result was not peace, but a large-scale domestic war.

Abdi Pasha began his governorship in 1849 by appointing district administrators according to the administrative laws issued earlier for empire-wide application, bringing the province of Baghdad into compliance with the Tanzimat movement. But the absolute authority of the sultan over the province was incomprehensible to the tribesmen, who had never recognized the government's authority. The most abhorrent measures to them were Abdi Pasha's changing each tribe's domains into a district and a unit of a tax farm, then appointing the paramount tribal sheikh as the district governor-tax farmer. This reorganization confused local administrators, upset tribal sheikhs, and fuelled the uprising of peasant tribesmen. In Hindiya, reducing a high top-up tax on Wadee, the paramount sheikh of the Zubaid, to 2,000 lira failed to appease the rebels, and in 1850, the Khazaʿil and Madan tribesmen attacked Wadee in Diwaniya, while all available troops were operating in Sulaymaniya. Eventually, Abdi Pasha cancelled the tax-collecting right that Necip Pasha had granted to Wadee, in return for that large top-up tax, paid in a lump sum. Angered by the government's inconsistency, Wadee himself took up arms and became the leader of the rebellions.[32]

Another cause of the internal war was the failure of Abdi Pasha's divide-and-rule approach to the Muntafiq tribe. After the death of Sheikh Bundar in 1848, the district governor in Basra recognized Sheikh Faris b. Ajeel as the paramount sheikh of the Muntafiq, since Basra had traditionally ruled over the Muntafiq region. But Abdi Pasha overturned the decision and appointed Mansur as the paramount sheikh after the latter made a better offer on the tax payment. Faris then took up arms against Mansur in a clash of two powerful sheikhs that halted almost all economic activities in the region until Abdi

32 Reports on the tribal situations are numerous. For examples, see TNA: FO 195/367, pp. 186–93, from Commander Felix Jones to Lieutenant Consul Rawlinson, attached to No. 3, 25 Feb. 1852; FO 195/334, No. 17, 23 May 1849; No. 8, 13 Mar. 1850; FO 195/367, No. 5, 26 Feb. 1851; No. 27, 8 Oct. 1851; No. 1, 28 Jan. 1852; No. 14, 2 Feb. 1852.

Pasha captured Faris and officially appointed Mansur as the paramount sheikh of the Muntafiq, whom the whole tribal group acknowledged. Faris, however, immediately escaped from captivity and took refuge with the Bani Lam tribe in al-Jazira, from which he, along with rebels in Hindiya and Hilla, resumed the attack against Abdi Pasha and Mansur.[33]

In the midst of the tribal uprisings throughout the province, in January 1851 Abdi Pasha was called up by the Porte to serve as the commander-in-chief of the Ottoman army; Vecihi Pasha was appointed the new governor in the following month. To put down the rioting in Hindiya, Vecihi Pasha appointed Reşit, the deputy governor under Necip Pasha, as the district governor in Hilla and entrusted him with the tribal administration. Concurrently, Vecihi Pasha granted the right of tax farming to Reşit instead of Wadee. In order to strike a decisive blow against the revolting tribesmen, the Pasha called the commander-in-chief of the Sixth Army, Namık Pasha, away from Sulaymaniya to Hindiya, where he reinforced the Sixth Army with about 1,500 foot soldiers from the Army of Anatolia for successful campaigns in Hindiya and seized seven sheikhs of the rebellious Khazaʿil and Madan tribes in Hilla, sending them to Istanbul for trial. Vecihi Pasha tried to make an armistice with the tribal sheikhs, but he failed to persuade Namık Pasha to effect a ceasefire. Instead, against the will of Vecihi Pasha, Namık Pasha insisted on a traditional policy of divide and rule over the tribesmen and finally took over the government from Vecihi Pasha in 1851, whereupon he worsened the tribal uprising.[34]

A military man incapable of political compromise with Arab tribesmen, Namık Pasha refused to accept the Muntafiq tribesmen's choice of Mansur as their ruling sheikh. He selected Salih as the paramount sheikh and district governor and incorporated the tribal domain into the Ottoman unit of administration as a district, intending to institute the tribal sheikh as an appointee of the Ottoman government, contrary to the tradition of tribal consensus. Now, even Mansur joined Wadee's forces in military attacks against the pasha; in the north-east, Tay and Ubaid tribesmen took advantage of the turmoil to challenge the government. With rebellion widespread in the province, Namık Pasha mobilized large numbers of troops and added a detachment of three hundred men from the Army of Anatolia. Quarrelling with the military commander of Sulaymaniya, Şakir Pasha, over his tardy and inefficient operation,

---

33 There are numerous Ottoman documents on busy correspondence between the Porte and the Baghdad government on tribal uprising. For examples, see BOA, İ. Dahiliye 13804, 9 Cemaziyelevvel 1267; İ. Dahiliye 15445, 12 Receb 1268; İ. Meclis-i Vâlâ 7406, 19 Zilkade, 1267.

34 BOA, İ. Meclis-i Vâlâ 7043, 24 Şevval 1267; İ. Dahiliye 14068, 11 Receb 1267; İ. Dahiliye 14508, 10 Zilkade 1267; İ. Dahiliye 15673, 19 Ramazan 1268; İ. Dahiliye 15714, 8 Şevval 1268.

Namık Pasha superseded him but encountered a solid union of rebellious tribesmen, who took advantage of the roads and bridges constructed by Necip Pasha, particularly a bridge on the Hay River that carried a road into the Muntafiq territory. As the Amir and the Zubaid tribes rose in support of Faris, the rebellious ex-chief of the Muntafiq, only the south of the Hay on the Tigris was comparatively quiet.[35]

The Sublime Porte finally stepped in to arbitrate affairs in Baghdad. Namık Pasha was removed from office in March 1852 to head the Imperial Arsenal of Ordnance and Artillery in Istanbul. Reşit Pasha, named the new governor in the same year, immediately made a truce with Wadee and Mansur. He also addressed conciliatory letters to various Arab chiefs, promising an amnesty for past offences and generous treatment in the future, including respect for their internal authority within the tribe. Mansur was invested as the ruling sheikh of the Muntafiq and as the district governor and tax farmer of his domain, which was incorporated as a district. Salih, the appointee of Namık Pasha, became refractory but immediately was suppressed. As a limit on the sheikh's power, however, Reşit Pasha established a rule of auctioning the chieftainship every three years. He also separated Samawa from the Muntafiq domain and formed it into a sub-district of Diwaniya, appointing the military official as the governor of Diwaniya with the right of tax farming and a financial clerk, a vice-judge, and an Arabic scribe to assist him. The troops withdrew to Samawa, leaving some two thousand men in Suq al-Shuyukh.[36] It was a monumental decision for the Muntafiq tribal sheikh to accept the right of tax farming as tribute in place of state money, not to mention the removal of Samawa from his domain.

Designation of the powerful Muntafiq sheikh as the district governor and tax farmer for the first time in tribal history intensified the tribesmen's bitter

---

35 Namık Pasha bolstered the military force by adding the irregular troops in Diwaniya and a battalion of the Third Cavalry Regiment, a battalion of the First Infantry Regiment of the Anatolian Army, two battalions of the Second Infantry Regiment, and a battalion of the First Infantry Regiment in Baghdad. He scorned conciliation, deprecated all compromise, and avowed his determination to vindicate the sultan's honour by carrying fire and sword into the rebellious tribal domains. BOA, İ. Dahiliye 14081, 13 Receb 1267.

36 Ahmet N. Sinapli, *Mehmet Namık Paşa* (Istanbul: Yenilik Basımevi, 1987), pp. 156–57; James Felix Jones, "Province of Baghdad," in *Selections from the Records of the Bombay Government*, no. 43 (Bombay: Bombay Education Society's Press, 1857), pp. 359–69; Heinrich Petermann, *Reisen im Orient 1852–55* (Leipzig: Veit, 1860–61), pp. 90–96. A document on cutting pay for officials in Hindiya suggests that they had been paid well. For example, the monthly salaries of members of the administrative council were cut from 800 kuruş to 500 kuruş and that of the Arabic scribe from 600 kuruş to 400 kuruş, reduced levels that were still high for the time. BOA, İ. Meclis-i Vâlâ 18446, 18 Muharrem 1276; İ. Meclis-i Vâlâ 20550, 28 Rebiyülevvel 1278.

feelings against the government. Then, in 1855 Ottoman soldiers from Suq al-Shuyukh raided the Abouda (Abu Uda) tribe; entered the domicile of the Shiite *ʿālim* Sayyid Ibn Jerjees, who was much revered by the Shiite population; ravished his wives and daughter; and plundered the valuables stored in his house. As a consequence, Mansur's brother Nasir and his myrmidons from the Shabib families rose against Mansur in Suq al-Shuyukh, and a few days later, the whole Muntafiq tribe rose against the government once more.[37] Mansur agreed with Nasir, without the consent of Reşit Pasha, to remove half of the two thousand Ottoman troops in Suq al-Shuyukh to Samawa and to share the tax revenues and stipends of the ruling sheikh with him. Joined by a large number of militant tribesmen, they marched to Suq al-Shuyukh and defeated the troops in the town. Meanwhile, in Basra, the Bani Malik, the Bani Tamim, and the Bani Nehed tribes of the Muntafiq rose against the government, plundering the date-palm groves. In addition, peasant tribesmen in Hindiya took up arms against the oppressive commander of the irregular troops, Muhammad Aga, who had obtained the tax-farming right for three years in 1854–55. The Albu Muhammad also were uniting under Sheikh Faisal against the government's extravagant tax claims, and the Bani Tamin, the Shammar, the Aniza, the Tay, and the Ubaid resumed their depredations on the Upper Tigris.[38]

Knowing the preponderance of Russian influence at the court of Teheran, Reşit Pasha understood the danger that Persia posed to Baghdad. In 1855, he mobilized about sixteen thousand men and the artillery in Kut al-Amara against the refractory Muntafiq, repaired the fortifications of Baghdad, constructed four more fortresses between Hilla and Suq al-Shuyukh, and, raising horsemen and musketeers from Kurdistan, augmented the military force in order permanently to station regular troops of the First Cavalry Regiment there.[39] His swift action enabled him easily to suppress the Muntafiq uprising. While Nasir took refuge with the Defyr tribe in Shamiya and his tribesmen scattered, Mansur was replaced as paramount chief and district governor by the family head of the Sadun, Sheikh Bundar, who thus obtained the right of tax farming in the whole Muntafiq domain for three years. As the Sadun

37 The Shabib families comprised eight families who had migrated from Nejd 150–200 years earlier: the Sadun, the Rashid, the Saqer, the Aziz, the Salih, the Isa, the Ali, and the Uthman. The ruling sheikh of the whole Muntafiq tribe had traditionally been elected from among the sheikhs of these Shabib families. Hurşid Pasha, *Seyahatnâme-i Hudûd*, pp. 55–56.

38 BOA, İ. Dahiliye 27525, 17 Safer 1275; İ. Meclis-i Vâlâ 17443, 21 Muharrem 1275; İ. Meclis-i Vâlâ 18469, 6 Safer 1276.

39 TNA: FO 195/442, No. 22, 14 Sep. 1855; No. 25, 17 Oct. 1855; No. 26, 14 Nov. 1855; No. 39, 18 Aug. 1855; Petermann, *Reisen im Orient*, p. 78.

family's hold on the power of the paramount sheikh proved permanent, Nasir and Faris came to Baghdad for submission, and more complete subjection of the Muntafiq followed.

After implementing tax farming in the large Muntafiq domain, Reşit Pasha banned the illegal charges imposed by tribal sheikhs in the other tribal domains. In 1856, for example, he ordered Sheikh Ferhan of the Shammar to stop his blackmail of caravans and rafts, which traditionally had been overlooked. Instead, the governor officially paid Ferhan and his brother for keeping guards on the roads from Orfa to Basra. The sheikh was allowed free migration from Mosul down to lower Mesopotamia on condition that Ferhan's son was left as a hostage in Baghdad. As for the Bani Lam, the pasha forced their rebellious section across the Kerkha River into Persian territory and farmed out their land for support of the garrison in its district.[40]

In Muhammara, Reşit Pasha had been alerted to the Kaab rivalry in 1851 by the survey of Derviş Pasha, the commissioner for the delimitation of the Ottoman-Persian border. Although the sheikh Jabir tried to keep his distance from the Baghdad governor, Reşit Pasha attempted to extend his influence over the town on the side of Jabir for commercial reasons. However, he failed to undermine Persian dominance over the town. In 1854, the Persian authority imprisoned Jabir, whose tribesmen escaped to the protection of the Muntafiq sheikh Mansur, a staunch friend of Jabir, but Jabir was soon released from confinement and restored to the chieftainship in Muhammara. The Shahzade returned to Ahwaz in 1856, giving Jabir a new title in Muhammara and a troop of eight hundred men, with a few guns to protect the forts that were reconstructed by French engineers dispatched from Teheran. In response, Jabir's rival, a Kaab chief who had taken refuge at Zain, invaded Muhammara to fight against this movement. When Persian troops occupied an island in the river near the Haffar Canal to build a fort, Reşit Pasha ejected them by force. So again, the tranquillity of the region was disturbed. After the Crimean War, it was confirmed that the Shatt al-Arab belonged jointly to the Ottoman and Persian governments, while small vessels of the British Indian navy navigated permanently on the Shatt al-Arab to protect British interests in the region, as well as communication between Basra and the Gulf. Although the Persians respected the neutrality of the Shatt al-Arab, they continued to claim Muhammara as their territory.[41]

From 1852 to 1856, many Arab tribal sheikhs who previously had been almost independent of the government accepted the authority of Reşit Pasha,

40 TNA: FO 195/521, No. 5, 4 Feb. 1857.

41 TNA: FO 195/521, No. 17, 30 Apr. 1856; No. 19, 30 Aug. 1856; FO 195/624, 22 June 1859.

recognizing the government's enhanced military power and the high cost of rebellions against it. Both parties had exhausted their men and money in the battles of 1847–52, which also had cost them their incomes from agriculture, trade, and river transportation. Thus, instead of fighting the governor, they served him as tax farmers or district governors, or both. In large part, it was the pasha's personality that had allowed him to subdue the rebellious sheikhs, except for Mansur of the powerful Muntafiq. At the height of his acclaimed career as governor, however, Reşit Pasha suddenly died of natural causes in Baghdad. His post was taken over in 1857 by Ömer Pasha, the renowned commander-in-chief of the Third Army in the Balkans. As an experienced career officer with little knowledge of the Arab tribes he was to govern, Ömer Pasha fully relied on his military power and spent almost all his time in campaigns against the tribes. Unlike that of his predecessor, which was alternately severe and gentle, his policy of "pay the tax or prepare for a fight" embedded abhorrence of the government among the tribesmen.

4 Changes in the Status of Arab Tribal Sheikhs, 1857–1860

As governor, Ömer Pasha first moved to reinforce the Sixth Army. In 1857, he established a military school and made additions to the forces, such as a gun-laden steam flotilla on the Tigris River. He formed a body of irregular troops by recruitment among the Ugail tribesmen and enforced conscription in the lottery. While reinforcing the military force, he embarked on securing the routes of communication and transport for the troops, especially in the tribal domains destabilized by the change in governor. As the restless commander, he himself led the campaign throughout the province and affirmed the Ottoman officialdom.[42]

Upon restoring peace, Ömer Pasha began reorganizing the districts within the tribal domains and replacing their officials with members of his retinue at high monthly salaries. In 1852–53, for instance, the domain of the Dulaim tribe had been organized into the district of Dulaim from the tribal tax farm that had been established in 1849–50. The paramount sheikh of the Dulaim, İsmail Aga, was appointed initially as the district governor under Ömer Pasha. He was replaced by a civil official with a proposed salary of 5,000 kuruş, though

42 For conscription among tribesmen for military reinforcement, see Ceylan, *Ottoman Origins of Modern Iraq*, pp. 58 67.

İsmail Aga was allowed to keep the right of tax farming.[43] In Hilla in 1857, the pasha discharged the district administrator, citing as an excuse his oppression and corruption, and appointed a colonel of the artillery regiment, Hüseyin, at a monthly salary of 6,000 kuruş. In the following year the oppressive military official Hüseyin was recalled to Baghdad because he lacked experience in civil administration, and the pasha appointed the former governor of the Karbala district, Yaqub Efendi, to the governorship and a former financial clerk in Baghdad, Fathi Efendi, as the financial clerk in Hilla, the latter at a proposed monthly salary of 3,510 kuruş. In the district of Diwaniya, which had been unsettled by the maladministration and oppression of its governor, a Kurdish ex-tribal chief named Abdullah, Ömer Pasha made the colonel of the troops stationed in the district, Sibli, the new governor with a salary paid by the Baghdad treasury. Diwaniya, Ufak, Dughara, Shamiya, Khazaʿil, and Haska in the Middle Euphrates region were united into one district called Diwaniya, under the command of the district governor in Diwaniya. The rights of tax farming given to Abdullah and his retinue were all cancelled, and a special committee was organized to collect the tax arrears until the appointment of a new tax farmer.[44]

More drastic changes took place in the Bani Lam domain on the Lower Tigris River, which had long been troubled by freebooters. Ömer Pasha reorganized it as a district administered by Muhammad Beğ, the colonel of the First Regiment of Cavalry in Kut al-Amara, and the Albu Muhammad tribe was removed from the authority of the paramount sheikh of the Bani Lam and placed under direct administration of the Basra government. The tribal sheikh of the Albu Muhammad, Faisal, was given the right of tax farming at the amount of 130,000 shami (1,105,000 kuruş), of which 7,000 shami (59,500 kuruş) was to be paid to the Basra government. In 1861 the powerful sheikh Faisal managed to reorganize his tribal domain as a sub-district known as Albu Muhammad in the Kut al-Amara district. Meanwhile, the areas of Mandali, Badr, Jisan, and Zurbata, including the Ottoman-Persian boundary zone, had been separated from the district of Kut al-Amara and placed in the new district of Bani Lam. The head of the imperial stable in Baghdad, Yaqub Efendi, was appointed the district governor of Bani Lam at a high monthly salary of

43 Ömer Pasha himself made an expedition to Hindiya and Diwaniya against the Khazaʿil tribe, and a member of the pasha's entourage, İskender, restored the tranquillity between Hilla and Diwaniya. BOA, İ. Meclis-i Vâlâ 18358, 24 Ramazan 1275.

44 BOA, İ. Dahiliye 27060, 11 Zilkade 1274; İ. Meclis-i Vâlâ 17719, 18 Muharrem 1275; İ. Meclis-i Vâlâ 18497, 16 Safer 1276; TNA: FO 195/624, No. 14, 2 Mar. 1859; FO 195/577, No. 31, 5 July 1858; Dr K. [Josef Koetschet], *Erinnerungen aus dem Leben des Serdar Ekrem Omer Pascha* (Sarajevo: D.A. Kajon, 1885), pp. 47–120.

6,000 kuruş, equivalent to that of the colonel of the artillery regiment, while another official, Murad Effendi, was appointed as the sub-district governor of Mandali at 3,500 kuruş.[45]

Kut al-Amara was given to Osman Beğ, who was transferred from Samarra, at a monthly salary of 1,500 kuruş. All its other civil officials, such as a financial clerk, a population census scribe, and an Arabic scribe, were appointed by the Baghdad government, and the tribal sheikh was granted only the right to tax farming, with no administrative responsibility in his tribal domain.[46]

Meanwhile, in 1858 the vessels of both the Ottoman and British navies withdrew from Muhammara, allowing the Persians permanently to establish authority there. The strategic and commercial importance of Muhammara increased rapidly, however, after the river steamer *Baghdad* arrived in 1859 and began transporting passengers and light goods between Baghdad and Basra. Boundary disputes arose ceaselessly afterwards, due to the military and commercial interests of the two governments.[47]

Ömer Pasha, in contrast to Reşit Pasha, turned a blind eye not only to the customs and traditions unique to Arab society but also to local corruption and tyranny. The most notorious example was the chief of police in Baghdad, who was appointed by the pasha. His salary was officially 1,000 kuruş per month, only half of which came from the public treasury, while the remaining 500 kuruş were the expected fees of the office.[48] In another example, the taxes imposed on the Muntafiq tribe increased 500 per cent in fifteen years. Some smaller tribes were hurt even more directly when the pasha sought to destroy their military forces and closed the mouth of the Hindiya Canal, which carried water into the marshes of the Madan tribesmen after they revolted.[49]

---

45 BOA, İ. Meclis-i Vâlâ 17443, 21 Muharrem 1275; İ. Meclis-i Vâlâ 18469, 6 Safer 1276.

46 Ömer Pasha assigned the secretary of the municipal council, Hüsni, to carry out a comprehensive survey in Samawa, Suq al-Shuyukh, and Basra. The strategic importance of the Lower Tigris as an outlet to the Gulf had already become public after a British captain, Selby, made a topographical survey of the Albu Muhammad district. The British consul frequently reported the plunder of merchandise carried on the steamer *Comet*. The pasha also dispatched Hüsni on a mission to Kuwait and Bahrain, as one of the elders of the Bani Khalid tribe in Nejd had come to Baghdad to solicit assistance from Ömer Pasha in retaking Ahsa, whose ruler he claimed to be. BOA, İ. Dahiliye 27060, 11 Zilkade 1274; İ. Meclis-i Vâlâ 17443, 21 Muharrem 1275; İ. Dahiliye 27525, 29 Rebiyülevvel 1275; İ. Meclis-i Vâlâ 18358, 24 Ramazan 1275; İ. Meclis-i Vâlâ 18469, 6 Safer 1276; İ. Meclis-i Vâlâ 18472, 6 Safer 1276; İ. Meclis-i Vâlâ 20030, 27 Ramazan 1277; İ. Meclis-i Vâlâ 20148, 28 Muharrem 1278.

47 TNA: FO 195/624 (Baghdad, 1859–60), No. 2, 4 Jan. 1860.

48 TNA: FO 195/624, No. 5, 5 Jan. 1859.

49 The claim of Ömer Pasha for tax arrears in the tribal districts was exorbitant, as summarized in the table below.

Without irrigation water, their farms suffered a sharp drop in production, and entire tribes fell into unprecedented poverty.[50] It was in this period, as a consequence, that the people began to air their grievances against the governors for their treatment of the local Arabs.

Taking over from Ömer Pasha, who was replaced owing to his aggressive tribal policies in 1859, Nuri Pasha nevertheless benefitted greatly from the new tribal policies. The chief of the Muntafiq paid his respect at Nuri Pasha's arrival, and the prideful chief of the Hamawand, Faki Kadir, came to Baghdad in response to an official invitation to settle the disputes among the chiefs of Kurdistan.[51]

The only trouble was with the Bani Lam, whose sheikh was a rival of Sheikh Faisal of the breakaway Albu Muhammad. When Faisal died, Nuri Pasha promptly acknowledged Faisal's brother Menshed as the new sheikh to prevent internal conflict. Menshed, however, boldly attacked the Ottoman troops at Hudd. Although that regiment of eight hundred soldiers with three artillery guns was assisted by the commander of another regiment from Kut with five hundred soldiers, three hundred regular cavalrymen, and two guns, only when another sheikh of the Bani Lam, Mizban, joined them, could they strike a decisive blow against Menshed. As a reward, Mizban was acknowledged as the paramount sheikh of the Albu Muhammad. Now Nuri Pasha's prestige and

Governor (year)	Hindiya	Diwaniya*	Hilla	Samawa
	Kuruş	Kuruş	Kuruş (wheat & barley in tagar)**	Kuruş (wheat & barley in tagar)
Necip Pasha (1264/1847–48)	3,130,718	750,399	1,295,234 (53 & 45)	
Abdi Pasha-Namık Pasha (1265–67/1849–51)	5,330,802	1,930,283	1,531,896	
Reşit Pasha (1268–72/1852–56)	6,599,261	2,268,098	1,795,243 (4,518 & 6,144)	3,137,235 (159 & 630)
Total	15,060,781	4,948,780	4,622,373 (4,571 & 6,189)	3,137,235 (159 & 630)

* Includes the sub-districts of Shamiya, Khazaʿil, Ufak, and Dughara.
** Wheat and barley to be collected for military use.
SOURCE: BOA, İ. DAHILIYE 27211, 28 MUHARREM 1275.

50 A British consular report suggests that the tax was 2,000 purses (1 million kuruş), less than the average assessment of 6,700 purses (3.35 million kuruş). TNA: FO 195/577, No. 31, 5 July 1858.

51 TNA: FO 195/624, No. 20, 6 June 1860.

authority had become unassailable. Massacres of Christians in Damascus had raised great fear among the Christians in Baghdad, but even they calmed down under the stable government.

By 1860, improved communication and transportation had shifted the balance of power between the government and the Arab tribal sheikhs to the advantage of the former. A new telegraph line between Istanbul and Baghdad swiftly delivered orders from the Sublime Porte and allowed the governor to mobilize massive military forces against tribal rebellions in the region, while the use of steam vessels along the Tigris River enabled the government to oversee the Bani Lam and Albu Muhammad tribal conflicts.[52] Those vessels also allowed traders to expand commerce on the rivers and generated lucrative profits for the tribal sheikhs by carrying their commodities to market. The Arab tribal domains were now integrated into the Ottoman state system, and the tribal sheikhs became the backbone of government officialdom, although the peasant tribesmen began to nurture a grudge against the government.

5 Instability in Kurdistan

Tribes in southern Kurdistan also experienced drastic changes, albeit in different ways than those in the Arab domains. In the Soran emirates, the hereditary chiefs Muhammad Beğ, or Muhammad Pasha Kör (1826–38), Ahmad Beğ (1838–40), Süleyman Beğ (1840), and Rasul Beğ (1840–48) were powerful enough to maintain peace and order in the region. The only disruption occurred when Necip Pasha expelled Rasul as hereditary ruler in 1847 and replaced him with a member of his own retinue, Hussein Aga, a Kurd by birth but brought up in the governmental service. All the chiefs of the Soran then confederated against the pasha with the assistance of the tribal troops of Badr Khan Beğ. After they were defeated, Rasul was forced to retire in Baghdad, and the commander of the Ottoman troops took over the district government in Rawanduz. In Amadiya, the chief of the Bahdinan surrendered to the governor of Mosul in 1848 and fled into the interior mountains of Kurdistan. The chiefs never restored their own rule after that. Only the Baban chief Ahmed continuously annoyed the pasha by reinforcing his defences with support from the governor of Kermanshah, Mirza Hedayat.

52 Mustafa Kaçar, "Osmanlı Telegraf İşletmesi," in Ekmeleddin İhsanoğlu and Mustafa Kaçar, eds., *Çağını Yakalayan Osmanlı!* (Istanbul: İsâm Tarih, Sanat ve Kürtür Araştırma Merkezi, 1995), pp. 45–120; Ceylan, *Ottoman Origins of Modern Iraq*, pp. 187–92; Herzog, *Osmanische Herrschaft*, pp. 341–57.

The chief of the Baban had served concurrently as the governor of Shahrizor province and as the district governor in Sulaymaniya since construction of the military base there by the governor of Baghdad, Süleyman Pasha, in 1780. In order to regain his authority as Baban chief, independent of the Ottomans, during Necip Pasha's term as governor, Ahmed secretly purchased guns from foreign traders and paid Turkish officers and instructors lucrative sums of about 2,000 toman a year to train his tribesmen. As British Consul Rawlinson estimated in 1844, Ahmed had two regiments with fourteen artillery guns, holding three thousand horsemen in service.[53] Although this situation had made Necip Pasha uneasy, as long as the Babans paid him large sums of tribute, he did not dare destroy the status quo.

Ahmed's dominance, however, was not acceptable to the next governor, the military man Abdi Pasha, who set out permanently to dissolve the Baban domain. He discharged Ahmed as district governor in Sulaymaniya in 1850 and confiscated his family's private holdings – a number of villages, including watermills and the other fixtures attached to the villages. The villages, including their tax farms, which had been awarded to local officials, ulema, and notables, were also confiscated if they had been granted by the chief of the Baban as a part of salary payments or as a special reward. Abdi Pasha then reduced the province of Shahrizor to a district and incorporated it into the province of Baghdad. Accordingly, Rawanduz and Sulaymaniya, which had been districts of Shahrizor province, were reorganized as one district subordinated directly to the governor in Baghdad, and the military commander in Shahrizor was appointed as the new district governor, concurrently responsible for tax collecting. The local officials were all paid, according to their positions and ranks, from district revenues.[54]

---

53 The Baban chief had paid an annual sum of 5,000 toman to the Baghdad governor from the revenues of Sulaymaniya and Köysanjaq during the 1830s. Consul Rawlinson's estimate of the disbursement on the Baban government in the Sulaymaniya district in 1843 amounted to 2,185,000 kuruş. It was composed of the following: the revenue of Sulaymaniya charged to remit to the Baghdad treasury, 750,000 kuruş, of which Necip Pasha granted a remission of 120,000 kuruş (leaving 630,000 kuruş) and the revenue of Köysanjaq, 400,000 kuruş. In addition, it included expenses charged on the account of the district. They were fees to officers of the Baghdad court, 350,000 kuruş; expenses of 2 regiments of infantry and 14 guns, 750,000 kuruş; and pay for Turkish officers and troops, 55,000 kuruş. Lieutenant Colonel Robert Taylor, political resident in Baghdad until 1843, deemed the tax assessment on the Baban punitive. BOA, İ. Dahiliye 2133, 21 Receb 1257; İ. Mesail-i Mühimme 2039, 23 Rebiyülâhir 1261; İ. Mesâil-i Mühimme 2044, 19 Receb 1262; TNA: FO 195/237, No. 38, 10 July 1844; FO 195/237, No. 39, 24 July 1844.

54 Ceylan, *Ottoman Origins of Modern Iraq*, pp. 51–52.

The termination of the Baban's reign in Shahrizor changed the balance among the Kurdish tribes, so that the large Jaf and Hamawand tribes gained power instantly, while the Ottoman troops were unable to prevent their dominance over the plains of Shahrizor. The military commander who had become governor of Shahrizor farmed out tax collecting to his own relatives and dependents, who, in turn, sublet the tax farms to the petty chiefs of the Jaf and Hamawand tribes, without any security for payment or any provision for the maintenance of general order. In almost every case, these tribal tax farmers defaulted, and revenue declined by at least three-quarters. The continued wrangles of the Baghdad government with the Persians over the control of the tribesmen on the border left it unable to win the upper hand over the chiefs of the Jaf and the Hamawand.[55]

The Jaf was a confederation of numerous Kurdish and Persian tribesmen domiciled in wide areas from Köysanjaq towards the Persian border. Clans were closely connected by intermarriage and had been permitted to migrate across the border between their winter and summer locations. The collapse of the Baban had given them full liberty to appropriate tax revenue and exercise the real functions of government. Despite instigating the Jaf's rebellions against Ottoman authority, the Persian government had trouble with the Jaf tribesmen during their summer residence in Ardalan, where they accommodated outlawed and disaffected Persian Kurds in their camps. In 1853, the governor of Kermanshah attacked and expelled them by force from the Persian territory, with the full consent of the Ottoman ambassador but without consulting the Baghdad government.[56] The government of Kermanshah claimed sovereignty over the Persian Kurdish tribes, including the Jaf, according to the Treaty of Erzurum, but the Baghdad governor, Reşit Pasha, claimed that the tribes in question possessed a prescriptive right to pasture in his province and so were obliged to pay tax to his government. Locally, the governor of Sulaymaniya had been arguing with the government of Senna about pasturage dues, which the latter had claimed from the Jaf. In 1854, Ottoman negotiations with the Jaf had progressed to the payment of tax arrears and the restitution of Persian plundered property, and the issue of suzerainty over the tribe was raised for the first time. Reşit Pasha ordered Rasul, the former head of the Rawanduz district now residing at Baghdad, to gather horsemen under his personal influence and to retaliate against the Persians for their attack against the Jaf. Nevertheless, neither the governor of Sulaymaniya nor Reşit Pasha was able to march against

55 Sinan Marufoğlu, *Osmanlı Döneminde Kuzey Irak* (Istanbul: Eren Yayıncılık, 1998), pp. 121–26, 163.

56 TNA: FO 195/442, No. 30, 3 Sep. 1854.

the Jaf encamped within Persian lines or to punish the delinquent Jaf, who had sought asylum in the camps of the Persian tribes to shelter their families' cattle from plunder by the tribes of the rival Hamawand.[57]

Regarding the Hamawand, shortly after the collapse of the Baban emirate in Sulaymaniya in 1848, Namık Pasha, then commander-in-chief of the Sixth Army, determined to take more aggressive divide-and-rule measures over the Hamawand and other tribes. He was in close communication with the governors of Sulaymaniya and Shahrizor. Because of the Hamawand's influence in large areas from Kifri to Köysanjaq, along a main route from Baghdad to Mosul, their subjection was vital to securing the roads and maintaining order in the districts.[58]

British Consul Arnold Burrowes Kemball, watchful of Ottoman-tribal relations in this area, made a detailed report on the situation. According to it, the Baghdad governor had recognized Imam Suleiman as the chief of the Hamawand tribe with a monthly stipend and a certain allowance of grain in return for his keeping order and collecting taxes in the tribal domain. He was succeeded by his brother Faki Kadir, who was displaced by Reşit Pasha in favour of Aziz Kala. Two other powerful chiefs, Hussein Kala and Yahya, were also paid handsome allowances. From 1855 to 1858, order was generally maintained by these means, and Reşit Pasha even brought these Hamawand chiefs to his side against the Jaf. When Ömer Pasha became governor, however, Faki Kadir raised a revolt against him and killed all the Ottoman officials (*müdir*) of the districts of Bazilan and Karadag, except for the district governor of Karadag, and plundered these districts. The road to Sulaymaniya was blocked, and the ensuing disorder spread into the district of Kirkuk. Although Faki Kadir surrendered, his brother Naka, the *kahya* of the Hamawand, murdered the brother of Aziz Kala and also fatally shot Aziz Kala. Naka, in turn, was killed by the brother-in-law of Aziz Kala. Shortly afterward, when the Kermanshah government established friendly relations with the Jaf tribesmen on the frontier and claimed their allegiance for Persia, Ömer Pasha compromised with Faki Kadir and restored him to favour on the pension previously enjoyed by Aziz Kala. Ömer Pasha then turned his attention to a campaign against the rebellious Jaf.[59]

The traditional strategy of divide and conquer underlay Ömer Pasha's tribal policy in other districts of Kurdistan. In 1859, an infestation of locusts between

---

57 TNA: FO 195/367, No. 11, 17 May 1853; No. 26, 24 Aug. 1853; No. 34, 16 Nov. 1853; FO 195/442, No. 14, 31 May 1854.

58 TNA: FO 195/442, No. 14, 31 May 1854. For a list of Kurdish tribes in Mosul and Shahrizor, see Marufoğlu, *Kuzey Irak*, p. 69.

59 TNA: FO 195/624, No. 20, 28 Mar. 1859.

Mosul and Kirkuk damaged the grain crop, considerably reducing the taxable produce of the peasants, and even the Dulaim tribe refused to pay an increased tax on sheep. Ömer Pasha appointed an unknown member of his cadre, Rifaat, to be governor of Rawanduz, dismissed İsmail as governor of Shahrizor, and restored the powerful Muhammad Khosrow to the chieftainship of the Jaf to prevent the break-up of its confederation.[60] The pasha also used his command as a check on the Hamawand by appointing Khosrow to be the tax farmer of the Hamawand districts that had been yielding no revenues for the government in return for a tax payment of 50,000 purses (25 million kuruş) a year, with responsibility to maintain safe roads and general tranquillity. Ömer Pasha appeared in person, accompanied by considerable forces, for this settlement in Sulaymaniya in late 1859, having postponed departure to his new assignment in Istanbul. Other than the Hamawand in Sulaymaniya, southern Kurdistan enjoyed perfect tranquillity. But Ömer Pasha's approach to the Kurdish tribal chiefs had prolonged after-effects.[61]

6 The Impacts of Political Centralization

Although the complete subjugation of rebellious paramount sheikhs to the government was the costly challenge, Ottoman authority gradually penetrated into the tribal domains and became unwavering. Tax farming played an important role in this process. Ali Rıza Pasha had attempted initially to merge the tribal domains into his province by force, divide and rule, or an enforcement of taxation, but his authority was executed through face-to-face contact with tribal sheikhs rather than by operation of the Ottoman state system. Under his regime, tax farming was a somewhat privatized venture whose revenues entered into the governor's pocket directly. The next governor, Necip Pasha, proved more capable of authorizing the imposition of tax farming on the tribesmen and had a new vision of provincial administration beyond the traditional divide and rule. His appointment of the powerful sheikh Wadee of the Zubaid as the tax farmer in the Hilla region proved the usefulness of tax farming both for tribal administration and also as a business that dramatically increased his revenues. At the same time, favouritism in the granting of tribal tax farms tended to cause oppressive tax collection on the peasant tribesmen, who rose up in arms and forced Necip Pasha's eventual resignation.

60 TNA: FO 195/624, No. 26, 13 Apr. 1859.
61 TNA: FO 195/624, No. 20, 28 Mar. 1859.

Abdi, Vecihi, and Namık Pashas resorted to the traditional policy of divide and rule to crush rebellious tribesmen. They reorganized the tribal domains into districts and sub-districts under extended administration but provoked a more serious uprising of resentful tribesmen against these measures. The battles lasted longer than expected and turned into violent military clashes that severely curtailed local production, causing costly damage to agricultural infrastructure and loss of profits. Consequently, their successor, Reşit Pasha, made peace with the sheikhs at the outset. He devised an effective way of district administration and made progress in centralizing the province. Above all, he achieved military supremacy in the Arab tribal domains, which allowed Ömer Pasha to establish an enduring system of district administration there. The district government became free from the influence of the paramount tribal sheikh, as its head was appointed from among the officials, and the sheikh was made only the tax farmer in the tribal domain. In Kurdistan, however, the Baghdad governors were unable to implement a tribal policy more effective than divide and rule and so granted the tax-collecting privilege for a chief's lifetime, yielding him a high return. Similarly, in Muhammara, on the Shatt al-Arab, the governors failed to settle boundary disputes with Persia. But outside these two trouble-laden regions, tribal uprisings no longer threatened the Ottoman regime, as long as the regime did not threaten the sheikhs' profits.

Thriving on political centralization, the Ottoman government gained the ability to plan and implement a feasible policy for administration, economic growth, agriculture, and land tenure in the province of Baghdad. The integration of the Arab tribal domains into the province, moreover, led to a reallocation of the tribal labour force from within tribal society to more extensive areas, enabling tribesmen to migrate between tax farms and fields, from one project to another, serving as workers. The resulting increase in labourers enabled the government to pursue labour-intensive projects for water control, irrigation, and land reclamation, just as it allowed private individuals and tribal sheikhs to hire tribesmen for labour-intensive agricultural activities. The ensuing progress brought peace and order in the agricultural areas and moved semi-settled peasant tribesmen to settle on the land, while the sheikhs' expanded role in tax farming and production activities helped to improve the local economy still further.

CHAPTER 2

Agriculture

Agriculture was a perennial target of development for the Ottoman governors of Baghdad, for its produce provided the largest portion of tax revenues. From the early days, even while carrying out military campaigns against the tribal confederations, the government rehabilitated the destroyed barrages and irrigation canals in the irrigated areas and tax farms. At the same time, it encouraged tax farmers, tribal sheikhs, and village headmen to improve water channels, land fertility, land use, and the labour force. Agriculture, however, was subject to the vagaries of climate, peasant work habits, and the availability of implements. Poor agricultural conditions were difficult to overcome without investment capital, proven techniques, and expertise. In addition, the traditions of tax farming, crop sharing, and a share in private (*harâç* or *öşür*) land called *ukr* (Ar. *uqr*) controlled the production of crops and distribution of revenues at various stages and made the government's involvement less effective.[1] By the end of Mustafa Nuri Pasha's term (1859–61), it became obvious that the government had to overcome the inefficient distribution of irrigation water, reclaim patches of dry land, reorganize the ownership of agricultural land, and enhance private sector investment. To understand the agricultural problems and policies of the early Tanzimat period that led to that conclusion, this chapter examines the overall agricultural situation, the indigenous practices of crop sharing, and *uqr* among the constraints on agricultural development in the province of Baghdad.

1 Geography, Climate, and Agriculture

Agricultural performance was, above all, influenced by the topography and climate of the province. Most cultivated lands were located on the alluvial plains of the Tigris and Euphrates Rivers. Production other than animal breeding was inactive in the high mountains of the north-east and in the desert in the north-west between the two rivers. According to today's standards, the climate was Mediterranean in the northern region, and continental, semi-arid,

1 Details on *uqr* can be found in TNA: FO 371/4150/187296, Administration Report, Revenue Board, Baghdad, 22 Mar.–31 Dec. 1917 (Baghdad: Printed at Government Press, 1918), pp. 11–12.

 | DOI:10.1163/9789004384347_004

and subtropical in the central and southern regions.[2] Rainfall, which occurred from November to April, was insufficient for most regions. A line representing 300 mm of annual precipitation, drawn from Ramadi to Khanaqin, divided the province into zones of rainfall agriculture and irrigation agriculture. In the central and southern areas, the rainfall season lasted only from December to February, and the precipitation averaged less than 100 mm per year. In the mountain areas in the north, by contrast, the annual precipitation reached 1,200 mm, and rain-fed lands were located in Derbend, Mosul, Rawanduz, Shahrizor, Sulaymaniya, and Zangabad.[3]

The deficiency of rainfall was addressed by drawing water from the Tigris and Euphrates, from streams in the mountain area, and from springs. With occasional flooding, as well as drought, even in the rainfall zone, the supply of water fluctuated. The water of the Euphrates generally rose to its highest in May; that of the Tigris, in April. Through the impact of these natural conditions on land use, forests and wooded lands were limited to the rain-fed mountain area; the croplands, permanent meadows, and pastures were scattered on the alluvial plains of the rivers and in the foothills of the mountain areas.[4]

The Tigris River flowed from its headwaters in the Taurus Mountains of south-eastern Anatolia across the province of Baghdad from the north-west to the Gulf. It meandered constantly between steep banks, well below plain level, so that water lifts or other irrigation facilities were needed to make its water available for agriculture. It had six tributaries on its left bank: the Greater

---

2 Among numerous sources on agriculture, Francis R. Chesney, *The Expedition for the Survey of the Rivers Euphrates and Tigris* (London: Longman, Brown, Green, and Longmans, 1850); Michael George Ionodes, *The Régime of the Rivers Euphrates and Tigris* (London: E. & F.N. Spon, 1937); Hans Heinrich Boesch, *Wasser oder Oel: Ein Buch uber den Nahen Osten* (Bern: Kummerly & Frey, 1944); Eugen Wirth, *Agrargeographie des Irak*, Hamburger Geographische Studien Im Selbstverlag des Instituts für Geographie und Wirtschaftsgeographie der Universität Hamburg (Hamburg, 1962); S.S. Johl (ed.), *Irrigation and Agricultural Development: Based on International Expert Consultation, Baghdad, Iraq, 24 February–1 March 1979* (Oxford: Pergamon Press, 1980); Nadhir A. al-Ansari, "Water Resources in Iraq," *Journal of the Geographical Society of Iraq* 14, no. 1 (1981), pp. 35–42.

3 The area of rainfall agriculture is distributed over present-day northern Iraq and the provinces (*muhafadha*) of Nineveh, D'hok, Erbil, Sulaymaniya, Ta'meen, and northern Diyala. Irrigation agriculture is broadly practised in central and southern Iraq. According to modern data, an annual rainfall of at least 200–300 mm is necessary for dry-farming agriculture. D. Hywel Davies, "Observations on Land Use in Iraq," *Economic Geography* 33, no. 2 (1957), pp. 125–29.

4 Travel books give a short overview of the province in this period. For example, James S. Buckingham, *Travels in Mesopotamia* (London: H. Colburn, 1827); Anthony N. Grove, *Journal of a Residence at Baghdad* (London: James Nisbet, 1832); Claudius James Rich, *Narrative of a Residence in Koordistan during the Years 1830 and 1831* (London: Duncan and Malcom, 1839).

Zab, the Lesser Zab, the Adamiya, the Diyala, the Nahr, and the Karkha. Among them, the Diyala, flowing from the Persian border in the north-east to south-west of the city of Baghdad, was of unequivocal importance, because its steady water flow was reliable.

The Euphrates River also had its headwaters in Anatolia, flowing from the province of Aleppo into the province of Baghdad from the north-west. The Euphrates was longer than the Tigris, and more than half of its course ran through the province. There were steep, high banks along the upper part of the river, a slow wide channel in the middle part, and large marshes formed after flooding along the lower part, known as the Upper Euphrates, Middle Euphrates, and Lower Euphrates respectively. The river flowed smoothly through the latter two regions on a level with the banks or higher, and its regular flooding began around the end of March and peaked in mid-May. The waters then receded rapidly, reaching their lowest level during November and leaving behind the marshes and conditions less suitable for grain production in the south. The Karun River, which ran from Iran into the Shatt al-Arab, carried fresh water before reaching the Gulf.[5]

Irrigation water that was not diverted from the rivers into canals was extracted from the rivers either by water lifts, which were waterwheels worked by the force of the current, or by water hoists, which were pulled up by animals. The waterwheels (*karûd*) operated on the Upper Euphrates, where the fields were located above the river, and along the west bank of the Hilla Branch. Water hoists were more commonly used on the Middle Euphrates and in scattered places along the Tigris River. On the Middle and Lower Euphrates, where large marshes had appeared in the flooding season, norias (*nawāʿīr*, s. *nāʿūra*), or Persian waterwheels, more commonly pulled up water into canals. The canals were divided into many subordinate branches by regulators to distribute the water into the fields. The canals ranged in width from a few metres to over 10 metres or, in some cases, up to 90 metres for maximum capacity during flood season.[6] Although maintaining water flow in these canals was crucial

5 John G. Lorimer, *Gazetteer of the Persian Gulf, Oman, and Central Arabia* (Calcutta: Superintendent of Government Printing, 1915), ii, pp. 793–96; Nuri Barazi, *The Geography of Agriculture in Irrigated Areas of the Middle Euphrates Valley* (Baghdad: Al-Aani Press, 1961), pp. 70–92; A.P.G. Poyck, "Farm Studies in Iraq," *Mdedelingen van de Landbouwhogeschool te Wageningen, Nederland* 62, no. 1 (1962), pp. 18–19.

6 E.g. the Dughara Canal was estimated to be 70 yards in width, the Yusufiya Canal 80 yards, the Machariye Canal 5–6 yards, and the Alaj Canal, which joined the Hindiya Canal below Kifli, 25 yards. J.B. Bewsher, "On Part of Mesopotamia Contained between Sheriat-el-Beytha, on the Tigris, and Tel Ibrahim," *Journal of the Royal Geographical Society of London* 37 (1867), p. 181; Great Britain, Admiralty War Staff, Intelligence Division, *Handbook of Mesopotamia* (London: The Division, 1916–17), i, p. 128; TNA: FO 195/752, No. 16, Baghdad, 22 Apr. 1863.

for agriculture, the canals were regularly clogged by weeds and silt or suffered from salinity.

The Euphrates River supplied large quantities of irrigation water. Above the Hindiya Barrage, the Saqlawiya Canal, constructed in the ʿAbbāsid period to release water from the Euphrates at Falluja, ran towards the Tigris through the Aqr Kuf depression.[7] Below it were the Nil Canal, nearly parallel to the river on its left bank, and the Husayniya Canal towards Karbala. The Euphrates was later diverted by the Hindiya Barrage into the Hilla and Hindiya Branches below Musaib, after the reopening of the Saqlawiya Canal by Midhat Pasha in 1871.[8] The government's repair of the Hindiya Barrage in 1911, according to the proposal of William Willcocks, raised the water level on the Hilla Branch to ensure a supply of irrigation water that had dried up because of a change in the flow of river water from the Hilla to the Hindiya Branch. Major canals on the left bank of the Hilla Branch towards Diwaniya, pulled at a right angle to the right bank, were the Nasiriya, the Mahawil, the Wardiya, and the Tahmasiya. The Muhannawiya and the Hawas Canals were on the left bank of the river. On the Lower Euphrates, around the Hawr Beyt natural reservoir and the marshes, irrigation more commonly occurred through flooding, without structural works. The major irrigation canals of the Diyala River were the Mahrut, the Shahriban, and the Khorasan. Along the Tigris River was the Dujaila Canal below Samarra.[9] The Lower Tigris also formed many marshes, but they were not always suitable for crop production. Numerous streams that flowed from the mountain inhabited by the Persian tribe of Kalhur down to Mandali irrigated large plots of land for cultivation, resulting in one or two notable conflicts over control of the water supply between the cultivators and the Persian tribesmen (see Maps 2.1 and 2.2 at the end of this chapter).[10]

The contemporary survey maps made by British surveyors from the Indian navy give us some insight into water resources, irrigation, and agricultural land use along the Euphrates and Tigris Rivers. According to *A Memoir of Indian*

---

7 The canal, originally called Nahr Isa, had been widened by Sultan Süleyman the Magnificent and had been constantly improved since, both as a public project and by private funds. Great Britain, Naval Intelligence Division, *Iraq and the Persian Gulf* ([London]: Naval Intelligence Division, 1944), p. 31.

8 Ebubekir Ceylan, *The Ottoman Origins of Modern Iraq: Political Reform, Modernization and Development in the Nineteenth-Century Middle East* (London: I.B. Tauris, 2011), pp. 200–1; Charles Issawi, *The Fertile Crescent, 1800–1914* (New York: Oxford University Press, 1988), pp. 353–55.

9 William Willcocks, *The Irrigation of Mesopotamia* (London: E. & F.N. Spon, 1911), pp. 12–15; Ahmed Sousa, *Irrigation in Iraq: Its History and Development* (Baghdad: New Publishers, 1945), pp. 34–39.

10 TNA: FO 195/318, No. 33, 20 June 1848.

Surveys by Clements A. Markham (1878), Lieutenant Ormsby first surveyed Mesopotamia in 1826–30, and Colonel Chesney followed on the Euphrates River.[11] Captain Henry Blossse Lynch in 1837 traversed the whole course of the Tigris from its source in Anatolia to Baghdad, Babylon, and Ctesiphon. In 1841, he did the same for the Euphrates, by three steamers, the *Nitocris*, the *Nimrod*, and the *Assyria*, assisted by Lieutenants Felix Jones, Campbell, Selby, and Grounds. His map (Map 2.1) presents the first sight of irrigation along the Tigris River, though it shows only large canals such as Ishaki, Dujail, Mahawil, Nil, Saqlawiya, Abu Ghraib, and Melik.

After Lynch retired from the survey in 1843, his assistant lieutenant, Felix Jones, continued the laborious survey, mostly single-handed, in command of the steamer *Nitocris* for surveying and carrying out other duties.[12] He stayed in Baghdad, where the energetic governor Necip Pasha actively improved irrigation and land reclamation, and seized on any chance that offered for excursion and survey. In 1844, now Captain Felix Jones accompanied Sir Henry Rawlinson on a journey to collect information about the boundary between Persia and Turkey. In 1846, he made an ascent of the Tigris from Baghdad to Samarra and, in 1848, undertook a journey to determine the course of the ancient Nahrawan Canal, by then desolate and almost impassable wasteland. In April and September 1850, he surveyed the old bed of the Tigris, discovered the site of the ancient Opis, and made researches in the vicinity of the Median Wall and Phyfcus of Xenophon. In 1852, he made a trigonometrical survey of the country between the Tigris and the Upper Zab, including the ruin of Nineveh. In 1853, Captain Felix Jones, assisted by young Collingwood, then a midshipman, completed a large-scale map of Baghdad, including the country from Musaib, north of Hilla, down to the north-west end of the Sea of Najaf, with a memoir on the province full of statistical information. Captain Jones retired from the Mesopotamian Survey to take up the post of political resident at Bushire, in the Persian Gulf, in 1855.[13] His efforts in Baghdad finally came to light

11 The notes and relations of Lieutenant Ormsby of the Indian navy were prepared for the press and published by Wellsted. James Raymond Wellsted, *Travels to the City of the Caliphs, along the Shores of the Persian Gulf and the Mediterranean*, 2 vols. (London: Henry Colburn, 1840).

12 James Felix Jones had served in the Red Sea Survey, in the Maldives, Ceylon, and the Manar Gulf, and had reported on the harbour of Kuwait in 1839 before serving under Captain Lynch on the Euphrates in that year.

13 Markham acclaimed James Felix Jones's achievement, mentioning, "For the work of the Mesopotamian Survey several acquirements were essential in addition to those of a surveyor; such an acquaintance with the language ad ancient history of the country, tact and judgement in dealing with wild Arab tribes, and capacity for enduring fatigues an privations. All these were possessed by Felix Jones in an eminent degree." Clements R.

when he edited the map in 1874 drawn by his assistant, Commander Selby, and Lieutenants Bewsher and Collingwood. (See Map 2.3 at the end of the chapter.)

As a successor to Captain Jones, in 1855, Commander Selby, now a captain, took charge of the Survey of Mesopotamia.[14] (In the spring of 1842, he had ascended the Persian Karun and Dizful Rivers to Shushtar on the steamer *Assyria*, thus demonstrating their navigability.) Lieutenants Collingwood and Bewsher assisted him. The tribal uprisings had come to an end under Reşit Pasha's governorship, and peace and order had been restored in the tribal domains. These officers made a trigonometrical survey of the region west of the Euphrates, including the Sea of Najaf, which is fed by that river, and embracing the classic sites of Meshed Ali, Birs Nimrud, Karbala, Kufa, and Babylon, and the portion of Mesopotamia from Samarra, on the Euphrates, to a point about 10 miles above Baghdad on the Tigris. The former portion was completed and sent home in 1861, with an elaborate memoir by Captain Selby. However, both maps and memoir were lost. The original maps and field books were procured from Baghdad, and the maps were redrawn by Lieutenant Collingwood and engraved. The ground they covered was most important, showing the region into which the waters of the Euphrates drained.[15] Their maps of the Middle and Lower Euphrates River also helped the Ottoman governor and his officials to understand the irrigation network, set up telegraph lines along the rivers, and start navigation by river steamship on the Tigris River.

Towards the end of 1862, Captain Selby retired, and Lieutenant Bewsher took charge of the survey from above Baghdad to Tel Ibrahim and from Tel Ibrahim to Samarra. Completing the survey in 1865, he published his memoir, which contains an interesting account of the ancient canals and irrigation. Makhram continued, "The ability and learning shown in this memoir are proofs that Lieutenant Bewsher would have been a worthy successor of the earlier surveyors; but he died of diseases contracted during the service, and the Government abruptly put a stop to the survey, leaving it incomplete, and with much work still to be done."[16]

With the progress of surveys on the Euphrates and Tigris River basin, the Baghdad government carried out irrigation and land reclamation projects. Although irrigation canals were necessary to provide sufficient water for

---

Markham, *A Memoir on the Indian Surveys*, 2nd ed. (London, 1878), pp. 29–33. The life of Felix Jones is detailed in Charles Rathbone Low, *History of the Indian Navy (1613–1863)* (London: Richard Bentley and Son, 1877), ii, pp. 394–411.

14 The life of Selby is also summarized in Low, *History of the Indian Navy*, ii, pp. 413–16.

15 Markham, *Memoir on the Indian Surveys*, p. 412.

16 Markham, *Memoir on the Indian Surveys*, p. 33.

agriculture, many of them were dry because they had not been maintained regularly by digging. Those irrigation canals, especially near Baghdad, drew the governor's serious concern from the beginning of Ali Rıza Pasha's governorship in 1831, because flooding of the Tigris River caused much damage in Baghdad. Large projects had progressed since then, and by the governorship of Midhat Pasha, extensive areas on the Diyala River basin and near Baghdad were irrigated and cultivated. On the Lower Euphrates, large floodwaters formed into numerous marshes and lakes, making public flood-control works difficult. As a reason, the consular report suggests that the Khazaʿil and Muntafiq tribes had so far refused to supply their tribesmen to keep the sheikh's authority against the government.[17] The canals, once reopened, brought lucrative revenues for both the government and the tribal sheikhs. Water resource waste, unsolved during the Tanzimat period, continued throughout the Ottoman period, as the survey map in 1874 (Map 2.3) still showed many dry canals and marshes in the Middle and Lower Euphrates.

Land in the area of perennial irrigation was generally cultivated in a two-year rotation, during which half the field was cultivated and half was left fallow. In the area where rainfall was sufficient for agriculture, winter crops of wheat, barley, beans, peas, and lentils were produced by dry farming, as were some small summer crops and vegetables. Crops of better quality and summer crops, such as rice, millet, maize, beans, sesame, tobacco, cotton, fruit, and vegetables, were produced along both the natural and artificial watercourses. In the area where the government's irrigation projects were focused – in Khanaqin, Shahriban, Abu Ghraib, and Karbala – after the winter grain crops were harvested, some portions of the winter fields were cultivated with the summer crops of maize, millet, rice, sesame, or cotton. In the vicinity of Baghdad and Karbala, instead of grains, peasants preferred to raise cash crops or broccoli, cabbage, carrots, celery, cucumbers, cauliflower, lettuce, mushrooms, onions, potatoes, pumpkins, radishes, spinach, turnips, and tomatoes for market in Baghdad.[18] Where a liberal supply of water was available throughout the year,

---

17 TNA: FO 78/1768, No. 16, 22 Apr. 1863.

18 James Felix Jones, "Province of Baghdad," in *Selections from the Records of the Bombay Government*, no. 43 (Bombay: Education Society's Press, 1857), pp. 342–45. Naval Lieutenant J.B. Bewsher, who surveyed in autumn 1862 with Commander Selby in Mesopotamia, observed that the water was drawn up in leather buckets by horses or oxen and diverted over in small channels to irrigate fields no more than two miles from the river bank. Near Baghdad, wheat, barley, millet, sesame, castor oil, beans, cucumbers, melons, and other beans and vegetables were cultivated. Bewsher, "On Part of Mesopotamia," pp. 180–81. The map included in his report was made by Jones, Selby, Collingwood, and Bewsher based on the survey. James Felix Jones himself resided in Mesopotamia for a long period, when Henry Creswicke Rawlinson also was resident for twelve years. See Lieutenant

high-return crops of dates, fruits, and vegetables were produced. As a main cash crop, dates were widely produced, but those grown in the groves along the Husayniya Canal and in Mandali were known for their premier quality. Tobacco was grown only in mountain areas, although it was another important cash crop.

The annual report of the Treasury Board in 1917 provides a detailed view of crop rotation and harvesting (see Table 2.3). On flow land, wheat was generally grown for local consumption only; that for sale was usually grown on the land irrigated by lifts. Barley was the most popular winter crop, whose harvest was usually cleared by the end of May, while the wheat harvest could be delayed until the middle of June. The barley of Mandali, generally considered the best in the province, was sown on lift-irrigated lands from mid-September, on the lands along perennial canals from mid-October, and on the lands along the inundation canals after the first winter rain. Barley could be sown throughout January, but it was estimated that fields sown after December would yield approximately 10 per cent less than those sown earlier. Sowing on flood-irrigated land usually began after the first rain and could be delayed until December or as late as the end of February. In many lands irrigated by lifts, from Ramadi to Mahmudiya, wheat and barley were cropped at a half and half. In Hilla, the proportion of wheat to barley was 1:3, but in some later years it reached 1:10. Further down the Euphrates, in Shamiya, very little wheat was grown. The decline in wheat production in the irrigated area caused few problems, however, as a shortage of wheat of up to some 7,000 tons annually could be made up from Mosul and Sulaymaniya.[19]

Rice was cultivated along the Ruz Canal in the Diyara River basin, along the canals above the Hindiya Barrage in the Euphrates, to a small extent in the Hilla district and extensively in Shamiya. It was possible to sow rice after barley production but not after wheat. The rice of Shamiya was of the highest quality in the province, that of Ruz of the lowest. Maize was not a popular crop, probably because of its low yield. As the local maize had a short cob and a small grain, its only merit was a short growing period. On inundation canals it had to be planted in March or April, but on irrigated lands or perennial canals it could be planted as late as mid-August. The most popular summer crop, millet, required less water than others and ripened sooner. Cotton was grown mainly in Khanaqin, but limited cultivation occurred throughout the province. Only

---

J.B. Bewsher, "On Part of Mesopotamia, between Sheriat-el-Beytha, on the Tigris, to Tel Ibrahim," *Proceedings of the Royal Geographical Society* 11, no. 1 (1867), pp. 155–59.

19 TNA: FO 371/4150/187296, Administration Report, Revenue Board, Baghdad, 22 Mar.–31 Dec. 1917, pp. 18–20.

some was considered excellent, having a long staple with great strength. The best fruit gardens were found in Karbala, where there were Persian gardeners, who also rendered service in other areas when a new garden was being planned. Baʿqūba contained the best orange groves; Balad and Sumaicha produced the best grapes and pomegranates.

Livestock production was a significant economic activity for peasants and tribesmen, although many peasants had only a draft animal. Livestock animals were left in pasture to forage for themselves. Camels and horses were held primarily by nomadic tribes (*bedevî*), and sheep and goats by totally pastoral or semi-settled pastoral tribes (*şâvî*). Cattle and water buffaloes were the main livestock of semi-settled and sedentary pastoral tribes (*maʿdân*) on the basin of the Lower Euphrates and Tigris Rivers. Production of poultry and other domesticated animals was rare, except for beehives for honey making. Ranching was rarely practised in this period, and the productivity of livestock was very low because of poor breeding, disease, and insufficient shelter. Yet as main capital stocks, these livestock were priceless to tribesmen. They tilled soils and transported grain from the field to the threshing place, granary, and marketplace. Some livestock, particularly horses, increased in commercial value, bringing nomadic tribesmen a good income in cash as a major export commodity and a carrier of goods and persons in urban areas.[20]

The province's plentiful agricultural resources were not fully used to maximize production because of the difficulty of managing water control on the rivers. For example, Ahmed Fahmi's estimate of land use in the best rice-raising areas in Shamiya in 1926 is shown in Table 2.1.

According to Fahmi's data, the area used for production of rice, dates, and other crops was 134 square miles, about one-third of the total cultivable land. In Shamiya, in which the area covered by marshes was 96 square miles, or 70 per cent of the cropped area, overflowing water in flood season periodically damaged crops before harvesting, but in drought season, the water level was too low to supply canals and ditches.

---

20 John T. Chalcraft, *The Striking Cabbies of Cairo and Other Stories: Crafts and Guilds in Egypt, 1863–1914* (Albany: State University of New York Press, 2004), pp. 59–63; Hala M. Fattah, *The Politics of Regional Trade in Iraq, Arabia and the Gulf, 1745–1900* (Albany: State University of New York Press, 1997), pp. 162–71; Michael Tuchscherer, "Some Reflections on the Place of the Camel in the Economy and Society of Ottoman Egypt," trans. S. Faroqhi, in Suraiya Faroqhi, ed., *Animals and People in the Ottoman Empire* (Istanbul: Eren Yayıncılık, 2010), pp. 175–77. Livestock were important capital stocks in the Baghdad province for peasant tribesmen who worked as land cultivators. For a case in Egypt, see Alan Mikhail, *The Animal in Ottoman Egypt* (New York: Oxford University Press, 2014), pp. 19–63.

TABLE 2.1 Land use in Shamiya

Type of land		Square miles
Exploited lands	rice grown lands	88
	date gardens and lands of summer and winter crops	46
(Sub-total)		134
Marsh lands		96
fallow lands (isolated and unirrigated)		200
Total area		430

SOURCE: TNA: CO 730/121, A REPORT ON ʿIRAQ BY AHMED FAHMI, ACCOUNTANT GENERAL, BAGHDAD, PART II, P. 33.

Because water control usually required large-scale projects with large budgets, abundant labour, and technical expertise, the government traditionally organized projects under the supervision of an irrigation official (*sedd agası*) in Baghdad. Still, its methods were extremely primitive. The crucial Hindiya Barrage, constructed at Musaib on the Middle Euphrates, frequently collapsed and was repaired by tribesmen and the Ottoman military forces stationed there, under the supervision of the district office of their project area. When it broke during the flood season, it caused severe damage to crops in large areas downstream. Maintaining the barrage required much labour, so was particularly costly, as the chief of the tribesmen who did the work received a portion of the reclaimed land, and the tribesmen received stipends as payment. The government of Abdi Pasha (1849–50) paid only the stipends to the tribesmen and stopped giving land to their chief, retaining all the reclaimed lands, which eventually led the chief and his tribesmen to join the uprising against the government.

In other areas of Baghdad province, irrigation and land reclamation generally had been assigned to the local officials and tribal sheikhs, whose methods of cleaning and levelling the canals differed from area to area. Consequently, the government found it difficult to coordinate projects and to effectively allocate the water. In the Diyala River basin, peasants in the villages dug and cleaned the canal as a part of their labour dues. There, the village official in charge of organizing the peasant workers in cooperation with the headman examined the canal and its regulators annually and assigned repairs to the villages along the canal according to the availability of their labour force.[21] Along the Saqlawiya Canal, in Aqr Quf, a watchman was employed to check the conditions of the canal and the regulators. Whenever a breach was found, it was repaired by nearby tribesmen, under the supervision of the district administrator. During the flood season, five to six households of tribesmen assigned to strengthen the embankment and do other emergency work were given a tax-exempt privilege, which was abolished by Namık Pasha in 1852.

Increasing land productivity was further hindered by the conservative mindset of the peasants, who were extremely poor and sceptical of the merit of investment. The price of seed was the same as the selling price of the crop, so the peasants often could not afford to purchase the seed they needed. The price of vegetable seeds was especially high because the seeds were cleaned in the towns and offered for sale in small quantities. The peasants used a breaker plough, harness, spade, hoe, sickle, and fork, all of which had to be repaired or replaced after a year of use, except for the steel point of the plough, which needed replacing more often. Many farmers paid a carpenter a fixed amount of barley per year to maintain their implements. Only the water-lifting devices would last from twenty to forty years. The peasants also provided their own draft animals, but the average life of a horse or donkey was ten years, and depreciation costs were high. Usually the peasants helped each other and also provided the labour supply for the land of pious foundations and hired services for some individual landowners.[22]

Methods of cultivation were extremely primitive. Rice was seldom transplanted, and crop fields were not properly cleaned. Manuring was not practised, and the rotation of crops was not generally understood. Briefly put, there was a lack of incentives to improve productivity above subsistence. For example, peasants were not willing to grow fodder when they had no livestock of their own. In the tribal fields, where the tribesmen were used to shifting cultivation, they were reluctant to improve the soil because they were not certain they would get back the same parcel of land for farming in the following year. Similarly, peasants might be persuaded to follow a given crop rotation only if assured tenure of the same land over a sufficiently long period. Governmental storage facilities were not used, in Hilla because they were often raided by

21 The official in the village was publicly recognized as the *zabit*. For comparison of the irrigation system and its maintenance with those of other regions, see Alan Mikhail, *Nature and Empire in Ottoman Egypt: An Environmental History* (New York: Cambridge University Press, 2011), pp. 38–81.

22 Iraq, Department of Agriculture, *Cultivation for Winter or Shitwi Crops in Iraq* (Baghdad: Government Press, 1919), pp. 4–5.

rebellious tribesmen, and generally because peasants feared that giving the government knowledge of their stocks would expose them to taxation and confiscation or that their grains would be mixed with inferior or dirty stocks deposited by others. Even in the early twentieth century, grain threshed by hand, according to the prevailing custom, contained 15–40 per cent foreign matter and 5–15 per cent dirt.[23]

Adding to the problems, peasant tribesmen readily abandoned their land when exposed to intertribal raids, drought, epidemics, and locust attacks, or heavy taxation. They then migrated, seeking pay and other reimbursement from employers, and water. The government had done little to cope with behaviour that originated in tribal tradition or to coerce the peasant tribes to settle. Only the crop sharing extensively practised in the irrigated areas set a sort of regulatory discipline on the peasant tribesmen and workers. The tax farmer, his agent, and the tribal sheikh organized production from seeding to harvesting and allotted individual tasks and the profits that the government could not regulate. Thus, although the government was unable directly to implement various development measures, it did manage to sustain some land productivity through the custom of crop sharing.

2 Agricultural Taxation

Taxation involved the government in the local population's economic activities through middlemen who carried out assessment, gathering, remittance, bookkeeping, and claims. In agriculture, besides the poll tax, heavy taxes were imposed on the production of food and fodder crops; on stocks of sheep, buffaloes, and camels; on the use of natural resources such as irrigation water, grasses, and ponds for fishing; and on the use of infrastructure, including waterwheels, bridges, and granaries. Still other taxes were collected indirectly in the process of marketing, among them a gate tax and a market sales tax. There was no clear dividing line between some different tax categories, of which the tithe accounted for the largest portion of total revenues, followed by various dues and the sheep tax. On irrigated farms, the tax was called the "state share," and its ratio was conventionally determined by the local custom of crop sharing. In the tribal domain, the government collected the tax from the tribal sheikh as "state money" at the amount fixed at the time it acknowledged the tribal sheikh as the paramount sheikh of the tribal confederation. Finally, other taxes were collected informally as extraordinary charges allocated and collected directly

23 TNA: FO 371/4150/187296, Administration Report, p. 20.

from the peasant cultivators by village headmen, local administrators, leaders of the community, or military commanders.

Officially, the tithe on grain crops was one-tenth of the produce from a dry-farming field and one-fifth from an irrigated field. For summer crops on irrigated fields, however, the tax varied from crop to crop: one-fifth of the produce for grain crops such as millet and maize, and one-fourth, one-third, or even one-half of the produce for commercial crops. For fruit and vegetables, the tax was uniformly one-fifth of the produce but was reduced to one-tenth for an orchard of lower productivity, for vegetables produced in a dry-farming field, or during drought and other natural disasters. In addition to the tithe, the peasant paid household dues of around one-tenth of the produce, or 75 kuruş and 100 kuruş per feddân in dry-farming and irrigated fields respectively.[24] In the tribal areas in the north, instead of household dues, migrating tribesmen were subject to registration dues (*mukayyid rüsûmı*) according to the number of members in their household and the amount of their livestock. Along a watercourse in the irrigated area, an owner of private land paid a fee for using water from the stream (*nehr-i icâr*), and the owner of a watermill also paid a fee (*değirman rüsûmı*) for using the water, determined by the capacity of the mill and the term of its operation.

Tax assessment was additionally complicated by wide regional differences in the measurements of area, weight, and length; their unit names; the market value of the money; and various customs of allocating land, seeding, and harvesting. In the crop-sharing area, the tax assessment was made on the threshing floor, after harvesting but before distributing the crops among the share claimants. The tax farmer, the official, or the tribal sheikh supervised the gathering of the crops into the threshing place and their distribution among share claimants. No grain could be taken away from the threshing floor until the threshing operation was completed. Shares were then divided on the spot, and the amount of the state share (i.e., the tax) was determined at the ratio of the share to the total produce or to the produce after the deduction of certain shares. After that, the grain was taken to the granary by the peasant. Because threshing floors were numerous and vulnerable to theft and plundering by nearby tribesmen, police guards or watchmen were assigned to each floor while threshing was completed.

---

24 A feddân was a unit of area cultivated for winter grain crops by a peasant household using a pair of oxen; it was approximately equivalent to the area of a dönüm (0.618 acre; 2,500 sq m). The fields of tribal domains were measured in müşâra, and the date grove of 100 palm trees, in cerib (Ar. *jarib*). Issawi, *Fertile Crescent, 1800–1914*, p. 480.

By contrast, in the area of settled agriculture, where the village was the unit of taxation, officials examined and assessed the output of the crops in the fields before they were harvested to determine the tax. Peasants could appeal tax assessments before the crop was harvested, within a fixed period (reportedly three days) from the original assessment. A new official would then make a reassessment, and if the two estimates differed widely, a final committee might be appointed. This system allowed for such a wide margin of error that it caused trouble and the loss of harvested crops.

In certain limited areas, usually in the irrigated fields of the tribesmen, an assumed output was calculated in a customary manner. The crop field was measured by a 25-metre rope, and the actual cultivated field was determined. The assessors classified the crop according to how many müşâra (a local unit of area equivalent to a dönüm; 0.25 hectare) it contained of first-, second-, and third-class produce. Deduction of the government's share was then made on the following scale: one-fifth from the first class, one-fourth from the second class, and one-third from the third class.[25] By the early twentieth century, this method commonly prevailed in Abu Gharaq, Yusufiya, Malik, Bughaila Umm al-Hawa, Abu Araijis Muftah, Abu Chamaghn, Shamiya, and Khawwas al-Maidan in the Hilla district and in the Shamiya sub-district, and it was similar to the crop sharing applied to rice fields in the irrigated areas. In fields of other grains, the ratio of the government's share differed, and the method of measurement was more complicated.

The custom and routines of crop sharing, called *müzâra'a* in Ottoman documents, had drawn the concern of the Baghdad government from the early days of the Tanzimat. Thus in 1860 Hurşid Pasha briefly reported its local practice, which he had observed in the Diyala River basin in 1846:

> In Khanaqin, for winter fruits, one-fifth, for summer products, one-third. For *serkâr*, that is superintendent or agent, one-tenth.... In Khorasan, crops were divided into five shares, of which three were taken by the owner, the government, or *vakıf*, and two shares were taken by the peasants.... the seeds were given by *serkâr* and for it *serkâr* was given one feddân out of five feddân as reward.[26]

25 This deduction was customarily known as *tajbir* or *haq talfiyah*.

26 Mehmed Hurşid Paşa, *Seyâhatnâme-i Hudûd* (Istanbul: Takvimhâne-i Âmire, 1277 AH [1860]), pp. 145–46.

While the government share was repeatedly estimated in various parts of official reports, a clear overall picture was not obtained until a survey report issued by Namık Pasha in 1866 identified the practice of *uqr* by area.

3 The Custom of Crop Sharing

In 1861, Governor Ahmet Tevfik Pasha organized a committee of survey specialists from the Porte and local officials, including the director of agriculture, the director of the treasury, and a treasury official, to survey the agricultural situation in Baghdad. The survey on crop sharing also carried out by this committee, in cooperation with the district administrators, was reported to the Porte in 1866 by Namık Pasha. It apparently was meant to investigate the breakdown of crop-sharing contracts in order to put under rule the unearned share of *uqr* taken by the landowner as rent or lien. The committee examined the share of winter crops, summer crops, vegetables, dates, and fruit in all administrative districts, except for the district of Sulaymaniya and the tribal domains in the southern part of the province. Because members were well acquainted with local methods of farming and crop sharing, confidence can be placed in their method of survey and its results. In addition, there was little chance for the surveyors to fake the data, since most data were presented as a proportion of total produce. In fact, a geographical survey of Khanaqin by Hurşid Pasha in 1846 had produced similar results, and the British Civil Administration also reported a similar method of crop sharing for the Hilla district in 1918.[27] Because the survey of Namık Pasha used the same method and the same standard of measurement throughout the province, it may be considered trustworthy for estimating the proportions of the crop shares in each unit of area and for comparing their results by region.[28] The report of that survey is descriptive, as indicated in the following translation of a text on the Khanaqin area:

---

27 BOA, İ. Meclis-i Vâlâ 24610, 24 Şevval 1282; Hurşid Pasha, *Seyâhatnâme-i*, pp. 144–46; The British Library (BL): India Office Records and Private Papers, IOR/L/PS/20/250, *Reports of Administration for 1918 of Divisions and Districts of the Occupied Territories in Mesopotamia. Volume 1* (1919), pp. 134–36. For the practice of crop sharing in other countries during the twentieth century, see Abraham Granott, *The Land System in Palestine: History and Structure* (London: Eyre & Spottiswoode, 1952), pp. 286–314; Ann K.S. Lambton, *Landlord and Peasant in Persia* (London: Oxford University Press, 1969), pp. 306–29.

28 The survey was titled "Baghdād eyāletinde kā'in bi'l-cümle mukāta'ātıñ 'ahd müzāra'asını mübīn defteridir" (The record of the agreement of crop sharing in all farms in the province of Baghdad), and together with the draft of the regulation, it was submitted to the Supreme Council in Istanbul. The record of the survey, now available in the *irâde* collection of the Prime Ministry General Directorate of State Archives in Istanbul (dossier

> In Khanaqin Farm, when winter crops were gathered, 2 shares out of 25 shares were taken as *uqr* fee and thresher each. From the rest of the produce, 3 shares out of 100 shares were taken and given to carpenter, goldsmith, and barber. In addition to them, measurer and police guards were given 15 okka per feddân of wheat and barley each in Istanbul standard of measures. The rest of the produce was divided into three shares. One was given to seed owners, tax farmer, or the other owner if any, one was the state share, and the third share was given to the peasant cultivator of the farm.[29]

To understand indigenous crop sharing, the survey report of 1866 is examined for winter grain crops in the northern districts (Table 2.4), the Diyala River basin (Table 2.5), the central region and mountain area (Table 2.6), the Middle Euphrates River basin (Tables 2.7 and 2.8), and for summer crops (Table 2.9). In the districts and sub-districts of Abu Ghraib, Karbala, Samarra, and Mandali (Table 2.6), crop sharing was carried out in the same way as in the Diyala River basin. The survey result for the district of Mosul is not included in Table 2.4 because the breakdown of the share distribution is not clear in the document. For the same reason, crop sharing in Ana, Haditha, and Kibisa on the Upper Euphrates and in Basra in the southern region is not be examined here. Analysis of the data in the tables provides a crude estimate of the average returns of agricultural holdings, how agriculture and Ottoman land taxation were practised, what regional differences existed, and what the government aimed at in its reform programmes.[30]

---

number: İ. Meclis-i Vâlâ 24610, 24 Şevval 1282 AH/14 Mar. 1866), presents first-hand information on agricultural situations in the mid-nineteenth-century province of Baghdad rarely described by contemporary travellers or foreign residents.

29 The transliteration of a text on the Khanaqin area in the Ottoman Turkish is:

> "Nefes Khānaqīn Muqāṭaʿası
>
> Muqāṭaʿa medhkūruñ şitvī ḥāṣılātī meydāna gelence yirmī beş ḥiṣṣede ikī ḥiṣṣesi bi'l-ifrāz birī ʿuqr bedeline ve değerī khirmen bāṣīcī ōlān devvāsa verildikden ṣonra mā-bāqī maḥsūldan yüz ḥiṣṣede üç ḥiṣṣe çiqārılaraq birincisi neccāra ikincisi tīmūrciye üçüncüsi berbere aʿṭā qulunaraq ve būnlārdan mā-ʿadā keyyāl ve ṣaḥneye verilmek üzere behr feddāndan bi-ʿibāre āstāne on beşer qiyye ḥinṭa ve şaʿīr baʿda al-ʾikhrāc quṣūr ḥāṣılāt üç ḥiṣṣeye taqsīm olunarak birisi tukhmi ṣāḥibī mültezim veyā emlāk īse onā ve değerī cānib mīrīye ve üçüncī ḥiṣṣesi dakhī fellāha verilmekte olduğu…."

BOA, İ. Meclis-i Vâlâ 24610, 24 Şevval 1282.

30 The survey's result is handwritten in a *defter* (notebook) of forty-five pages about 18 cm wide and 42 cm long. BOA, İ. Meclis-i Vâlâ 24610, 24 Şevval 1282.

In Ottoman usage, weight was to be measured according to the Istanbul standard, but in practice the measure varied from source to source. One batman ranged from 6 to 12 okka; one vezne was either 4 or 5 batman; and one tagar varied between 600 and 1,200 okka. Based on the survey record and other Ottoman documents (BOA, İrade, Mesâil-i Mühimme 2054, 2 Muharrem 1263), the following equivalents are used in this chapter: 1 okka = 1.282 kg (Istanbul standard); 1 batman = 10 okka = 12.82 kg; 1 vezne = 4 batman = 51.28 kg; 1 tagar = 20 vezne = 1,025.6 kg.

The area of a feddân in the survey record was determined according to the quantity of seed sown. In Khanaqin, for example, the feddân was the area in which 12 vezne of wheat seed, 15 vezne of barley seed, 2 vezne of cotton seed, or 2 batman of millet seed were sown. The corresponding amounts of wheat and barley seed per feddân in Karbala were 10 vezne each (measured by the Karbala standard), while along the Dujail Canal, 1 tagar equaled 10 vezne of wheat or barley seed. Hurşid Pasha had reported that 1 tagar (or 600 okka in Hurşid Pasha's estimation) of wheat seed and 2 tagar of barley seed could be sown in a feddân (which he estimated to be 20,000 square zirâ [1 zirâ = 65 cm]). Cuinet defined the feddân as the area in which seed for 500 okka of wheat or 700 okka of barley could be sown.[31] Regardless of the regional differences, the feddân is considered equivalent to the dönüm (0.25 hectare) in this chapter.

4 The Northern Districts

The system of agriculture in the northern districts of the province was distinct from the area of irrigation agriculture in the central and southern districts in several aspects. Rawanduz, Derbend, and Sulaymaniya were located in mountainous areas in the north and north-east of the province, in which agriculture occurred in limited areas in valleys and basins, and on lower hill slopes. Mosul, Shahrizor, and Zangabad were situated in foothills, built on Miocene deposits that were more suitable for cultivation than the high mountainous areas. Rainfall was sufficient for agriculture throughout the northern districts, and on the rain-fed fields (*dâim-i mezraʿa*), winter crops of wheat, barley, beans, peas, and lentils were produced by dry farming. Crops of better quality and summer crops of rice, millet, maize, beans, sesame, tobacco, cotton, fruit, and vegetables were produced in the fields along the natural and artificial watercourses (*sûlı mezraʿa*) whose water flowed from mountain streams, the Tigris River, and

31 Mehmed Hurşid Paşa, *Seyâhatnâme-i*, p. 145; Vital Cuinet, *La Turquie D'Asie* (Paris: E. Leroux, 1892–1900), iii, p. 44.

its tributaries, the Great Zab, Lesser Zab, and Amadiya. The river in this region, however, flowed well below plain level, and their water became available only through water lifts or other irrigation facilities.

The peasants settled in the villages and along rivers, canals, streams, and springs. The tax was both a tithe of either one-tenth of the produce on the dry-farming field or one-fifth on the irrigated field, which the tax farmer collected from the total produce as allocated by the village headman. For summer crops, the share varied from crop to crop: one-fifth for grains such as millet and maize, and for commercial crops one-fourth, one-third, or even a half of the produce. The tax farmer often cultivated summer cash crops such as cotton, rice, and sesame by providing the peasant with seeds. He took most of the produce, from five-sixths to eight-ninths, giving the rest as a labour fee. For fruit and vegetables, the share was uniformly one-fifth of the produce, which was reduced to one-tenth for an orchard of low productivity and for vegetables produced in a dry-farming field, or when production decreased because of drought or other natural disasters.

The tax farmer also collected a household due (*çifthane vergisi*) from the peasant in cash (75 kuruş per feddân or 100 kuruş per feddân in the irrigated field); in tribal areas in Derebend and Shahrizor, he collected a registration due (*mukayyid rüsûmı*) from migrating tribesmen according to the number of the household and of livestock. From privately owned land along the watercourse, the tax farmer collected a fee for using water from the stream (*nehr-i icâr*); from the owner of a watermill, a fee (*değerman rüsûmı*) depending on the capacity of the mill and its operation period.

The tax farmer increased his profit by rewarding a portion of the government share and household due (one-tenth or one-fifth in the dry-farming or irrigated field) to the tribal chief for his cooperation with Ottoman authority, or to the village headman who recruited migrating peasant tribesmen for cultivating more fields. The share in the reward was higher in tribal areas: in Köysanjaq, one-third of the government's share was given to the chiefs of the Bilbas, Aku, and Menkur tribes, and one-half of the government's share was given to the chiefs of the Sinn and Ramak tribes. Where police guards were employed, the village headman made a payment (called *me'kelât* or *meşrûbât*) to them as a collective unit. The tax farmer himself engaged in agriculture on uncultivated fields. In Zangabad, for example, the tax farmer employed an irrigation specialist (*sûcu*) for land reclamation and recruited a *serkâr* (a tribal sheikh-bailiff) and his tribesmen for farming on condition of giving him a portion (usually one feddân of five feddân). The land also was cultivated by the peasants in the village near the field as a part of their unpaid labour due. From the harvested produce, the tax farmer paid the *uqr* share (one-fiftieth of the produce), made a payment to the irrigation specialists (one-twentieth of the produce), and retained the rest.

According to the survey, a number of grain fields were held by the landholder (*eshâb-ı zemîn*) in the districts of Kirkuk and Erbil. The peasant paid the rent (*zemîn icâri*) – between one-tenth and one-fifth of the total produce in Kirkuk, and between one-fifteenth and one-third in Erbil, depending on the landholder's residence. The *uqr* share, if any, was between one-thirtieth and one-forty-fifth of the total produce for grain, summer crops, fruit, and vegetables. Such *uqr* land was situated around the towns along the major road from Baghdad to Mosul, Kifri, Qaratepe, Altun Köprü, and Kirkuk, and in irrigated areas along the streams flowing from Tuz Hurmatu and Jamali. Some grain fields were *temlîk* land, as observed in the Zangabad district, in which the owner (*eshâb-ı temlîk*) received the owner's share at one-tenth of the produce on dry-farming lands or one-fifth on irrigated fields. He paid the tax of *öşür*, at the rate of one-tenth or one-fifth of the owner's share, to the tax farmer.

After the payment of all these shares, the produce belonged to the peasant cultivator (*eshâb-ı zirâi*). In many fields, especially those surrounding a large town, however, the peasant could not afford the cost of irrigation, seeds, and other expenses incurred during farming. In order to finance these expenses, he obtained a cash loan (*kuvvet-i akçe*) or provisions in kind from another person, usually a tax farmer or a person dwelling in a town or village near the peasant's fields.[32] The partner (*şerîk*) claimed a share (*hakk-ı müzâra'a*) according to the partnership contract (*ukde-i şirket*), usually a half-and-half division of the produce (Table 2.4, col. 12). The peasant's net share, after all deductions, was small – usually much less than in the central and southern districts.

5 The Diyala River Basin

Located near Baghdad, with a stable water supply from the Diyala River, the Diyala River basin was more productive than other districts. Different from the partnership arrangement in the north, the tax farmer was a key man in crop sharing because he not only provided the seeds for cultivation but also shared political control over the cultivating peasant tribesmen with the government. Irrigation, land tenure, and land productivity influenced the tax farmer's

32 A loan in cash (*kuvvet-i akçe*) in the Mosul district did not cover the investment for land reclamation and maintaining the watercourses necessary for increasing land productivity. The government paid such costs as aids or as a part of public projects. BOA, İ. Meclis-i Vâlâ 15452, 28 Şevval 1272.

involvement in farming, and under complicated practice of agriculture, the government could hardly interfere the tax farmer's activities in the field. During Reşit Pasha's governorship (1852–57), the importance of agriculture increased as the main source of tax revenues. He implemented more irrigation and land reclamation projects and provided tax farmers with financial support such as a grant-in-aid for the cost of seeds and of cleaning the irrigation canals, a reduction in the tax owed, or in some cases a tax exemption for some years. By Namık Pasha's governorship, large tracts of land in Khalis, together with Abu Ghraib, were reclaimed in this way. The tax farmer by then was an actual executor of Ottoman authority through his collection of the large government share from tribesmen.

The surveyed areas of the Diyala River basin were located near towns and villages in Khanaqin, Qizlarbat, Zawiya, Hajji Qura, and Bungudra or in irrigated areas along the major canals of Khorasan, Mahrut, Shahriban, and Baladruz. In the village areas, either tent-dwelling peasant tribesmen or peasants settled in the village were the cultivators. They largely belonged to the Shammer Toga tribal confederation, but their tie to the paramount sheikh had become rather nominal. For the land cultivated by unsettled peasant tribesmen, the field was divided into a number of units measured by feddân and allocated to the tribesmen by a *serkâr*. The seed was provided by the tax farmer, while the production was supervised by the bailiff, who was usually the chief of the cultivating peasant tribesmen but occasionally the village headman. For his payment, the bailiff was entitled to cultivate about one-tenth of the land as his free land. When the bailiff increased production by cultivating more land or recruiting migrating peasant tribesmen to work, he received an additional portion of land as a reward or gift (Table 2.5, col. 1).[33]

The crops were divided among the various share claimants based on their rights in land, or according to their services as thresher (*devvâs*), barber (*berber*), blacksmith (*demirci*), carpenter (*naccâr*), measurer (*keyyâl*), scribe (*kâtip*), police guard (*şahne*), hydraulic engineer (*kârih*), irrigation specialist (*sâkî*), or coffee maker (*kahveci*). Fees and *uqr* shares varied from field to field but either were a proportion of the total produce or were determined by the area of cultivation.[34] The rest of the produce was divided between the tax

33 The record distinguishes two kinds of reward: free land (*mutlak*) and a portion of land in addition to the prearranged reward (*ekrâm*). It was calculated as an area of one feddân out of eleven but subject to payment of the government's share to the tax farmer.

34 The share of *uqr* was 1/20 in Hajji Qura and 1/25 in Khanaqin, Qizlarbat, and Zawiya. The thresher received the same share for his service. After deduction of the *uqr* and thresher's shares, the service persons received their fees from the produce. The fees for the barber, blacksmith, and carpenter were 1/100 of the total produce; those for the measurer and all

farmer (i.e., the government's share) and the peasant tribesmen at a ratio of two-thirds for the tax farmer, including his share as the seed provider, and one-third for the tribesmen (Table 2.5, cols. 3–8).

The seed was furnished usually by the *mallâk* (meaning either landholder or seed supplier).[35] The price of the seed was the same as the selling price of the crop, except for higher-priced vegetable seed. The peasant provided his own breaker plough, harness, spade, hoe, sickle, and fork and paid for their repair or replacement, often in kind. Threshing also was paid for in kind at a customary compensation of 100 kg per 2 tons of crop threshed; for sorghum and millet, which were easier to thresh, 50 kg per 2 tons. Camel drivers charged 12.5 kg per 200 kg to transport the threshed crop out of the field.

In most cases, a landholder purchased a right of possession in the land from the government, and he furnished the seed to the peasant who cultivated it.[36] From the produce of this land, the *uqr* share and various fees were paid at the same proportion as mentioned above, and the remainder was divided among the tax farmer, peasant, and landholder at the ratio of one-fifth of the produce for the tax farmer, two-fifths for the peasant, and two-fifths for the landholder as seed provider. This was a better arrangement for the peasant than the one in which the tax farmer furnished the seed (40 per cent vs 33 per cent), but in it, the landholder received only about 40 per cent of the crop in return for the seed, whereas the tax farmer received an additional 46–47 per cent of the crop above his basic 20 per cent when he furnished the seed. While the government's share taken by the tax farmer was one-seventh of the produce in rain-fed fields, the rest was divided half-and-half between the peasant and the *mallâk*.

From the crops produced by a landholder and from peasants settled in villages of the Diyala region, the tax farmer received a commission, or fee, for tax collecting. Since there was no custom in which the tax farmer took the seeds from the harvested crops in that region, he might have collected this commission to offset the costs of seed in parts of his tax farm where no landholder furnished it. The amount of the commission was usually high: in the Khanaqin sub-district, it was 3 vezne of wheat or barley per feddân in the irrigated fields, and 3 batman of either crop per feddân in the rain-fed fields (Table 2.5, col. 2).

In the irrigated areas along the Khorasan, Mahrut, Shahriban, and Baladruz Canals, agriculture was largely performed by tent-dwelling peasant tribesmen,

the police guards were 15 okka of both barley and wheat per feddân. In Bungudra and Dakka, where there was no *uqr* holder or thresher, only the measurer and police guards received fees from the produce (15 okka of barley and wheat per feddân).

35 *Mallâk* is a transliteration of the Ottoman Turkish word in the record. In Arabic, the landholder was called *mâlik* (pl. *müllâk*).

36 The seed owner was called *mübâzirci* in the survey.

with the seed provided by either the tax farmer or the landholder. Except in the Baladruz area, crop sharing was practised in the same way as in the Khanaqin sub-district. The *uqr* share was paid in cash by the tax farmer, and the fee for the thresher was paid by the peasant from his share, but the commission of the tax farmer was higher in these areas, and the peasant paid a fee to a hydro-specialist who was employed in Khorasan, Mahrut, and Baladruz to distribute water among the fields. In Shahriban, a fee also was paid to a coffee maker (*kahveci*) from the tax farmer's share of the produce.

As presented in Table 2.6, cols. 3–4, in Abu Ghraib, Karbala, Musaib, Samarra, and Aziziya in the central region, no *uqr* share and no fee for the thresher were deducted from the produce. The payment for the bailiff was higher there because he received a special gift of 1 feddân when he cultivated an area of 10 feddân. In the farms along the Husayniya Canal in Karbala, Abu Usaid, Iskandariya, and Musaib, the government supported half the cost of digging and cleaning the canals in the fields held by landholders, who consequently received a lower share and gave more of the crop to the tax farmer.[37] This smaller share for the landholder was one of the main reasons why the sale of land for reclamation was delayed in this region.

6 The Middle Euphrates River Basin

The practice of crop sharing was complicated even further in the Middle Euphrates River basin by the influence of tribal custom and the government's land policies. On the west bank of the Hilla Branch, for example, the bailiff received his reward in crops, instead of land, for maintenance. This reward was paid by the tax farmer or by both the tax farmer and the seed owner from their shares. In addition, the bailiff received the right to sow a certain quantity of seed for his own use on land adjacent to the crop field.[38] Half the seed, which altogether was about one-fifth to one-tenth the amount sown in the area of a feddân, was often gifted to him by the government. The produce of the bailiff's gift was subject to crop sharing, but the bailiff was exempt from the government's share if he could manage to cultivate more land for the tax farmer. Some seed owners also received a gift for supplying the seed to the tribesmen (Tables 2.7 and 2.8, col. 1).

37 In Abu Ghraib, the tax farmer and the peasant paid the fees of the service persons from their shares when the total production reached 10 tagar in an area of 2 feddân. When the production was lower, the tax farmer paid the fees from the total produce.

38 In this area, the reward was called *şikâret* or, if tax exempt, *şikâret-i muâf*.

Another unique custom on the west bank was giving a special fee to the tax farmer, *serkâr*, seed owner, or landholder who provided the seeds to the peasant tribesmen. The fee for the tax farmer, called *berâtîl* (commission; lit., a bribe), was usually 2.5–3.5 vezne per tagar, or 10–15 per cent of the harvested crops. From 10 to 15 per cent of the fee, called *ekrâm* or *şikâret*, was granted to the bailiff and the seed owner, according to their contributions to the production (Table 2.7, col. 3). The landholder also supplied the seeds in his land, receiving the commission or reward.

In addition to the tax farmer's fee, the cost of the seed, the *uqr* share, and various service fees were deducted from the total harvest. The fees for the service persons, which were detailed only for Muhannawiya, were given to the thresher, barber, blacksmith, carpenter, measurer, scribe, police guards, transporter (*nakldâr*), and watchman of a dyke (*bekçi*).[39] The comparatively high rate of *uqr* in this area was one-eleventh of the produce, of which one-fifth was given to the bailiff as his reward (Table 2.7, cols. 4 and 5).

After the required deductions and fees, the produce was divided between the tax farmer and the peasant tribesmen, or among the tax farmer, peasant tribesmen, and seed owner. Because the government did not give the right of land possession to private individuals in this region, the seed owner received the *mübâzirci*'s share. Usually, the seeds necessary for farming in the next season were reserved as a stock.[40] If the tax farmer took responsibility for them, the resulting produce was divided at the ratio of two-thirds to one-third, or three-fifths to two-fifths, between the tax farmer and the peasant tribesmen respectively. Where a separate seed owner was responsible for the seed, he received one-third to one-half of the government's (tax farmer's) share. If the peasant tribesman provided the seed himself, he obtained one-half of the produce, while the remaining half was taken by the tax farmer as the government's share (Table 2.7, col. 6).

On the east bank of the Hilla Branch, the bailiff received his reward in land and in kind.[41] The service fees were subtracted from the total harvest at amounts ranging from 2 to 8 vezne per feddân, depending on the productivity of the land. The *uqr* share was usually paid by the tax farmer at one-eleventh of the government's share. In Mahawil, Abu Hasan, Niyasiya, and Wardiya on the east bank of the Hilla Branch, owing to the establishment of a government

---

39 The fee was 6 batman per vecih (a local unit of area equal to 2 feddân) of barley each for the blacksmith and carpenter, a total of 10 batman per vecih for the police guards, 2 batman per vecih for the watchman, 4 batman per vecih each for the measurer and scribe, and 10 batman per vecih (1/6 of which was paid by the tax farmer) for the transporter.

40 Seed reserved for the next year's cultivation was recorded as *demirbaşı* (stock).

41 The reward in kind was called *şikâret* as it was on the west bank of the Euphrates River.

office in Hilla, a number of fields were privately held as *temlîk* land. In such fields, the holder of the land, also called a *mallâk*, received the holder's share of the crops, even though he was not involved in the production and the seed was furnished by the seed owner or by the peasant tribesmen.[42] A government official (a *zabit* in a village or a *müdir* in a sub-district town) collected the tax of tithe from the total produce of these fields. From the rest of the produce, the *uqr* share and the service fees were subtracted at the same rate as for other fields; then the remainder was divided among the landholder, peasant tribesmen, and seed owner.

In Khatuniya and Mishmis, the whole area was held by one private individual as his property. The crops there were distributed in the same way as elsewhere, except that the government's share was taken by the owner (Table 2.8, col. 6).

7 Summer Crops

Maize, millet, sesame, cotton, rice, dates, and vegetables were cultivated in the limited parts of the Diyala, Middle Euphrates, and Mandali regions, where irrigation water was available in the farming season (Table 2.9). Maize, millet, sesame, and cotton were produced mainly in the Khanaqin sub-district and Mandali district, in which the tax farmer or the landholder provided the seed to the peasant tribesmen. Service persons were employed as needed, and the harvested crops were divided in a way similar to the winter crops. Rice was intensively cultivated in the sub-districts of Budair, Diwaniya, Samawa, and Shamiya in the Middle Euphrates. There, the rice fields were divided into a number of small units measured in müşâra (equivalent to 42.25 sq m) and cultivated by the peasant tribesmen according to their tribal custom. Because the seeds were saved and prepared by the tribesmen, the crop was subject to a half-and-half division between the tax farmer and the tribesmen. In addition to his half of the crop, the tax farmer collected a fee and dues (called *hafr rüsûmı*) for digging a water runnel. The tax farmer's fee was 2 or 2.5 vezne per tagar, while the digging fee cost 100 qiran (1 qiran = 5 kuruş) per vasle (40 müşâra); they were a respective 5 qiran per müşâra and 25 qiran per hane in Dughara; 60–75 qiran per müşâra for digging in Ufak, and 250 qiran in Samawa, and one-fortieth of the produce for the tax farmer and 5 kuruş per feddân for digging in Shamiya.

42 *Temlîk* land was granted in the pre-Tanzimat era in the same way as the land of *eshâb-ı temâlük* in the northern districts.

Vegetables and dates were produced on both state-owned farms and private land. The vegetables produced in the state gardens were subject to crop sharing. For example, in Khawas and Nahr Shah, the bailiff received rewards in land and in kind: 1 bustan per every 10 bustan (the unit of area for a vegetable garden cultivated by one household), and one-fifth of the government's share of the produce. One-tenth of the total produce was subtracted as a fee for services, and the rest of the produce was divided between the tax farmer (government) and the tribesmen at the ratio of two-thirds to one-third, or if there was a separate seed owner, he, the tribesmen, and the tax farmer each got one-third. In Annana, in which the government owned the date groves, the tax farmer received five-elevenths or one-half the produce, and the peasant the remainder.

In the privately owned date groves, fruit orchards, and vegetable gardens, the owner paid the tax of *hums* (one-fifth of the produce) to the tax farmer or to a government official, often in cash. In Khanaqin, for example, the tax was 42.5 kuruş per bile (equivalent to a bustan) or 32.5 kuruş per bile. The fees for service persons were usually one-tenth of the produce or a cash equivalent. In the Upper Euphrates basin, the tax was charged on each tree, 100 para (5 kuruş) per tree in Hit, 70 para (3.5 kuruş) per tree in Kibisa, and between 40 and 100 para per tree in Ana. In addition to the tax of *hums*, in the Mandali district a landowner who drew water from mountain streams flowing from the Ottoman-Persian border paid a fee for water use.[43] That fee was collected by the government official in charge of water management (*sû memuru*) according to the quantity of produce and the amount of water consumed. An annual fee of 300 toman (750 kuruş) in total had been agreed upon by the governments of Baghdad and Kermanshah in 1824, and the landowner's share of it was in proportion to his consumption and production.[44]

8 Estimations of the Quantities of Shares

The quantities of seed sown in a feddân, as described in the record for Khanaqin, were 615.36 kg (12 vezne) of wheat seed and 769.2 kg (15 vezne) of barley seed. As approximately five times each amount of the seed was harvested, we can

43 The fee for water use was *sû bedeli*.

44 The annual fee for water use in the Mandali district was 2,800 qiran (1 qiran = 5 kuruş), which was paid by the landholder either to the government in Kermanshah or to the Persian tribe of the Khalhur that dominated the high mountain areas. BOA, İ. Mesâil-i Mühimme 2067, 23 Receb 1263; TNA: FO 195/318, No. 33, Baghdad, 20 June 1848.

estimate the production of 3,076.80 kg (60 vezne) of wheat and 3,846 kg (75 vezne) of barley per feddân. The total amount of the *uqr* share and service fees was approximately 369 kg of wheat and 462 kg of barley, or 12 per cent of the total produce. The shares of the tax farmer were 1,005 kg of wheat and 1,256 kg of barley (33 per cent of the total), and the shares of peasant tribesmen were 851 kg of wheat and 1,064 kg of barley (28 per cent of the total). The seed owner's share also was 28 per cent of the total produce, but subtracting 20 per cent of the total for the quantity of seed sown reduces his net revenue to 8 per cent. In Khanaquin, where it was 12 per cent, the unearned income of the *uqr* owner was high; in the Diyala area, it was only 4 per cent; and in the Middle Euphrates, 9 per cent.

Applying the same ratio of crop per seed as in the Diyala River basin, we can figure the distribution of the shares in the Middle Euphrates. The quantities of seed, the tax farmer's fee, the *uqr*, and the service fees were estimated to be 20 per cent, 15 per cent, 9 per cent, and 8 per cent of the total produce respectively, on the west bank of the Hilla Branch. On the east bank, the tax farmer's fee was only 3 per cent of the total produce after these costs were deducted. On both banks, the rest of the shares were divided equally among the tax farmer, the seed owner, and the peasant tribesmen: 697 kg of wheat and 872 kg of barley for each on the west bank of the Hilla, and 820 kg of wheat and 1,026 kg of barley on the east bank.

According to survey data compiled in the Hilla region in the 1950s, food intake per person per day was 32 g of wheat, 112 g of barley, and 164 g of dates.[45] Farm owners exchanged their surplus dates with their tenants for grain, as tenants were not allowed to plant date palms. Applying these figures for the 1950s to the previous century, the necessary quantities of food per person a year would be 11.7 kg of wheat, 40.9 kg of barley, and 59.9 kg of dates. Assuming five persons in a household on an area of a feddân, they would be 58.5 kg of wheat, 204.5 kg of barley, and 299.5 kg of dates. The peasant's estimated shares were 700–850 kg for wheat and 870–1,000 kg for barley (the exchange ratio between grains and dates being unknown), rough estimates that suggest that the peasants earned more than a subsistence level in the mid-nineteenth century.

Regarding the government's share accredited to the tax farmer, in a grain field without an owner's share and with the household dues paid by the peasant, the survey indicates it was roughly 10–20 per cent of the total produce. After the government's share was deducted, the produce was divided half-and-half between the peasant and any partner, becoming 40–45 per cent of the total produce respectively. In order to collect produce equivalent to the quantity of

45 Poyck, "Farm Studies in Iraq," p. 67.

the seed he furnished, the partner had to harvest at least 2.2 times the amount of the seed on dry-farming fields and 2.5 times the amount on irrigated fields. When the tax farmer provided the seed to the peasant, he obtained the government's 10 per cent share and partner's 45 per cent share, or 55 per cent of the total produce on the dry-farming fields. On irrigated fields, where the government's share was 20 per cent and the partner's 40 per cent, the tax farmer who provided seed received 60 per cent of the total produce. The harvest consequently had to be at least 1.8 times the amount of the seed for the dry field and 1.7 times for the irrigated field.

The average rate of return to the tax farmer can be calculated on the assumption that the tax farmer's investment was the quantity of the seed (20 per cent of the total produce), while his return on investment was the seed owner's net share. As estimated in Table 2.2, assuming the seed owner's share as 28 per cent on the Diyala basin, 23 per cent on the west bank of the Hilla branch, and 27 per cent on its east bank, the tax farmer's return from investment in seeds became, after the deduction for the seed, 8, 3, and 7 per cent of the total produce in the three respective regions. In order to cover the cost of the seed from his share as the seed owner, the tax farmer had to attain production of at least 3.4 times the amount of the seed sown in the Diyala River basin, 2.9 times on the west bank of the Hilla branch, and 3.1 times on the east bank. These numbers suggest that because the tax farmer risked sustaining a loss on his investment, he might attempt to increase his rate of return on productive land, without investing for the long term in the marginal portion of the farm, thus increasing the uncultivated portion of the land in the marginal area.

TABLE 2.2 Estimated shares in irrigated areas

Share	Diyala basin			Hilla branch basin: west bank			Hilla branch basin: east bank		
	Wheat (kg)	Barley (kg)	%	Wheat (kg)	Barley (kg)	%	Wheat (kg)	Barley (kg)	%
Tax farmer's fee	154	192	5	461	577	15	92	115	3
Service fees	246	308	8	246	308	8	246	308	8
Uqr fee	123	154	4	277	346	9	277	346	9
Tax farmer's share	851	1,064	28	697	872	23	820	1,026	27
Seed owner's share	851	1,064	28	697	872	23	820	1,026	27
Peasant's share	851	1,064	28	697	872	23	820	1,026	27
Total	3,076	3,846		3,076	3,846	100	3,076	3,846	100

TABLE 2.3 Agricultural calendar in the Baghdad district

	January	February	March	April	May
Sown	wheat (late) barley (late) red urfa onions (120)*	wheat (late) short cucumbers (65) long cucumbers (60) sugar melons (90) okra (lady's fingers) (90) tomatoes (90) gourds (90) pumpkins: Var Askala (90) White Stamboul (90) kidney beans (90) dwarf French beans (60) coriander (70) cumin (70) aniseed (70) fenugreek (70) fennel (70)	millet (60) maize (70) sorghum (90) long cucumbers eggplants (brinjal) (100) water melons (90) chillies (90)	millet coriander (110) long cucumbers (90) eggplants (brinjal) (80)	millet maize coriander mash (90) broad beans (90) long cucumbers (90)
Harvested				cucumbers long cucumbers mulberry	barley wheat maize long cucumbers apricots yellow plums purple plums Persian apples

* Expected number of days until harvest.

SOURCE: TNA: FO 371/4150/187296, ADMINISTRATION REPORT, REVENUE BOARD, BAGHDAD, 22 MAR.–31 DEC. 1917 (BAGHDAD: PRINTED AT GOVERNMENT PRESS, 1918), P. 19.

June	July	August	September	October	November	December
millet maize mash broad beans long cucumbers sesame red kidney beans	millet maize long cucumbers	millet (65) maize (65) long cucumbers (65) beetroot (90) carrots (120) cabbage (120) spinach beets (90)	garlic (150) broad beans (var Falea) broad beans (var local) turnips (90) green onions (80) radishes (30) spinach (90)	imported wheat (210) barley (210) broad beans (150)	local wheat (195) barley (170)	wheat (180) barley (150)

wheat millet maize long cucumbers eggplants (brinjal) apples pears nectarines	millet maize long cucumbers eggplants (brinjal) figs	millet maize mash broad beans long cucumbers pomegranates figs grapes dates	millet maize long cucumbers coriander mash broad beans dates	millet maize long cucumbers quinces dates	millet sweet limes sour limes sweet oranges sour oranges turunj (citrons)	

TABLE 2.4 Share distribution in the northern districts

District or Subdistrict/Town	State share				
	(1)	(2)	(3)	(4)	(5)
	Winter crops*	Winter crops**	Summer crops	Vegetables	Fruit
Rawanduz/Dashtidiyan, Daira, Harir		1/5	1/2^{S}	1/2^{S} 1/2	
Darband/Köysanjaq	1/10		2,500k/y 1/3, 2/3^{S}		1/5
Khalakan/Khaydaq, Ayzub	1/10		5/6^{S}, 1/6 1/5, 1/4, 1/3		1/10
Khushnawi/Ishtar, Khabrain	1/10		5/6^{S}, 1/6 1/5, 1/4, 1/3		1/10
Shahrizor/Kirkuk	1/10		1/2 5/6–8/9^{S}	1/10	1/5
Shaydan/Sheykh Bezi	1/10		1/2 5/6–8/9^{S}	1/10	1/5
Tuz Khurmatu	1/10		1/2 5/6–8/9^{S}	1/10	1/5 1/10
Erbil	1/10		1/10	1/10	
Altun Köprü	1/10			1/10	
Zangabad/ Kifri	1/10	1/5	3/5, 2/3^{S}	1/10	1/5
Qaratepe	1/10	1/5	3/5, 2/3^{S}	1/10	1/10
Makatibad, Bardan, Qizlar, Hajjilar, Kashgawil	1/10 of owner's	1/5 of owner's	1/5 of owner's		

* rain-fed land; ** irrigated land.
S: seeds provided by the tax farmer; k: kuruş; f: feddân; y: year; m: month.
SOURCE: BOA, İ. MECLIS-I VÂLÂ 24610, 24 ŞEVVAL 1282.

Taxes and dues			Other shares			Division	
(6)	(7)	(8)	(9)	(10)	(11)	(12)	
Household	Watermill	Irrigation	Landowner	*Uqr*	Landholder	Peasant	Partner
75k/f	80k/y 40k/6m					1/2	1/2
75k/f							
Mukayyid Rüsûmı							
100k/f	31.5k/y 20.5k/6m	45k/y– 163k/y	1/5–1/10	1/30		1/2	1/2
Mukayyid Rüsûmı	31.5k/y 20.5k/y					1/2	1/2
100k/f	100k/y 50k/6m	75k/y 225k/y			1/10	1/2	1/2
175k/f	100k/y 60k/6m		1/3–1/15			1/2	1/2
100k/f	36k/y			1/30		1/2	1/2
75k/f 100k/f	30–100k			1/40		1/2	1/2
75k/f 100k/f	30–100k			1/40		1/2	1/2
75k/f 100k/f				1/40	1/5 1/10		

TABLE 2.5 Crop sharing in the Diyala river basin

Mukâtaa	(1) *Serkâr* (Bailiff)	(2) *Vasıta* (Fee)	(3) *Uqr*	(4) Thresher	(5) Barber, carpenter, blacksmith	(6) Measurer (M) Police (P)	(7) Division Tax farmer	 Peasant	 Land-holder
Khanaqin	1f/11f *ekrâm*	3v/f-b 3v/f-w 3m/f (*dâim*)	1/25	1/25	1/100	150/f-b 150/f-w	2/3^{S} 1/3 1/5 (1/7 *dâim*)	1/3 1/3 2/5	1/3^{S} 2/5^{S}
Qizlarbat Zawiya	1f/11f *ekrâm*	3v/f-b 3v/f-w 3m/f (*dâim*)	1/25	1/25	1/100	150/f-b 150/f-w	2/3^{S} 1/3 1/5 (60k/f *dâim*)	1/3 1/3 2/5	1/3^{S} 2/5^{S}
Hajji Qura	1f/11f *ekrâm*	3v/f-b 3v/f-w	1/20	1/20	1/100	7.50/f-b 1.50/f-w (M) 150/f-bw (P)	1/2 (1/7 *dâim*)	1/4	1/4^{S}
Bungudra Dakka	1f/11f *ekrâm*	3v/f-b 3v/f-w 3m/f (*dâim*)				150/f-b 150/f-w	1/5 (1/7 *dâim*)	2/5	2/5^{S}
Khorasan Mahrut		10v/f-b 5v/f-w	1/30	1/30	2v/f-b 1v/f-b	2v/f-b, 1v/f-w (P& *Kârih*)	2/3^{S} 1/3	1/3 1/3	1/3^{S}
Shahriban		6v1m/f-b 3v1m/f-w	1/20	1/30	1/100-b 0.5/100-w	2v/f-b & 1v/f-w (P), 1/100-b & 0.5/ 100-w (M), 1m/f-bw (*kahveci*)	2/3^{S} 1/3	1/3 1/3	1/3^{S}

TABLE 2.5 Crop sharing in the Diyala river basin (*cont.*)

Mukâtaa	(1) *Serkâr* (Bailiff)	(2) *Vasıta* (Fee)	(3) *Uqr*	(4) Thresher	(5) Barber, carpenter, blacksmith	(6) Measurer (M) Police (P)	(7) Division: Tax farmer	Peasant	Land-holder
Baladruz		13v/f-b 6.5v/f-w	27.5k/f	1/25-b 1/30-w	2v/f-b 1v/f-w	4v/f-b & 2v/f-w (P), 1v/f-b & 0.5 v/f-w (M), 2v/f-b & 1v/f-w (*kârıh*)	2.5/4^{S} 1/3	1.5/4 1/3	1/3^{S}

v: vezne; m: batman; o:okka; k: kuruş; b: barley; w: wheat
dâim: rain-fed land; *ekrâm*: reward; *kahveci*: coffee maker; *kârıh*: hydraulic engineer
SOURCE: BOA, İ. MECLIS-I VÂLÂ 24610, 24 ŞEVVAL 1282.

TABLE 2.6 Crop sharing in the central region and mountain area

District or Sub-district/ *Mukâtaa*	(1)	(2)	(3)	(4)
	Serkâr (Bailiff)	*Vasıta* (Fee), seed	*Uqr*	Threshe
Abu Ghraib/Abu Ghraib Mahmudiya Ridwaniya	1f/11f *ekrâm hedâvî*	6m/f-b 3m/f-w		
Karbala/Husayniya Abu Usaid		Seeds or 1t/f		
Musaib/Musaib Abu Luka Iskandariya	1f/6f *ekrâm hedâvî*	Seeds		
Samarra/Dujail	1f/11f *ekrâm*	Seeds		
Aziziya/Aziziya	1f/6f *ekrâm*			
Mandali/Mandali	1f/11f	2v/f-b 1.5v/f-w	1/20	1/20
Mandali/Qazaniya Dusheykh			1/20	1/20
Mandali/Badra Jisan Zurbata	2f/12f 18 qirân 1t-seeds			

t: tagar; v: vezne; m: batman; o: okka; f: feddân; k: kuruş; b: barley; w: wheat; S: seed
çift: unit of land; *dâim*: rain-fed land; *dulâb*: waterwheel; *ekrâm*: reward; *hedâvî*: reward; *kârıh*: hydraulic engineer; qirân: local unit of currency (=5 kuruş)

SOURCE: BOA, İ. MECLIS-I VÂLÂ 24610, 24 ŞEVVAL 1282.

(5)	(6)	(7)	(8)		
Barber, carpenter, blacksmith	**Measurer (M) Police (P)**	***Çift*** **(Ç) &** ***Dulâb*** **(D) dues**	**Division**		
			Tax Farmer	**Peasant**	**Landholder**
3v/t-b 1.5v/t-w	2yük-b 1 yük-w		1/3	1/3	1/3^{S}
2m/f	2m/f		2/3^{S} 1.5/3^{S}	1/3 1/3	0.5/3^{S}
from 0.5/5.5 3v/t	from 0.5/5.5 3v/t		1/5.5 3.5/5.5^{S}	2/5.5 2/5.5	2/5.5^{S}
2v/t	2v/t		2/3^{S} 1/3	1/3 1/3	1/3^{S}
		175k (D)	1/5	4/5^{S}	
1/100		25k/f (Ç)	2/3^{S} 1/6 1/6	1/3 5/6^{S} 1/6	4/6^{S}
1m/f-b 0.5m/f-w	1m/f-b 0.5m/f-w (*kârih*)		8/9^{S} 8/45	1/9 1/9	32/ 45^{S}
		25 qirân/ f (Ç)	11/13^{S}	2/13	

TABLE 2.7 Crop sharing on the west bank of the Middle Euphrates River

Mukâtaa	(1) ***Serkâr*** **(Baillif)**	(2) **Seed** **(S)**	(3) ***Berâtîl***	(4) ***Uqr***	(5) **Service fees**	(6) **Division** **Tax Farmer**	 **Peasant**	 **Landholder**	(7) ***Çift* (Ç) & *Dulâb* (D) dues**
Muhannawiya Annana Khawwas	3/11 of *miri* 3/11 of (Ç) 1/8 of (D) 1m40 of *berâtîl şikâret* (2m/f)	(S)	2.5v/t 3.5v/t		10.5v/2f	$2/3^{S}$ 1/3	1/3 1/3	$1/3^{S}$ 2m of *berâtîl şikâret* (2m/f)	2 şâmî/f (Ç) 120 qirân (D)
Tahmasiya Tajiya	3/11 of *miri* 1/5 of *uqr* 1m of *berâtîl şikâret*	(S)	3.5v/t	1/11	10.5v/2f	$2/3^{S}$	1/3		2 şâmî/f (Ç)
Nahrshah	3/11 of *miri* 1/5 of *uqr* 1m40 of *berâtîl şikâret*	(S)	3v/t	1/11	10.5v/2f	$2/3^{S}$ 1/2 1.5/3	1/3 $1/2^{S}$ 1/3	$0.5/3^{S}$ 1m of *berâtîl şikâret* (2m/f)	2 şâmî/f (Ç)
Dur Humayniya	3/11 of *miri* 1/5 of *uqr* 1m40 of *berâtîl şikâret*	(S)	2.5v/t	1/11	10.5v/2f	$2/3^{S}$ 1/2 1.25/3	1/3 $1/2^{S}$	$0.75/3^{S}$ 1.5m of *berâtîl şikâret*	100 qirân

TABLE 2.7 Crop sharing on the west bank of the Middle Euphrates River (*cont.*)

Mukâtaa	(1) *Serkâr* (Baillif)	(2) Seed (S)	(3) *Berâtîl*	(4) *Uqr*	(5) Service fees	(6) Division			(7) *Çift* (Ç) & *Dulâb* (D) dues
						Tax Farmer	Peasant	Landholder	
Alaj	3/11 of *miri* 1/5 of *uqr* *şikâret*	(S)	2.5v/t	1/11	10.5v/2f	$2/3^{S}$ 1/2 1.25/3	1/3 $1/2^{S}$ 1/3	 $0.75/3^{S}$ şikâret	3 şâmî/f or 6 şâmî/f (Ç)
Jurbuiya	3/11 of *miri* 1/5 of *uqr* *ekrâm* (1f/11f) şikâret (2m/f)		2.5v/t	1/11	4v/2f-b 2v/2f-w	1/2	$1/2^{S}$		

t: tagar; v: vezne; m: batman; o: okka; f: feddân; k: kuruş; b: barley; w: wheat; S: seed
çift: household; *dulâb*: waterwheel; *ekrâm*: reward; *hedâvî*: reward; *şikâret*: reward; *kârıh*: hydraulic engineer; *miri*: government share; qirân: local unit of currency (=5 kuruş); şâmî: local unit of currency (=8.5 kuruş)

SOURCE: BOA, İ. MECLIS-I VÂLÂ 24610, 24 ŞEVVAL 1282.

TABLE 2.8 Crop sharing on the east bank of the Middle Euphrates River

Mukâtaa	(1) *Serkâr* (Baillif)	(2) *Vasıta* seed (S)	(3) *Uqr*	(4) Service fees	(5) Division (*Miri* land)			(6) Division (*Temlîk* land)			
					Tax farmer	Peasant	Seed owner	Tax farmer	Land holder	Peasant	Seed owner
Nasiriya	2f/12f	(S)	1/3 of 1/5.5	2/3 of 1/5.5 3v/2f (*bekçi* & *nakldâr*)	2/5.5^{S} 1/5.5	2.5/5.5 2.5/5.5	1/5.5^{S}	*öşür*	2/5.5^{S} 1/5.5	2.5/5.5 2.5/5.5	1/5.5^{S}
Haswaniya	1f/12f *şikâret*	(S)	1/20 f 1/5.5	1/2 of 1/5.5 2v/2f (*bekçi* & *nakldâr*)	2/5.5^{S} 1/5.5	2.5/5.5 2.5/5.5	1/5.5^{S}				
Mahawil	3f/13f *şikâret*	(S)	1/30	4v/2f	3/5^{S} 2/5	2/5 2/5	1/5^{S} *şikâret*	*öşür*	3/5^{S} 2/5	2/5 2/5	1/5^{S} *şikâret*
Nil	3f/13f *şikâret*	3v/2f-b 1.5/2f-w	1/11	2v/2f	3/5^{S} 2/5 1/2	2/5 2/5 1/2^{S}	1/5^{S} *şikâret*				
Khatuniya	1/6 *şikâret*		from 1/6	from 1/6				*öşür* from 1/6	2.5/6 2/6	2.5/6^{S} 2/6	1/6^{S} *şikâret*
Wardiya Niyasiya	*şikâret*	(S)	1/11	3v1m/2f	1/2 2/5	1/2^{S} 2/5	1/5^{S}	*öşür*	1/2 2/5	1/2^{S} 2/5	1/5^{S}
Abu Hasan	*şikâret* (2m/2f)	(S)	1/11	6v/2f	3/5^{S} 1/2 1.5/5	2/5 1/2^{S} 2/5	0.5/5^{S} *şikâret*	*öşür*	3/5^{S} 1/2 1.5/5	2/5 1/2^{S} 2/5	0.5/5^{S} *şikâret*
Mishmis	3f/13f *şikâret* (2m/f)	(S)	1/11	8v/2f				*öşür*	1/2 3/5.5^{S}	1/2^{S} 2.5/5.5	

TABLE 2.8 Crop sharing on the east bank of the Middle Euphrates River (*cont.*)

Mukâtaa	(1)	(2)	(3)	(4)	(5)			(6)			
	Serkâr (Baillif)	*Vasıta* seed (S)	*Uqr*	Service fees	Division (*Miri* land)			Division (*Temlîk* land)			
					Tax farmer	Peasant	Seed owner	Tax farmer	Land holder	Peasant	Seed owner
Bayrumana	*şikâret*	3v/f-b	1/11 from 1/5	2v/2f from 1/5	$2/5^{S}$	2/5					
Rubyana	3f/13f *şikâret* (1/2t)	(S)	1/11	8v/2f	$3/5^{S}$ 1/2	2/5 $1/2^{S}$					
Shumali	3f/13f *şikâret* (2m/2f)		1/11	5v/2f	$2/3^{S}$ 1/2	1/3 $1/2^{S}$					

t: tagar; v: vezne; m: batman; o: okka; f: feddân; k: kuruş; b: barley; w: wheat; S: seed
çift: household; *dulâb*: waterwheel; *ekrâm*: reward; *hedâvî*: reward; *şikâret*: reward; *bekçi*: watchman; *nakldâr*: transporter; *miri*: state land; *temlîk*: private landholding; qirân: local unit of currency (=5 kuruş); şâmî: local unit of currency (=8.5 kuruş)

SOURCE: BOA, İ. MECLIS-I VÂLÂ 24610, 24 ŞEVVAL 1282.

TABLE 2.9 Crop sharing for summer crops

		(1)	(2)	(3)	(4)	(5)	(6)			(7)
							Division			
Mukâtaa	Crops	*Serkâr*	*Berâtîl*	*Uqr*	*Devvâs*	*Amûle* (dues)	Tax farmer	Peasant	Seed owner	*Hafr* (tax)
Khanaqin	maise	1f/10f		1/25	1/25	6m/f	2/3^{S}	1/3	1/3^{S}	
	millet					(*vasıta*)	1/2	1/2^{S}	2/5^{S}	
	sesame						2/3^{S}	1/3		
	cotton			1/25		150/f	1/2	1/2^{S}		
	rice	1v-seeds				(*keyyâl*)	1/3	1/3		
						4–50	2/5	1/5		
						(*şahne*)				
Shahriban				1/20	1/30	1m/f	2/3^{S}	1/3	1/3^{S}	
						(*keyyâl*)	1/3	1/3		
						2m/f				
						(*şahne*)				
Baladruz	cotton			1/30			3/4^{S}	1/4	1/4^{S}	
	sesame						2/4	1/4	3/7^{S}	
	rice						6/7^{S}	1/7		
							3/7	1/7		
Badra Jisan	millet					15–20	3/4^{S}	1/4		
Zurbata	sesame					kile	1/3	2/3^{S}		
	cotton					(*bekçi*)	9/10^{S}			
							1/2	1/2^{S}		
						1/10				
						(*sâki*)				
Annana	rice	1/5					2/3^{S}	1/3		
Khawwas		*şikâret*					1/2	1/2^{S}		
Alaj	rice	1/5	2.5v/t		2v/vasle		1/2	1/2^{S}		100q/ vasle
Daghara	rice	1/5- 1/10	2v/t			2m/t (*bekçi*)	1/2	1/2^{S}		5q/ müşâra
Afaj	rice	1/5; 1/6	2.5v/t		1/5; 1/6		1/2	1/2^{S}		6.25- 7.5q/ müşâra

TABLE 2.9 Crop sharing for summer crops (*cont.*)

		(1)	(2)	(3)	(4)	(5)	(6)			(7)
							Division			
Mukâtaa	Crops	*Serkâr*	*Berâtîl*	*Uqr*	*Devvâs*	*Amûle* (dues)	Tax farmer	Peasant	Seed owner	*Hafr* (tax)
Shamiya	rice	1/5	1.5–3v/t			1.5–2v/ müşâra	1/2	1/2^{S}		5k/ müşâra
Samawa	rice	1/8	2.5v/t		1t–114v /vasle	1v/t (*vasıta*) 0.5v/t (*nakliye*)	1/2	1/2^{S}		200q/ vasle

t: tagar; v: vezne; m: batman; o: okka; f: feddân; k: kuruş; b: barley; w: wheat; S: seed; q: qirân *amûle*: servicemen; *keyyâl*: measurer; *şahne*: guard; *şikâret*: reward; *bekçi*: watchman; *nakliye*: transport; *sâki*: hydraulic engineer; *vasıta*: fee; qirân: local unit of currency (=5 kuruş); şâmî: local unit of currency (=8.5 kuruş).

SOURCE: BOA, İ. MECLIS-I VÂLÂ 24610, 24 ŞEVVAL 1282.

9 Agricultural Policies

The government's measures to cope with agricultural issues were inadequate in the early Tanzimat period. While public works were undertaken on the rivers and major canals, small-scale irrigation projects on branch canals were kept in private hands. Investment in the land to enhance yields was also a private function, for which the government gave only incentives such as tax privileges and technical advice. Under the governorship of Necip Pasha (1842–49), the first public project to bring lasting benefit was to utilize the floodwaters of the Saqlawiya Canal, which had originally been dug as a water outlet from the Euphrates River to the Tigris. Previous governments had constructed embankments along the canal and pulled branch channels from the canal for irrigating lands nearby. However, large quantities of water still flooded wastefully, so that the area of the canal produced only about 2,000 tagar of grain a year at the sum of 1,000 kese akçe (0.5 million kuruş).[46]

46 Issawi, *Fertile Crescent, 1800–1914*, pp. 353–55.

Necip Pasha allocated a budget of nearly 10,000 kuruş for annual maintenance of the Saqlawiya Canal to prevent the overflow of water from it. He also repaired the decrepit dykes and water channels of the Mahmudiya, Radwaniya, Iskandariya, Abu Ghraib, and Dawdiya Canals, below the Saqlawiya, and made more water from the Euphrates River available to them. Lands near the Radwaniya and Iskandariya Canals were estimated to harvest 7,000 tagar of grain annually, and those near the Abu Ghraib, 5,000 to 6,000 tagar, if the canals were in good repair. Because the price of wheat was 850 kuruş per tagar and that of barley 525 kuruş at the time, Necip Pasha could expect large profits after the Saqlawiya Canal was embanked. Upon establishing control of the irrigation water in the area, he farmed out the irrigated lands one by one to tax farmers and thereafter obtained the anticipated large sums of tax revenue.[47] When Necip Pasha reinforced the embankment of the Hindiya Barrage and opened a new canal near Karbala, he made himself tax farmer of the new lands, achieving a surplus more than sufficient to reimburse the cost of the projects. He awarded the sheikh of the Zubaid Arab the right of tax collection on the farms along the Hindiya Canal and his own son Ahmet Pasha the right for the outskirts of the Muntafiq domain.[48] The various other farms were let out, for from one to five years, to Necip Pasha's relatives and retinue members, public officials, notables, and tribal sheikhs, without public auction and at less than their market value. When the large size of the farms were given at the fixed amount of tax, they brought in large profits.[49]

Because so many tax farms were offered to the sheikhs of peasant tribesmen or to local notables, or rented out to their agents for tax collecting, tax farming was localized but increasingly oppressive.[50] The most notorious abuser of the privilege of tax farming was Sheikh Wadee at Hindiya, who obtained

47 BOA, Muallim Cevdet Tasnifi (CT), İktisat 1723, 15 Cemaziyelahîr 1260; TNA: FO 195/272, No. 67, 18 Aug. 1847.

48 The tax was assessed in shami (*şâmî*), local currency circulated among tribesmen, and raised 100,000–200,000 shami a year. TNA: FO 195/237, No. 9, 4 Feb. 1846.

49 It was proposed to grant any speculative capitalist who might put it under cultivation a lease of five to ten years on such land, if the governor guaranteed the lease against possible forfeiture of his right. It was reported that capital was so redundant at Baghdad that there was difficulty in finding good investment opportunities and obtaining advantageous leases. TNA: FO 195/334, No. 7, 11 Mar. 1850.

50 As an example of growing interest in tax farming as a lucrative investment, the private granary in the city contained 3,000 tagar of grain belonging to the government, 5,000 tagar belonging to private individuals, and 5,000 tagar for stock. TNA: FO 195/272, No. 67, Baghdad, 18 Aug. 1847.

his privilege in return for payment of one-tenth of the estimated value of the tax farm.[51] After that payment was increased by half, the sheikh recovered his losses through higher charges on the inhabiting tribesmen and ignored the custom of crop sharing, thus reducing them from a state of comparative affluence to complete destitution.[52] In 1848, when the harvest yielded only one-fifth of the usual cereal produce because of a drought, worsening discontent among the peasant tribesmen against the oppression of Wadee prompted the Porte to auction tax farms under the strict supervision of the Imperial Treasury, separating fiscal affairs from civil administration.

The governor's concern with agriculture continued even while his violent battles with the tribal sheikhs interfered with production. Necip Pasha organized a committee on agricultural improvement and had it survey the contemporary situation in order to recommend measures for improvement. The committee's relatively brief report offered a broad blueprint for agriculture-related projects and affirmed the need to encourage commercial production activities and so to diversify crops. It emphasized that while wheat and barley were the chief staples, other commercial products (e.g., rice, wool, cotton, and animal products) were equally important targets for encouragement, and it proposed improving their quality, distributing seed, and dispatching technicians to local areas.

During his first term as governor (1851–52), in keeping with the committee's blueprint, Namık Pasha planned to grant money for improvements and to provide stock to cultivating peasants. Transfers of tax farms on the secondary market were carefully monitored, so that aid was used for the intended projects. Peasants who previously had had no choice but to leave the land fallow, due to lack of money and seed, could apply for the government aid themselves, and a tax farmer was allowed to recruit peasants from other farms if his land was unoccupied. Where the land had been productive but had lost fertility because of the tax farmer's short contract or the high costs of land clearing, the government provided the tax farmer with animals, tools, and other necessities,

51 According to the British consular report, Sheikh Wadee of the Zubaid tribe farmed revenues at Hindiya that were fixed at 2,000 purses (1 million kuruş). It appeared that the lands watered by the Hindiya Canal and the other offshoots from the right bank of the Euphrates were assessed in the registry at a sum of 3,500 purses (1.75 millon kuruş), yet the sheikh had been permitted to collect 21,000 purses (10.5 million kuruş) from them. TNA: FO 195/334, No. 17, 23 May 1849.

52 During the period in question, 10,000 purses (5 million kuruş) in excess of the registered sum of 3,500 were given to the Porte. TNA: FO 195/334, No. 18, 23 May 1849. An additional 2.5 per cent duty, called *sarrahieh*, was collected by the *zabit*, who had paid enormous fees for being appointed to the sub-district.

and it extended the term of his tax farm by one or two years, or longer if necessary. Repayment of the aid money at harvest involved various schedules, typically one-eighth of the total produce on the land cultivated the first year, one-seventh the second year, followed by one-sixth, one-fifth, and one-fourth, before stabilizing at one-third of the produce each year. Land for date groves and gardens was transferred without fee in return for installment payments over three, four, or five years, and the buyer was permitted to build a new village for workers.

As people became more involved in agriculture by lending money, supplying seed, tools, or housing, or purchasing tax-farming rights, Reşit Pasha (1852–57) recognized the trend established during the brief term of his predecessor. He resolved to use the crop-sharing custom to encourage tax farmers to extend land cultivation with peasant tribesmen. He also frequently toured the agricultural areas along the Diyala River, personally supervised the cleaning of one or two canals by forced labour, and settled the Shammer Toga tribesmen for cultivation. To incentivize tax farmers to undertake irrigation and land reclamation projects on their farms, he offered grants-in-aid for the costs of seed and cleaning the irrigation canals, a reduction in the tax owed, and, in some cases, a tax exemption for some years.[53] Through crop sharing, the tax farmer could secure his return on these improvements at a pre-fixed rate. Such encouragement of private investments in land subsequently became a main feature of agricultural development.

The tax farmer's profit or loss depended not only on the auction price of his tax farm but also on the quantity and value of the harvested crops, which reflected economic and natural conditions.[54] As a result, the tax farmer himself, his agent, or the bailiff-*serkâr* was actively involved in production activities in the areas of crop sharing, where the rate of return was customarily established.

In the villages of the north, where the tax farmers engaged in commercial production, they made their profits from the cultivation of summer cash crops such as cotton, rice, and sesame by providing the peasants with seed, then

53 In repairing Abu Hanafi Mosque in 1857, as an example of Reşit Pasha's benevolent policies, he built a fort surrounding the tomb and connected the dyke therewith to protect the city from flooding on that side. The whole expense of the work was set at 3,000 purses (1.5 million kuruş), of which the *nakif* of the establishment contributed one-third and the government two-thirds. Non-Muslims were exempted from this contribution. TNA: FO 195/521, No. 4, 4 Feb. 1857.

54 Claudius Rich observed that a peasant could produce eight to twenty times the amount of seeds he planted in Mosul in 1820, while British Consul Henry Rawlinson estimated that the crop-seed ratio was about 5:1 in Shahriban in 1848. Rich, *Narrative of a Residence in Koordistan*, ii, p. 63; Great Britain, Royal Geographic Society, Private Papers, Sir Henry C. Rawlinson, MS.

taking most of the produce (from five-sixths to eight-ninths), and giving the rest to the peasant as a labour fee. They returned a proportion of the government's share and the household dues (one-tenth on dry-farming fields and one-fifth on irrigated fields) to the tribal chief as a reward for his cooperation with the Ottoman authority or to the village headman who recruited migrating peasant tribesmen and thus cultivated more fields for the tax farmer. On a deserted field in Zangabad, where the tax farmer employed an irrigation specialist for land reclamation, he turned over cultivation of the reclaimed land to a *serkâr*, giving him one feddân of the reclaimed land when he cultivated five feddân.[55]

The land was worked by peasants from the nearby village as a part of their unpaid labour dues. From the produce harvested on the reclaimed land, the tax farmer paid the *uqr* share of one-fiftieth of the produce, paid the irrigation specialist one-twentieth of the produce, and retained the rest for himself.

For a field on which no prospective tax farmer wanted to bid because of its infertility or a danger of tribal raids, particularly on the east bank of the Hilla Branch and in the Mandali district, the government had put the field under *emânet*, or direct collection by the local official or by the military commander. It had then dug and dredged canals and, after restoring them, farmed them out for tax collecting.[56] As an alternative, Reşit Pasha attempted to sell vacant lands to private individuals according to the new land legislation. The purchaser was expected to carry out irrigation and land reclamation on his field and to take responsibility for supervising peasant tribesmen with their sheikh (*serkâr*) according to the local practice. The government gave him various kinds of financial support for such expenses as cleaning irrigation canals and constructing houses for settlement of the peasant tribesmen cultivating the field. The profit was large, for the purchaser received an average net return of 45–70 per cent on his investment in seed, but this sort of transfer took place in limited areas near the cities.

The sale of land was popular only in areas where irrigation was less costly. For instance, numerous fields cultivated by settled peasants using seed from the landholder were reclaimed in the Diyala River basin. In contrast, the transfer of vacant land was delayed where the cost of irrigation was high or where the tax farmer was of political consequence or closely associated with the peasant in farming. Having a new private landholder diminished the share of the tax farmer in the produce and consequently lessened the influence of the

55 The irrigation specialist is referred to by the local terms *sûcu, kârıh, sedd agası*, etc., in the record.

56 The field whose taxes were collected by the official was called *zabit-i mezraʿa*.

tax farmer in the field, while the large government share of the produce kept the net profit to the land purchaser small.

Tax farming always had been accompanied by sequences of problems in the Ottoman society and economy, but from the late 1850s, those problems were overshadowed by mounting local deficits and the slow growth of the overall economy. In general, the tax farmer's short-sighted behaviour had discouraged private investment and had curtailed other economic activities, because he bound the peasants to the land, preventing them from moving to non-agricultural sectors. In irrigated areas, where a diminishing rate of return could have been solved by irrigation and land reclamation, the tax farmer had been indifferent to land development without guaranteed profits. He had no incentive for long-term investment in the land itself, as his tax-farming right was not inheritable, and he was similarly disinclined to apply technological innovation beyond the term of his deal. What he practised was a sort of slash-and-burn agriculture on less fertile exterior fields, by permitting the peasant tribesmen free use of the land, which was easily worn out from overuse and abandoned without incurring penalty. Eventually, the problem of barren land began to draw the concern of the Ottoman government, which urgently needed to improve its fiscal position by increasing revenues, and it initiated a comprehensive reform of the state land system in the 1860s.

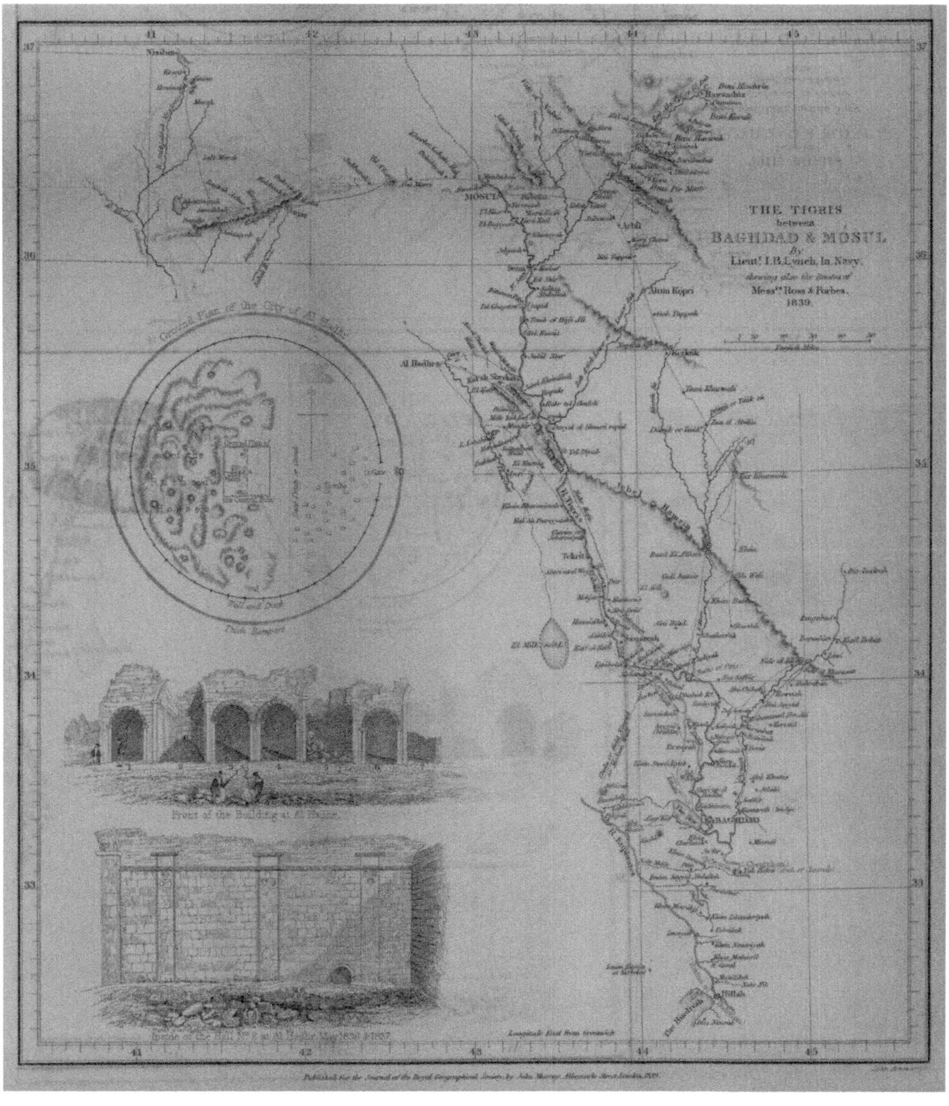

MAP 2.1 The Tigris between Baghdad and Mosul in 1839

SOURCE: BLOSSE H. LYNCH, *THE TIGRIS BETWEEN BAGHDAD AND MÓSUL*, 1 CM = 5 MILE (PUBLISHED FOR THE JOURNAL OF ROYAL GEOGRAPHICAL SOCIETY BY JOHN MURRAY, 1839), IN BLOSSE H. LYNCH, "NOTE ON A PART OF THE RIVER TIGRIS, BETWEEN BAGDÁD AND SÁMARRAH," *THE JOURNAL OF THE ROYAL GEOGRAPHICAL SOCIETY OF LONDON*, 9 (LONDON, 1839), PP. 471–76.

MAP SOURCE: PRINCETON UNIVERSITY LIBRARY: HTTPS:// CATALOG .PRINCETON.EDU/CATALOG/7682964

COURTESY OF ROYAL GEOGRAPHICAL SOCIETY

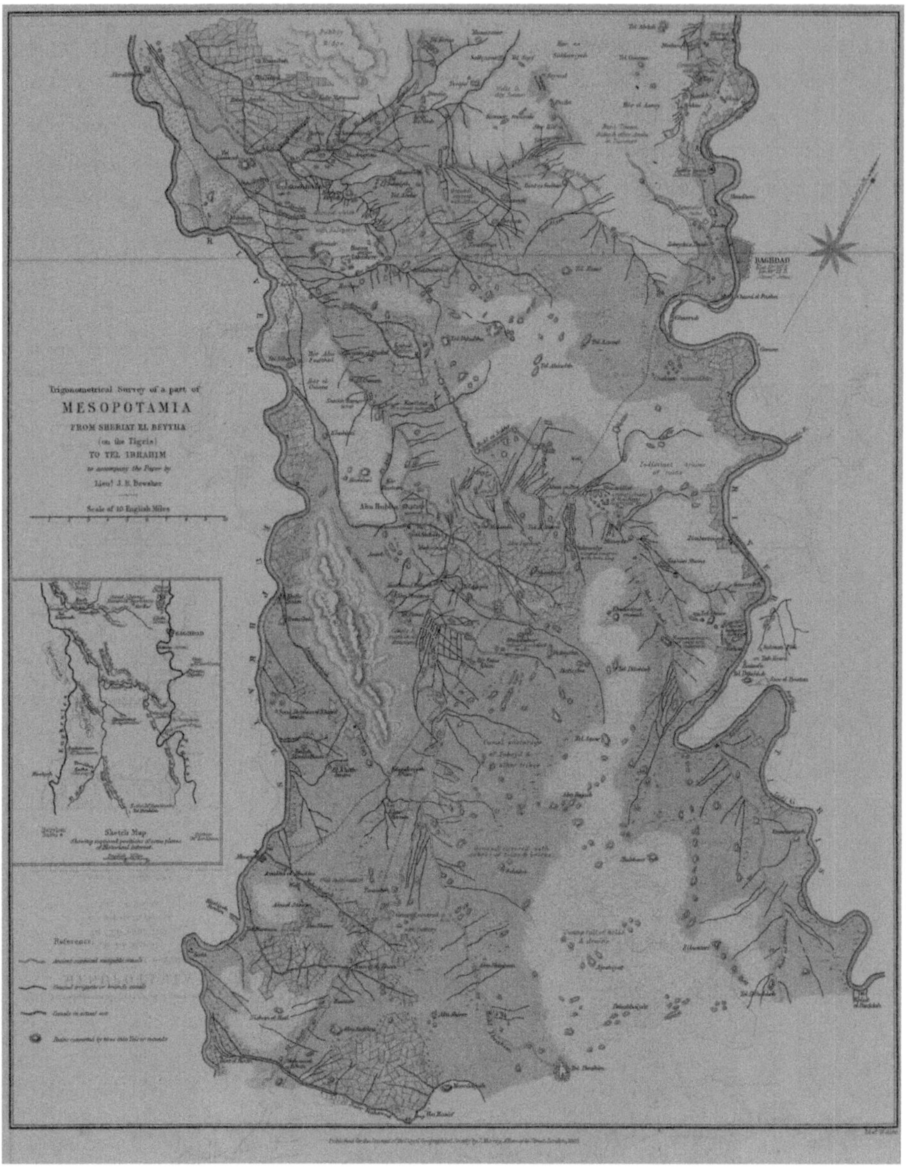

MAP 2.2 Trigonometrical survey of a part of Mesopotamia in 1867

SOURCE: W. B. SELBY AND J. B. BEWSHER, *TRIGONOMETRICAL SURVEY OF A PART OF MESOPOTAMIA FROM SHERIAT EL-BEYTHA (ON THE TIGRIS) TO TEL IBRAHIM WITH THE RIVERS EUPHRATES AND TIGRIS IN 1862–65* [MAP] 6 MM = 1,000 YARDS (LONDON, N.D.), TO ACCOMPANY THE PAPER BY LIET. J. B. BEWSHER/ [ENGRAVED BY] EDWD. WELLER, IN LIUTENANT J. B. BEWSHER, "ON PART OF MESOPOTAMIA, FROM SHERIAT EL-BEYTHA, ON THE TIGRIS, AND TEL IBRAHIM," *THE JOURNAL OF THE ROYAL GEOGRAPHICAL SOCIETY* 37 (LONDON, 1867), P. 326 IN PP. 325–48.

MAP SOURCE: PRINCETON UNIVERSITY LIBRARY: HTTPS://CATALOG.PRINCETON.EDU/CATALOG/7113274

MAP 2.3 A plan of the ruin of Babylon and of the surrounding country in 1874
SOURCE: JAMES FELIX JONES, *A PLAN OF THE RUIN OF BABYLON AND OF THE SURROUNDING COUNTRY* [MAP] DRAWN FROM THE SURVEYS OF COMMR. SELBY I.N., LIEUTS. BEWSHER & COLLINGWOOD I.N., ED. CAPTN. FELIX JONES, I.N. (LONDON: JOHN MURRAY, 1874), SCALE: 1:253,440, IN *DR. WILLIAM SMITH'S ANCIENT ATLAS*, ED. WILLIAM SMITH (LONDON: JOHN MURRAY, 1872–74).
MAP SOURCE: PRINCETON UNIVERSITY LIBRARY: HTTPS://MAP.PRINCETON.EDU/MAPVIEWER/#8W32R806S

CHAPTER 3

Tax Farming and Public Finance

Tax farming was routinized as a main method of tax collecting from agricultural produce in the early Tanzimat period. As observed in previous chapters, among the benefits of its application in the tribal domains were increased state revenues collected from the tribes, the incorporation of the paramount tribal sheikh into the Ottoman administration as a tax farmer or a district governor, and the exploitation of new taxable resources. Although these effects were partly offset by tribal uprisings, oppressive tax collection by the tax farmer, bribe taking, and fraud, they strengthened the government's authority and political centralization. In the irrigated areas outside the tribal domains, tax farming also improved the position of the sheikh of peasant tribesmen because the local practice of crop sharing required the tax farmer to cooperate closely with the sheikh, from tilling through harvesting, and in distributing the produce among the shareholders. Working together, they stimulated agricultural progress and a rise in income that the government had been endeavouring to promote without other effective measures. Yet the revenue collected by tax farming was slow to increase. This chapter examines the reasons why, while highlighting the original function of tax farming, its local practice, and the economic factors that affected its role in public finance.

1 The Origins of Tax Farming

The basic procedure of tax farming was simple and applicable to any taxable resources in the province of Baghdad. The government divided the tax farming area into units called *mukâtaa* and commissioned private individuals to collect the tax in each for a prepayment and a fixed tax. The conditions of assignment differed according to the period of contract, the amount of the deposit, the manner of sale, and the number of farmers and agents in the tax unit. The privilege was awarded for the farmer's lifetime or for a limited period, depending on the amount of deposit that the farmer made at the beginning as a guarantee and on the amount of tax he paid annually. For a lifetime farm in an urban area, the deposit was roughly eight times the tax farmer's annual profit.[1] If the tax farmer could increase production in subsequent years, he could

1 Mehmet Genç, "Osmanlı Maliyesinde Malikâne Sistemi," in Osman Okyar and Ünal Nalbantuoğlu, eds., *Türkiye İktisat Semineri* (Ankara: Hacettepe Üniversitesi, 1975), pp. 236–42;

 | DOI:10.1163/9789004384347_005

keep the increase as profit because the initial deposit had been based on the average annual profit. Only when the contract of a lifetime farm was renewed by the deceased tax farmer's son or shares in it were resold on the auction market, could the government increase the deposit and the price of the tax to gain more revenue.[2] In case of short-term tax farming, the government set the non-refundable deposit paid in the beginning at about 10 per cent of the tax price, much lower than for a lifetime tax farm, but the tax on the short-term tax farm was higher and sometimes increased annually. The small deposit made auctioning competitive, and profits fluctuated considerably depending on production.

The procedure of tax farming was modified periodically. The general trend before 1831 was towards longer periods of farming, preferably for the farmer's lifetime. Only wealthy merchants, traders, bankers, high-ranking military and civil officials, and local notables could afford to pay the high initial payment. For them, tax farming was a lucrative business if the amount of the tax was fixed for their lifetime. It was practised over most taxes, including customs duties, taxes for the boat bridges over the Tigris River, the poll tax charged on non-Muslim residents, transit duties, taxes on bakeries and sugar factories, fees

---

Yavuz Cezar, *Osmanlı Maliyesinde Bunalım ve Değişim Dönemi (XVIII. yy dan Tanzimat'a Mali Tarih)* (Istanbul: Alan Yayıncılık, 1986), pp. 151–280; Ariel Salzmann, "An Ancien Régime Revisited: Privatization and Political Economy in the Eighteenth-Century Ottoman Empire," *Politics & Society* 21, no. 4 (1993), pp. 393–423; Baki Çakır, *Osmanlı Mukataa Sistemi (XVI–XVIII. Yüzyıl)* (Istanbul: Kitabevi, 2003), pp. 115–73.

2 The government later invented a new method of shareholding (*esham*) for lifetime tax farms, under which the increased portion of the revenue could be divided into shares and sold publicly. After the sale, the government could increase the initial payment from both the tax farmer and the new shareholders, while the yearly tax payment became smaller. Attracting widespread subscription from the public, shareholding benefitted the government's urgent fundraising efforts. According to Mehmet Genç, in 1777, in order to finance an indemnity owed Russia following defeat in the Ottoman-Russian War of 1768–74, the Ottoman government introduced shareholding over the tax farm on tobacco in Istanbul. The original tax amount of the tobacco farm was 159,000 kuruş, and owing to increases in its production, the government could collect 559,000 kuruş–400,000 kuruş more than had been charged to the tax farmer for its collection. The government divided the increased portion of the revenue into 160 shares, each of which bore 2,500 kuruş of dividend per year. Each purchaser paid five times the annual dividend (i.e., 12,500 kuruş) at the time of purchase, or 2 million kuruş. As the shareholding system was able to increase revenues because productivity was increasing in the early nineteenth century, the revenues from *esham* accounted for nearly 10 per cent of total state revenues. It is unclear whether *esham* was ever practised in Baghdad, but it was an important means of domestic finance for the Porte until its abolition in 1864.

Mehmet Genç, "Esham," in *Islam Ansiklopedisi* (Istanbul: Türkiye Diyanet Vakfı İslâm Ansiklopedisi Genel Müdürlüğü, 1995), xi, pp. 376–80; Cezar, *Osmanlı Maliyesinde Bunalım*, pp. 79, 169–74, 242; BOA, Maliye Nezareti Defterleri, Vâridat Muhâsebesi Defterleri 3043, 1274 AH; CT, Maliye 1622, 24 Cemaziyelevvel 1250.

for the issue of domestic passports, and stamp duties.[3] In agriculture, it was used for collecting tithe on crops, household dues, poll taxes, and sheep taxes, and the dues on pasture land, threshing fields, and forests, whose unit of payment was the village, irrigation canal, tribal community, or field. The tithe was the largest among the taxes, whose actual rate fluctuated from area to area, and it was paid in kind, cash, or both. The tax on highly productive lands in Khalis, in north-east Baghdad, had to be paid in *zolota kuruş* (Polish silver coins).[4] The tax farmer, who resided in the area of the tax farm or had an agent there, arranged community projects, the allocation of forced labour, and agricultural marketing with the merchants. He paid the tax to the tax-collecting official in the district, while the farmer of a large tax farm paid directly into the provincial treasury.[5] Such large tax farms were rare in the agricultural area – the tax farms were partitioned usually into plots along water channels and sold to other tax farmers on secondary markets. These smaller tax farms were villages or portions of villages, rain-watered fields, or irrigated fields along streams, canals, springs, wells, and marshes. In many places the new tax farmer received only a portion of a canal or stream or a part of an agricultural field.

According to an entry list of a survey Ali Rıza Pasha commissioned in 1831–32, the number of individual tax farms registered with the land registry (*defterhâne*) as a divided unit (*maktûa*) totalled about 456: five *timar* holdings in the Zangabad district; 171 farms in the Hilla region on the Middle Euphrates; 198 farms in Mahrut, Khorasan, Khanaqin, and Khalis in the Diyala River basin; 34 farms in Mandali and Jisan in the mountain area; and 53 farms in Dujail, north-west of Baghdad along the Tigris River. Two of the five *timar*s in Zangabad were merged into the tax farm; two were turned into farms with shareholding; and one was farmed out to the military official for tax collection. The backgrounds of the tax farmers varied. The military men (*asker*) were beg,

3 Mehdi J.H. al-Bustani, "Bağdad'daki Kölemen Hakimiyetinin Te'sisi ve Kaldırılması İle Ali Rıza Paşa'nın Vâliliği (1749–1842)," Ph.D. diss., Istanbul University, 1979, pp. 180–83; Thomas Lier, *Haushalte und Haushaltpolitik in Bagdad, 1704–1831* (Würzburg: Ergon, 2004), pp. 195–98, 204–5.

4 BOA, CT, Maliye 19034, Ruznamçe Sureti, 20 Rebiyülâhır 1228 (23 Apr. 1813). For the *zolota* coin, see Şevket Pamuk, *A Monetary History of the Ottoman Empire* (Cambridge: Cambridge University Press, 2000), pp. 160–61.

5 The tax farmer's application (*arzhal*), the deed of authorization (*dîvân-ı tezkire*), or the deed issued by the Islamic court (*ilam*) can be used to understand the status of the tax farm held by the tax farmer (*der- uhdeci*) listed in the tax record. The government attempted to control the tax farming process. A document on tax farms along the Abu Jedid Canal in Mahrut shows that even the agent purchased the tax-collecting right from the government, not from the tax farmer in the secondary market. BOA, İ. Dahiliye 2932, 12 Rebiyülevvel 1258; İ. Mesâil-i Mühimme 2037, 17 Cemaziyelevvel 1260; İ. Mesâil-i Mühimme 2038, 4 Cemaziyelâhir 1260.

çavus, ağa, and paşa; the government officials (*kalemiye*) were efendi, kâtib-i hazîne, kâtip, emin, mir-i cemâat, muhâsebeci, and halîfe; the employees of religious institutions (ulema) were müderris, imam, hâtib, müftü, and mulla; and the notables (*ayân*) were haci, zâde, karısı, hatûn, sayyid, and varîd. Those listed with no distinguishing epithets were *reaya* (Ottoman subjects), but since their wealth was great enough to purchase the tax-farming right, they may be classified as notables. Members of mystic orders were designated as *şeyh* or *derviş* in the record, and in the same category were entries on the tekkes of the Nakşbendi and Bektaşi orders to which the government assigned tax farms. Tribes (*aşîret*) were listed under the name of the tribal sheikh but can be distinguished by the size of the tax farm and its location.[6]

Tax farming gave rise to a variety of tax-collecting schemes. One was tax sharing between the government and the lifetime tax farmer at the proportion of half and half, or of four to six in favour of the tax farmer. In it, the government share was collected by the local official in cash and directly remitted to the provincial treasury. In some cases, the government share was assigned to public facilities, such as inns and postal stations, for their operating expenditures. In other cases, private individuals shared the whole tax by obtaining their shares through the market or through partition, inheritance, or gift. These shareholders' lands were located near the city of Baghdad, where production was stable and less risky, and it was assumed that their shares would be based on long-term contract and incorporated into the custom of crop sharing. Thus, those with less capital could purchase tax-farming rights. In fact, such shares were held by women, orphans, minor government officials, and urban dwellers and under Islamic law could be transferred as a private right to all children, whether male or female. Eventually this sort of shareholding caused numerous disputes between the government and shareholders as the former exerted more direct control over tax farming.[7]

To make lifetime farming more complicated, the tax benefits also were given out widely as a privilege, reward, or stipend for service. Under the *mamlûk* governors, about three-fifths of all tax farms were granted a whole or partial tax exemption. In the Dujail district in particular, all but six farms claimed a tax privilege. Almost all tribal sheikhs and many of the ulema and dervishes enjoyed such tax-exempt privileges, as did military men and government

6 BOA, Bâb-ı Defteri Başmuhasebe Kalemi, Bağdat Hazinesi, 16748, 1247 AH; 16749, 1247 AH. For the details, see Keiko Kiyotaki, "The Practice of Tax Farming in the Province of Baghdad," in Colin Imber and Keiko Kiyotaki, eds., *Frontier of Ottoman Studies* (London: I.B. Tauris, 2005), i, pp. 91–107.

7 Salzmann, "Ancien Régime Revisited," pp. 393–423.

officials. Meanwhile, public inns, postal stations, and mosques had the use of tax revenues for stipends, salaries, or the operating costs of their facilities. In the case of smaller tax farms, as were found in Mahrut, the farmer was either an authorized tax collector or a tax-collecting agent of the tax farmer, but even such an agent had purchased the tax-collecting right directly from the government, and not from the tax farmer of the larger tax farm on the secondary market. He had entered into a contract for his lifetime by paying the initial deposit and fees requested by the government, although he paid his tax to the tax-collecting official for the place in which his tax farm was located.

Along the irrigation canals, the government partitioned the large tax farms and granted the tax-collecting rights for the smaller units to different tax farmers, who paid their taxes to the tax farmer of the large tax farm. These individual farms, called *maktûa* and registered with the land registry (*defterhâne*), were mostly one or two feddân and no larger than eight feddân. They were held either under a single name or by two to four different tax farmers, usually notables. The same family often purchased the contract for such a smaller farm, which could be renewed upon inheritance or sale for generations. Otherwise, the farm was merged into one of the larger units of the tax farm. In reality only two-fifths of these tax farmers paid taxes into the treasury; nearly three-fifths received the privilege of tax exemption and other tax benefits. When the tax was paid, it was in cash, grain, or both, depending on the farm's location.[8]

British Consul in Baghdad Henry Creswicke Rawlinson described the tax-farming system in Shahriban in the travel diary he kept on his excursion from Baghdad in 1847:

> The farming system seems tolerably simple. The farmer supplies seed and the cultivators labor and the produce is divided at the rate of two between the former and the latter. Cattle, implements of husbandry are supplied by the farmer but charged to the *fellāh*s at the harvest. The interior distribution including the levies on the villages are however somewhat complicated. The return of seeds varies from 20 fold to nothing. I suspect 5 fold is about the average. The sowing seed for Shahriban is 200 tagars. The *zabit* complained grievously [about] the state of the canal which was running every year more checked and unless thoroughly cleaned and worked, should be declared useless.[9]

---

8 BOA, İ. Dahiliye 2932, 12 Rebiyülevvel 1258; İ, Mesâil-i Mühimme 2037, 17 Cemaziyelevvel 1260; İ. Mesâil-i Mühimme 2038, 4 Cemaziyelâhir 1260.

9 Royal Geographical Society Archives, H.C. Rawlinson Collection, No. 10 [Excursion from Baghdad? 1850].

In this valuable diary, Rawlinson implied complicated "interior distribution" and agricultural production was affected by unpredictable natural conditions. Maintenance of irrigation canals and land reclamation made by the combined efforts of the tax farmer, local official *zabit*, and peasant tribesmen *fellâh* together prevented significant loss of revenues. Their combined efforts had formed into indigenous custom bearing prosperity in this area in later periods.

The tax farmer's role in agriculture, behind the simple method of tax farming, was inseparable from the government's tax policies. Tax benefits were common and were obtained by putting down a larger initial deposit upon purchase of the tax farm as a premium for service, reward, or stipend. Confiscation of tax farms also was frequent, as occurred during Ali Rıza Pasha's period on 'Abd al-Qādir Gīlānī's *vakıf*. The government terminated assignment of a tax farm to a dervish lodge (tekke) or its members and paid them monthly stipends from the local treasury in compensation. It indicates that the government may have remained a party to the tax-farming contract and retained the power to authorize any transfer of the farm.[10]

Lifetime tax farming had been a rational decision by the government, for the farmer of a small tax farm was expected to encourage profitable activities, supervise agricultural production, improve the maintenance of such resources as irrigation canals and drainage, and recruit peasant workers. As noted earlier, he was often actively involved in agricultural practices as the seed owner or supervisor of farm management, and the fields along the branch canals and watercourse were well maintained and fertile as a result of the tax farmer's involvement.

After the collapse of the *mamlûk* regime in the 1830s, lifetime tax farming began to disappear, and short-contract farming was practised over the confiscated farms. The deposit was estimated in proportion to the tax value that was auctioned off publicly, so it was lower and the tax higher. Consequently, the tribal sheikhs, notables, and merchants, who had better access to the production activities, acquired the rights of tax farmer, but turnover was frequent due to the influence of politics. The procedure of the transfer itself was simply regulated by state laws, but this change had profound effects in agricultural areas, as observed below.

10 BOA, CT, Maliye 9258, 17 Cemaziyelevvel 1250; CT, Evkaf 27168, 11 Cemaziyelevvel 1250; CT, Evkaf 1185, 27 Cemaziyelâhir 1260.

2 The Reform of Tax Farming

In 1831, Ali Rıza Pasha took over the government without altering its basic systems. The treasurer auctioned confiscated private properties and distributed the confiscated tax farms among members of the pasha's retinue, officials, and local notable residents for the time being. Lifetime tax farms whose contracts had expired were auctioned only for a limited number of years. In those cases, the government auctioned off the tax due from the tax farmer, based on the tax revenues in the previous years, instead of requiring payment of a deposit based on the estimated future profit of the tax farm. In theory, as the amount of the deposit decreased, the tax would increase rapidly year by year. The public auctions, however, took place at the administrative council, which had been set up in Baghdad under the supervision of the governor, rather than at the local treasury, where the auction of the lifetime tax farms had taken place.[11] Lacking experience in local tax administration, Ali Rıza Pasha sold the tax farms to those who offered the highest deposits, in the same way that the lifetime tax farms had been sold, and the annual amount of the tax was fixed at a low level in the contract. He also transferred tax farms illegally to the governor's inner circle of office holders, without the required payment or authorization, leading to frequent turnover in tax farmers due to politics.[12]

Eventually, there was a crucial change, under which the confiscated tax farms were consolidated into larger farms and transferred to tax farmers who could deliver large portions of the assigned revenues to the provincial treasury in regular instalments for a shorter term of from one to three years. Otherwise the procedure remained almost unchanged. The whole process of tax farming was performed locally, under nominal authorization from the Porte. After the prospective purchaser of the farm had submitted an application to the governor's office, the treasury was to prepare an official memorandum on the terms of the contract and forward it to the central authority for the sultan's authorization to finalize the contract. In reality, however, the treasury often ignored the formal procedure, and based only on the memorandum, the governor of Baghdad issued an authorization of the contract. The tax farmer made a partnership contract with his agent, which was registered with the Islamic court

11 BOA, CT Maliye 19034, 20 Rebiyülevvel 1228; İ. Meclis-i Vâlâ 5488, 20 Zilkade 1266; Halil İnalcık, ed., with Donald Quataert, *An Economic and Social History* (Cambridge: Cambridge University Press, 1994), ii, pp. 64–66; ʿAbdul Rahmān ʿAbdul Rahīm and Yuzo Nagata, "The İltizām System in Egypt and Turkey," *Journal of Asian and African Studies* 14 (1977), pp. 179–83; Ahmet Tabakoğlu, *Gerileme Dönemine Girerken Osmanlı Maliyesi* (Istanbul: Dergâh Yayınları, 1985), pp. 122–35.

12 Cezar, *Osmanlı Maliyesinde Bunalım ve Değişim Dönemi*, pp. 281–301.

upon payment of a deposit as required by the contract. The procedure was official but frequently deficient. Because the letter of authorization often was not precise in prescribing the details of the contract, the treasury became involved in many confusing disputes.[13]

The continuous application of tax farming, however, was beneficial to the government. Because the tax farmer or his agent made direct contact with the peasants in the fields, they represented the state authority at that level and made up for the lack of administrative officials after the domestic war, enabling the government to carry out its routine of administration in rural areas with less confusion. The government's willingness to preserve the traditional taxation method also relieved the anxiety of local people, who allowed it to proceed without much political resistance or many administrative difficulties. Indeed, given the lack of employment and business opportunities in rural areas, tax farming made the government the largest employer in many areas and kept some revenue within the local economy at the various stages of tax collection.

During the governorship of Necip Pasha (1842–49), the Porte more immediately got involved in agriculture and tax farming. After the province of Baghdad was officially proclaimed to be under the regime of the Tanzimat in 1844, the Porte began appointing agricultural directors and officials in the province, districts, and sub-districts to supervise agricultural activities according to a regulation, Derûn-ı Kitâbda Doksanıncı Sahîfede Mestûr Zirâat Müdîrleri Ta'lîmnâmesidir (29 July 1844).[14] But the Porte's attempt to centralize agricultural development failed in the province of Baghdad because of the predominance of tax farming. As British Consul Rawlinson reported, "The ordinance in question has been hitherto entirely inoperative in the Pashalic [*Paşalık*; pasha's province] of Baghdad."[15] Observing indigenous agricultural

13 For the authorization of the contract, the tax farmer's agent (*kefil*) was registered and recorded in *dîvân-ı tezkire*. BOA, CT, Maliye 19794, 12 Rebiyulâhir 1250; CT, Maliye 9618, 28 Zilkade 1252; İ, Mesâil-i Mühimme 2044, 19 Receb 1262. Murat Çizakça, *A Comparative Evolution of Business Partnership: The Islamic World and Europe, with Specific Reference to the Ottoman Archives* (Leiden: E.J. Brill, 1996), pp. 146–59.

14 For the effective beginning of Tanzimat in 1844, see Ebubekir Ceylan, *The Ottoman Origins of Modern Iraq: Political Reform, Modernization and Development in the Nineteenth-Century Middle East* (London: I.B. Tauris, 2011), p. 103. For the text of the regulation, see Ahmed Lûtfî Efendi, *Vaka'anüvîs Ahmed Lûtfî Efendi Tarihi*, translit. Yüncel Demirel (Istanbul: Türkiye Ekonomik ve Toplumsal Tarih Vakfı, 1999), vii, pp. 1174–76.

15 The title of the ordinance is not clear in the inquiry, in which the British ambassador in Istanbul described "the nature and extent of the encouragement given by the Governor of Baghdad to agriculture in conforming with the ordinance issued by the Sublime Porte upon the subject on the 4th of last September [1844]." Rawlinson reported that the

practices associated with tax farming, Rawlinson pointed out the need for public irrigation and land reclamation works and suggested that, "according to the present revenue system, the easiest available method of promoting and encouraging agriculture would be for Government to undertake the cleaning out of some of the numerous canals."[16] Necip Pasha's irrigation and land reclamation measures also relied on tax farmers, benefitting those who received tax reductions, aid, and other incentives for the work.

While agriculture improved and yielded larger revenues to the provincial government and tax farmers, the Porte began more strictly to regulate tax farming so that it could receive increased tax revenues. According to the published rule, the provincial government closely monitored tax farm transfers – from 1844, any farm without the sultan's authorization was regarded as illegal. The rule officially abolished lifetime tax farming, except for those farms transferred before the Tanzimat until its termination.[17] Its control over tax farming subsequently brought large increases in agricultural production and revenues to the Baghdad treasury and Necip Pasha himself.

By the period of Reşit Pasha, after domestic tribal disturbances had been settled, more tribal sheikhs, including the paramount sheikh of large tribal confederations, became tax farmers. Because the area of tax farming expanded and transferred to tax farmers from a wider backgrounds, including merchants, urban notables, and tribal sheikhs, the Baghdad government implemented the

---

appointment of agricultural directors was not possible, because of predominance of tax farming in Baghdad:

"Neither have any officers been deputed to the province to afford protection and encouragement to the agriculturalists, nor have pecuniary advances been made on reasonable terms to enable the peasantry to lay fresh lands under cultivation. The provisions indeed of the art[icles] of September 4, 1844 appear to be scarcely applicable to the present working of the revenue system of the Baghdad province, for the government is not in any case brought in contact with the poorer classes of agriculturalists. The various estates which compose the Pashalic [*paşalık*] are let out annually to the capitalists of the city, who are alone responsible to Government for the revenues of the districts entrusted to their charge, and who make their own arrangements with the cultivators of the soil, according to the various systems of farming, which obtain in different places, and which usually secure to the peasantry a full moiety of the net produce of the lands, in return for the labor and expenses of husbandry."

TNA: FO 195/237, No. 2, From Rawlinson to Canning, Baghdad, 8 Jan. 1845.

16 TNA: FO 195/237, No. 2.

17 BOA, İ. Mesâil-i Mühimme, 2044, 7 Rebiyülâhir 1262; İ. Dahiliye 25697, 8 Rebiyülevvel 1274. For tax reforms during the Tanzimat period, see Nadir Özbek, *İmparatorluğun Bedeli: Osmanlı'da Vergi, Siyaset ve Toplumsal Adalet (1839–1908)* (Istanbul:Boğaziçi Üniversitesi Yayınevi, 2015), pp. 48–50; Abdüllatif Şener, *Tanzimat Dönemi Osmanlı Vergi Sistemi* (Istanbul: İşaret, 1990), pp. 41–45.

proclaimed rule in 1855, as summarized below. It put in order the transfer of tax farms by law, which made tax farming a high-return investment for the local people.[18]

Because the rule regulated mainly the procedure of auctioning tax farms, as distinct from the previous lifetime farming, it allowed the Baghdad government to determine the tax payable according to capacity of agricultural production. The initial auction price was publicly announced one or two weeks in advance, and the auction took place from two to four days a week in the presence of bidders, their agents, an official of the administrative council in the province, and officials from both the Imperial Treasury and the Ministry of Commerce. The successful bidder, his financial agent (*sarrâf*), and his bidding price were announced a week before the closing. The initial price was estimated by calculating the average tax in the past years and increasing it by at least 2 per cent. The prices of the previous and the current years' contracts and the names of the present tax farmer and his agent were reported to the administrative council of the province and then to the Treasury. If there was no bidder, that information was posted for eleven days in the province, and another auction was held for ten more days at the Imperial Treasury in the capital, where it was announced in the official newspaper, *Takvîm-i Vakâyi*. No change was allowed after the closing, and the auction was finalized by the sultan's issuing an imperial edict. The transfer of the tax farm for a longer period, payment in foreign currencies, lowering of the auction price, and illegal transfer without auction were prohibited. In case of fraud, a new price was offered by the Treasury, and the Code of Penalty was applied.[19]

According to the legitimized procedure, the tax-farming contract was valid for one year for the tithe and dues; two years for customs, olive-oil pressing, and fishing; two to five years for state estates; and five years for salt sale. The auction of these contracts began in September and lasted until mid-February but could be held until April for the dues and until June for the tithe. The tax farmer was to be a resident in the area where his farm was located and was considered a high official in the province. Only he, his agent, or his financial agent could supervise tax collection. Resale of the tax farm to another agent was allowed, but the tax farmer and his financial agent remained responsible for paying the tax according to the contract. If he wished to hold it jointly with another person, the names of the joint holder or holders were all to be listed upon the transfer, and after issue of the sultan's authorization, partition to a new partner was not allowed. The partners were equally responsible for the tax

18 BOA, İ. Dahiliye 25697, 8 Rebiyülevvel 1274.

19 BOA, İ. Meclis-i Mahsus 232, 20 Rebiyülevvel 1272.

payment. The amount of 0.5 million kuruş was the maximum amount of tax a single farmer could bid, and if he borrowed money, he had to report its amount for record keeping. The financial agent issued a warranty of deed for the loan to the tax farmer, but he also could lend the money with another agent. In case of the tax farmer's default, his agent, children, relatives, or custodian was obligated to pay the amount due. The financial agent's debt was repaid from the surety he gave to the administrative council. A governor, district governor, treasurer, or other provincial official was not allowed to bid on tax farming or to influence the sale. Officials who violated this regulation were fined by the administrative council in the province. If their fraud was discovered after the auction, the tax farm was confiscated.[20]

Reşit Pasha began to enforce the new tax-farming regime in the tribal areas in 1855. As observed earlier, he expanded sovereign authority in the Arab tribal domains by putting the tribesmen under a tax obligation. Because he thus considered taxation a display of his power and justice, he attempted to set rules for it. For example, the standard rate of tax was based on the average tax in past years, and the tax farmer could not take any revenue beyond the auctioned price. The tax on the tribes, even if it was called state money, was collected from the tribes by officials the administrative council trusted to take special care to prevent theft. The tax due the treasury and the locations of the tax farms were recorded in a record book that the provincial treasurer submitted to the governor. The collected revenues were deposited in the cashier's box in the treasury, and the head scribe of the accounting office gave proof of the deposit to the treasurer. The arrears were recorded separately, along with the reasons for them, and reported to the Imperial Treasury. The local official who collected the tax arrears received a reward of one-one hundredth of the collected revenues, which was also recorded in the account book as a cost. In case of resale of the tax farm, the tax farmer had to find a purchaser from among the residents of the farming area or a person who was familiar with the agricultural conditions and local customs in the fields. The actual share and the way of collecting it in the fields were determined according to the local crop-sharing custom, which was complicated and very different from area to area.[21]

The new measures sustained Reşit Pasha's tax and agricultural policies in the mid-1850s, and he managed regularly to pass profits to the Imperial Treasury. By prohibiting the award of tax-farming privileges to government officials as salaries and rewards, he stopped the diversion of revenues from the tax

20 BOA, İ. Meclis-i Mahsus 232, 20 Rebiyülevvel 1272; İ. Meclis-i Mahsus 532, Gurre-i Cemaziyelevvel 1274; İ. Meclis-i Mahsus 928, 23 Receb 1277.

21 BOA, İ. Dahiliye 25697, 8 Rebiyülevvel 1274.

resources in the fields to them. Having avowed in an official report "to seize the initiative of tax administration from the tax farmer and transfer it to the treasury," the pasha made his provincial treasury responsible for collecting taxes and holding the public auction of the tax farms. Such duties included deciding the price, distributing the taxes in cash and in kind, handling the produce paid in kind, bookkeeping, and managing unsold tax farms. The return of peace and order to the province allowed the auctioning of farms from then on.[22]

Reşit Pasha's new approach to tax-farm auctioning had noticeable impacts on agriculture. The small, non-refundable deposit required on less productive farms drew more interest in them. If the purchaser of a tax farm could achieve more than the estimated amount of production or could hold on to the farm for more than the estimated number of years, he could reap handsome profits since he had deposited only 20 per cent of the tax value and could make his payments to the government in two or more instalments. The profitability of his tax farm would, in turn, benefit the government because the tax-farming contract could be renewed at a higher price in the next auction. (See Appendix A at the end of the chapter.)

Although tax farming had become more speculative when it was subjected to more frequent auctioning, a farmer could make a longer contract on infertile land, then make a longer-term investment and attain a higher rate of return through committing to production activities. Another noteworthy trend was benefit taking by the tax farmer from an agricultural infrastructure improved by public works, especially in the irrigated areas along canals where the tax farmer could gain from increased productivity. As tax farming became a profit-making business in the irrigated area where operation costs were reduced by crop sharing in the field, it also formed secondary markets. When that occurred, division of the tax farm into pieces on which the tribal sheikh and other agents held subcontracts with the tax farmer made the tribal sheikh of the peasant tribesmen a significant figure in agriculture and increased the role of the sheikh in smaller tribes, an equally important development in agricultural history.

---

22 BOA, İ. Meclis-i Mahsus 44, 13 Şevval 1270. Necip Pasha's policy of regaining control over tax farming involved commerce, trade, and the Persian pilgrimage. In 1854, Reşit Pasha abolished the accounts of the tax farms and monopolies relating to the Persian pilgrims, namely, the rights to supply grain to them en route from Baghdad to Samarra (10,000 kuruş), to provide them lodging (20,000 kuruş), and to supply barley to them at Kadhimiya (60,000 kuruş); the diminution of the ferry tax on the pilgrims; the grain monopoly at Musaib (70,000 kuruş), and various taxes and transit duties at Najaf (100,000 kuruş), in all some 260,000 kuruş annually (more than 5,000 toman). TNA: FO 195/442, No. 26, 3 Oct. 1854, Enclosure of No. 34, 4 Oct. 1854. Ceylan, *Ottoman Origins of Modern Iraq*, pp. 198, 202–4.

In terms of public finance, however, tax farming was not an ideal method of taxation. It spilled out money in bribes, tax overcharges, and oppressive tax collecting by the tax farmer, and its contracted revenue could not increase at the same rate as expenditure. Consequently, a fiscal deficit began to amass, creating a more structural problem. Although the government's loss appeared to be the tax farmer's gain, considering the tax farmer's contributions to agriculture and the local economy, his gain did not solely reflect abuse of his privilege at the cost of the government. Regardless, the problems of tax farming related to fiscal issues, such as tax prepayment and arrears, had become serious by the late 1850s, as had the lingering problems of local currency and grain prices.

3 Tax Prepayment

Tax farming's scheme of tax prepayment began to wear on the government after the pace of tax increase slowed. The tax farmer's deposit and tax payment at the pre-fixed amount determined at auction provided large sums of initial payment to the provincial treasury. Nevertheless, this system also caused habitual fiscal deficits and internal debt for the provincial treasury, because the prepayments implicitly were the government's borrowing from taxpayers by clearing off the principal amount of the prepayment made in past years in the fiscal year in which the tax was due. This created a built-in system of fiscal deficits and debt, which became a serious problem in the 1860s. If the government had received in advance the full amount of tax estimated to be due by the end of the contract, it would have had little problem. But instead, it often granted deductions or even exemptions for certain years as an incentive for prepayment, and such reductions caused a deficit in the flow variables of the current year that could accumulate year after year.

Understanding how the problems with tax prepayment intensified in the Tanzimat period requires looking first at the two-calendar system that had led to fiscal crisis during Ali Rıza Pasha's administration of Baghdad. According to Halil Sahillioğlu's important study, the Ottoman government used two fiscal years, a solar year (365 days) for revenue collection and a lunar year (354 days) for spending, so it had to skip one fiscal year out of every thirty-three fiscal years due to a lack of revenue to finance expenditure:[23]

---

23 Halil Sahillioğlu, "Sıvış Year Crises in the Ottoman Empire," in M.A. Cook, ed., *Studies in the Economic History of the Middle East* (London: Oxford University Press, 1970), pp. 230–52; Tabakoğlu, *Osmanlı Maliyesi*, pp. 241–46.

> Since the lunar and the solar year do not contain the same number of days, we would have to make a correction in this solar-lunar calendar every 33 years ... the eleven days' difference between the two systems produces one additional lunar year in every 32 solar years. Therefore, for 32 budgets there will be 33 lunar years. Since no budget will be made for this 33rd year, it will be discarded or skipped.[24]

Those skip years were 1839–40 during Ali Rıza Pasha's term, and 1871–72 in the last year of Midhat Pasha's term, which actually was not skipped.[25]

Sahillioğlu's interpretation of the two-calendar system as a built-in measure of public finance in favour of the government helps explain the scale of fiscal deficits as a consequence of the skip year.[26] For thirty-three years, the government collected extra revenues equivalent in total to the expenditures of one lunar year, and it can be assumed that the revenues collected in advance became 0 per cent of the expenditure. From this point, another period of advanced collection of revenues would begin and continue until the next skip year. Thus, the average prepaid amount of revenues was estimated to be the average of 0 per cent and 100 per cent (i.e., 50 per cent) of the total annual revenues. Because of the cumulative deficits, the government resorted to forcing donations, confiscating private property on default of inheritance or as penalty, prearranging a savings fund for spending in the skip year, imposing extraordinary taxes, expanding the tax base by conquering new land, or simply defaulting on payments. In the provinces, where fiscal policies were less effective without centralized fiscal administration, the local government resorted to the monetary policy of debasing currencies and using them to meet payrolls.[27]

Experiencing the skip year of 1839–40 in Baghdad, Ali Rıza Pasha found himself in severe financial trouble, so borrowed from local notables and

24 Sahillioğlu, "Sıvış Year Crises," p. 233.

25 The year 1255 AH was Mar. 1839–Feb. 1840 on the lunar (*hicrî*) calendar, and a *sıvış* (skip) year on the solar (*malî*) calendar; 1288 AH was Mar. 1871–Feb. 1872 on the lunar calendar, and Mar. 1872–Feb. 1873 on the solar calendar, a designated *sıvış* year that was not actually skipped.

26 Sahillioğlu, "Sıvış Year Crises," pp. 237–47.

27 Genç, "Malikane Sistemi," pp. 231–96. Pre-nineteenth-century budgets are well surveyed in Cezar, *Osmanlı Maliyesinde Bunalım*, pp. 20–22; Sahillioğlu, "Sıvış Year Crises," pp. 230–52; and Tabakoğlu, *Osmanlı Maliyesi*, pp. 77–113, 178–81; Keiko Kiyotaki, "Ottoman State Finance: A Study of Fiscal Deficits and Internal Debt in 1859–63," Working Paper No. 90/05, Department of Economic History, London School of Economics, September 2005, p. 14, published in Kaan Durukan, Robert W. Zens, and Akile Zorlu-Durkan, eds., *Hoca, 'Allame, Puits de Science: Essays in Honor of Kemal H. Karpat* (Istanbul: The Isis Press, 2010), pp. 97–120.

moneylenders a sum that amounted to 5 million kuruş by the time he was replaced by Necip Pasha in 1842. The ever-increasing spending for military campaigns, civil administration, and public works meant the administration could not afford to set up a savings account for the next skip year of 1871–72. When that year was not officially skipped, the provincial government in Baghdad could not shift completely to the new fiscal calendar because of its heavy use of tax farming and confusion in the accounting system. Even the acclaimed benevolent reformer Midhat Pasha (1869–72) failed to find a solution for the accumulated fiscal deficits.

The concept of the skip year provides a clue for understanding the role of tax farming in the problem of implicit deficit. If the tax farmer paid both his non-refundable deposit and his tax in advance of the tax-collecting date, both might be counted as a tax prepayment for the revenue. Similarly, if the recipient of expenditure received payment at the end of the fiscal year or from the next year's tax prepayments, it might be entered in the arrears of spending. Because the Baghdad government collected prepayments for taxes due in future fiscal years, its receipts of current revenues were always larger than the revenues that appeared in the budget, and the Baghdad treasury ran an unrecorded budget deficit each year due to the tax prepayment.

Another problem of tax prepayment for the Baghdad treasury was the discount of tax revenues at a disadvantage to the government. Its taxable resources consisted mainly of agricultural produce that was collected at source and earmarked for local spending. Since production and prices fluctuated unpredictably from year to year, depending on the availability of agricultural water and other natural conditions, the real amount of the taxes also fluctuated after the tax prepayment. In short, the volatility of revenues from direct taxes was high because nearly 70 per cent of the total revenue was collected as a tithe on grain and commercial produce. Besides the direct taxes, the treasury received profits from the sale of state properties and forest products and fees for land registration. The revenue from indirect taxes, such as payment for exemption from military service, customs duties, stamp duties, and other miscellaneous taxes, was more stable, but it was far less significant than that from direct taxes. The provincial government officially changed the beginning of its fiscal year from February to March in 1855–56 under Reşit Pasha and accordingly arranged for taxes to be paid in instalments and tax arrears incurred by this change to be collected at the end of the fiscal year.[28] Although Reşit Pasha's

28 Revenues were remitted to the central treasury twice a year, on 11 March (*Nevruz*) and at the beginning of August. See Sahillioğlu, "Sıvış Year Crises," p. 233. Reşit Pasha claimed the tax arrears of Arab tribesmen amounted to 6.6 million kuruş in Hindiya, 2.3 million kuruş

measure increased revenues, they were insufficient to cover a rapid increase in spending.

The large amount of tithe revenue indicates that the tax revenues derived from the tax farmer were also large, but the tax farmer still enjoyed abundant profits, as the tax rate was usually discounted after his prepayment. In due course, the profitability of tax farming led to the corruption of officials, who asked for kickbacks and bribes from the farmer. As examined earlier, Governor Nuri Pasha (1859–61) was a notorious bribe taker, who thwarted efforts to foster a competitive market for tax farming, yet he managed to escape prosecution and preserve the fortune he had amassed in Baghdad.[29] The taxes and bribes paid by the tribal sheikhs, however, did have a detrimental effect on the lives of the tribesmen. For instance, in Khalis, Musaib, Dujail, and Samarra, where a number of irrigation and reclamation projects took place in cooperation with the tribesmen, the taxes were generally undervalued due to bribes paid to the governor and other high officials. As a result, their revenue was insufficient to fund the projects, and the Baghdad government levied additional charges on the tribes. Nevertheless, while the spill of money provoked fiery denunciations, and although the use of the tax farmers' prepayments for current expenditures may have exacerbated the problem, the main source of the shortfalls was the rapid growth of extraordinary governmental expenditures.

4 Increased Expenditures

Most revenues collected through tax farming were earmarked for spending as prearranged in the annual budget, so could not be used for increasing expenditures. Amid rising expenditures for military troops, public works, investments in infrastructure, and purchases of goods abroad, however, the Baghdad government proceeded with two new ventures that required large investments: the purchase of steamboats for river and ocean navigation and the construction of telegraph lines. Reşit Pasha purchased two steamboats from Belgium and France, at a price of 82,936 francs, for commercial navigation on the Tigris River from Baghdad to Basra.[30] One, named *Baghdad*, arrived late in 1859, when Ahmet Pasha was acting governor; the other, named *Basra*, arrived in 1860, during Nuri Pasha's term. Both operated as merchant vessels for regional

in Diwaniya, 1.8 million kuruş in Hilla, and 3.1 million kuruş in Samawa. BOA, İ. Dahiliye 27211, 28 Muharrem 1275.

29 BOA, İ. Meclis-i Vâlâ 20409, 21 Ramazan 1278.

30 BOA, İ. Meclis-i Vâlâ 16755, 6 Rabiyülâhir, 1274.

trade in the Gulf and for the export of dates from Basra to Bombay. During his second term as governor, in 1862, Namık Pasha purchased two 800-ton vessels from Belgium to navigate the Red Sea and the Gulf, and resumed the improvement of port facilities at Fao, a few miles east of Basra, which had been begun over a decade earlier, under Necip Pasha.[31]

The first telegraph lines were constructed between Varna and Balıklava by the British and between Rusçuk and Varna by the French in 1854. In the same year, the Porte planned lines from Istanbul to Şumnu through Edirne, and from Edirne to Niş through Filibe and Sofya, and construction progressed rapidly throughout the empire until there was a completed connection from Istanbul to Baghdad by 1860. Namık Pasha extended the line from Baghdad to Basra, in conjunction with a British plan to connect it with Karachi, and he frequently used the line for official correspondence.[32] The construction costs were partly reimbursed by the Porte; the rest was financed by the province from customs duties and loans from the British India Office, but the revenues from the line were insufficient to cover its operating costs without support from the provincial treasury.[33]

On top of the on-going projects, the governor hired more paid officials for expanded district administration in 1859–60 and 1862–63, increasing the outlay for salaries and projected pension costs. The deficits from this were addressed with short-term loans from local financiers, the governor and other high officials, foreign residents, tax farmers, and even the treasuries of other provinces. The provincial government also imposed new taxes on the tribesmen at the risk of tribal disturbances against it.

Still, revenues were inadequate to cover the shortages. As noted, tax farming was no help in coping with extraordinary expenditures because most taxes had been earmarked for current expenditures. The provincial government put large portions of its itemized expenditures on arrears, but as their sums increased and their repayment was delayed, it incurred heavy financial burdens. The entries on payment arrears recorded in the book of liabilities for the

31 Stephen Hemsley Longrigg, *Four Centuries of Modern Iraq* (Oxford: Clarendon Press, 1925), pp. 280–84.

32 In 1865, Namık Pasha planned to establish a railway company in which no less than half the shares would be allotted to Ottoman subjects. He projected construction of the line from the Shiite shrines at Najaf and Karbala to Baghdad and its eventual extension to the Persian frontier at Khanaqin.

33 BOA, İ. Meclis-i Vâlâ 5500, 22 Zilkâde 1266; İ. Meclis-i Vâlâ 16755, 6 Rabiyülâhir, 1274. Mustafa Kaçar, "Osmanlı Telegraf İşletmesi," in Ekmeleddin İhsanoğlu and Mustafa Kaçar, eds., *Çağını Yakalayan Osmanlı!* (Istanbul: İslâm Tarih, Sanat, ve Kültür Araştırma Merkezi, 1995), pp. 48–51.

fiscal year 1862–63 were broadly demarcated as military expenses, administrative expenses, purchase of grain for export, and direct receipt of revenues by the local treasury. Their total of 100.8 million kuruş was 176 per cent over the current revenue of 57 million kuruş in the fiscal year. The sums of 59 million kuruş for military expenses and 39 million kuruş for administrative expenses together accounted for 97.5 per cent of the arrears. Most payments were made within a few years, but some, only after many years because of shortages in repayment funds. Even if the figures included a discount, they would still have been large because of the high weighted values of outstanding payments.[34]

Ultimately, the increased expenditures were financed by the natural increases in revenues that took place when political stability prevailed under Reşit Pasha (1852–57) and by extraordinary revenues from grain exports, customs duties, improved tribal collection, and indirect taxes in the urban areas, such as bridge tolls, taxes on manufacturing profits, and the like. The traditional ways of addressing deficits by forced aids, extraordinary taxation, and the forced collection of tax arrears, however, were ineffective for long-term borrowing. Instead, the government encouraged the export of grain. Observing the large profit of 16.5 million kuruş that the viceroy of Egypt made from exporting about 10,000 tons of grain to Hijaz, Reşit Pasha began exporting grains to Jidda and Yemen, renting the steam flotilla that had been used to transport pilgrims. Although this trade reportedly yielded 6.5 million kuruş or more in cash revenue for the treasury, due to the unusually high price of grain, that was not enough fully to fund current expenditures.[35] Successive governors attempted to solve the deficit, which had existed annually and had been carried forward to the next account, by borrowing, aids, and confiscation of income-bearing properties as a penalty or for arrears of payments, but those measures had already been heavily used.

After the Porte's massive issues with paper money, the values of Ottoman currencies in foreign exchange markets dropped significantly. The currency

---

34 The liability was recorded in the account book called *Zimmet Defteri*. The government would have incurred larger payment obligations than the original amount if it had been obliged to offer compensation for the arrears. BOA, Maliyeden Müdevver Defterler Tasnifi, 10953; Kiyotaki, "Ottoman State Finance," pp. 19–21; Kiyotaki, "Ottoman State Finance," in Kaan Durukan, Robert W. Zens, and Akile Zorlu- Durkan, eds., *Hoca, 'Allame, Puits de Science*, pp. 109–11.

35 The committee of trade (*meclis-i ticâret*), established to increase trade activities, consisted of ten members, of whom four were Ottoman Turks, two Persians, and four *reaya* (two Christians and two Jews). It was reorganized with eight members, of whom six were Ottoman Turks and two were *reaya* (one Christian and one Jew) when the Persians declined to send representatives because they objected to the president of the committee, who was an Ottoman Turk. TNA: FO 195/521, No. 12, 22 July 1857; FO 195/1370, 11 Feb. 1881.

devaluation, which saw grain prices increase, had mixed consequences on the local economy and society. The provincial government had little influence over the Porte's financial policies but had to cope with the problems in the province that ensued from them (although tax farming itself had been unaffected directly from the worsening situation). Understanding the problematic currency, the Porte's policies, and their impacts on grain prices, agriculture, and trade are necessary in the following, as they eventually influenced the provincial government's land policies.

5 Currency and the Issue of Paper Money

The financial problems of the provincial treasury were aggravated by the Porte's frequent currency debasements and the illegal use of paper money for some payments. The circulation of debased coins, albeit limited and in small amount, showed that even though it was on the empire's frontier, Baghdad could not avoid the problems that reduced fiscal deficits but caused inflation.[36] In addition, as pointed out by Şevket Pamuk, a large variety of coins, each with different standards, had circulated since the beginning of the century, which consequently increased the use of European coinage in international trade and for private saving.[37] After the Tanzimat period, the Porte set out to adopt the bimetallic standard of the silver kuruş and the new gold lira as legal tender and to stabilize the currency by announcing the official rate of exchange. However,

36 The deteriorating balance of payments in the period 1859–62 caused financial trouble for the Porte. The Ministry of War, the largest consumer of revenues, accounted for 30.7 per cent of the total expenditures. Adding in the sum of the navy brought the war expenditures to nearly 40 per cent of the total. The Ministry of the Interior, at 13.7 per cent, and the Civil List (i.e., the sultan's private account), at 11.3 per cent, followed. Another important expenditure, though it had not yet become burdensome, was for interest payments on and amortization of foreign and internal debts, which accounted for 14.2 per cent of total expenditures in 1859–60, or 16.2 per cent of total revenue. Spending on public works, infrastructure, and education was extremely low but increased in later years. TNA: FO 424/24, "Report on the Financial Condition of Turkey"; Tevfik Güran, *Tanzimat Döneminde Osmanlı Maliyesi: Bütçeler ve Hazine Hesapları, 1841–1861* (Ankara: Türk Tarih Kurumu Basımevi, 1989), pp. 107–8.

37 Pamuk, *Monetary History of the Ottoman Empire*, p. 207. For currency debasement, see also Şevket Pamuk, "From Debasement to External Borrowing: Changing Forms of Deficit Finance in the Ottoman Empire, 1750–1914," in Ş. Pamuk and R. Avramov, eds., *Monetary and Fiscal Policies in South-East Europe: Historical and Comparative Perspective (Conference Proceeding)* (Sofia: Bulgarian National Bank, 2006), pp. 7–22 in Şevket Pamuk, *The Ottoman Economy and Its Institutions*, Variorum Collected Studies Series (Farnham, Burlington, UK: Ashgate, 2009).

it could not withdraw some old silver coins from circulation, as observed in Baghdad as well, and the new measures largely failed to mitigate the complexity of the money market.[38]

Issues of paper money caused another external shock on the provincial government in Baghdad. In 1840, the Porte first issued treasury bonds (*esham kavâimi*) with nominal values ranging from 50 to 1,000 kuruş and an annual yield of 12.5 per cent. A second issue, with reduced nominal values of 50, 100, and 250 kuruş, was used to pay the salaries of military personnel.[39] Also in 1840, the government made a third issue with a total nominal value of 50 million kuruş. Although these bonds were not backed by gold or any other hard currency, they were highly popular among investors because of their high interest rate. The Porte continued to issue new bonds but decreased the interest rate to 10 per cent in 1843 and 6 per cent in 1844 before finally issuing no-interest-yielding paper money in 1851 in denominations of 20 and 50 kuruş. By March 1853, out of a total of 177.5 million kuruş in bonds and paper money that had been issued by the government, 45.5 million kuruş of paper money yielded no interest. It was possible to pay tax obligations to the government with the paper money, making the bills de facto tax discounts.[40] Nevertheless, in 1859 the Porte issued 1,250 million kuruş in new paper money, of which 650 million kuruş was used to repay short-term borrowing; the rest was allocated to the Ottoman Imperial Bank to replace the old paper money and fund public works. The new paper money depreciated rapidly against the pound sterling and even against the old paper money in the domestic money market.[41]

The problem of paper money became part of the much greater problem of Ottoman foreign loans, which affected even the empire's remotest province of Baghdad. The Porte's debt finance in international markets began and worsened the domestic financial problems caused by the paper money. It acquired a foreign market loan of £5 million for the first time during the Crimean War (1853–56), at 80 per cent of the face value with an interest rate of 6 per cent.

---

38 Pamuk, *Monetary History of the Ottoman Empire*, p. 208.

39 Paper money was called variously *evrak nakdiye, kâğıt para, kaime-i nakdiye*, or *kaime*. Ali Akyıldız, *Osmanlı Finans Sisteminde Dönüm Noktası: Kâğıt Para ve Sosyo-ekonomik Etkileri* (Istanbul: Eren Yayıncılık, 1996), pp. 41–51; Mine Erol, *Osmanlı İmparatorluğunda Kâğıt Para (Kaime)* (Ankara: Türk Tarih Kurumu Basımevi, 1970), pp. 38–59; Pamuk, *Monetary History of the Ottoman Empire*, pp. 209–11; Zafer Toprak, "Osmanlı Devleti'nde Para ve Bankacılık," *Türkiye Ansiklopedisi* (1991), iii, pp. 760–70.

40 Akyıldız, *Osmanlı Finans Sisteminde Dönüm Noktası*, pp. 43–46.

41 The official rate of Ottoman currency to the pound sterling was 110 kuruş, but Hobart and Foster used in their report the depreciated rate of 125 kuruş to one pound sterling. TNA: FO 424/24, "Report on the Financial Condition of Turkey," Mr. Foster and Lord Hobart to Earl Russell, Constantinople, 7 Dec. 1861; FO 195/521, No. 12, 22 July 1857.

In 1855 it borrowed another £3 million in London, with a premium of 2.625 per cent and an interest rate of 4 per cent, a better effective rate than the previous loan. It borrowed a further £5 million in 1858 and 2 million francs from Paris in 1860. A new loan of £8 million, borrowed in 1862 at an issue rate of 68 per cent and an interest rate of 6 per cent, was the largest ever, despite the disadvantage of its high real interest rate. That loan of 1862, which was a turning point in the history of Ottoman foreign loans, was used to withdraw paper money from the domestic market.[42]

In the province of Baghdad, where only hard currency – usually silver coins (beşlik) – was used, and paper money was not supposed to circulate, issues of paper money seriously affected the local economy. In spite of this restriction, paper money had been used for payment of the official payroll, for commercial transactions, and for commercial transfers between Baghdad and the outlying districts. While the silver coins were debased at a rate of 8 to 10 per cent and paper money was discounted 50 per cent lower than the debased coins, paper money was accepted for payment of taxes by the tax farmers, often without discount, causing a large exchange loss to the Porte.[43]

The Porte's monetary policies hit hard the Baghdad government, which had been coping with fiscal deficits of its own. Numbers of high officials and notables in Baghdad bought interest-bearing paper money, whose value declined sharply. The tax farmers who managed to use circulated paper money to pay their taxes made large profits. Meanwhile, the devaluation of coins in the local market, which will be discussed shortly, influenced grain prices and greatly affected urban residents, salaried officials, and peasants. In addition, on various occasions the Porte called on the Baghdad governor to remit more than the established annual sum of 60,000 kuruş – to liquidate state debts incurred during the war, to establish the Ottoman Imperial Bank, to make interest payments, or to make the forced purchase of paper money. These required loans totalled 2.9 million kuruş, but to aid the governor, a group of notables and principal merchants offered to pay the whole sum demanded as a free gift to the sultan if the paper money was definitively abandoned.[44] Still, such temporary measures could not relieve the government and its people of the serious

42 For the historical context from the standpoint of international finance, see Donald C. Blaisdell, *European Financial Control in the Ottoman Empire* (New York: Columbia University Press, 1929), pp. 27–35.

43 TNA: FO 424/24, "Report on the Financial Condition of Turkey," p. 39; BOA, İ. Meclis-i Mahsus 596, 29 Receb 1275; İ. Meclis-i Vâlâ 21066, Sulh Şevvel 1278; İ. Meclis-i Mahsus 1099, 17 Muharrem 1279.

44 TNA: FO 196/676, No. 28, 9 Oct. 1861.

financial distress that stemmed from the domestic problems of debased coinage, increased grain prices, and an inland transit trade that benefitted foreign traders.

6 Debased Coinage and Increased Grain Prices

The depreciation of coins in the local market had disturbed the Baghdad government since the early days of Ali Rıza Pasha. Previous governors had gathered coins that had been counterfeited or had been debased by wear, battering or cutting on the edge of the coin in order to forge them into new ones at a local mint, but although the new ones were usually smaller, they were put into circulation and used for paying soldiers and irregular troops. In Baghdad, even the *mahmudiye*, a gold coin issued by Sultan Mahmud II (1808–39) with a high percentage of metal, had been debased by cutting off as much as half the coin, and it was devalued badly after the collapse of the regime. In 1834 Ali Rıza Pasha received a permit from the sultan to strike new coins to counter the debased ones in just a limited area of the province, while the Arab tribal domains continued to use a local coin called shami (*şâmî*).[45]

After the exchange rate of his new coins deteriorated against the old coins, Ali Rıza Pasha withdrew the new ones and circulated coins received from the Porte. He then invited a minting specialist from the imperial mint to supervise the local mint and penalized the exchange of Ottoman coins for foreign coins at arbitrary rates set by merchants. This meant a heavy loss for the merchants who had specified payment in the Persian silver Nassir al-Din Shah keran or gold toman. It also caused the depreciation of Ottoman currencies and constant exportation of silver coins to Kermanshah to be re-coined into the Persian silver coin of reduced weight that was used as a substitute for the Turkish lira as the standard money in the local money market.[46] The coinage problem lingered into the 1840s, when the value of the kuruş and beşlik (5 piaster) dropped steeply against foreign coins in the Baghdad market.[47] The volatility of the

45 Bustani, "Bağdad'daki Kölemen Hakimiyetinin Te'sisi ve Kaldırılması İle Ali Rıza Paşa'nın Vâliliği," p. 339.

46 Ibid., pp. 337–52.

47 In 1844, one Indian rupee was exchanged at 11.5 kuruş, and 100 kuruş were exchanged at 206 Persian keran. However, the kuruş was devalued against the Persian currency in the local market. The exchange rate between Baghdad and London, payable at thirty days after sight, was 22 Persian keran to a pound sterling, instead of 21–21.25 keran (22 or 21.5–22) to a pound sterling; 109 kuruş to a pound sterling; and 5.0625 kuruş to a keran in Baghdad. In Baghdad the rate was 19.0263157 keran to a pound sterling or 42,076.5

currencies negatively affected the many officials, pensioners, and wage workers who received salaries, pensions, or stipends in kuruş. The circulation of gold and silver mecidiye in the province had been very limited, so their value was not much affected.

Meanwhile, the beneficiaries of weak official currency were foreign nationals, traders, and merchants, and the tribal sheikhs who could receive payment in foreign currency. The increased market value of the Persian keran, for instance, enabled Persian subjects to speculate in real estate by purchasing houses, land, and other properties in Baghdad, Karbala, Najaf, and other Shiite shrine towns and by endowing charities with large sums. In case of state land, whose acquisition by foreign nationals was prohibited by Ottoman state laws, the purchase was made through an informal contract with an Ottoman national as the nominal owner. When the government made a sale of vacant agricultural land in the 1840s, it could not prevent the land from passing to the Persians. In 1867, foreign nationals were officially allowed to purchase real property in the province under state law, but the government often raised disputes against the Persians' acquisitions.

Among the other beneficiaries were the tribal sheikhs whose domains were located along the rivers, telegraph lines, bridges, and other facilities that needed supervision. For the guardianship of a telegraph line entrusted to a sheikh, the British paid a monthly allowance of about 100 pounds sterling for the distance of an hour. The sheikh of the Tay tribe, who was assigned a distance of nine and one-half hours, was paid 1,000 pounds sterling monthly, which became even more lucrative when the kuruş was devalued.[48] On the

keran to 2,000 pounds sterling. In 1856, the value of a şâmî in Baghdad was 8.5 kuruş (34 R piaster [sic]) (1 şâmî = 18 pence). However, about two months before, the same coin had risen in the market to 8–8.125 kuruş (35 ¼ R piaster [sic]), a difference of about 3.5 per cent. Official exchange rates in Baghdad were set in 1866–67 (1283 AH) at 216 şâmî/100 German kronen, 44 şâmî/100 Persian keran; 102 şâmî/100 rupees; 10 1/2 kuruş per şâmî; and 110 kuruş per pound sterling. TNA: FO 195/803A, No. 30, 18 May 1864; Enclosure No. 3 in Dispatch No. 67 from Baghdad, "Report on the Trade of Basra in Turkish Arabia for the Year Beginning 13th March 1866 Ending 12th March 1867" by H.M. Vice Consul at Basra, Mr. P. Johnstone, Basra, 27 July 1867.

48 Monthly allowances for the guardianship of the telegraph line in 1861 were proposed as follows:

From	To	Tribe	Distance in hours	Allowance (sterling pounds)
Lau Su [*sic*]	Teemar (Timar)	Tay	9 ½	1,000
Teemar (Timar)	Yerdelan	Dezair	7 ½	750
Yerdelan	Altun Köpru	Beldivli	2 ½	250
Altun Köpru	Kirkuk	Al-Zerai	9	600

trade route on the Tigris, the local sheikh collected an informal toll for safe transport but proved more interested in his own profit-making investments in land than in the safekeeping of the cargo.[49]

While paper money, whose use the Porte had prohibited in the region, began to be sold in Baghdad, the rapid expansion of foreign trade led to the circulation of large quantities of foreign currencies in the local market. British traders, for example, began to use the Indian rupee, which had gradually displaced the Persian keran at the ports of Persia and Arabia. When an order to fix the fluctuating prices of Ottoman coins issued in 1861 proved unenforceable, Namık Pasha imposed penalties on the arbitrary rates of exchange, a measure that nearly halted transactions except in the local *şâmî* coin.[50]

In addition to the currency problem, the government struggled with an increase in grain prices. The brisk grain market in Baghdad made the transit trade a lucrative business for many foreign and local traders, and the domestic trade became not only safer, as peace and order were restored in rural areas, but also more profitable, owing to the low 3 per cent import tariff and unchanged 3 per cent transit tariff under the Treaty of Balta Liman of 1838.[51] Consequently, local traders and merchants were able to realize large profits

(*cont.*)

From	To	Tribe	Distance in hours	Allowance (sterling pounds)
Kirkuk	Taha Khurmatu	(official)	3	
Taha Khurmatu	Dakuk (Dühûk)	(Dühûk)	5	500
Dakuk (Dühûk)	Tuz Khurmatu	(Dühûk)	7	500
Tuz Khurmatu	Kifri	Beiati	9	600
Kifri	(Kifri)	(Kifri)	2	
(Kifri)	Kashlla	Kerawi		600

SOURCE: TNA: FO 195/676, NO. 8, "TELEGRAPHIC LINE AND ITS SECURITY BETWEEN MOSUL AND BAGHDAD," 10 APR. 1861.

49 The tribes along the trade route collected illegal tolls such as the *galibiye* (transit dues) imposed on British merchant boats by the Bani Lam tribe on both the Middle Tigris and the Zab Rivers. As a solution, Necip Pasha attempted to annex the Bani Lam domain to that of the Muntafiq and to pay the Bani Lam 100,000 şâmî to stop the *galibiye*, but the Bani Lam proved difficult to put under control. TNA: FO 195/676, No. 8, 10 Apr. 1861; FO 195/676, No. 29, Basra, 16 July 1861; FO 195/717, No. 27, 18 June 1862.

50 TNA: FO 195/803A, No. 30, 18 May 1864.

51 Before the Balta Liman Treaty, the tariff on trade had been 9 per cent of the estimated value for import and 3 per cent for export, but for foreign traders with a licence, the tariff was 4 per cent. For foreign traders without a licence and local merchants alike, it was 5 per cent, with possible extra charges on transit, issue of a licence, and sales, plus a stamp duty (*damga*) of 2.5 per cent and town dues (*ihtisâb*). In the treaty, the tariff was set at 3 per cent on imports with an additional 2 per cent for internal tax, 12 per cent on

from the weak Ottoman currencies, increases in grain prices, and shortage of grain supplies. For goods exported from Baghdad to Persia, an export duty of 4 per cent was charged to the Persian merchant, irrespective of whether the goods were Ottoman products or European goods that had been imported into Baghdad by a foreign merchant for the transit trade. Added to a 3 per cent duty paid at the port of entry, the tariff for export to Persia subjected British products imported into Persia through Baghdad to a duty of 7 per cent when they changed hands at Baghdad from the importer to the exporter. That was much lower than the 12 per cent formerly levied on the export of domestic products to Persia. Now, for exports to Persia, other than British goods brought to Baghdad for transit to Persia, the traders paid only the 3 per cent transit duty, avoiding the 4 per cent export duty.

When Necip Pasha attempted to collect the full 5 per cent import tariff for the local market, the British consul and merchants protested that they were not subject to a duty of 9 per cent, or to the import (5 per cent) or export (4 per cent) tariffs, based on the Treaty of Balta Liman. According to an additional article of that treaty, the British goods, having paid the full 5 per cent import tariff, could be exported without being liable to any additional charge. Although the 4 per cent export tariff was not levied directly upon them, it caused arguments between the government and the traders. At least one half of the British goods imported into Baghdad were ultimately transited to Persia, and the British claimed that their goods could not support a 9 per cent duty in the Persian market and that a discount of 4 per cent was not affordable for doing business at Baghdad.[52]

Locally the grain trade both for local markets and for export became a profitable government activity as well under Necip Pasha. While water-related projects drew private investment to tax farming, some tax farmers then engaged in marketing grains to merchants when their prices increased.[53] When grain was withheld by tax farmers for speculation, the shortage of grain in the market increased prices for consumers. It consequently led more people to become involved in agriculture by purchasing tax-collecting rights, lending money, or supplying the necessities of seed, tools, and housing.

Reşit Pasha, who had collected large quantities of staple grain for export to Jidda and Yemen, became more watchful of grain prices in the markets and of the form of payment, in kind or in cash, by the tax farmers. Particularly in

---

exports, and 3 per cent on transit. TNA: FO 195/237, No. 30, 12 June 1844; FO 195/237, No. 37, 9 July 1844.

52 TNA: FO195/334, No. 18, 23 May 1849.

53 For example, an official tax report for Baghdad, Basra, and Rawanduz in 1264–65 AH (1848) shows a voluminous tax collection of wheat, barley, and rice in kind, 7,967 tagar in total, of which 5,807 tagar of wheat and barley exceeded the tithe payment.

1857, owing to the Crimean War, the value of the kuruş against the Turkish lira declined from the official value of 110 kuruş to 130 kuruş in the local money market. At the same time, two or three favoured merchants were permitted to buy the bulk of the grain for speculation, pushing up grain prices to three times more than the average price, or double the price of the last year, and sharply decreasing the supply of grain for local consumption. The pasha hastily imported grain from Persia, but not in a volume sufficient to meet the increased demand.

The government was encouraged, however, by the increasing capital accumulation in the private sector, which enabled people to raise their income through investment. The profit from tax farming increased at the market price of the Ottoman currency because its purchasing price was arranged at the current price of the kuruş, whose future price would decline on the local market. As a secure source of income, the right to tax farming became an interest-bearing investment, but it was the tax-collecting right itself that attracted investors rather than the productivity of the cultivated land. Not until the 1860s were investors drawn to acquire uncultivated state land, which became more affordable than tax farming and a secure target of investment by tribal sheikhs, traders, merchants, and other notables who had accumulated capital with the development of the economy.[54]

54 The account balance of the trust fund between 1868–69 (1285 AH) and 1869–70 (1286 AH) shown below indicates the accumulation of capital among the people.

Receipt (Kuruş)				
	As of 2/1285	3–5/1286	6–8/1286	As of 9/1286
Balance	1,938,208	763,074	642,959	3,344,241
Interest	10,692	8,463	92,220	111,275
New Deposits	133,265	67,620	613,983	814,868
Total	2,082,165	839,157	1,349,162	4,270,484

Payment (Kuruş)				
	As of 2/1285	3–5/1286	6–8/1286	As of 9/1286
Lending	1,544,575	653,860	856,761	3,055,196
Interest	2,758	3,498	18,318	24,574
Withdrawal	376,133	172,058	433,811	982,002
Total	1,923,466	829,416	1,308,890	4,061,771

SOURCE: *ZEVRÂ*, NO. 6, 10 REBIYÜLÂHIR 1286; NO. 15, 15 CEMAZIYELÂHIR 1286; NO. 27, 10 RAMAZAN 1286; NO. 41, 4 MUHARREM 1287; NO. 54, 25 REBIYÜLEVVEL 1287; NO. 62, 24 REBIYÜLEVVEL 1287; NO. 78, 21 CEMAZIYELÂHIR 1287.

Tax farming practised in harmonization with crop sharing functioned effectively for tax collection, agricultural production activities, farm management with *serkâr* (tribal sheikh), distribution of earnings among peasant tribesmen, irrigation, and land reclamation in tax farming areas in the province of Baghdad. Collecting most revenues through tax farming, however, the government could not collect enough revenues to finance rapidly increasing expenditures. The fiscal deficit worsened as the currency devalued and the Porte amassed volumes of paper money. As a consequence, grain prices increased, which hurt urban residents (e.g., wage earners), even as it benefitted a certain group of merchants and traders. Tax farmers and tribal sheikhs who collected the tax in kind gained by selling grain at market. It certainly motivated them to use uncultivated areas of their farms for agricultural production. However, their investments in agriculture still were insufficient to meet the increasing expenditures. The expansion of land under cultivation itself caused disputes with the original landowners, who had neglected cultivation but continued to request rent. Inefficient land use, as Chapter 4 details, affected the governor's land policies and triggered reform.

CHAPTER 4

Land Problems

In the midst of the province of Baghdad's financial deficits, agriculture was an economic sector with great potential for growth owing to its abundant water resources, large numbers of tribal peasants, practical agricultural customs, and large areas of uncultivated land. As explained in previous chapters, in order to raise revenues by taking advantage of this potential, the government had carried out numerous projects for flood control, irrigation, and land reclamation and had encouraged tribal sheikhs, tribesmen, tax farmers, and other private individuals to involve themselves in agriculture. The projects did lead to increased production and tax revenues, but in many places, the increases were not enduring. This inability to sustain progress in agriculture stemmed from the difficulty of water control, the empire's shortage of technical expertise, and the invisible deficiencies of a land-tenure system ruled by custom and tradition. Among these constraints, the problem of land tenure, which caused patchy land use and slowed the extension of land use in the irrigated areas, is examined in this chapter.

1 The Origins of the Land Problems

In principle, agricultural lands were governed by the Ottoman customary practice of land tenure. The state and the private individual had absolute ownership of state land (*arâzi-i miriye*) and private land (*arâzi-i mülkiye*) respectively.[1] The state, however, had rarely claimed its right as long as it could collect taxes on its land, while the right of the private owner had been fully protected by Islamic law. Besides these two categories, some state-owned land was reserved for common use, classified as public land and subject to a different scheme of rules and taxation; wasteland was occupied largely by tribes, who often claimed it as their land. The tribes used such land for grazing domestic animals or seasonally cultivated the marsh areas by using floodwater. Agricultural holding on these tribal lands involved tribal tradition and local custom, which

1 The land was officially classified into state land (*arâzi-i miriye*), public land (*arâzi-i metrûke*), waste- or barren land (*arâzi-i mevât*), land belonging to a religious endowment (*vakıf*), and private (*mülk*) land.

 | DOI:10.1163/9789004384347_006

complicated the practice of land tenure and made it almost impossible for the government to regulate.[2]

According to British Consul in Baghdad Arnold Burrowes Kemball's rough estimation in 1861, state land in agricultural areas, including the lands of religious institutions, accounted for 82 per cent of all the land, private land 12 per cent, and the land called *temlîk* – privately held state land – 6 per cent of the total.[3] But state land was not under the effective control of the government. Rather, the trend was towards a higher percentage of private landholding, as the title to state land passed into private hands along rivers and canals and on fertile lands. The transfer was made mainly by way of gift and reward from the sultan or as a result of the reclamation of barren land for the cultivation of date palms and fruits. When the government set out to control state land by means of land legislation, it usually failed to regain these privatized state lands until the land became vacant. The private (as opposed to privatized) lands were governed by Islamic law, so that the problem was even more complex and lingered without solution.

Most private land was used as date groves, fruit gardens, and grain fields, and the owners generally paid a tax assessed by the area of cultivation for dates; a tithe of one-tenth or one-fifth of the produce for fruits and vegetables; or a tax of one-fifth, one-fourth, one-third, or one-half of the produce for grain fields.[4] Because of their higher taxes, grain field owners often defaulted on their tax payments and abandoned cultivation. Part of the private land, however, had been entrusted to the religious institutions and was to be supervised by the Islamic court, although in practice the land administrator was assigned by the religious institution's endowment. The peasant cultivators' desertion from the private land and inefficient land use damaged its productivity and made its recovery expensive.

The problem of uncultivated land also was serious in the northern districts, where rainfall agriculture was practised. There, state land accounted for a large proportion of the agricultural land, and a number of fief holdings in the districts of Erbil, Kirkuk, and Mosul were retained as fief until the mid-nineteenth

2 Less attention was paid to tribal landholding before the Land Code of 1858, and it was usually inscribed only as the tribal domain in official records. BOA, İ. Meclis-i Vâlâ 24610, 24 Şevval 1282; Mühimme Defterleri 262, pp. 166–67 (20 Safer 1283); Abudurrahman Vefik, *Tekâlif Kavâidi* (Istanbul: Matbaa-yı Kader: Kanaat Matbaası 1328–30 AH [1910–12]), i, p. 21.

3 TNA: FO 602/35, "Question Relating to the Financial System of Turkey." The survey reports of British Consul Arnold Burrowes Kemball are included in TNA: FO 78/1633, Enclosure Nos. 1–4 of Dispatch No. 41, 29 Aug. 1861 (hereafter, "Kemball Reports").

4 For *harâc* land, the tax was either *harâc-ı mukâseme*, from one-fifth to one-half of the produce, or *harâc-ı muvazzaf*, assessed by the area measured in *cerîb, dönüm*, or other units.

century. The fief given to the Kurdish tribal chiefs had merged into the tribal lands, where the government was unable to collect taxes.[5] Along the major road from Baghdad to Mosul, in such major towns as Kifri, Tuz Khurmatu, Kirkuk, and Altun Köprü, a number of private holdings had been converted from other categories of land or retained from the Islamic period.[6] By the mid-nineteenth century, some of them were deserted; others had merged into state land or had been transformed into land on which the owner was entitled to claim a certain proportion of the produce as the owner's share.

In the northern districts, the state land regime had been troubled by deficiencies in administration and legislation as well. In Mosul, for example, large areas of agricultural land abandoned by peasants had been neglected since the beginning of the nineteenth century. Then, after the Tanzimat, because of the political instability involving Christian peasants and oppression by the tribal chief-tax farmer, a number of villages were destroyed, and their land became vacant. The government sold the cultivation right on such vacant lands in accordance with the Law of Land Registration of 1847, either transferring it from the state to a private individual or between individuals by inheritance or sale. It was a pioneering attempt to put the vacant land into use and collect tax from the produce, although the land registration had been slow.

The agricultural director appointed from among the local notables took charge of land administration and sold the cultivation rights on vacant land in exchange for a large proportion of the sale revenues as his commission. Issue of the new title deed (*tapu senedi*) was delayed because of the complex procedure for land registration, which confused local officials and led to errors. If the purchaser incorrectly assumed that he had to bear the mailing cost of the title deed sent by the Imperial Treasury, he might not register the land. Or the government official might fail to report a land sale to the treasury, so that the title deed did not always arrive in the province. When land was transferred to the tribal chief as a gift, sometimes a peasant's cultivated land also was transferred illegally. As the transfer of land went on, the government consequently faced a number of troubles.[7] The district governor of Mosul forwarded his complaints about the situations to the Porte in 1855–56:

5 BOA, Mâliye Nezâreti, Mâliye Defterleri, No. 187, Kerkük, Musul ve Erbil Sancaklarında Bulunan Tımarların Yoklama ve Tevcihine Dâir Defter (1256 AH).

6 BOA, İ. Meclis-i Vâlâ 24610, 24 Şevval 1282.

7 Land disputes occurred most often over inheritance. BOA, İ. Meclis-i Vâlâ 3069, Gurre-i Receb 1264; İ. Meclis-i Vâlâ 9563, 7 Rebiyülevvel 1269; İ. Meclis-i Vâlâ 10179, 11 Cemaziyelevvel 1269; İ. Meclis-i Vâlâ 15174, 14 Safer 1272; İ. Meclis-i Vâlâ 16818, 8 Rebiyülevvel 1274; Bâb-ı Âlî Evrâk Odası (BEO), Sadâret Evrâkı Mektûbî Kalemi, Umûm Vilâyet Kismi (A.MKT.UM) 66–17, 9

> In Mosul district [*sancak*], official requests for *tapu* title deeds were submitted, but many of them did not arrive. The lands transferred in this form were deserted villages and fields where no peasant tribesmen cultivated. Their transfer by *tapu* is necessary to make them cultivated and produce revenues to pay officials as salaries.... In Mosul, some vacant fields and villages were sold in auction with payments of fees and transferred by *tapu* to Muhammad, Tahir, Khalid Riza, Kabet, and other people. They cultivated their transferred lands and managed them. There are still large areas of unregistered lands.[8]

In order to hasten an issue of *tapu* title deed, the land committee in Mosul submitted *mazbata* to the Meclis-i Vâlâ requesting that the minister of finance make a quick decision. As mentioned in the quote above, selling land and issuing registered *tapu* title deeds to the purchaser was a useful measure to encourage land cultivation, so the government assigned, according to the law, 2,500 kuruş for salaries and 7,500 kuruş for expenses to the local land registry office (*defterhâne*). Asım Effendi was appointed to carry out the official order and issue the undelivered title deeds with a provisional committee. However, as the district governor complained, the issuing of *tapu* title deeds was delayed considerably.[9] Moreover, as the above document of complaint suggests, one person was not alone allowed to acquire a whole village or its fields, so the land was subdivided into smaller units. Thus the expectation of private investment led to smaller and smaller subdivision, inadvertently devaluing land prices and impoverishing peasant cultivators.

In the irrigated zone, landownership developed into even more complicated forms of tenure, for which the land laws were wholly inadequate. In the central and southern areas, irrigation agriculture prevailed along dry canals, in marshlands, or in rice fields watered by little runnels. In parts of that area, where agriculture was undertaken only during flood season, tribes claimed ownership as their tribal land. In other parts of the area, those that were irrigated perennially by canals or watered by water lifts, the lands were officially state land

---

Ramazan 1267; A.MKT.UM 215–72, 6 Rebiyülâhir 1272; A.MKT.UM 229–47, 19 Cemaziyelevvel 1272; Buyruldu ve İlmühaber Defterleri 3, p. 128 (10 Rebiyülevvel 1269).

8 BOA, A.MKT.UM 215–72, 6 Rebiyülâhir 1272.

9 BOA, A.MKT.UM 215–72, 6 Rebiyülâhir 1272. Vice-consul of Great Britain in Mosul Christian Anthony Rassam also details the problems of the *tapu* system, particularly on peasant cultivators, in his consular reports. For an example, TNA: FO 195/394, No. 28, Mosul, 3 Dec. 1855.

but actually included private land or land entrusted to a religious institution.[10] Surrounding the cities and towns, along the Diyala River, the Abu Ghraib Canal, the Husayniya Canal, and the Hilla Branch of the Euphrates, a number of private landholdings were cultivated for date palms, fruit, and vegetables. The private land of the religious institutions was mostly put under the administration of the Ministry of Religious Endowment by Ali Rıza Pasha (1831–42), but that belonging to the mosque of ʿAbd al-Qādir Gīlanī was returned to the administration of the mosque in 1844.[11] The remaining cultivated fields, which largely belonged to the state, were divided into different units of administration and tax collection and farmed according to local practice. Land tenure in the irrigated and the cultivated zones developed differently, causing patchy land use. The uncultivated arable lands were located predominantly in the irrigated zone in the mid-nineteenth century.

In Basra and along both banks of the Shatt al-Arab, abandoned lands that were originally private land gradually fell barren and were taken over by the government. In Basra, peasants had left their villages because of frequent attacks and plunder by nearby tribesmen belonging to the Bani Malik, the Bani Tamin, and the Bani Nahd. In one instance, a privately owned garden granted by the governor as a reward was exposed to frequent tribal raids and was put on the market, together with the seller's other profitable garden. The purchaser left the uncultivated garden abandoned, paying its tax from the produce of the productive garden. Other abandoned gardens were taken over and cultivated by the government, but when no one wanted to bid on them for tax farming, they were eventually farmed out to a tribal sheikh at a discount. Due to his exploitation, however, peasants fled, and the gardens again became uncultivated. Annual flooding in spring and subsequent plagues also caused a number of wealthy people and merchants to leave all their landed properties for refuge in Muhammara, Muscat, Kuwait, and Yemen. Before the collapse of the military regime in 1831, the irrigation official and tribesmen had cooperated on

10 The perennially irrigated areas included those along dry canals (*şitvî*), marshlands (*kibî*), and rice fields watered by little runnels (*çertik*), as well as perennially cultivated areas located along irrigation canals (*saih*) or watered by water lifts (*karûd*). Great Britain, War Office, Intelligence Division, *A Handbook of Mesopotamia* (London: The Division, 1916–17), i, p. 128; Defterdar Ahmed Fahmi, *Baghdād Vilāyeti Dākhilinde Arāḍininñ Sūret-i Idāre ve Taṣarrufuna dā'ir Ta'limāt <Lā'iḥası>dir* (Baghdad, n.d.), p. 1.

11 BOA, İ. Dahihiye 4717, 24 Zilkade 1260; İ. Dahiliye 5134, 22 Rebiyülâhir 1261; İ. Dahiliye 7038, 18 Safer 1263; Mehmed Hurşid Paşa, *Seyâhatnâme-i Hudûd* (Istanbul: Takvimhâne-i Âmire, 1277 AH [1860]), translit. into Turkish in Alâattin Eser, *Seyâhatnâme-i Hudûd* (Istanbul: Simurg Kitapcılık ve Yayıncılık, 1997), pp. 104, 180.

public works, but after the regime collapsed, damage from flooding was rarely repaired, and the damaged areas were deserted.[12]

Private grain fields fell into vacancy in default of inheritance or because the owner's minor heirs were unable to cultivate the land. Sometimes the owner himself was unable to cultivate it because he could not afford to maintain canals and pay higher taxes imposed on the land, or because tribal raids, battles, epidemics, flooding, or other natural disasters prevented cultivation. Since the early seventeenth century, with the consent of the owner, such uncultivated land had been taken over by the government. It then was cultivated by way of tax farming, leasing, or share cropping, either at the expense of the government or at the tax farmer's risk, or was transferred to another person by sale or gift. Usually between one-fourth and one-fortieth of the produce still was given to the original owner of the land as *uqr*, depending on the local custom. The land with the owner's *uqr* share, called *akâr* in the Ottoman documents, was often called *uqr* land.[13]

In the rainfall zone in the north, over the course of time, large portions of unused agricultural land were cultivated and merged with state and private lands in which the original owner claimed only the *uqr* share. Such lands were mostly grain fields, fruit orchards, and vegetable gardens situated around the towns along the major road from Baghdad to Mosul, Kifri, Qaratepe, Altun Köprü, and Kirkuk and in irrigated areas along streams flowing from Tuz Khurmatu and Jamali. There, the share was between one-thirtieth and one-forty-fifth of the total produce and was collected at the same rate for winter grain crops, summer crops, fruit, and vegetables.

By contrast, in the irrigated zone the conversion of privately owned uncultivated land to state land was less common due to the difficulty of maintaining canals, complicated farming practices, unstable tribal situations, and natural disasters. Large tracts of land were left abandoned throughout the mid-nineteenth century and proved to be one of the major land tenure problems. Consequently, measures to deal with infertile land in the irrigated zone formed

12 BOA, İ. Mesâil-i Mühimme 2071, 22 Rebiyülâhir 1264; İ. Meclis-i Vâlâ 22368, 4 Cemaziyelevvel 1280; İ. Meclis-i Mahsus 943, 4 Şevval 1277.

13 BOA, Mühimme Defterleri, 263, pp. 11–12 (23 Şevval 1287); İ. Meclis-i Mahsus 943, 4 Şevval 1277; TNA: FO 371/4150/187296, Administration Report, Revenue Board, Baghdad, 22 Mar.–31 Dec. 1917 (Baghdad: Printed at Government Press, 1918), pp. 11–12; Turkey, *Mecelle* (*Mecelle-i Ahkâmı Adliye*), prep. Himmet A. Berki (Ankara: Banka ve Ticaret Hukuku Araştirma Enstitüsü, 1959), p. 215; Shākir Nasir Haider, *Aḥkām al-Arāḍī wa-l-Amwāl Ghair al-Manqūla* (Baghdad: Maṭbaʿat al-Iʿtimād, 1941–42), pp. 17–27; Hüseyin Hüsnü, *Arâzi Kânûnnâmesi Şerhi* (Istanbul: Kanaat Kitaphanesi 1324 AH [1908–09]), pp. 17–19; Ibrāhīm Nājī, *Kitāb Ḥuqūq al-Taṣarruf wa Sharḥ Qānūn al-Arāḍī* (Baghdad: Dār al-Islām, 1923), pp. 17–18.

part of the Porte's plan to cope with the problem of vacant land and apply the basic principle of the new land legislation. These laws were implemented effectively once people became accustomed to the idea of a private property right in land and familiarized themselves with its merits.

Illegally held state land was located mainly in productive areas and was relatively well maintained. Until the mid-nineteenth century, the government had been unable to prevent its vacant land from falling into private hands.[14] Much of it had begun as *temlîk* land on fertile grain fields that private people had obtained from the sultan by an imperial edict, such as *temlîk-nâme, emr-i âlî*, or *berât*, which permitted them to hold the land for private use. The recipient of such a grant was entitled to the owner's share from the produce and had to pay a relatively low tax from his share. In the Zangabad district, for example, he received one-tenth of the produce from a dry-farming field and one-fifth of the produce from an irrigated field, and the tax farmer collected the government's share from him as a tithe of one-tenth of the owner's share from the dry-farming field or one-fifth of the owner's share from the irrigated field. The government claimed that the actual ownership was retained by the state and that only the cultivation right had been transferred, so full payment of the tax was due. If the recipient, however, had registered his grant with the Islamic court as a private property or had turned it into the property of a religious institution, the government could not exercise any power over the land. Instead, the land's transfer and succession took place according to either Islamic law or the deeds given to the institution's trustee, and the government could not collect any fees from the transaction.[15]

According to British Consul Kemball in 1861, there were four kinds of privatized state land entrusted to a religious institution in Baghdad: (1) *vakf-ı nebevîye*, or a bequest to Mecca and Medina of which a superintendent called *nazîr-i evkâf* assumed the administration; (2) *vakf-ı sadaka*, or a charitable bequest for the benefit of a school and mosque, in which the creators of the trust nominated a representative (*müvekkel*) and regulated the succession to the trust; (3) a bequest of which a designated administrator (*mütevellî*) assumed the administration and its accounts were open to inspection by the director of religious endowments, the *nazîr-i evkâf*, who appropriated one-fourth of the net surplus income for the government; and (4) *vakf-ı zürriye*,

14 The title of the property was guaranteed by an issue of official documents. Such titled property was called *emlâk-ı mazbûta* or *emlâk-ı kayd*. The record in an official memorandum, such as *ilmühaber*, was also valid evidence of landholding.

15 Halil Cin, *Mirî Arazi ve Bu Arazinin Özel Mülkiyete Dünüsümü* (Konya: Selçuk Üniversitesi, 1987), pp. 21–22; Vera P. Moutafchieva, *Agrarian Relations in the Ottoman Empire in the 15th and 16th Centuries* (New York: Columbia University Press, 1988), pp. 61–77.

or a bequest for the benefit of the heirs and descendants of those creating the trust, who themselves were the executors and trustees.[16] Entrusting his right in state land to a religious institution, while including his family among its beneficiaries, allowed the owner to transmit it to more heirs, including daughters, sons, and other family members, and the land was free from government confiscation as long as it remained under the supervision of the Islamic judge's office. Upon the death of the owner and his heirs, the land became the quasi-property of the religious institution, despite the state's claim of ownership, and was administered by the judge's office independently from the government. State land that had thus become that of a religious institution was called *vakf-ı gayr-i sahîh* (lit. "the illegitimate endowment," even though that kind of endowment had become a deeply entrenched custom by the time that the government set out to enact preventive measures against it).[17]

In the mid-nineteenth century, Persians and other foreign nationals began to acquire land in the province of Baghdad. Although it had long been customary for foreigners to possess landed properties and receive rents from them in the province, the purchase had been effected in the name of an Ottoman subject, who afterwards gave bond that the property in question belonged entirely to the foreigner and that he himself had no claim upon it.[18] It had also been an unquestioned custom for the foreigner to receive the rents or to hold in his own name a mortgage on the property.

The first governor to intervene in foreigners' landholding was Necip Pasha, who in 1847 officially prohibited foreigners from purchasing or holding land and severely punished individuals who lent their names to the transfer of property to them. The first case to result involved properties left by a Persian woman without heirs. When the local chief Shiite judge (*mujtahid*) executed a formal written decree according to Shiite law, it was brought to the pasha by a Sunni priest, who argued that the Persians should be forced to sell or abandon

16 Kemball Reports, TNA: FO 78/1633, No. 41, 29 Aug. 1861.

17 Ahmet Akgündüz, *İslâm Hukukunda ve Osmanlı Tatbikatında Vakıf Müessesesi* (Ankara: Türk Tarihi Kurumu Basımevi, 1988), pp. 423–57; John R. Barnes, *An Introduction to Religious Foundations in the Ottoman Empire* (Leiden: Brill, 1986), 45–46; Bahaeddin Yediyıldız, *Institution du Vaqf au XVIIIe Siecle en Turquie* (Ankara: Société d'Histoire Turque, 1985), pp. 21–23; Moutafchieva, *Agrarian Relations*, pp. 77–130.

18 The restriction on landholding caused great damage to the Persian subjects, as their population was large. In 1845, the province's Shiite Muslim population was estimated to be at least three hundred thousand under the *mujtahid* of Karbala, Najaf, and Kadhimiya, including some six thousand Persians. Foreigners possessing landed property also were subject to other official controls such as a domestic passport fee of 4 kuruş for travel within a province and 40 kuruş for travel to another province (5 kuruş = 1 shilling). TNA: FO 195/237, No. 26, 25 June 1845.

their property under an imperial edict that publicly declared that foreigners could not hold land or houses in the empire. The decision of the Shiite judge was cancelled, the transaction was voided, and the judge was summoned to Baghdad for deportation to Persia.[19]

Subsequently the pasha applied a strict rule for the compulsory sale of landed property held by foreigners and ceaselessly attempted to regain the ownership of land illegally conferred on private individuals. As a penalty and escheat to the government in default of inheritance or for abandonment of land use, confiscations were frequently imposed despite the discontent they caused. In 1845, all foreigners possessing land or houses in the empire were made subject to all state laws and local regulations. Since those laws prohibited Persians and other foreign nationals from privately holding land, their land then was transferred to Ottoman subjects.[20] This measure was applied not only to the Persian merchants of Baghdad, almost all of whom were landed proprietors, but also to a considerable number of British subjects and to the scions of the royal house of India, who had long been settled in the province and who possessed considerable land, houses, and gardens. Nevertheless, because foreigners had frequently transferred their land, their titles to it tended to be defective, hindering the government's efforts to regain control over the land and transfer it to Ottoman subjects.[21] The law permitting all natives of the Ottoman empire, without reference to religion, to purchase land and houses was modified in 1846. A new regulation in that year allowed Ottoman Christians and Jews to transfer their property only within their group. Any sale of land by them to Muslims would be invalid and subject to penalty.[22]

---

19 TNA: FO 195/237, No. 28, 12 June 1844.

20 In civil, criminal, and religious matters, Persian subjects residing in the province were entirely subject to Ottoman law, which was administered according to the forms and usages of Sunni tribunals. The vice-judge (*nâib*) who resided in each quarter was the only constituted authority on questions of civil law in the district. All deeds for the sale or transfer of property had to be drawn and registered in his office, and a decree or written instrument issued by any other party was invalid. BOA, İ. Mesâil-i Mühimme 2070, 17 Cemaziyelâhir 1263; İ. Meclis-i Vâlâ 9647, 17 Rebiyülevvel 1269; TNA: FO 195/237, No. 26, 25 June 1845; No. 6, 4 Feb. 1846; FO 195/272, No. 23, 7 May 1847; FO 195/272, No. 67, 18 Aug. 1847.

21 The deed (*hüccet-i şeriye*) issued by the Islamic court was accepted for valid title to private land.

22 TNA: FO 195/237, No. 26, 25 June 1845; No. 6, 4 Feb. 1846; FO 195/272, No. 23, 7 May 1847; FO 195/272, No. 67, 18 Aug. 1847.

In 1848, a tax of 2.5 per cent was imposed on contracts for the lease or the hire of landed and household property.[23] Mortgage deeds now had to be registered at court, and if the deed could not be found at court, a sale was regarded as illegal, and the premises had to be vacated. Ömer Pasha (1857–59) reasserted the prohibition on the acquisition of landed property by foreigners, and a provision of the commercial code that required documentary evidence of a land sale was given precedence over Islamic law, which admitted oral testimony to prove the alleged sale of a house without reference to the date of the transaction.

The problems of privatized state land and of private holding by Persian and other foreign nationals had involved land use, taxation, and lack of supervision on the transfer of state land. As the government's capital investments in agricultural infrastructure, water control, irrigation, and land reclamation increased, the owners of these lands benefitted greatly, but because their tax rates and various fees were lower than those on the original state land, the government could not obtain a full return on its investments.

The government, therefore, tightened its regulation of land tenure, which had been governed by tribal custom, regional practices, and Islamic, as well as Ottoman, laws. Late in the governorship of Reşit Pasha (1852–57), tax farming came under stricter state laws, as did the transfer of state land. Not long after Ömer Pasha replaced Reşit Pasha, the Land Code of 1858 was proclaimed by the Porte and issued to the Baghdad government with the sultan's order for its application. Although Ömer Pasha had been extending district administration in the agricultural areas, his application of the code was initially slowed by ceaseless skirmishes with tribesmen, but in the next few years, the code's significance for agriculture was increasingly acknowledged by the governor and local officials. Its main principles supported the appropriation and transfer of uncultivated private land, though some of them proved impossible to apply in the province.

2 The Land Code of 1858

Replacing Ottoman state laws based on customary rules, the first major land law applied in Baghdad had been the Law of Land Registration of 1847, also

---

23 British Consul in Baghdad Henry Creswicke Rawlinson complained that levying this tax on European lessees through a nominal levy on the Ottoman proprietor was illegal based on Article 27 of the capitulation, which provided them protection of their property and exemption from all government fees. TNA: FO 195/318, No. 71, 22 Nov. 1848.

known as the Tapu Law of 1847. It expanded the right of succession from the owner's eldest son to all his female and male children. It also imposed a commission fee on land title transfers of 1.5–3 per cent of the land value for transfer by inheritance, and 5 per cent of the land's cultivation value for transfer by sale. When a new title deed was issued for the possession of state land, the person claiming the title had to pay the costs of registration – 3 kuruş for the cost of the paper, and 1 kuruş for the scribe. When a right of possession on vacant land was sold at auction, a commission was charged at the rate of 10 per cent of the land value. If the land was uncultivated and land reclamation was necessary for cultivation, the purchaser paid only the registration costs of 4 kuruş and was exempt for one year from the tithe on any grassland that had never been cultivated, and for three years on any land in stony areas. Half the revenue from the sale of the vacant land was given to the district administrator as his commission, and another portion of the purchase money was given to the auctioneer.[24] A mother was permitted to transfer her ownership right over land to her sons and daughters for payment of the land's cultivation value. If no offspring exercised that right, the land could be transferred for cultivation to other relatives of the owner, but if it was held in partnership, it was transferred to the other partners for payment of the market value of the land. Government officials – an agricultural director and a district administrator – were put in charge of selling the right of possession on vacant state land. Handwritten title deeds issued by other land administrators or by the tax farmer became invalid and were replaced by newly printed title deeds. The fees for land transactions were fixed and were collected by government officials.[25]

---

24 The land's cultivation value was called *tapu misli* to distinguish it from the land's market value (*bedel-i misl*). *Takvîm-i Vakâyi*, No. 539, 25 Cemaziyelevvel 1272; BOA, İ. Meclis-i Vâlâ 3584, 17 Safer 1265. For the principles of the Tapu Law of 1847, see Serkiz Karakoç, *Tahsiyeli Arâzi Kânûnı ve Tapu Nizamnamesi* (Istanbul: Kitaphane-yi Cihan, 1340 AH [1924]), pp. 307–11; BOA, Buyruldu ve İlmühaber Defterleri 4, pp. 55–56 (4 Cemaziyelevvel 1263).

25 Prior to the Tapu Law of 1847, when the land became vacant without a landholder and the land value was under 2,000 kuruş, the right of possessing and cultivating the land was sold by the local land administrator – the cavalryman, tax farmer, or other tax-collecting agent – and upon the transfer, a handwritten title deed was issued by him. This sale did not involve the ownership of the land, which was vested in the state. Half of the purchaser's payment, or *muaccele* (immediate payment, i.e. land value), sales commission, and registration fee was taken by the administrator who handled the sale. The provincial government conducted the transfer of the possession and cultivation right in vacant state land whose value was over 2,000 kuruş, but in many cases, the land was estimated at less than that amount and sold by the local land administrator. This practice was voided by the new *tapu* law, and all vacant lands were sold by a government official under the supervision of the Imperial Treasury. Ömer Barkan, "Türk Toprak Hukuku Tarihinde Tanzimat ve 1274 (1858) Tarihli Arazi Kanunnamesi," *Türkiye'de Toprak Meselesi* (Istanbul: Gözlem

The new law provided a different method of land registration. The administrative council of the sub-district prepared an official report, including the buyer's and seller's names and the land's location, boundaries, and value. Based on that report, another report was prepared by the administrative council of the district. After payment of the land value and the registration fees, the second report was submitted to the deputy governor and agricultural director of the province. They sent it to the Central Office of Land Registry in Istanbul and received a new title deed printed in the printing house of the Office of Land Registry and issued with the seal of the director of the office. The old title deed was void and replaced by the new deed upon the land transfer.[26]

In areas remote from Baghdad, land purchasers had to deal with district officials who were unfamiliar with the new procedure. As land tenure became an even more vital issue in the 1850s, the government assigned land issues to the agricultural director and other officials, and in 1857 appointed a government-salaried land official, who specialized in the transaction of the land title or of the possession right, in each of the major district towns.[27] As a result, by the time the government publicly announced the Land Code of 1858, these officials were familiar with the land problems and the previous legislation of the Porte relevant to them and able to cope with the rapid increase in applications for the title deed as the Code affected agricultural lands.

The Land Code of 1858 was not a newly created scheme, but a codification of various laws issued prior to 1858 for state-owned lands, such as state land, public land, and wasteland. It did not apply to privately owned land, which continued to be regulated by Islamic law, or to land whose possession right was assigned to religious institutions. The Code was composed of three parts, with a preface. The first part was the most important, as it was concerned with the right of possession in state lands transferred to private individuals. In it, the right of ownership in state land was retained by the state. At the same time, the government attempted to recognize a right of possession in state land as a quasi-property right, rather than as the peasant's traditional right of

---

Yayınları, 1980), pp. 323–71; İstanbul Üniversitesi, MS. TY 748, *Tanzîmât Hayriyeden İtibâren 1278 Tarihine Kadar Nesr Olunan Kavânîn ve Nizâmât*; BOA, CT, Maliye 1356, 16 Cemaziyelâhir 1257; İ. Meclis-i Vâlâ 15174, 8 Cemaziyelevvel 1272; İ. Meclis-i Mahsus 446, Safer 1274.

26 BOA, A.MKT.UM 65–100, 7 Şaban 1267; A.MKT.UM 100–46, 8 Şevval 1268. The *tapu* revenue of the Porte continued to increase steadily from the enactment of the Tapu Law of 1847 until that of the Land Code in 1858. In 1847–48 (1264 AH), it was 266,015 kuruş, only 0.04 per cent of total revenues, but it had increased to 7,858,000 kuruş, or 0.7 per cent of the total by 1859.

27 BOA, İ. Meclis-i Vâlâ 15709, 7 Muharrem 1273.

using and cultivating state land, thus expanding the sphere of the possession right and elaborating the rules governing its transfer by sale, inheritance, and escheat.

Still, like the right of ownership (*rakaba*), the right of possession (*tasarruf*) was vested in the state and transferred to the peasant only on condition that he use and cultivate the land and pay the commission immediately. A title deed was issued upon registration of the deed, and the peasant could transmit the title deed by inheritance to his eldest son. If the peasant died without a son, his right was transferred to his daughter, father, or brother upon payment of the land value, measured in terms of the cultivation right.

A peasant was entitled to claim the possession right only if he could prove he had continuously cultivated the land for ten years without legal dispute. Even if the peasant held the land illegally but had continuously cultivated it and regularly paid the taxes, he was granted the right of possession after a payment of the land value, measured by the value of the cultivation right. If the peasant's heir was a minor or the peasant had become disabled, a guardian could apply for the right on his behalf. A person leasing the land to a peasant for cultivation, however, was not qualified to claim the right, and neither was the lessee. Foreign nationals, mosques, churches, municipalities, and corporate bodies likewise were not allowed to claim possession of the land.[28]

Traditionally in the province of Baghdad, the peasant had a right to cultivate deserted or abandoned land. He also could transfer that right to another person by sale, gift, or mortgage, but first had to obtain the permission of the cavalryman and then undertake the transaction at the Islamic court office, paying various fees for the transaction and the registration. The land, moreover, had to be maintained as a grain field; no other land use was permitted. If the peasant disappeared, died without an heir, or was unable to meet his tax obligations, his right temporarily reverted to the state, which officially deemed the land escheated or vacant (*mahlûl*) and transferred the right to another cultivator through a sale by the cavalryman.[29] In reality, the right often passed from the peasant or actual cultivator of the land to a tax farmer, moneylender, or urban resident, who did not cultivate the land himself but received a share

---

28 Arts. 9, 23, 52, 78, and 122 in Frederick Ongley, trans., *The Ottoman Land Code* (London: W. Clowes and Sons, 1892), pp. 1–70; BOA, Muktezâ Defterleri 1, p. 294 (9 Cemaziyelevvel 1284); Ayniyât Defterleri 1012, p. 26 (8 Safer 1290). Pastureland (*yaylak* and *kışlak*) was distinct from grassland (*otlak*). Unregistered pastureland was considered vacant state land and sold at auction, but one could apply for the possession of grassland in accordance with the Land Code.

29 Barkan, "Türk Toprak Hukuk," pp. 294–95. For a definition of *mahlûl*, see Halil Cin, *Osmanlı Toprak Düzeni ve Bu Düzenin Bozulması* (Istanbul: Boğaziçi Yayınları, 1985), p. 223.

of the produce. Such land easily fell out of the legal control of the government, and the restrictions imposed on its use and transfer became less effective.

Under the Code, state land that had become uncultivated was considered to be vacant and was sold to the highest bidder at a government auction. If the uncultivated land was vacant private land without an owner, the ownership reverted to the state and was sold in the same way as state land. In both cases, the purchaser received the possession right on condition that he cultivate the land and pay the tax according to the Code.

Arable barren land was classified as wasteland when it was grassland, stony, or hilly and neither owned by anyone nor designated as public land. Such land also was supposed to be located far from any town or village, but in practice, land near villages was given to cultivators as wasteland. A right of possession in this land did not exist unless the government created that right for a person who obtained official permission to reclaim and cultivate the land for agricultural production and paid the cultivation value for a grant of the possession right. Unregistered pasturelands were considered vacant state land, and one could apply to buy their possession rights and those of unused grassland at auction. An applicant who had already opened up the land for cultivation could claim possession following ten years of consecutive cultivation without dispute, after he paid the registration fee.

In addition, the Code dealt with the common land of the tribal group. For features such as a pond, the possession right was conferred on everyone who had interests in the common land before it was parcelled out as cultivated land. Similarly, the whole of the land in the town or village was not sold to individuals, and the remaining commonly owned land could neither be made into a garden or vineyard nor be turned into a housing lot.[30]

The Code acknowledged the right to inheritance in the following order: on the death of the owner, the possession right went to his male and female children equally; if he died without children, it went to his father; and if his

---

30 Arts. 9, 19, 24, 25–31, 41, 68, 72, 101, 103, 104, and 106 in Ongley, *Ottoman Land Code*, pp. 1–70; BOA, Buyruldu ve İlmühaber Defterleri 3, pp. 187–88; Mukteza̋ Defterleri 1, p. 249 (19 Muharrem 1284); Muktezâ Defterleri 3, p. 71 (8 Rebiyülevvel 1287); Muktezâ Defterleri 4, pp. 155 (10 Şevval 1288), 186–87; Ayniyât Deferleri 1014, pp. 133, 135–36. The customary practice of the acquisition of land as estate (*çiftlik*) was forbidden, except when the construction of houses and fixtures was necessary for recruiting peasants and settling them on the land in order to cultivate it. In this case, the owner had to obtain permission from the government before construction. The owner of the *çiftlik* could not establish ownership of the land. The transfer and transmission of the *çiftlik* were carried out according to Ottoman land laws in the same way as the state land. Arts. 8, 31–33, 72, and 130 and "Tapu Law" in Ongley, *Ottoman Land Code*, pp. 71–110. BOA, Muktezâ Defterleri 2, p. 238 (27 Zilkade 1286); Muktezâ Defterleri 4, p. 181 (11 Safer 1289).

father was not alive, to his mother. If the owner died without children or parents, the right was transferred to his other relatives upon payment of the land's cultivation value. Inheritance by any non-Muslim was forbidden, and if the owner's children or parents were foreign nationals, they were forbidden to inherit even if they were Muslims. Instead, the owner's land was sold at auction to an Ottoman subject. In the case of a foreign subject who died in an Ottoman land or of an Ottoman national who died in a foreign country, the rule of succession followed the provisions of the treaty between the two countries. Consequently, when Persian subjects residing in the Ottoman Empire died without heirs, their possession rights were put under the custodianship of the Islamic court for one year. If no inheritor or his agent showed up in this period, the right was sold according to the Treaty of Erzurum.[31]

To transfer a possession right on state land from one person to another by sale or gift, only the permission of the land official was sufficient. After the person transferred his possession as a gift, he could not claim payment, and after payment for a transfer by sale was complete, the seller had no right to take back the land. If the possession right was sold for payment of the landholder's debt, however, with an acknowledgement from the land official, the debtor could reacquire the right when the debt was paid in full, and heirs of a deceased debtor could inherit his right by paying the debt.[32]

In 1859, the government enacted another law of land registration, which put each district's financial official, land official, and clerk in charge of land registration. They prepared a memorandum that included the land's location, boundaries, area, type of field, and market value, as well as the type of transaction and the assessed value of the tax. The memorandum then was sealed by the members of the administrative council in the district and sent to the office of land registry in the province. Upon receiving the memorandum, the land official examined the old title deed, inquired into the accuracy of the survey, and estimated the fees for completing the transaction. The registration fee was 5 per cent of the land value, and the costs were 3 kuruş for the paper and 1 kuruş for the clerk for ordinary transactions. If the land was transferred for the payment of a debt, an additional fee of 2.5 per cent of the debt was charged to the debtor.[33] After payment of the registration fees, the provincial administrative

31 Arts. 54–59 and 110–11 in Ongley, *Ottoman Land Code*, pp. 1–70; BOA, Muktezâ Defterleri 2, p. 131 (13 Safer, 1287).

32 Arts. 115–16 in Ongley, *Ottoman Land Code*, pp. 1–70; BOA, İ. Meclis-i Mahsus 518, 5 Cemaziyelevvel 1274; *Takvîm-i Vakâyi*, No. 562, 9 Şevvel 1274; Barkan, "Türk Toprak Hukuk," pp. 347–50.

33 "Tapu Law" in Ongley, *Ottoman Land Code*, pp. 71–110. The registration fee actually was charged at rates from 2 to 4 per cent and sometimes up to 10 per cent of the land value.

council prepared the official report, including all the necessary information about the land, and that report, copies of the land official's memorandum, and the council's report were sent to the Office of Land Registry in Istanbul, which issued the title deed and sent it to the provincial treasury. The land official sent all fees collected for land registration to the Imperial Treasury in Istanbul and was not allowed to take any portion of the fees as a commission.[34] The administrative council in each province was responsible for organizing the auction sale of vacant land. For land between 100 and 500 dönüm, the council had to prepare the official report for completing the transaction. For land over 500 dönüm, the result of the auction was reported to the Ministry of Finance and, if necessary, another auction was held by the ministry in Istanbul. After the land transfer was authorized, the land official registered the title in the same way as for other state land. The new title deed was issued for only the registration cost, as the government paid the auction costs (of up to 10 per cent of the land value) from the purchase money.

3 Consul Palgrave's Report on Land Problems

Although the Land Code of 1858 is regarded as the first major law on property rights on land during the Tanzimat, which protected the use of land and its transfer by the private individual, it was not very effective in mitigating land problems. The survey of British Consul in Trabzon W. Gifford Palgrave in 1869, which Şevket Pamuk deems a "very important and useful survey of land ownership and tenancy patterns in the Asiatic provinces of the Ottoman Empire in the late 1860s," summarizes the problems in eastern Turkey, Anatolia, Kurdistan, the northern region of Iraq above Baghdad, and Syria.[35] According to Palgrave's report, problems arose from changes in proprietorship, the subdivision of land, the depreciation of land values, and the modification of tenancy. Although his

---

BOA, Ayniyât Defterleri 1014, pp. 124 (26 Cemaziyelâhir 1290), p. 135 (19 Rebiyülâhir 1291), p. 144 (9 Şevvel 1291).

34 The title deeds were issued at the office of land registry (*defter-i hâkanî*) in the province after 1873 (1290 AH). BOA, Ayniyât Defterleri 1014, pp. 101 (11 Receb 1289), 116 (5 Şaban 1290).

35 Great Britain, House of Commons, "Reports from Her Majesty's Representatives respecting the Tenure of Land in the Several Countries of Europe: 1869–70, Presented to both Houses of Parliament by Command of Her Majesty, Part II," in *Accounts and Papers*, vol. 67 (London: Harrison and Sons, 1870), Enclosure 2 in No. 15, Trebizond, Consul Palgrave (signed W. Gifford Palgrave), esp. pp. 276–92 on conditions of land tenure. Şevket Pamuk scrupulously elaborates on this report in *The Ottoman Empire and European Capitalism, 1820–1913* (Cambridge: Cambridge University Press, 1987), pp. 82–107, 182–90.

survey included only Mosul and the northern districts of Baghdad, where large estates had belonged to military fiefs described as *beğlik*, *zeamet*, or *timar* and resold piecemeal after their confiscation, Palgrave found that the subdivision of land worsened after the application of inheritance law. This problem caused subsequently the depreciation of land values and the modification of tenancy, acutely affecting the peasants' subsistence.[36]

Depreciating land values made it difficult to place a mortgage on the land, though houses, shops, and other objects were acceptable. The reasons for the depreciation were many: the subdivision of land; the loss of public confidence in investment because of the arbitrary withdrawal of grants and privileges long enjoyed by estate holders; and existing laws on the inheritance, purchase, sale, and transfer of land. Especially, the Land Code tended to lower the value of land by imposing heavy government dues on every transaction connected with the land and by invariably giving a legal preference to the contingencies and transfer over those of possession and permanence. In addition, although the Code hampered occupation and invalidated proprietorship throughout, Palgrave found land registration was still deficient:

> On the purchase of land from the Government, no title deed is granted but in its place, the purchaser's name is entered as such on the official register, and a premium of 10 per cent *ad valorem*, over and above the cost price of the land, is paid by him on the spot. On this payment he receives a paper of quittance; which, apart from the registry-book itself, over which he has no control, is his only title.
>
> Should he desire to re-sell, he must provide the new purchaser with the original paper of quittance; and, on its production at the Registry Office, the intended transfer is entered on the lists, and a fresh premium of 5 per cent is claimed by Government. But should the quittance paper have by any accident been lost, or be otherwise not forthcoming the premium rises to 10 per cent, as at the original sale, and so on through all further sales and transfers, *ad infinitum*.[37]

In case of private land sales, as in public sales, no legal deed was required to persons concerned. Proof of ownership, as an example, was receipt of payment of the last 5 per cent or 10 per cent of the sales value and the registry book, of which no copy or extract was given to either the buyer or the seller. They were

36 TNA: FO 83/346, Land Tenure Reports, vol. 8. Turkey, 1870, "Report on Land Tenure in Eastern Turkey."

37 House of Commons, Accounts and Papers, "Reports respecting the Tenure of Land," p. 283.

the only valid documents that often caused trouble and dispute.[38] Besides the deficient method of land registration, the most serious reason for the depreciation was excessive taxation on the land and its produce. In some areas, its impact was increased by direct and indirect official "spoliation," such as the confiscation of land for the construction of a road, barrack, or other public works, without any return or compensation, and the recurring requirement of forced labour from the peasants on all possible occasions, which diverted them from cultivating the land. Observing that "the excess of large estates is an evil; the excess of small ones is perhaps a worse,"[39] Palgrave, however, considered the negative effects of subdivision worse than the system in the previous period, because the proprietors of large estates disappeared, so that nobody could support their "lesser co-landlords" over a difficulty. Such small peasant landholders collapsed almost into "produce-sharing beggars" to bear the yearly burden of expenditure, and taxation fell into great trouble upon bad harvest.[40] As observed in the district governor in Mosul's official complaints, the northern districts in Mosul region experienced similar land problems:

> Such is the condition into which the greater part of the landowners in Eastern Turkey are already sank, and into which the small and decaying remnant of the better sort are rapidly sinking. Meanwhile agriculture wanes on every hand; its quality and its quantity alike deteriorate and diminish; pasture-land encroaches on plough-land, waste-land on both; cottage-roofs drop in, and the country population emigrates or dies away. A sad landscape, but a true one. I have seen the original in "Irak" from Baghdad to Mosul, in Syria from Damascus to Aleppo, and in Anatolia from Erzurum to Angorah, and can neither forget nor overdraw it.[41]

In central and southern Baghdad province, where large portions of cultivated land were tribal land, the custom of *müzâra'a* (crop sharing) spared the land and its peasant cultivators from the degradation Palgrave saw in the north. Recognizing the mutual trust over crops, the governors left this established practice untouched in their land policies, so that the application of the Land Code had different sorts of consequences outside the northern districts observed in Palgrave's report.

---

38 Ibid.

39 TNA: FO 83/346, "Report on Land Tenure," p. 285.

40 House of Commons, Accounts and Papers, "Reports respecting the Tenure of Land," pp. 284–85.

41 Ibid.

4 The Land Policies of Reşit Pasha and Ahmet Tevfik Pasha, 1852–1861

The matter of state land had drawn the interest of Baghdad governors since the governorship of Ali Rıza Pasha, who confiscated private properties as punishment. Although the next governor, Necip Pasha, was concerned with political issues and the revenues from agricultural produce, not the property right on the land, landholding became part of the political agenda during his term, when the Porte issued a series of laws on the inheritance and registration of land. Consequently, by the time the first *tapu* law was enacted in 1847, land issues had also become a realistic concern of the people. The customary right on cultivated land that had been vaguely asserted by its holder now became more a definite right for him. In addition, the transfer of land that was held by Persian subjects was more closely scrutinized and often subject to interference by officials.

Subsequently, years of political and economic turmoil diverted the attention of Baghdad's governors from agriculture and land rights until the term of Reşit Pasha (1852–57). In his promotion of such industrial and cash crops as indigo, hemp, silk, white cotton, madder root, safflower, opium, sugarcane, ginger, and saffron, Reşit Pasha prioritized that of indigo and white cotton. To enhance the cultivation of indigo, he brought in agricultural specialists and instructors from Egypt and exempted its imported seeds from customs duties. As a result, an estimated 150 okka of indigo, with a total market value of 9,750 kuruş, was produced and sold in Baghdad during Reşit Pasha's governorship.[42] While his promotion efforts did not extend to the grain-producing areas, the governor's attention to cash crops signalled a growing interest in land and its cultivation beyond tax farming, and the expanding, more competitive markets for staple and commercial products made grains profitable trade goods. In addition, because merchants could pay the export duty on their merchandise at the place of production, at any customs house in the course of transit, or at the port of shipment, they could avoid paying it at a place covered by treaty. They also could receive a discount on the stipulated rate of the tariff due to competition among the tax farmers of the customs duties at the optional payment locations.

Others besides the merchants and traders benefitted from the government's promotion of agricultural progress. A tax farmer who had arranged prepayment of the tax could profit not only from the difference between his lower collecting price and the crop's increased selling price on the market, but also from retaining a portion of the grain, speculating that the selling price would

42 BOA, İ. Meclis-i Vâlâ 14224, 27 Şaban 1271.

rise even further. Although the government made tax collection in kind or in cash a policy choice in an effort to gain control of the grain markets, it could not prevent speculative investment by the tax farmer. Only when Ömer Pasha ordered a compulsory sale of grain did the grain price stabilize in the market.

As interest in agriculture remained high, despite Ömer Pasha's stabilization of the selling price for grain, the auction price of tax farms and the leasing price of productive land both continued to rise.[43] According to British Consul Kemball, in rice fields in the Hindiya district, the tax had been farmed for a quite profitable 2.35 million kuruş before Ömer Pasha let it to another person for 4.875 million kuruş, which was raised to 6 million kuruş by Governor Ahmet Tevfik Pasha (1861). Because this extreme profit making on a commercial crop, reinforced by the rise in grain prices, commonly occurred on productive farms, the government increased the volume of the tax payment in kind for some profit making of its own. It also took advantage of the increasing grain prices when it recorded revenues and expenditures in its account books, particularly for military expenditures, eliciting complaints from suppliers, military men, pensioners, and officials.[44]

Still, the government's rising revenues from trade and tax farming were no match for its mounting expenditures. Because agricultural production was failing to keep up with demand, the government sought private investment in agriculture, and investors responded – the decreased market value of the currency and increased grain prices favoured private investment in a secure source of lucrative revenue such as agricultural land. As a result, the affordable acquisition of a *tapu* title deed on state land became an attractive, secure target of investment for tribal sheikhs, traders, merchants, and other notables.

After lifetime tax farms were abolished, large numbers of tax farms were merged into a larger unit of tax collection called *mukâtaa*, complicating the issue of land tenure. The only examples of a *mukâtaa* held wholly by a private owner were one along the Khatuniya Canal, owned by the family of a vice-judge in Baghdad, and another along the Mishmis Canal, owned by a chief treasurer of Baghdad. The typical *mukâtaa* contained many blocks of fields that included state land, estates of religious institutions, and land that was owned privately by official permission of the sultan. Consequently, certain portions of the land were uncultivated, because the tax farmer could fulfil his tax payment from the productive land, without delving into the complicated

43 Reşit Pasha issued an "Instruction for Implementing the Law of 1855 concerning Revenues and Expenditures in the Province of Baghdad and Basra," which was based on the Law of 1855 on tax and fiscal administration. BOA, İ. Dahiliye 27525, 17 Safer 1275.

44 BOA, İ. Meclis-i Vâlâ 7726, 21 Safer 1268.

tenure on uncultivated land. For this reason, Reşit Pasha reclaimed land in the tax farming areas around the city of Baghdad – Khalis, Khorasan, Shahriban, and Hilla – most of which had been private land (i.e. *harâç* land that had fallen into disuse).[45] He transferred the land to tax farmers, along with financial support such as grants for seed or for maintaining the irrigation canals, a tax reduction, and, in some cases, a tax exemption for some years. If no one wanted the land because of its infertility, it was placed under direct official administration, and the canals were dug and dredged to revitalize it. After the revitalization, unlike previous governors, Reşit Pasha claimed the profits from the state's investments for the state as tax.

On other infertile land, Reşit Pasha had to deal with land tenure on the tax farms. Under Necip Pasha, money had been invested in residential land, houses, and other immovable properties, but not in agricultural land. Since then, agricultural conditions had changed as instability in tribal domains became less frequent and the rural infrastructure improved rapidly, but emerging investors avoided purchasing agricultural land because the market was small and transactions were insecure.

Desiring to sell uncultivated lands in the market to be revitalized by the purchaser, Reşit Pasha sold those near Baghdad to wealthy townspeople who were capable of maintaining land productivity and tax payment. The title deed was issued to the purchaser of the land in accordance with the new land legislation. The resulting demand from new investors drove up the market price of land there. Now, for example, along the canal, 10 feddân of irrigated land was estimated at 20,000 kuruş, and uncultivated arable land was about half the price of cultivated land. The price of uncultivated private land, which had long been out of use, was no more than four times the market value of its annual produce. The value of a date-palm grove was estimated according to the number of trees, each being worth 80–200 kuruş. The value of such a grove in the immediate vicinity of a town was about twenty times that of its annual produce, but if a grove had orange, lime, pear, or other fruit trees, instead of date palms, its value increased by 20–50 per cent. The value of either a date-palm grove or an orchard declined by as much as half according to the distance from the town.[46] Nevertheless, the sale of uncultivated land under Reşit Pasha was

---

45 This *harâç* land also was described in the records as "ownership of watercourse (*temâlük enhârı*)" or "land of ownership-like possession (*malikane-i uhde-i tasarruf*)." BOA, A.MKT. UM 202–26, 5 Zilkade 1271; İ. Meclis-i Mahsus 943, 4 Şevval 1277; TNA: FO 195/521, No. 12, 22 July 1857; No. 37, 12 Nov. 1856; ʿAbbās al-ʿAzzāwī, *Taʾrīkh al-ʿIraq baina Iḥtilalain* (Baghdad: Maṭbaʿat Bagdād, 1935–56), vii, 109–110.

46 BOA, İ. Meclis-i Mahsus 943, 4 Şevval 1277; TNA: FO 78/1633, Enclosure No. 4 of Dispatch No. 41.

limited to Basra, the Shatt al-Arab, and the places along the Diyala and Middle Euphrates where Ottoman authority was firmly established, and the sales prices were not high enough to bring significant profits to the government. On uncultivated land farmed out to tax farmers, moreover, long-term investments were scarcely made by the tax farmers, so the land tended to become infertile again.

In the few tribal areas where land sales were undertaken, the land's market value became high enough to allow Reşit Pasha to use the land sale as a means of tribal policy. As gifts to the tribal sheikhs who accepted Ottoman authority, he granted a large area of date-palm groves in Basra and the Shatt al-Arab to the paramount sheikh of the Muntafiq in Suq al-Shuyukh, and to the sheikh of the Kaab in Muhammara, as their private properties. Reşit Pasha also gave the sheikhs *tapu* title to their cultivated lands upon their payment of the land's *tapu* value, much as Vecihi Pasha had attempted to sell the land to the Jaf tribe in its winter dwelling places. But the sheikhs were inclined to sell the *tapu* to others, especially to Persian and non-Muslim subjects, in spite of the prohibition against them doing so.[47]

The Land Code of 1858 immediately became significant as the epitome of Ottoman sovereignty and a symbol of modernization in the province of Baghdad. It, however, was neither applicable to most state land that had remained vacant without titleholders nor enforceable without supplementary regulations.[48] The right to any vacant land depended on whether it was originally state land or private land. If it had been state land, the government either sold it to a person capable of using the land and making tax payment, or, in most cases, farmed it out to a tax farmer. If it had been private land, the government confiscated the land and merged it into state land before transferring it to a private person as it did other state land. But confiscation often raised disputes. Because the local practice of land tenure over such private land had

47 Ahmad Ibn Nūr al-Anṣārī, *Al-Nuṣrah fī Akhbār al-Baṣrah*, ed. Yūsuf ʿIzz al-Dīn (Baghdad: Maṭbaʿat al-Majmaʿa al-ʿIlmī al-ʿIrāqī, 1969), pp. 19–25; BOA, İ. Hariciye 3915, Gürre-i Zilhicce 1267; İ. Hariciye 9430, 6 Rebiyülevvel 1276; İ. Meclis-i Mahsus 943, 4 Şevval 1277.

48 Huri İslamoğlu-İnan, *State and Peasant in the Ottoman Empire* (Leiden: E.J. Brill, 1994); Sir Ernest N. Dowson, *An Inquiry into Land Tenure and Related Questions* (Letchworth: Garden City Press, 1931); Saleh Haider, "Land Problems of Iraq," Ph.D. diss., London School of Economics, 1942, pp. 556–660, reprinted in Charles Issawi, ed., *The Economic History of the Middle East 1800–1914* (Chicago: University of Chicago Press, 1966), pp. 164–78; Albertine Jwaideh, "Aspects of Land Tenure and Social Change in Lower Iraq during the Late Ottoman Times," in Tarif Khalidi, ed., *Land Tenure and Social Transformation in the Middle East* (Beirut: American University of Beirut, 1984); Albertine Jwaideh, "Midhat Pasha and the Land System of Lower Iraq," *St. Antony's Papers*, no. 16, Middle Eastern Affairs (Oxford: Oxford University Press, 1963), pp. 106–36.

been in disarray due to conflicting claims based variously on Islamic law, tribal tradition, and local custom, the government was unable to assert effective ownership of unoccupied land, which deferred its revitalization.

In 1861, Ahmet Tevfik Pasha resumed official efforts to improve agricultural land and, above all, to resolve immediately the problem of uncultivated private land. To this end, he set up a committee, chaired by Münip Pasha, the district governor of Basra, that included Ata Bey from Istanbul, who was investigating the alleged bribery of the previous governor, Nuri Pasha; an accounting director; a chief treasurer; other government officials; and notables in Baghdad.[49] Its reports, submitted to the Special Council of Ministers in Istanbul, proposed reclaiming uncultivated private land (*harâç* land). Its other recommendations largely copied policies undertaken by previous governors, especially Reşit Pasha – in particular, combining an improved method of tax farming with transfer of the right of possession to a person willing to cultivate the land either gratis or upon payment according to the Land Code. The committee also endorsed Ahmed Tevfik Pasha's resolve to deal with the land problems by farming out land to tax farmers for longer terms, with financial support, direct administration of the land by government officials, the application of leasing, and transferring full private ownership to a person who would perform irrigation and agriculture. It further recommended transferring *harâç* land by *tapu* to tent-dwelling Arab tribesmen and people from cities and villages, provided that a new watercourse was opened, and it advocated the formation of a Committee of Land Reform. As a result, it predicted, large numbers of tribesmen would be settled and put under control, production of crops for export would increase, and a growing demand for land sale would be addressed.

A report enclosed in BOA, İ. Meclis-i Mahsus 943 recommended:

> *Harâç* land had been transferred to tax farmers piece by piece for digging canals and organizing peasant cultivators, and cultivated, but water is being blocked little by little and left uncultivated. In order to cultivate these lands, such uncultivated land should be transferred by *tapu* to tent-dwelling Arab tribesmen and people in city and village on condition of opening new watercourse according to the land code. For this purpose, a commission, Meclis-i Islâhât-ı Arâziye [Committee of Land Reform] is formed with a chairman, a secretary, and staffs locally appointed with paid salaries of from 1000, 1500, to 2000 kuruş. The revenue of transfer by *tapu* is estimated 40,000–50,000 kese piaster. With this measure, large numbers of tribesmen will be settled and put under control. Production

49 TNA: FO 195/676, No. 15, 5 June 1861; No. 33, 6 Nov. 1861.

> of crops will increase to be exported to Hicaz.... Reşit Pasha began to pay attention to cultivation of arable barren land, but after him no measure was taken and land again became vacant. As a measure, costs of canal cleaning and seeds are given to peasants as aids, tax discount for one year, or direct management *emânet* by the government, and land sale as people who want lands are many.[50]

Among the recommendations, the transfer of the possession right was most important, for the government preferred to assume ownership of uncultivated private land and create a new form of tenure on it over putting the land under tax farming, even though new landowners would have less experience in irrigation and agriculture than the tax farmers. Such new owners were expected to bear the costs of irrigation and reclamation work because their lands were subject to the uniform tithe, which was much less than the tax obligation imposed on the tax farmer. Moreover, their irrigation work would be more efficient than a tax farmer, who usually did not invest his own money in irrigation. It was these advantages of private landholding over tax farming that led the committee to suggest uncultivated private land be sold and the Land Code be applied to the transferred lands.

Following on the committee's recommendation, uncultivated private land was sold at auction to be cultivated at the purchaser's risk, and completely infertile land was given gratis to cultivators. The tax imposed on the land was a tithe of either one-tenth or one-fifth of the produce, but a few years' tax exemption was conferred on the purchaser, along with a variety of subsidies from the government, such as the provision of seed and of construction materials for housing. Land for raising date palms, fruit, or vegetables also was auctioned off. As with other private land, the purchaser acquired full private ownership with a tax obligation. If a cultivator met the condition of prescriptive rights, the land was transferred to him in accordance with the Land Code. Land sold in these ways was located where reclamation was easier and less costly for the cultivator – in the suburban areas of Baghdad and along the Diyala, Middle Euphrates, and Middle Tigris Rivers. In Hindiya, Musaib, and Diwaniya, which the powerful Khaza'il and Zubaid tribal groups dominated, state land was not sold. Instead, some was leased at an annual fee of 5–50 kuruş per dönüm, according to the productivity of the land, and land that could not be cultivated easily was rented out, but without fees for one or more years.[51]

50 BOA, İ. Meclis-i Mahsus 943, 4 Şevval 1277.
51 Ibid.

As land reclamation continued, serious problems beset the government's forced sale of private land. According to Islamic law, if an owner of private land died without heirs, left minor heirs unable to cultivate the land, or was unable to cultivate it himself, the government could take one of several measures to ensure the payment of taxes: It could grant the land to another person for cultivation and receive the tax from the owner's share, or lease the land to peasant tribesmen and collect the tax from the rent. Or it could cultivate the land on its own account and take its share of the produce as the tax, or sell the land and deduct the tax from the sale money. As Islamic law provided for lands where agriculture was costly and difficult because of water problems, the government became involved in cultivating ownerless or uncultivated private land by selling the land to a new owner or by leasing out the land on behalf of the original owner. When the land was sold and made productive by the new owner's effort, it was customary that the original owner still receive a certain proportion of the produce as rent, either from the new owner's share or from the total produce. When the government cultivated the land by leasing or on its own account, the owner of the land received the rent from the total produce. As long as the original owner shared in the produce, he or she was not inclined to raise any legal questions over the title in land, even though the land was sold or cultivated by the government.[52]

British Consul in Baghdad Kemball noted in 1861 that there were two kinds of private land, distinguished by whether or not the owner had the right to charge *uqr*. According to Kemball's report, the *uqr* share took one of three forms: the proprietary rent to which the landowner was entitled; a portion of the rent reserved by the owner upon the sale or transfer of the property to another person; or a lien held by the owner upon land to which the property right was otherwise vested in the state. In this third case, the *uqr* share assumed the character of a grant or assignment in perpetuity to the owner of 3–5 per cent of the produce, taken before the tax. In the other two cases, where the owner's share represented the whole or a part of the rent, its appropriation was made after payment of the taxes.[53]

As to tenure, on the land on which the owner took the *uqr* share as a rent, as indicated in the first case of the consul's report, he held ownership of the land as his private property. The land in the second case was also private land, but

52 Hüsnü, *Arâzi Kânûnnâmesi*, pp. 15–19; Kuyucaklızade Mehmet Âtıf, *Arâzi Kânûnnâme-i Hümayün-i Şerhi* (Istanbul: Mahmut Bey Matbaası, 1319 AH [1900 or 1901]), pp. 25–26; Haider, "Land Problems of Iraq," p. 193.

53 Kemball Reports, TNA: FO 78/1633, No. 41, 29 Aug. 1861.

its ownership belonged to the new owner, and the original owner reserved the *uqr* share as a portion of the rent. In the third case, in which the government cultivated the private land on its own account as recognized by Islamic law, the ownership changed from the original private owner to the government. The government then transferred the land as vacant state land or as wasteland to an individual who could carry out land reclamation and agricultural production. In that case, the *uqr* share was granted as a kind of the owner's right attached to the land, which is the reason it was subtracted from the total produce before the payment of taxes.

Usually, the owner's rent was taken after the tax deduction at a ratio of one-tenth to one-fifth of the produce, depending on local practice. But his share could be larger when the government collected the tax from the owner's rent or when the rent was assessed on the total produce. By contrast, if his land had been confiscated by the government, his *uqr* share was between one-thirtieth and one-twentieth of the produce. For this reason, as land reclamation went on, the original owners of reclaimed land began to assert their right of ownership under Islamic law, arguing that the legal status of uncultivated land as private land had been unchanged, even though it had fallen into the government's hands and had been put into use at others' expense. Such claims impeded implementation of the measures recommended by the committee Ahmet Tevik Pasha had convened and severely inhibited investment in land.

Outside the areas of tax farming, crop sharing, and tribal lands, lands were mostly unused, and no one was liable for or capable of tax payment. In the 1850s, Reşit Pasha had initiated use of such land, but the original owners' claims for a large share of the produce decreased the return on investment in that land. Those claims also discouraged private irrigation projects on rivers and major canals and thus any small-scale irrigation development on farm and branch canals, for the government contributed only such incentives as tax privileges, aids, and technical advice to those projects and relied on private investment for the bulk of the work.

Uncultivated private land in irrigated areas in Basra, the Shatt al-Arab, and along the Diyala and the Middle Euphrates began to be transformed into state land. In the areas of tax farming and crop sharing, the claim of the shareholder overrode an unclaimed individual right of possession. According to Saleh Haider, in tribal areas, the prohibition of communal ownership in the Land Code's Articles 8 and 9 raised the basic question of who could apply for the land based on the prescriptive right. Because tribesmen performed shift agriculture, they could not define land boundaries, and their conflicts of interest with the tribal sheikh and other involved parties left the tribesmen plainly unable to be landholders.[54] Yet, as long as the status quo imposed a certain level of order on the cultivation of land, the government did not dare to disturb it with the new law.

To be sure, with political centralization, the market economy penetrated deep into the tribal areas of Baghdad province and brought large returns from better agricultural conditions. Peasants began to use money to pay for seed, tools, food, and services, rather than barter, and so had to secure a certain level of production for cash income. The development of rural infrastructure and more accessible markets for agricultural produce, however, was limited to areas where the land was productive enough to yield profits. No one was willing to cultivate marginal land without government aid because its return decreased sharply after the owner's share was deducted. Land disputes increased year by year, demanding attention from the government, even as fiscal deficits mounted.

The efforts of Ahmet Tevik Pasha and his committee only bore fruit when Namık Pasha, during his second governorship (1862–67), undertook a legal solution to the problem of uncultivated land by applying the Land Code of 1858 first, ahead of Islamic law, to succession, transaction, and transfer. Midhat Pasha (1869–72) brought Namık Pasha's approach fully into operation, for both were passionate promoters of modernization, keen to encourage agricultural production by introducing the modern idea of private property rights.[55] Consequently, as will be discussed in Chapter 5, the Code's significance in Baghdad may have differed from what historians have described for the empire as a whole.

---

54 Haider, "Land Problems of Iraq," pp. 164–69.

55 The Land Code of 1858 has been reprinted and interpreted by dozens of Ottoman and European legal specialists since its enactment. For example, M. Belin, "Étude sur la propriété foncière," *Journal Asiatique* 5, no. 18 (1861), pp. 390–431, and 19 (1862), pp. 156–212; Ongley, *Ottoman Land Code*, pp. 1–70; Âtıf, *Arâzi Kânûnnâme-i Hümayün-i Şerhi*; Hüsnü, *Arâzi Kânûnnâmesi Serhi*; Serkiz Karakoç, *Tahsiyeli Arâzi Kânûnı ve Tapu Nizamnamesi* (Istanbul: Kitaphane-yi Cihan, 1340 AH [1924]), pp. 175–254; Ebül'ula Mardin, *Toprak Hukuku Dersleri* (Istanbul: Stad Matbaası, 1947).

CHAPTER 5

Land Reform

Although Reşit Pasha (1852–57) had embarked on a new scheme of rejuvenating agriculture and trade to replenish the treasury, the increase in revenues he generated was overshadowed by the unbalanced budgets of his immediate successors. It was not until Namık Pasha returned in 1862 that the governor resumed development policies focused on agriculture and trade in order to boost the economy and thereby increase state revenues. Prioritizing reform of the customary land system, Namık Pasha encouraged private investment in land by ensuring the holding right in the land based on land laws. Midhat Pasha (1869–72), continuing that approach, intensified the reform and established a new regime of *tapu*. His measures generated an immediate response among the people and triggered a rapid spread of *tapu* land in the province, until Sultan Abdülhamid II prohibited land transfer by *tapu* in 1881. This chapter digs into the historical evidence to identify the principles of Namık Pasha's land regulation that underlay *tapu* land tenure in the province. It then turns to Midhat Pasha's administrative, agricultural, and land policies, particularly the essence of his land reform, why that reform raised revenues for the government, and the consequences for *tapu* land tenure after his departure.

1 The Provincial Administration of Namık Pasha, 1861–1868

Roughly a decade after his brief first term (1851–52), Namık Pasha returned to Baghdad as an accomplished governor and political figure. Recalled to Istanbul in 1852, he became the commander-in-chief of the Imperial Artillery (Tophane-i Âmire), and then was promoted to minister of trade in 1853, the year the Crimean War with Russia broke out. In 1854, he was assigned as ambassador to London to secure foreign loans for war finance in London and Paris. Subsequently appointed as the governor in Hüdavendigar (Bursa) and in Kasmanonu and, for a short period, as the commander-in-chief of the Ottoman army, he returned as governor of Baghdad in 1862. Resolving to achieve what he had failed to do before, he was harsher in imposing his rule and pushed forward modernizing reforms that reflected his experiences in London and Paris.[1]

1 Ahmet N. Sinapli, *Mehmet Namık Paşa* (Istanbul: Yenilik Basımevi, 1987), pp. 156–74.

 | DOI:10.1163/9789004384347_007

In private correspondence, Sir Henry Bulwer, the British ambassador to the Ottoman Empire, had written in 1861 from Constantinople to Lord John (soon, Earl) Russell, foreign secretary:

> Namık was one of the first Europeanized Turks, a dashing young colonel, talking French like a Frenchman, and the phonic of the day. He went in this guise and was much admired as Ambassador to London whence he returned just previous to my coming here as secretary in 1838, when I remember bringing him a letter from Lady Blessington.
>
> As everyone in vogue began talking French and affecting French customs, he got disgusted with the idea of appearing rather a Parisian than a Turk, and with the part he had played as the former, becoming somewhat suddenly a rigid Mussulman in his habits and observances but still retaining his European notions as to the necessity of improvement. He is a good soldier, of undoubted probity, and fair abilities; but said to be obstinate, which may prove an inconvenience, since he is a cleverish man [but] he is not a superior one.[2]

As an established governor, Namık Pasha aimed to boost economic growth in order to increase state revenues without oppressive taxation. Repeatedly in his official correspondence with the Porte, he stressed reforms in administration, agriculture, and trade. Because tribesmen played a vital part in agriculture, they had to be settled on the land, even if coercive measures fuelled their discontent against him and his total grip on the appointive power in district administration.

Under Namık Pasha's administrative arrangement, the province was divided into the districts of Mosul, Shahrizor, Khorasan, Khanaqin, Bani Lam, Samarra, Dulaim, Diwaniya, Karbala, Hindiya, Samawa, Amara, and Basra. Each district had a district governor and his deputy, financial officer, an administrative council, a committee of investigation, and an office of Arabic records. Districts generating large tax revenues, such as Diwaniya, had a larger district

2 The letter of Henry Bulwer continues, referring to an incident at Jidda while Namık Pasha was the governor there:

"As to Jeddah, no one when the facts became known seriously accused him of having had anything to do with the unhappy occurrences which took place there. It would be absurd to suppose he had, but he happened to be governor of the town, and then absent at Mecca. This is always to be regretted, and is to a certain extent against his present nomination, but not sufficiently in the absence of any better person to name, to have justified interfering or preventing it."

TNA: PRO 30/22/89, 3 July 1861, Lord John Russell: Papers.

government, subject to tighter control by the governor, with officials to supervise the bridges of Musaib and Hilla and a government storehouse in Hilla. In Karbala, another important district because it governed the cities of the Shiite shrines – Karbala and Najaf – a director was put in charge of administration in Musaib and Najaf. Similar officials were appointed to the other districts, but their duties were not always assigned in the same way.[3] In order to exercise his influence over the legal system, Namık Pasha cleaned up corruption in the religious courts of Baghdad by replacing the chief judge (*mevleviyyet*), the inspector (*müfettiş*), and the vice-judges (*nâibler*) in Baghdad, Mosul, Kirkuk, Basra, and other districts with the ulema in Baghdad, on monthly salaries paid by the government.[4] He also dismissed a long-time troublemaker, the chief of police (*tufunkçu başı*) in Baghdad.

Financial affairs, another main concern of Namık Pasha, were carried out by the offices (*oda*) of *masraf* (expenditure), *vâridât* (revenue), *mâliye tahrîrât* (financial register), *hazîne* (treasury), *muvazzaf* (employment), and *hazîne-i sarrâf* (money-changing treasury). Other administrative duties were the responsibility of the office of administrative council (*meclis odası*), the committee of investigation (*meclis-i tehkikât*), and the office of Arabic records (*arabî tahrîrât odası*). The *defterdar, muhâsebeci*, and *zabit-i komandar*, in charge of the treasury, accounting, and the police respectively, continued to be high officials under direct command of the governor, except for the chief treasurer (*defterdar*), who was an appointee of the Imperial Treasury. Under the governor's supervision, minor officials became more vigorous managers of irrigation, flood control, construction, quarantine, the telegraph, hospitals, and land registration, and the director of the sacred towns Kadhimiya and Adhamiya.[5]

---

3 The administrative officials in the district of Hilla were a director of finance (*müdîr-i mâl*) and a money changer (*sarrâf*) in charge of financial affairs; a director of secretariat (*müdîr-i dîvân*), a scribe of council (*kâtib-i meclis*), and an Arabic scribe (*kâtib-i arabi*) for civil administration. In the district of Karbala, financial affairs were carried out by a scribe of finance (*kâtib-i mâl*), a scribe of tax (*kâtib-i bedel*), and a money changer, while civil administration was performed by a scribe of council, an Arabic scribe, a scribe in Najaf (*kâtib-i Nacaf*), an official of the sacred town (*memûr-u selâm*), and an official of village (*memûr-u kur'a*). BOA, İ. Meclils-i Mahsus 1011, 15 Rebiyülahîr 1278.

4 The positions of chief judge (*mevleviyyet*), inspector (*müfettiş*), and vice-judge (*nâib*) in Baghdad had been reorganized according to the judiciary reform after the Tanzimat. BOA, İ. Dahiliye 39494, 4 Cemaziyelâhir 1284; TNA: FO 195/1370, Baghdad, 11 Feb. 1881.

5 Christoph Herzog, *Osmanische Herrschaft und Modernisierung im Irak: Die Provinz Bagad, 1817–1917* (Bamberg: University of Bamberg Press, 2012), pp. 123–31; Keiko Kiyotaki, "The Implementation of the Administrative Law of 1864 in the Province of Baghdad," in Markus

Mosul was set up as an independent province, and Shehrizor and Basra as the type of district called *sancak*. The smaller unit of the district, locally called *kâimmakâmlık*, and the lesser unit, known as *müdîrlik*, were administered by the *kâimmakân* and *müdîr* respectively, both under the governor's direct supervision. The districts' officials differed in numbers, titles, salaries, and duties – a district that generated larger tax revenues had a larger district government. The tribal domains of the Muntafiq, the Dulaim, and the Bani Lam remained *kâimmakâmlık*, but Namık Pasha applied a tighter version of divide and rule by separating certain sub-districts from the paramount tribal sheikh's authority and putting them under his own direct supervision. They usually corresponded to tax farming units in which the tax farmer was the tribal sheikh, local governor, or military commander. Where the district governor used the military to collect taxes, the tribesmen generally suffered oppression, but the paramount tribal sheikh was unable to help them, as his privileges of jurisdiction over his tribesmen had been curtailed substantially. In the tribal sub-districts of Abu Muhammad, Shatt al-Arab, Kut al-Amara, Dulaim, Ufak, Dughara, Budair, Hindiya, and Diwaniya, in which civil and criminal courts were not established, the administrative council dealt with minor legal cases, either with or without the tribal sheikh's cooperation.

Although Namık Pasha succeeded in centralizing authority in tribal areas, he did not change the established system of civil administration associated with tax farming. Peasant tribesmen frequently rose up against local administrators and military commanders, but as long as those officials' salaries and expenses depended on tax revenues, they would not change the status quo.

With his powerful government, and with his military forces bolstered by conscription in the towns and tribal areas, Namık Pasha increased expenditures to extend his direct supervision over public finance, tribal administration, foreign trade, domestic commerce, agriculture, and the currency market. When agriculture was hit by drought and a huge drop in the harvest during his second year in office, he set up, without delay, a committee to conduct an economic survey and commenced projects for agricultural development and increasing state revenues. Among his innovations were a flat tax on date groves on the bank of the Shatt al-Arab as an incentive to encourage export, an experimental planting of Egyptian cotton seed in Basra, the distribution of samples of American cotton seed among landowners and tax farmers, and the employment of agricultural specialists from Egypt to assist cotton growers. He also attempted to improve the production of grains, despite a decline in their prices

Köhbach, Gisela Procházka-Eisl, and Claudia Römer, eds., *Acta Viennensia Ottomanica* (Vienna: Selbstverlag des Instituts für Orientalistik, 1999), pp. 216–17.

on international markets. In addition, 1,500 okka of seeds were imported from India, and although their distribution was limited to a few handfuls of seed for three to four persons, it introduced potatoes, other vegetables, and fruit from Europe and India, and like some of his other efforts that failed, still fostered among the people ideas of modern and commercial agriculture.

Foreign trade enlarged dramatically under Namık Pasha.[6] Better seed, modern equipment, and miscellaneous commodities were actively traded in the market, and the commercial crops of cotton, tobacco, and wool were in particularly high demand for export.[7] Supporting this improvement were the port facilities Namık Pasha had upgraded to accommodate more ocean- and river-going vessels, the shipping company he set up to carry pilgrims between Basra and Jidda as well as to trade goods, and a steamboat from Belgium put into use with the aid of Egyptian engineers. He also reorganized the customs house in Basra to speed up the process of quarantine and customs clearance for a greater number of ships, and, in order to prevent tribal sheikhs from illegally collecting tolls, he established new customs houses in Amara and Kirkuk along the Tigris River.[8] By 1863, the telegraph line was about to be extended from Baghdad to Basra through Hilla, Karbala, Najaf, and Suq al-Shuyukh along the Euphrates River, and a new commercial court in Mosul dealt with commercial disputes throughout the province.[9] In the following year, the governor established the Euphrates and Tigris River Navigation Company, which promoted the expansion of trade beyond the traditional transit commerce in the region.

Taking advantage of the improved infrastructure and lowered tariff, British and local traders enlarged the transit trade of grains with Persia.[10] When a merchant in the province purchased grains from one part of Persia and re-exported them to another part of Persia, the Persian import duty was 4 per cent and the reduced export duty was 1 per cent, for total 5 per cent tariff on the transit trade of grains. Compared to a tax of 8 per cent imposed on wheat brought to Baghdad from Mosul by river, the 5 per cent transit duty was far lower than the tax on internal trade as of 1865. Upset by the lucrative profits

6 The position of chief merchant (*re'is al-tujjār*) was given to the powerful native merchant Abd al-Wahab Chelebee.

7 In 1841, barley was 5 kuruş per kilo, and wheat was 9 kuruş per kilo. In 1842, they were 3 kuruş and 5.75 kuruş each. Market prices of these crops increased by five times after the Crimean War.

8 BOA, İ. Dahiliye 37186, 26 Zilkade 1281.

9 BOA, İ. Meclis-i Vâlâ 23361, 26 Cemaziyelahîr, 1281.

10 Namık Pasha had not yet interfered in private transactions nor enforced the penalty on the exchange of foreign coins for local currency at arbitrary rates influenced by supply and demand. TNA: FO 195/752, No. 51, 19 Dec. 1863.

of the transit trade with Persia, Namık Pasha seized the chartered boats of the Lynch and Hector companies on the Zab River and imprisoned their captains. The pasha then applied a strict new rule, under which the Persian grain re-exported by British traders was subject to an additional duty at the general rate of 4 per cent.[11] British and other foreign subjects who traded the produce or industrial goods made in their own countries, however, were not affected by this measure, which was aimed at foreign nationals who purchased Persian grain for re-export. In addition, the governor replaced corrupt officials at the Basra customs house with new officials and more assistants.

While encouraging trade, Namık Pasha made an effort to extend the cultivation of grain for export. His purchases of grain for export were large, especially in Abu Ghraib, which produced 7,000 tons of grain annually, and in Mahmudiya, which produced 5,000–6,000 tons in a good harvesting season.[12] As Ottoman, Persian, British, French, Swedish, and Belgian ships now carried passengers besides manufactured goods and wheat, barley, dates, animal skins, and woods for export, by the time Midhat Pasha took office in 1869, four to five vessels were arriving every day from major ports in the Gulf region, India, and

11 If a trader exported 141 tagar of wheat to Persia, his purchase price was 169,200 kuruş (141 tagar of wheat at 1,200 kuruş per tagar), and his duty, at 12 per cent, was 20,304 kuruş. Even if he received a discount of 20 per cent of that duty, or 4,060.80 kuruş, owing to competition of tax farmers on customs duties, he paid 9.6 per cent of the purchase price, or 16,243.20 kuruş, as the duty. It was still higher than the 5 per cent transit duty. TNA: FO 195/717, No. 20, 21 May 1862.

12 According to the memoir of J.B. Bewsher, the tax revenues were large, though they fluctuated depending on the enterprise and capital of the farmers, the rise of river water, and the flight of the locusts. He gave his estimation of the revenues in 1866 as follows:

Canals	Tax revenue (keran)
Abu Ghraib	22,500
Ruthwaniya	6,000
Mahmudiya	11,050
Iskandariya	1,150
Musaib	86,440
Nasiriya	3,041
Mahawil	17,500

Note: Tariff rate of Mehmed Shah keran was 5 piaster and current market rate was 5 5/40 piaster. TNA: FO 195/803 A, No. 30, 18 May 1864.

J.B. Bewsher, "On Part of Mesopotamia Contained between Sheriat-el-Beytha, on the Tigris, and Tel Ibrahim," *Journal of the Royal Geographical Society of London* 37 (1867), p. 181.

Persia. At the same time, numerous small boats transported local produce and occasionally passengers to those ports from Muhammara, Qurna, and other towns on the Shatt al-Arab; from Suq al-Shuyukh, Samawa, and Hilla on the Euphrates River; and from Kut al-Amara and Baghdad on the Tigris River.

Because grain exports yielded off-budget revenues for development projects and other extraordinary expenditures, Namık Pasha attempted to increase by 6,000 tons the wheat and by 4,100 tons each the barley and rice sent to ports on the Red Sea during 1863. He solicited the approval of the Porte to advance 1.5 million kuruş to induce merchants to invest in grain production. He issued orders to collect about 2,000 tons of wheat and barley in Hilla and Basra for export to Jidda and enough in the following year to achieve the export of 4,500 tons. In the shortage of grain production, the government's purchase of grains increased their prices in both urban and rural areas. Between 1857 and 1867, as a result, the real price (in shillings) increased by 41 per cent for local wheat, 72 per cent for barley, 68 per cent for superior rice, and 70 per cent for inferior rice.[13]

Although the price hikes in grain should have motivated producers to increase their production, supply was insufficient to meet demand in Baghdad. The grain shortage was partially solved by purchases from Mosul and Sulaymaniya, facilitated by improved river transportation, road conditions, telegraph communication, and safety in the tribal areas along the road. Still, it was necessary to increase local production in the irrigated area, in which the production cost was cheaper and the yield larger. In 1864, Namık Pasha approved the purchase of imported irrigation pumps and a floating steam engine from the Lynch trading firm at a cost of 2,000 pounds sterling.[14] The Porte, by then receiving an annual remittance of 9 million kuruş from Baghdad, asked Namık Pasha's opinion of a proposal, submitted by the Ottoman ambassador in London, to rent land in the province to a foreign company that would provide floating steam pumps for irrigation. The following year, the pasha had a waterway constructed on the Hindiya Canal, between Suq al-Shuyukh and Qurna, to facilitate navigation. The budget of 15 million kuruş for the project was funded by a 20 per cent tax on the value of all the wood cut for fuel on the

13 In Baghdad, 1 tagar had been equal to 1.216 tons, which became 1.816 tons in Hilla (1.5 times the original amount) and 2.469 tons in Basra (2.03 times). Within a decade, the price of barley became 25 kuruş per tagar in Baghdad, 60 kuruş in Mahawil (2.4 times), and 82.5 kuruş in Hilla (3.3 times). See also Charles Issawi, *The Fertile Crescent, 1800–1914* (Oxford: Oxford University Press, 1988), p. 478.

14 TNA: FO 195/803A, No. 20, 13 Apr. 1864; No. 40, 10 Aug. 1864.

bank of the Tigris. Nevertheless, again production remained slow to respond to the opportunities and incentives for rapid growth.[15]

Local people, particularly peasants, continued to suffer from the weakness of the kuruş in the local market, although it was stable against the British pound sterling in the Istanbul exchange market. Because the peasants had to pay their tax in cash, the shortage of good coins forced them to pay in devaluated coins.[16] In contrast, some tribal sheikhs enjoyed large increases in cash income from commerce, transportation, and trade. Those who had been drawn to tax farming also gained, but its market was small and affected by non-market factors. Some two decades earlier, Necip Pasha had expressed concern over the tendency to invest in residences, land, and other immovable properties before agricultural land had become a commodity of transaction.

Now that agricultural conditions had changed, with greater stability in the tribal domains, an improved rural infrastructure, and water-control projects, emerging investors began to purchase agricultural lands. Earlier, Reşit Pasha's desire to sell uncultivated land for revitalization by the purchaser was thwarted when the land legislation of the Porte failed to overrule Islamic law and customs in many transactions. Consequently, Namık Pasha realized the need to overcome such constraints in order to make the transaction of land and its title secure enough to attract enthusiastic investment in agricultural land. Confident in his provincial administration in Baghdad, as will be discussed in the following, he turned to land reform based on the Land Code of 1858 for a fundamental solution to the knotty problem of land tenure in the province.

2 Land Regulation under Namık Pasha

In the third quarter of the nineteenth century, an intervention in the customary practice of landholding was necessary to boost land use in the province of Baghdad. In the past, reform had demonstrated the sultan's symbolic authority without practical effect, but Namık Pasha backed up efforts to put landholding in order with changes in local administration, agricultural management, tax farming, and land legislation. In doing so, he took advantage of political centralization, the expansion of trade, better land laws, and greater popular

15 TNA: FO 195/803B, No. 9, 8 Mar. 1865.

16 TNA: FO 195/113, No. 26, 16 Apr. 1832; No. 56, 27 July 1832; No. 65, 29 July 1833; No. 67, 5 Sept. 1833; BOA, İ. Dahiliye 2133, 21 Receb 1257; Jean Baptiste Rousseau, *Description du pachalik de Bagdad* (Paris: Treuttel et Würtz, 1809), pp. 25–28; Mehdi J.H. al-Bustani, "Bağdad'daki Kölemen Hâkimiyetinin Te'sisi ve Kaldırılması ile Ali Rıza Paşa'nın Vâliliği (1749–1842)," Ph.D. diss., Istanbul University, 1979, pp. 330–35.

concern for agricultural development. His survey committee already had highlighted the effects of financial disarray, tense relations with foreign nationals, and inefficient land use and had suggested measures to deal with them. What remained was to make the drastic change of converting uncultivated private land to state land by creating a legal basis for determining ownership over the uncultivated private land.[17]

Namık Pasha's reforms provided private individuals a valid title deed that confirmed their new ownership over uncultivated land. Those reforms recognized *uqr* as the owner's right to its share in the land's produce and granted it to him officially. Because of this change in land tenure, the governor could take control of the uncultivated lands and put them under the regulation of the Land Code and other land laws. To reinforce the new measures, Namık Pasha drafted a memorandum spelling out regulations for land with *uqr* and sent it to the Supreme Council of Judicial Ordinances in Istanbul. The memorandum was examined, enacted as an official decree in 1866, and sent back to the Baghdad administration. Most articles of the decree duplicated the existing principles of Ottoman land laws, but others reconfirmed the conversion of uncultivated private land to state land governed by the Land Code of 1858 and the Law of Land Registration of 1859.[18] The decree, titled "Memorandum Including Seventeen Articles on Land in the Province of Baghdad and the Districts of Shahrizor and Basra," is summarized here to demonstrate how Namık Pasha would apply the code to uncultivated private land and state land:

(1) The private land, whose owners are extinct in default of inheritance, is converted to state land and sold to the individual in accordance with the laws.

(2) The purchaser should be an Ottoman subject, not a foreign national or his protector. Any transactions involving these people are invalid. He need not be an inhabitant of a town or village in which the land is situated; he need only ensure its cultivation.

---

17 BOA, İ. Dahiliye 37186, 26 Zilkade 1281; İ. Meclis-i Vâlâ 24610, 24 Şevval 1282.

18 In order to complete the land registration, whatever the purpose of the application was, the form of a *lâyıha* (memorandum), a temporary application form, and a transliteration of the *ilmühaber-i muvakkat* were sent with an official report (*mazbata*) to the Office of Land Registry (Defterhâne) in Istanbul. The local authorities dealing with the transfer of the title were the treasury official (*mâl memûru*) and the administrative council (*meclis-i kebîr*) of the district government. The land transactions included *ferâğ* (sale, cession, or alienation), *intikâl* (transmission by inheritance), and *mahlûlât* (vacancy, escheat). The fees for land transfer were *resm-i tapu, resm-i ferâğ*, and *resm-i intikâl*. BOA, İ. Meclis-i Vâlâ 24610, 24 Şevval 1282.

(3) For the transfer of the land, the area, the estimated production, and other information are surveyed and recorded in an application form. Based on this survey, an official report is prepared and sent to the Office of Land Registry in Istanbul. Upon its receipt, a *tapu* title deed and its counterfoil shall be sent back to the provincial government in Baghdad. They shall be kept in the provincial treasury in Baghdad, and at the time of the transfer, with supervision of the treasury official and the administrative council, are given to the purchaser.
(4) The land is first offered to the neighbours of the land for immediate payment, and if they do not want it, it is to be put up at auction. If no one purchases it, the land is given gratis to the person willing to reclaim it on the condition of its being farmed in the future.
(5) All transactions, such as sale, cession, alienation, and transmission by inheritance, vacancy, and escheat, should be duly recorded in the title deeds to the land.
(6) The land is escheated to the government and given to another person if it is not cultivated for three years.
(7) The block of the land irrigated by a single river or canal is transferred either piece by piece or as a whole to a single person or to two or more persons jointly. The transferred land should include all defective portions of the land.
(8) When the land is extremely infertile due to its distance from water runnels, the cost of digging and dredging a canal, if necessary, is paid only once by the government. For the land registration, the area, estimated production, and other information are to be surveyed and recorded in an application form.
(9) Based on this survey, an official report is to be prepared and sent to the Office of Land Registry in Istanbul. On receipt of the application, the title deed is sent back to the government in Baghdad and given to the purchaser under the supervision of the treasury official and the administrative council. The counterfoil is kept in the Baghdad treasury.
(10) A tithe tax is imposed on the transferred land and collected as the government's share of the produce, as practised locally.
(11) For the transferred private land, the old taxes (*harâç* and *öşür*) are cancelled, and a new tithe tax is imposed on a fair basis.
(12) On the private land, the owner receives the owner's share [of the produce] by means of leasing, share cropping, and tax farming. But his right is examined by a land committee. If the owner's title is invalid, it becomes null. If the owner can prove his ownership for a period of 100–150 years,

he is granted the right to claim the share. If he can prove his landholding for forty years by proper evidence, he can also take the share.

(13) The owner's share is granted to the owner whose title to the land is affirmed. The share varies from one-fortieth, one-thirtieth, or one-twenty-fifth, to at most one-twentieth of the produce, and the exact share is inscribed in the title deeds. Other than the right to the share, the land is transferred according to the Law of Land Registration, and thus the transaction fees are duly collected.

(14) Where the holder of the owner's share dies in default of inheritance, the arrangement is dissolved. In this case, the legal status of the land is not changed; the ownership is vested in the state, and possession is left to the person holding the land.

(15) Only the owner of the land with the valid title deed can claim the share of the produce.

(16) If the land is entrusted to a religious institution in a legal way, whose title is confirmed by the commission, the owner's share ascribed to such land is guaranteed.

(17) State-owned gardens can be auctioned in the same way as other state land.

(18) When there is no purchaser, the land is farmed out or administered by the government until its sale.[19]

Clearly, Namık Pasha's affirmation of the state's ownership of uncultivated private land put it under Ottoman land law instead of Islamic law. An owner's right to land was transformed into a right to claim an owner's share in the produce. This had no connection with ownership and possession of the land, for the pasha established the owner's claim to the share as *uqr* acknowledged by Ottoman land law rather than by local custom and tradition.[20] Any title deed, official edict, deed of trust in *vakıf*, or registered ownership deed to claim the *uqr* share was examined and confirmed by the government, not by the Islamic

19 BOA, İ. Meclis-i Vâlâ 24610, 24 Şevval 1282.

20 A structural change in the institution of the property right is considered one of the reasons for economic growth in Europe since it reduced the transaction costs, which pushed up the level of production. In the province of Baghdad, this approach could partially explain the development of agriculture after the land code. For the connection of the property right and the economy, see Douglass C. North and Robert P. Thomas, *The Rise of the Western World: A New Economic History* (Cambridge: Cambridge University Press, 1973); Armen A. Alchian and Harold Demsetz, "The Property Right Paradigm," *Journal of Economic History* 33, no. 1 (1973), pp. 16–27; Douglass C. North, *Institutions, Institutional Change, and Economic Performance* (Cambridge: Cambridge University Press, 1990).

courts. Namık Pasha's decree, moreover, set the maximum share of *uqr* while respecting the local practice of crop sharing.

The land commission investigated a claim to ownership of the land by occupation, based on the witness of birthplace recognized by Islamic law and regarded as sufficient evidence when the owner proved his actual holding of the land for forty years. The owner's share, *uqr*, however, was governed by Islamic law, under which the owner was entitled to the exclusive possession and enjoyment of his right. Although this entitlement to his share resembled the absolute ownership of private properties, the *uqr* shareholder was not allowed to interfere with the ownership or cultivation of the land and was not obliged to bear any reclamation costs.[21]

According to a regulation issued in 1874 on the title deeds of private properties, the Office of Land Registry issued the ownership deed to the owner of the private property in place of the deed issued by the Islamic court. Because the title deed and the ownership deed were issued on the same land, *uqr* land was called the "land of two title deeds" in a later period.[22]

The regulations laid down by Namık Pasha became the guidelines for implementing the principles of the Land Code of 1858 and the Law of Land Registration of 1859 in the province. In 1866, he appointed land officials for Baghdad, as he had for Mosul and Shahrizor in 1863. These officials registered the land in accordance with the Law of Land Registration and its supplementary regulations. The land was surveyed in terms of its location, size, estimated production, kinds of land tax, reasons for transfer, sales price, estimated land value, the amount of immediate payment, and costs of registration. Along with the name of the applicant and the date, all of this information was recorded on a land registration form.[23] A copy of the form and the official report were sent to the Office of Land Registry in Istanbul, and upon their receipt, the official

21 The title deeds used to claim the right of *uqr* included *berât, emr-i âlî, vakfiyye* (deed of trust in *vakıf*), or *müseccel-i hüccet-i şeriye* (registered ownership deed). The proof of occupation was based on the *şâhit ikâmesi* (witness of birthplace recognized by Islamic law). The new title deed issued by the Office of Land Registry was called *mülkiyet senedi*. The *uqr* land later was called *iki senedli*. BOA, İ. Meclis-i Mahsus 1641, 27 Şevval, 1287. TNA: FO 371/4150/187296, Administration Report, Revenue Board, Baghdad, 22 Mar.–31 Dec. 1917 (Baghdad: Printed at Government Press, 1918), p. 12; Saleh Haider, "Land Problems of Iraq," in Charles Issawi, ed., *The Economic History of the Middle East, 1800–1914* (Chicago: University of Chicago Press, 1975), p. 190.

22 The immediate payment in this case was *bedel-i misl* or *bedel-i müzâyede* and the costs of registration. The payment was also recorded on a form called *ilmühaber-i muvakkat*.

23 BOA, İ. Meclis-i Mahsus 743, 27 Receb 1276; BOA, İ. Meclis-i Vâlâ 21299, Selh-i Muharrem 1279; İ. Meclis-i Vâlâ 21913, 12 Şevval 1279; İ. Meclis-i Mahsus 1531, 13 Safer 1286.

title deed was sent back to the Baghdad administration and then officially given to the applicant to assure adequate protection of his right to the land.[24]

The landholder usually obtained the title deed (i.e., the possession or cultivation right) from the peasant as collateral for granting the peasant a mortgage or by government auction. He leased the land back to the peasant and received a fixed proportion of the produce as a land rent. The rent was between one-tenth and one-fifth of the total produce in the district of Kirkuk, and between one-fifteenth and one-third of the total produce in the district of Erbil, depending on the location of the residence of the landholder. But delays in administrative procedures and great confusion about land registration arose from the lack of competent authorities before an office of land registry was established in Baghdad. Consequently, a title deed (*tapu*) issued by the land registry was not sufficient to register state land with *uqr*, because the government had not yet concluded what inscription should be made on the deed and in what form the deed should be issued.

In addition, serious disputes erupted among the government, the purchaser of the land, the original owner, any co-owners, and neighbouring owners. The cases raised by landowners who based their right to uncultivated land on Islamic law posed particularly serious problems. Because of these disputes and the administrative difficulties, the transfer of land in *tapu* title had slowed by the time Namık Pasha left office in March 1868 to become the commander-in-chief of artillery of the Ottoman army.[25] Takiyüddin Pasha, formerly the district governor of Shahrizor and deputy governor under Namık Pasha, briefly took over the office, but it was not until Midhat Pasha's tenure that a legal

24 BOA, Ayniyât Defterleri 851, p. 135 (25 Zilkade 1288); İ. Meclis-i Vâlâ 24815, 6 Muharrem 1283; "*Tapu* Law," in Frederick Ongley, trans., *The Ottoman Land Code* (London: W. Clowes and Sons, 1892), pp. 71–110.

25 BOA, İ. Dahiliye 30043, 4 Ramazan 1276; İ. Meclis-i Vâlâ 25173, 12 Cemaziyelâhir 1283; İ. Meclis-i Vâlâ 24815, 6 Muharrem 1283. The market prices of grains per tagar (estimated 3,055 pounds) increased rapidly at the end of Namık Pasha's term (1284 AH [Mar. 1866–Feb. 1867]).

	3/1866 (shillings/tagar)	2/1867 (shillings/tagar)	% Change
Mesopotamian Wheat	119	168	+41%
Persian Wheat	180	227	+26%
Superior Rice	98	165	+68%
Inferior Rice	90	153	+70%
Barley	69	119	+72%

SOURCE: TNA: FO 195/803A, NO. 67, ENCLOSURE NO. 3, "REPORT OF THE TRADE," 24 JULY 1867.

solution was reached for the Code's application, and agriculture attracted private investment.

3 The Administrative Reforms of Midhat Pasha, 1869–1872

Midhat Pasha's achievements in Baghdad were testimony to the modernization that had taken place since the term of Reşit Pasha. The population in the urban areas had nearly doubled since Ali Rıza Pasha's conquest in 1831, although the estimated totals varied from 120,000 to 150,000.[26] Owing to the peace and order established during centralization, the rural population also had increased. This steady, continuous population growth, in turn, had required more government services and public works in cities and villages, as well as increased supplies of goods and food. It thus triggered development and change in agriculture, the economy, tribal society, and the system of administration itself.

Inspired by these demographic factors and the quest for modernization, Namık Pasha's eventual successor, Midhat Pasha, more thoroughly implemented the Provincial Administration Law (Vilâyet Law) of 1864.[27] He divided the province of Baghdad into ten districts: Mosul, Shahrizor, Sulaymaniya, Baghdad, Dulaim, Hilla, Karbala, Amara, Muntafiq, and Basra. Stationed in each district centre was a battalion of regular troops, reinforced by soldiers chosen by lottery in Baghdad, Karbala, and Diwaniya and by the incorporation of the dissolved irregular troops of tribesmen into the new Ottoman army. The districts were divided into sub-districts, each of which was further divided into villages as its smallest unit.

On each level of administration, the governor devised a system of hierarchical bureaucracy that put every district and sub-district centre under the direct control of the provincial centre of Baghdad. The provincial administration comprised six divisions, dealing with domestic affairs, finance, judicial

26 *Zevrâ*, no. 9, 2 Cemaziyelevvel 1286; no. 12, 23 Cemaziyelevvel 1286; no. 43, 18 Muharrem 1287. The 1869 census recorded the total number of households in Baghdad as 18,407. The total recorded male population of 63,672 included 52,689 Muslims, 9,325 Jews, and 1,258 Christians. The 2,411 foreign nationals comprised 2,126 Persians, 265 Britons, 14 Russians, 3 French, and 3 Austrians. According to Ceylan, a household was a housing complex that accommodated several houses. Ebubekir Ceylan, *The Ottoman Origins of Modern Iraq: Political Reform, Modernization and Development in the Nineteenth-Century Middle East* (London: I.B. Tauris, 2011), pp. 32–33.

27 For the Provincial Administration Law of 1864, "Vilâyet Nizâm-nâmesi," in *Düstur*, 1st series, (Dâr-i Saadet (Istanbul): Matbaa-yı Âmire, 1289–1335 AH), i, pp. 608–24; Roderic H. Davison, *Reform in the Ottoman Empire, 1856–1876* (Princeton, NJ: Princeton University Press, 1963), pp. 136–57; İlber Ortaylı, *Tanzimattan Sonra Mahalli İdareler, 1840–1878* (Ankara: Sevinç Matbaası, 1974), pp. 33–42.

and legal affairs, trade and commerce, education, and public works, as well as an additional specialized division for foreign affairs. In the district and sub-district centres, administrative offices for each division were set up under the direct control of the division's headquarters in Baghdad.[28] At the government house, constructed in every district and sub-district centre to carry out civil administration, were employed the assistant to the governor and the scribes, such as the document official, keeper of archives, and writing master. Even a small sub-district in a tribal area had a government house established under the chief administrator. An administrative council was organized in all centres to perform consultative functions, and a treasurer's office in all districts and sub-districts kept the account books, paid salaries to government employees, and supervised tax farming in conjunction with the local governor and members of the administrative councils.[29] In the district and sub-district offices of the administrative divisions of education, public works, trade, and foreign affairs, officials and staff appointed by the head department in Baghdad carried out the routine of administration. A considerably expanded department of public works reflected the development of communication and transportation. Telegraph lines connected all major towns in the province between Mosul and Basra, and the government subsequently extended them from Baghdad through Baʿqūba to Khanaqin and to Mandali in the south-east.[30] District telegraph officials in Mosul, Shahrizor, Baghdad, Hilla, Karbala, and Basra were to maintain and repair the lines under supervision of the department of public works (*nâfia*).

The penetration of financial officials into rural and tribal domains, which proved effective in tribal administration under Namık Pasha, was continued by Midhat Pasha. The governor appointed local treasurers (*muhâsebeci* for all the districts, and *müdîr-i mâl* and *katib-i mâl* for all the sub-districts) supervised by the *defterdar*. Their presence in local towns, combined with those of the administrators and military officials, conveyed financial affairs as a real business to taxpayers and tribesmen. These officials carried out all financial

28 Halil Sahillioğlu, "Osmanlı Döneminde Irak'ın İdarî Taksimatı," *Belleten* 54, no. 211 (1990), pp. 1233–57.

29 The increase of 1,216,123 kuruş in revenue for the tax farm (*mukâtaa*) of Karataş for the fiscal year 1868–69 (1285 AH) was used to pay the civil officials, whose numbers increased because of the administrative reform. BOA, İ. Meclis-i Mahsus 1664, 27 Zilkade 1287.

30 Construction began on a telegraph line connecting Baʿqūba, Shahriban, Quzlarbat, and Dali Abbas, and was about to begin on new lines in Sulaymaniya, Rawanduz, and Erbil, although the financing of construction and operating costs had not been completed. BOA, İ. Dahiliye 41857, 19 Receb 1286; Mustafa Kaçar, "Osmanlı Telegraf İşletmesi," in Ekmeleddin İhsanoğlu and Mustafa Kaçar, eds., *Çağını Yakalayan Osmanlı!* (Istanbul: Yıldız Matbaacılık ve Yayıncılık, 1995), pp. 73–78.

functions: keeping the account books, paying salaries to government employees, and distributing aid, stipends, and reimbursements. The growing role they played in tax farming, such as measuring, collecting revenue, and keeping records, along with the presence of the local governor and members of the local administrative council, intimately connected the government with local peasants, tribesmen, tribal sheikhs, and tax farmers.

The civil, criminal, and commercial courts were drastically reorganized, curtailing the tribal sheikhs' power. Civil and criminal cases were brought to the Superior Court of Revision and Appeal, and all commercial cases were dealt with in the commercial court. The Superior Court was divided into civil and criminal divisions, each with a paid judge and four unpaid juries. Each division's judge and two of its juries were Muslim, while the other juries were Jewish and Christian. In the district and sub-district centres, minor courts dealt with simple cases at the local level. To supervise the proceedings of the different courts and to prevent and correct irregularities, the government set up a Council of Justice, which was composed of a president and seven members. Two of its members were the public prosecutor and his assistant, and the other members were the presidents of different divisions of the courts. The public prosecutor and his assistant were required to attend all sittings of the council.[31]

Midhat Pasha also drove forward the modernization of the province. Population growth, political centralization, and peace and order in the tribal areas facilitated the modernization and began to involve the private sector in productive economic activities. In order to draw even more attention from private individuals, in 1869 the governor started a gazette, *Zevrâ*, which publicized his views on the modernization of the economy, society, policies, and programmes. In numerous issues, he called for progressive change in living standards, society, and the cultural way of life, as well as in agriculture, commerce, manufacturing, and foreign trade.

To improve the urban economy, Midhat Pasha restructured a municipality that short-term governor Takiyüddin Pasha had established in Baghdad in 1868. Responsible for performing services for the amelioration of urban life and various public duties, such as widening roads, cleaning streets, constructing pavements, installing streetlights, and renovating Necip Pasha's public park, it also built a new bridge across the Tigris River in the city centre and relocated the old one. A horse-drawn streetcar was introduced in Karkh for public transportation, and more elementary schools were opened throughout the city, in keeping with the Porte's scheme of developing an education system. In addition, facilities to provide drinking water were set up in residential

31 TNA: FO 195/1370, No. 17, 11 Feb. 1881; BOA, İ. Meclis-i Mahsus 1664, 27 Zilkade 1287.

areas.[32] Because the increased numbers of paid workers in the city and the overall population growth were expected to drive up both the demand for food and its price, in the suburban areas, lands were put to use for commercial crops, attracting peasants to cultivate them and affecting the tribal peasants' settlement on the land.

4 Tribal Settlement

Midhat Pasha's drive to establish his authority in the tribal domains began in Dughara, Budair, and Ufak, in the former district of Diwaniya, where a riot had broken out shortly before his arrival. In this area, the peasant tribesmen comprised a number of small tribal clans under the control of the paramount sheikhs of the large tribes of Zubaid, Khazaʿil, Albu Shil, Shalal, Azalan, Bani Hakim, and Albu Sultan. The district governor in Diwaniya had exercised his authority over the tribal sheikhs mainly through the operation of tax farming, but due to his incompetence and corruption, the sheikhs' tax payment was always delayed or often not made at all. The majority of the peasant tribesmen, moreover, were Shiites strongly tied to the Shiite ulema in Karbala and Najaf, who were only outwardly obedient to the Ottoman government. Namık Pasha had been unable to prevent the spread of this branch of Islam among the peasant tribesmen, and after the change in leadership in Baghdad, the tribesmen in Diwaniya took up arms to challenge Midhat Pasha into giving them a tax discount as a compromise. At that point, because most of the sheikhs did not pay their dues to the government, their collective tax arrears amounted to 10 million kuruş, about one-third of the total arrearage for the province.

Midhat Pasha immediately reinforced the Sixth Army in Baghdad and created an additional regiment of troops. The soldiers were uniformed and better equipped, and a textile factory had been built in Baghdad to produce their uniforms. He also dissolved the undisciplined irregular troops composed of tribesmen. The strengthened military forces were stationed in the districts of Mosul (including Samarra), Sulaymaniya, Shahrizor, Baghdad, Dulaim, Karbala, Hilla (in Diwaniya), Amara (in Kut), Muntafiq, Basra, and Nejd, while the newly formed regiment was sent to new fortresses in the Ottoman-Persian boundary area. Other new fortresses also were constructed along the Euphrates River.[33]

---

32 Ceylan, *Ottoman Origins of Modern Iraq*, pp. 183–86.

33 The troops were to be composed of 2,400 cavalrymen and 4,000 infantry men. Nearly 8,000 tribesmen reportedly joined the irregular troops, but they were undisciplined, and Midhat Pasha desired to dissolve the force. Approximately 2,095 men who were recruited

The fighting between the reinforced military troops and the tribesmen was the most violent confrontation in Diwaniya since the battle of 1847–52. The uprising of the tribes was nothing unusual, as they habitually took up arms to reduce their taxes and gauge the military power of a new governor in Baghdad. What made the uprising of 1868 exceptional was the reaction of the pasha, who made no compromise with the rebels and fully mobilized the troops.

Midhat Pasha replaced the corrupt district governor in Diwaniya, Qarbi Pasha, with Tevfik Efendi, who had successfully collected tax arrears in the sub-district of Yeni Köprü. In order to collect all the arrears in Diwaniya, Tevfik threatened to close the major irrigation canals and started constructing a barrage in the Diwaniya Canal with the help of military troops. Armed with modern weapons, the peasant tribesmen proceeded to the government headquarters in Diwaniya, cut the telegraph lines, and killed Tevfik and two other commanders.[34] Three battalions of the Sixth Army were dispatched immediately, but they failed to gain a decisive victory. Considering the uprising a threat to the Ottoman regime, rather than a mere regional riot, Midhat Pasha mobilized the regular troops of cavalry and artillery from the other regiments under the commander-in-chief in Mosul, Ahmet Pasha, and the tribesmen of Nasir, the Sunni governor-sheikh of the Muntafiq, now titled pasha. Midhat Pasha himself proceeded to Hilla, lifting the spirits of Ahmet and his troops, who soon captured the defiant sheikhs and pacified the tribesmen. After this battle, there occurred no serious tribal conflicts.

Having subdued the tribal rebellion in person, Midhat Pasha resolved to implement the Provincial Administration Law in the tribal domains and thus to incorporate the tribal sheikhs into the Ottoman state system.[35] To rule over

---

in 1861–62 were to serve until 1869–70. BOA, İ. Dahiliye 43045, 9 Cemaziyelâhir 1287; BOA, İ. Dahiliye 43370, 29 Şaban 1287; İ. Dahiliye 44880, 26 Zilkade 1288; *Zevrâ*, no. 2, 12 Rebiyülevvel 1286; no. 6, 10 Rebiyülâhir 1286.

34 The details of the tribal uprising (*Divâniye Sancağ-ı Vukuâtı*) were frequently reported to the Porte. For instance, one file, titled "The extract of telegraphic communication with the commander Samih Pasha and local officials on the disturbance in Diwaniya," contains forty-two pieces of correspondence dated from 19 Aug. 1868 to 19 Sept. 1869 (1285 AH), which spell out the Ottoman military operation against the Arab Shiite rebels. BOA, İ. Meclis-i Mahsus 1591, 19 Zilkade 1286; TNA: FO 195/949, No. 12, 29 Sept. 1869, No. 13, 13 Oct. 1869, and No. 14, 10 Nov. 1869.

35 In order to avoid Shiite agitation in the tribal area in the Middle Euphrates, Midhat Pasha tried to appease the Shiite ulema in Karbala and Najaf. His invitation for the shah of the Persian Qajar to visit the Shiite shrines in Karbala and Najaf succeeded in containing the Shiite Muslims, although he imprisoned a number of their rebellious elements while receiving the shah in Baghdad. The pasha also improved the means of transport and routes for the pilgrims. Ceylan, *Ottoman Origins of Modern Iraq*, pp. 201–4.

the large tribal confederations, he established departments of civil, fiscal, judicial, and military affairs in each tribal district, following the model of the successful reorganization of the Zor (Dayr al-Zūr) district in Aleppo province, which the Porte had initiated in the early 1860s.

In Zor, the district town of Dayr, on the Upper Euphrates River at a strategically important point on the roads connecting Aleppo, Damascus, Diyarbakir, Mosul, and Baghdad, had been a lawless area in which the Aniza and the Shammar Jarba tribes interrupted the traffic, disturbed peasants at harvest times, and plundered domestic animals. Since the governor Arsulan Pasha had constructed houses and had settled small groups of nearly 8,000–10,000 peasants in Hama and Hamas and the deserts of Aleppo, however, Dayr had become safer.[36] Implementing a similar policy in the tribal domains of the Muntafiq, the Dulaim, and the Bani Lam, Midhat Pasha attempted to settle the tribesmen in dwellings.

Furthermore, under the Provincial Administration Law the jurisdiction of the tribal sheikh over his tribesmen was cancelled and replaced by a fair trial at the government court. Instead of the sheikh, the district government maintained order and policed villages and farmsteads to protect the peasants' lives. The improvement of the infrastructure; the extension of electric telegraph lines, local roads, and river transportation; and the reinforcement of the military, both as a whole and on the district level, tremendously improved safety in the fields and enabled the peasants to settle and carry out agriculture on a large scale.

In the Muntafiq domain, for instance, sub-districts in Basra and in Diwaniya, created under Reşit Pasha's governorship, were formed into a single district of Muntafiq. The paramount sheikh of the Muntafiq, Nasir Pasha, was appointed district governor, and the district office was divided into departments of internal affairs, financial affairs, and religious affairs under the supervision of the corresponding offices in Baghdad. Such major officials as the assistant to the district governor, local treasurer, and vice-judge were appointed by the provincial governor from among the officials in Baghdad. To reduce tribal influence over the district administration, the new town of Nasiriya was constructed as the district centre and named after the district governor, Nasir Pasha. The district was divided into four sub-districts, each of which was administered by government officials and scribes, while the sheikh's jurisdiction over the tribesmen was abolished, and his imposition of arbitrary taxes and penalties was strictly

36 BOA, İ. Meclis-i Mahsus 1520, 12 Muharrem 1286; İ. Meclis-i Mahsus 1654, 12 Zilkade 1287; İ. Meclis-i Mahsus 1694, 4 Rebiyülâhir 1288.

prohibited.[37] The administrative system introduced in the Muntafiq domain was also applied to the tribal domains of the Bani Lam and the Dulaim, which became the districts of Amara and Dulaim respectively.[38]

In the district of Sulaymaniya, Midhat Pasha reorganized five sub-districts, one of which was established over the tribal domain of the Jaf tribe as the Kalanbar sub-district. The chief of the Jaf, Muhammad Beğ, was appointed as the sub-district governor at a lucrative monthly salary of 5,000 kuruş. He took responsibility for recruiting thirty soldiers annually, increased from eight, and guarded against the Persian tribes on the border. At the same time, he was ordered not to disturb the land settlement of the peasant tribesmen of the Jaf.

Midhat Pasha also vowed to settle in their winter places the tribesmen who migrated between the Ottoman plains in winter and the Iranian highland in summer. To do so, he transferred farmland to them piece by piece, on the condition of five years' tax exemption, except for the tithe and a tax on sheep and cattle.[39] The settlement facilitated land improvement and mobilization of the tribesmen for various public works, and the tribesmen benefitted from commercial and modern agriculture and the reorganization of administration.

5 Agricultural Policies

The successful implementation of the Provincial Administration Law was followed by agricultural improvement in wide areas. In dealing with agricultural policies in his troublesome province of Baghdad, Midhat Pasha relied on his experience as governor of the Tuna province, in today's Bulgaria, where he had witnessed the large-scale introduction of modern crop rotation and improved implements. In Baghdad, the pasha embraced every possible means for development, including the import of modern power-driven machines, fertilizers, and quality seeds; experimental planting of new crops; land settlement; and the improvement of infrastructure, marketing, and exports. Through his gradual introduction of better tools and other innovations to support intensive

---

37 *Zevrâ*, no. 11, 16 Cemaziyelevvel 1286.

38 In 1872, Midhat Pasha established the *sancak* of Ahsa in Nejid for district administration, and the paramount sheikh of the Nejid, ʿAbdullāh al-Faiṣal, was appointed district governor (*kâimmakâm*). When the district of Basra was separated from Baghdad as an independent province in 1875, Nasir Pasha, the paramount sheikh of the Muntafiq tribe, was appointed the new district governor of the Ahsa district in the province of Basra. BOA, İ. Dahiliye 44930, 15 Zilhicce 1288.

39 BOA, İ. Dahiliye 41931, 9 Şevval 1286; İ. Dahiliye 46314, 12 Zilkade 1290; *Zevrâ*, no. 16, 22 Cemaziyelâhir 1286.

agriculture, landholders were encouraged to invest in higher-yielding agriculture and to recruit peasants to operate the new equipment.

A worldwide increase in the supply of iron and steel contributed to the improvement. Previously, because iron had been used for military purposes, its supply and distribution had been under strict official control, but now streetcars, telegraph lines, and other infrastructure projects could take advantage of the greater supply. For peasant cultivators in Baghdad province, as for those in Europe, the reinforcement of ploughs with steel-tipped iron permitted deeper tilling of the soil and expanded cultivation of both heavy clay soil and vast areas of plain that had previously been used only for grazing.

A model farm that Midhat Pasha set up in Aziziya, near Baghdad, demonstrated imported machines, such as a small engine-driven plough that could furrow up to 50 dönüm a day, a tractor, threshing machines, and winnowing machines. The farm publicized the capacities of the machines, how many days they could be used, how they could be obtained, and how to arrange instruction on their operation and maintenance. When the vessel *Babel* arrived in 1868, it brought ten machines for harvesting, one for threshing, and many for ploughing, which were sold at cost. In the same way, imported seed was sold for trial and study. Midhat Pasha also continued Namık Pasha's efforts to install engine-driven pumps for irrigation, which gradually had begun to prevail in spite of the high cost and large initial investment.[40]

Other innovations, including artificial fertilizers, did not prevail. Mid-nineteenth-century advances in chemistry, moreover, could not help Baghdad battle its insects and fungi, particularly in the north, where devastating locusts and other voracious pests regularly damaged crops and animals. Winnowing and seed-cleaning machines were not used in Baghdad either, due to the slow expansion of the grain fields.

Despite the setbacks, contact with modern techniques and technology inspired an increasing commercialization of agriculture and diversification of produce. The twenty-fourth issue of *Zevrâ* featured an article on the importance of agriculture in the local economy that encouraged private investment in the production of cash crops, such as tobacco and cotton, and called for boosting grain production to meet the demand created by urban growth. As Midhat Pasha's policies increased the land's use value and productivity, along with agricultural incomes and tax revenues near Baghdad, investors began to look for similar opportunities in other regions. The most visible result was a government-organized shuffle of uncultivated land among private individuals.

---

40 *Zevrâ*, no. 36, 21 Zilkâde 1286.

The pasha, who may have been familiar with the enclosure of land in England a century earlier, aimed to reallocate private land from inefficient landowners to agriculturalists willing to cultivate it and pay taxes from the produce. His personal involvement in importing modern tools even indicates that he had looked at the enclosure movement carefully and observed its relationship to the introduction of new implements conducive to ploughing wider plots and crop rotation. Similarities to enclosure also are apparent in Midhat Pasha's approach to communal tribal lands. In the area of irrigation agriculture, where the costs of pulling the water channels from the canal and regularly cleaning them were high, he sought to identify the property right of the individual tribesmen in the land in order to determine each individual's liability for maintaining the watercourse.

Midhat Pasha, however, made a serious mistake that affected many peasant tribesmen when he carried out a flood-control project on the Saqlawiya Canal on the Euphrates River. This project was originally planned to revitalize the agricultural lands along the canal free of flooding and thus to attract private investment in commercial agriculture near the city of Baghdad, but it overlooked the traditional role of the canal as a route for water to escape from the Euphrates River. As a result, some 750 cubic metres of water per second were discharged from the Euphrates downstream of Falluja. The high-lying Hilla Branch was incapable of carrying this extra supply, which found its way into the low-lying Hindiya Canal, swept away the temporary dams across its channel, scoured into its bed, and permanently lowered the level of water at the bifurcation. The Hilla Branch immediately began to silt up because less water went down its channel and more down that of the Hindiya, but the barrage was not modified to suit the new conditions. The peasants in the Hilla and Diwaniya districts along the Hilla Branch suffered especially from the decrease in river water usable for irrigation. Not until some thirty-seven years later, in 1909, did the government began to correct this state of affairs by reconstructing the Hindiya Barrage.[41]

Nevertheless, Midhat Pasha's policies and projects were effective on other lands in the Euphrates River basin. Most important, the land irrigated by increased water flow became more fertile. As interest in agriculture increased in response, Midhat Pasha immediately began implementing Namık Pasha's regulation on state and uncultivated private land in order to control the

41 For the project on the Saqlawiya Canal, see Issawi, *Fertile Crescent*, pp. 353–55. The rebuilt structure was made of loose rubble cemented for about 1 metre in thickness along its crest and provided with an opening 20 metres wide in the middle of the river. TNA: FO 195/1076, 5 June 1875.

acquisition of infertile and uncultivated lands in the irrigated area. His goal was to establish a routine of orderly land registration and local issue of the *tapu* title that had eluded the previous governors.

6 The Institutionalization of *Tapu*

For state land, Midhat Pasha's reform was based on legally setting up the owner's share as *uqr* and instituting a firm system of land survey and registration throughout the province. His new regulation was descriptive and decisive in converting uncultivated private land to state land, and it entailed two important changes in the rights in the land. The first acknowledged the owner's share in private land as a property right of *uqr*, and the second changed the traditional cultivation right on the land to an ownership-like property right in the land. In short, the intent was to introduce the concept of private property in land. The principal law supporting these changes was the Ottoman Land Code of 1858, which had been introduced in the province upon its enactment, but which was rarely applied due to the complication of interests in landholding.

In contrast to other governors, Midhat Pasha left numerous writings that eloquently express his political philosophy. The articles in *Zevrâ* also articulate his government's ideas on modernization and land policies: "Lands in this region had been fertile, but now most lands are barren. We should regain the fertility of the past and at the same time, we should develop industry. We should also learn European technology and civilization for our improvement." Taking developed Western Europe as a model, Midhat Pasha apparently desired to introduce an idea of private property right in land in fertile regions such as the province of Baghdad, as the following translated quotation from the first article indicates:

> The protection of the people's rights, security, and justice are the responsibilities of the Sultan, whose tasks have been delegated to government officials. In this province, Reşit Pasha began to improve the state system, but he could not finish the work. Namık Pasha continued his task in the appropriate way. It is still going on. What we should do is to attain the peace and happiness of the state and the people. The quick way of bringing forth the fruit of the wealth and the improvement for the people is to make good conditions. In this way, the wealth is not [increased] cash nor cash hidden in the box. Cash, money, and transaction create the means. The essence of wealth is agriculture, trade, industry, culture, and welfare. The people's profit is the state's profit. The state's profit is the

> people's profit. The two are not different but one common problem. The state treasury gains profit by encouraging the people's wealth and their improvement. For the people's wealth and improvement, it is necessary for the state to improve the state system by reorganization of the administration. The government officials did not work for this purpose. The government employees, whatever their positions, should know they work for the people's happiness and the people should also cooperate with the officials in their work. Some of their work does not show good results directly.[42]

While Midhat Pasha invoked his predecessors' efforts to reform the provincial administration, he promised to prioritize improving the welfare of the people, who for the first time were expected to cooperate in the operation of the state system. He considered it the governor's responsibility to establish a provincial administration in which both the government officials and the people could play a role. In this regard, he believed one of the most important institutions was the property right that he called the *tapu* right (i.e., the possession right registered with the Office of Land Registry for issue of the title deed).[43] It was, therefore, the governor's task to lay down legislation to solve the increasing disputes over the possession right and give the possession right the function of a private property right.

Midhat Pasha deemed private ownership of land better than family or tribal ownership after witnessing how Arab tribesmen fettered to tribal lands were oppressed by their tribal sheikhs. Along with all tribal domains, he intended to liquidate the lands of feudal landowners and tax farmers, to get rid of oppressive taxation by the tax farmers and the heavy burdens of interest payments on the peasants, and to reduce the political and economic power of notable families and tribal sheikhs. Declining tribal traditions or local customs as rules for governing land, the pasha publicly decided to create and ensure an individual property right under the Ottoman land laws and the regulations that he, as governor, would lay down.

Specifically, Midhat Pasha prohibited the customary right of landholding and cultivation granted to a tribal sheikh who organized tax farming as the *serkâr* (bailiff). In place of that customary right, he attempted to create a possession right over the land granted by the state as a reward and to transfer it to the tribal sheikh. Upon this change, the government could apply Ottoman state laws in place of local customs and traditions and could rescind a tax-exempt

42 *Zevrâ*, no. 1, 5 Rebiyülevvel 1286.

43 The Office was called Defter-i Hâkanî.

privilege that had accompanied the grant of land for cultivation. Registration of the land by the tribal sheikh-bailiff accordingly took place in many areas in the Middle Euphrates region.

For Midhat Pasha, increasing the revenues from agriculture was indispensable for financing his other development schemes.[44] In addition, he believed that, unlike agriculture, industry, trade, and commerce were Western-oriented sectors, whose development could only be attained with a certain degree of relationship with Western European countries. Still, the greatest importance of a shift of land policies towards a large-scale application of the Land Code of 1858 would be the immediate income for the government it would generate through registration fees and the even higher revenues eventually returned by productivity due to the owner's investment in agricultural land.[45]

Midhat Pasha's desire for prosperity based on agricultural development was spelled out in an article for the third issue of *Zevrâ*, which was specially titled "Irâkın Esbâb-ı Tednîyesi ve Vesâil-i Terkîyesi" (The Need for Reform and Progress in Iraq):

> Improvement and revitalization of agricultural lands did not take place, because of lack of political authority and public security. Now, ... the prosperity of the state and people is one of the most important targets of the government of the Ottoman Empire. Military reforms and provincial reforms were attempted for this purpose. The consequences of these reforms were significant. In order to attain the glory, which the empire achieved in the past, and now we would wish the most, we should keep advancing reform in the Iraqi region. It is necessary to improve agriculture, industry, and trade to achieve the prosperous state. Especially, rapid improvement in cultivation of Iraqi land is desirous. But it will take place along with the development of industry and trade. For agricultural development, the Euphrates River should be cleaned, as well as to bring into force the system of land registration so that we could secure the possession right in land.[46]

Written early in the pasha's governorship in Baghdad, this article also analyzed the backwardness of the province caused by political instability and a lack of

---

44 ʿAbd al-ʿAzīz Dūrī, "Baghdad," in *The Encyclopaedia of Islam* (Leiden: E.J. Brill, 1960), i, p. 906; Stephen Hemsley Longrigg, *Four Centuries of Modern Iraq* (Oxford: Clarendon Press, 1925), pp. 298–99.

45 BOA, İ. Meclis-i Mahsus 1531, 13 Safer 1286; *Zevrâ*, no. 3, 19 Rebiyülevvel 1286; no. 24, 19 Şaban 1286; no. 36, 21 Zilkade 1286; no. 50, 7 Rebiyülevvel 1287.

46 *Zevrâ*, no. 3, 19 Rebiyülevvel 1286.

safety, which had persisted since the Mongolian invasion, and it reiterated the need for a land registration system for agricultural development. The pasha clearly connected protecting the possession right under the law to promoting agriculture and the economy.

Midhat Pasha knew the function of modern law from his experience as governor of the province of Tuna, when he and former prime minister Fuad Pasha drafted the Provincial Administration Law of 1864 and implemented it in his province. Later, applied throughout the empire, it served as the major state law for the centralization of provincial administration. In the province of Baghdad, where the Provincial Administration Law was implemented by its co-drafter Midhat Pasha, it drastically changed the system of government in the province. But the ultimate goal of that change was to secure the possession right in land for the sake of agriculture and the economy.

Midhat Pasha repeatedly used the *Zevrâ* to explain the benefits of holding land with a valid title deed. In 1867, the inheritance right was extended from female and male children to grandchildren, fathers, mothers, sisters, brothers, husbands, and wives. To remove potential purchasers' concerns about heavier taxation on the land, the governor assured a uniform rate of tax on the produce and guaranteed no additional charges. Declaring officially the difference between the possession right and *uqr*, he encouraged the cultivation of uncultivated land, most of which was previously private land.[47]

The disputes that arose with the progress of land reclamation and sale occurred when a purchaser claimed absolute ownership of the land, even though ownership had reverted to the state and the possession right belonged to another person. These disputes were usually complicated because ownership in uncultivated private land, as well as the owner's right to the share, was often shared by many individuals as a result of succession and transfer according to Islamic law.

Midhat Pasha's idea for coping with land disputes was basically identical to the regulation issued by Namık Pasha:

(1) Those who hold valid ownership deeds have conferred on them the right of *uqr* in the land, while those without deeds but who can prove a forty-year period of possessing the land are also given the right of *uqr*.

(2) Any claim to the *uqr* right is to be promptly examined by the land commission.

47 *Zevrâ*, no. 5, 3 Rebiyülâhir 1286; no. 14, 8 Cemaziyelâhir 1286; no. 50, 7 Rebiyülevvel 1287; no. 68, 15 Cemaziyelevvel 1287; "Copy of Imperial Khat," in Ongley, *Ottoman Land Code*, pp. 158–59.

(3) The *uqr* right is set up separately from the right of possession, and therefore both rights are not sold together by any of the joint owners or by a single owner.
(4) The sale of land is carried out according to the Ottoman practice of preference instead of the Islamic principle of pre-emption.
(5) The transferred land is subject to escheat in the case of non-cultivation for three years and sold to another cultivator at auction.[48]

To implement the crucial fourth regulation, however, Midhat Pasha needed to regulate the practice of preference on state land of which the original owner claimed his share – the Land Code provided no such rule for state land on which the *uqr* share was set up. He consequently drafted a regulation in an official report and submitted it, together with a memorandum from the administrative council in Baghdad, to the Council of State in Istanbul. Following the deliberation of the Council of State, an imperial edict was issued in 1869, and the regulation came into effect.[49]

According to the Land Code, the preference was a right to purchase land at its market value when it was going to be transferred to another person by way of cession, gift, or sale. The preferential right was given first to the owners of properties such as trees and buildings on the land; if they did not claim it, the preferential right was given to the co-owners of the land; if none of them claimed it, it then went to the inhabitants of the village in which the land was situated. The period in which the right could be exercised after the transfer was ten years for owners of trees and buildings, five years for co-owners, and one year for villagers. Those who refused the right once, lost their preference.[50] The right of pre-emption recognized in Islamic law was not applicable to the sale of state land.[51] For land held in partnership, each partner had the preferential right, and no partner could sell his share or give it to another person as a gift without the permission of the other partners. If he sold his share, the

48 BOA, Mühimme Defterleri 263, pp. 11–12.

49 *Zevrâ*, no. 50, 7 Rebiyülevvel, 1287.

50 Arts. 41–44 in Ongley, *Ottoman Land Code*, pp. 1–70; Frederic M. Goadby and Moses J. Doukhan, *The Land Law of Palestine* (Holmes Beach, FL: Gaunt, 1998), pp. 21–22.

51 The Islamic principle of pre-emption (*şufʿa*) was the right to claim private property that had been sold for the price at which it had been sold. A co-owner of the property, a shareholder if any, or a neighbour was entitled to pre-emption and could exercise his right at any time through a proper procedure. Turkey, *Mecelle* (*Mecelle-i Ahkâmı Adliye*), *1879*, prep. Himmet A. Berki (Ankara: Banka ve Ticaret Hukuku Araştirma Enstitüsü, 1959), Arts. 950, 1008–44. The Ottoman practice of preference (*hakk-ı ruçhân*) can be found in the Land Code, Arts. 41–45, in Ongley, *Ottoman Land Code*, pp. 1–70.

other partners had the right to take back that share for its market value during a period of five years.[52]

Based on the Code's principle on preference, Midhat Pasha laid down a new regulation that applied to transaction of the right of possession and the owner's share for the *uqr* land. It held that when the possession right was about to be sold by its owner, it was first offered to the holder of the owner's share. In the case of land without *uqr*, it was offered directly to the inhabitants of the village in which the land was situated. If they did not exercise their preference, the land was sold at auction to the highest bidder. When the owner's share was sold, it was first offered to the person holding the possession right in the land. The sale price was established by multiplying fifteen (fifteen years) by the average of the value of the share for the three preceding years. Those holding both the right of possession and the owner's share could not sell the right and the share separately. Transfer of the owner's share by sale or by inheritance required confirmation by the director of the office of land registry in Baghdad.[53] Because this regulation affirmed that the preference right was applicable to state land converted from private land, the government could reject the claims by the original owners of the land and by the owners of the neighbouring lands who had been entitled to nullify the transaction of the land under Islamic law's right of pre-emption.[54] By applying the rule of preference to the land in which the owner's share of *uqr* was set up, moreover, the government prevented the land from being sold to an outsider and becoming vacant for lack of cultivation.

In order to protect the purchaser's rights in the land, Midhat Pasha established a centralized system of land registration for the province according to the administrative reform of 1864.[55] In Baghdad, the centre of the province, the new office of land registry was supervised by the department of financial affairs. The director of the registry was responsible for land administration in the whole province, assisted by clerks for land registration. In the districts of Shahrizor, Sulaymaniya, Mosul, Hilla, Karbala, and Basra, similar officials were

---

52 BOA, Muktezâ Defterleri 1, p. 249 (19 Muharrem 1284).

53 The report of the administrative council in Baghdad on land use and current regulations on state land and uncultivated private land was submitted to the State Council. It noted that large areas of land had been farmed out to tax farmers who rarely made investment in the lands. Since 1868, for promoting land use and agricultural production, such uncultivated land had been sold according to the attempt to introduce *tapu*. However, in the larger areas of 40,000–50,000 dönüm, for example, the *uqr* owner had claimed the high sum of 3,000–5,000 kuruş as his *uqr* share, discouraging purchase of the land. BOA, İ. Meclis-i Mahsus 1641, 27 Şevval, 1287.

54 Ali Himmet Berki, *Açıklamalı Mecelle: Mecelle-i Ahkâmı Adliye* (Istanbul: Hikmet Yayınları, 1985), pp. 186–206, "Kitab-ül-Hacr vel-Ikrah veş-Şufʿa," Arts. 941–1044.

55 BOA, İ. Meclis-i Mahsus 1664, 27 Zilkade 1287.

appointed to carry out land registration on the local level, but no land officials were assigned to the tribal districts of Muntafiq, Dulaim, and Amara. Together with the members of the administrative councils organized in every district and sub-district, including the other tribal ones, these land officials surveyed the land, assessed its value, and registered it. The title deeds, which had been obtained previously from the Office of Land Registry in Istanbul through a complicated procedure, began to be issued locally at the office of land registry in Baghdad. Once the right to preference was enforced and the office of land registry was set up in Baghdad, the title to land became marketable, and the purchase of vacant land in the province increased dramatically. Even lands remote from Baghdad were sold for speculation, though some went unused due to the high cultivation costs.[56]

Believing that agricultural land could be cultivated more efficiently under private holding, Midhat Pasha also began to transfer cultivated areas of tax farms for payment of their land value, first offering the land to the *uqr* owner and then to the peasant cultivators or the inhabitants of the village where the land was situated. If no one wanted the land, it was sold at auction.[57]

The fiscal position of the province improved tremendously with the profits from the vigorous auctioning of abandoned and uncultivated lands. In 1869–70, the local land registry made 565,620 kuruş from the issue of official deeds, followed by 572,256 kuruş and 609,087 kuruş in the next two years. These amounts alone were nearly equal to the revenues from stamp duties. Revenue from *tapu* title deeds also rose rapidly, from only 43,753 kuruş in the first year of Midhat Pasha's term to 105,534 kuruş, 433,756 kuruş, and 227,975 kuruş in the successive years (Table 5.1). Their increases suggest that the sales of state land and vacant private land show the same trend.[58] In all, due to the increases in land sales, the total revenue of the province of Baghdad between 1862–63 and

56 Midhat Pasha reported that the transaction of *tapu* had been steadily increasing, so he needed to expand the local land registry by appointing two more capable officials. BOA, İ. Dahiliye 42557, 28 Muharrem 1287; İ. Meclis-i Mahsus 1531; İ. Meclis-i Mahsus 1664, 27 Zilkade 1287. BOA, Ayniyât Defterleri 849, p. 145 (20 Safer 1289); Ayniyât Defterleri 851, p. 201 (23 Zilkade 1290); *Zevrâ*, no. 68, 15 Cemaziyelevvel 1287; no. 69, 18 Cemaziyelevvel 1287.

57 TNA: FO 371/4150/187296, Administration Report, pp. 11–12.

58 Land revenue from the sale of state land and vacant private land, or payment of land value (*muaccele*) received for the special account, was 299,149 kuruş in March 1869, or only 16.8 per cent of the total monthly revenue of the province, and in April the figure amounted to 2,488,649 kuruş, or 63.2 per cent of the total. Subsequently the provincial government received 1,514,181 kuruş in May and 375,628 kuruş in June, or 38.3 per cent and 16.9 per cent of its total revenue respectively. BOA, Vâridât Muhâsebesi Defterleri, no. 3483; Mâliyeden Müdevver Defterler, no. 8846.

1871–72 grew at an average rate of 4.8 per cent, while that of agricultural tax revenues between 1846 and 1861 was 1.9 per cent. They indicate the major role land reform played in the improved fiscal position of the provincial government in Baghdad.[59]

7 The Privatization of State Land, 1872–1881

The reorganization of land registration led to the consolidation of scattered, unproductive plots and to better livelihoods for increasing numbers of peasants. Peasants also developed desirable managerial or planning skills when they cultivated the land with assurance of the fruits of their efforts. As the appeal of private investment in land acquisition and agriculture spread among the sheikhs of the peasant tribesmen, in particular, they began to settle in the irrigated area and to take up cultivation. A section of the Shammar Jarba tribe was detached from the authority of the paramount sheikh Farhan, who was given the title of pasha and made the district governor of his tribal domain. The tribal land on the west bank of the Upper Tigris then was granted piece by piece to his tribesmen by registered *tapu* title. Upon its registration, they were assured that they had to pay only the tithe and no other taxes on the land.[60] Other tribesmen, who took possession of state land called *mallâk*, began to distinguish themselves from the peasant tribesmen in socio-economic terms. In irrigated areas, peasant tribesmen were increasingly induced to settle by the prospects of a stable income and better living conditions than migration offered.

---

59 BOA, İ. Dahiliye 31563; İ. Mesâil-i Mühimme 2042; TNA: FO 195/676; Keiko Kiyotaki, "Ottoman State Finance: A Study of Fiscal Deficits and Internal Debt in 1859–63," Working Paper No. 90/05, Department of Economic History, London School of Economics, September 2005, p. 32, published in Kaan Durukan, Robert W. Zens, and Akile Zorlu-Durkan, *Hoca, 'Allame, Puits de Science: Essays in Honor of Kemal H. Karpat* (Istanbul: The Isis Press, 2010), pp. 97–120.

60 The Shammar tribe between Baghdad and Mosul had a troubled experience with land settlement. In 1868 they lost large numbers of livestock because of flooding and had only begun to recover when the tribesmen of Sheikh Farhan robbed the peasants along the Kanan (Kanʿān) Canal in Samarra and those on the Tigris of their cattle and money. A group of tribesmen settled on the west bank of the Tigris River and took up agriculture in response to a lucrative offer from the governor to charge only tithe tax on their produce and to grant the individual tribesmen the land by *tapu*, gratis. However, the incorporation of the whole tribe into the sub-district of Shammar was slow. BOA, İ. Dahiliye 43847, 29 Muharrem 1288; Anne Blunt, *Bedouin Tribes of the Euphrates* (New York: Harper & Brothers, 1879), i, pp. 238–43.

TABLE 5.1 Revenues in the province of Baghdad, 1278–1287/1862–1872 (in Kuruş)

		1278/ 1862–63	1279/ 1863–64	1280/ 1864–65	1281/ 1865–66
Vergi	income tax	6,152,694	6,182,818	5,811,724	6,438,02
Bedel-i asker	exemption from military service	288,137	289,137	420,175	408,12
Öşür	tithe	39,039,006	41,208,602	38,744,911	27,664,26
Ağnâm	sheep tax	2,738,902	2,215,508	2,244,957	2,754,12
Tapu	land title deeds	35,768	103,673	13,142	69,13
Varak-ı sahîh	stamp duty	503,598	536,154	573,263	800,16
Kontratu	contracts	89,417	102,712	84,546	153,16
Harac-ı vasâik	official deeds	0	0	0	
Rüsûm	fees, etc.	7,330,072	7,439,904	11,196,545	11,734,29
Emlâk-ı miri	state estates	0	131,894	23,758	
Orman	forests	0	0	0	
Hâsılât	misc. income	1,174,775	1,719,118	2,361,793	951,39
Total		57,352,369	59,983,520	61,474,794	50,972,68

SOURCE: BOA, MALIYE NEZÂRETI DEFTERLERI, VÂRIDÂT MUHÂSEBESI, 3483.

After Midhat Pasha left office in 1872, the provincial government pursued tribal settlement on a large scale for the next decade. In 1881, however, land sale for tribal settlement was severely curtailed by Sultan Abdülhamid II, and the system of state land developed differently from Midhat Pasha's idea of establishing and protecting the property rights of peasant tribesmen.

In 1873 the government had decided to give tribal lands gratis to nomadic tribesmen, expecting them to settle and farm the land, especially on the travel routes from Baghdad to Aleppo, Mosul, and other local towns. By contrast, the non-nomadic peasant tribesmen were required to pay the land value at its registration, and urban dwelling tribesmen and notables were allowed to purchase at auction only rice fields cultivated solely during flood season or vacant land.[61] That vacant land was divided into pieces of at most five feddân and sold at the low price of 25 lira per feddân, on the condition that purchasers would not resell the land for ten years.

In practice, settlement varied widely by place and by tribe. The Dulaim and Zubʿa tribesmen, who were willing to settle and cultivate the land, were given a

61 BOA, Ayniyât Defterleri 851, pp. 178–81 (Gurre-i Rebiyülevvel 1290).

282/ 866–67	1283/ 1867–68	1284/ 1868–69	1285/ 1869–70	1286/ 1870–71	1287/ 1871–72
3,701,224	5,790,863	5,655,663	5,759,563	6,234,245	5,862,090
427,110	408,233	408,233	512,131	514,491	519,059
4,426,219	38,332,727	27,858,393	37,907,667	51,406,917	65,788,193
1,283,559	2,925,467	2,737,447	3,040,502	4,086,200	4,488,941
52,887	29,430	43,753	105,534	433,756	227,975
371,171	776,911	607,970	672,712	630,567	458,941
48,198	6,144	4,615	59,702	(572,256)	37,699
0	0	0	565,620	572,256	609,087
6,341,142	12,967,001	10,006,875	8,169,783	7,557,283	7,276,498
0	0	109,227	2,159,884	7,500,000	5,777,784
0	0	0	72,971	161,280	168,279
632,511	1,460,913	2,161,622	1,229,944	874,957	641,517
7,284,021	62,697,689	49,593,798	60,256,013	80,544,208	91,856,063

bounty of 500 kuruş per feddân, and the government sent agricultural specialists and irrigation engineers to advise them.[62] Due to the government's efforts, a number of tribesmen in Hindiya, Dughara, and Samawa likewise began to settle to produce grain. The cultivable land that they were offered at moderate prices allowed them to commence seeding immediately, without the need to irrigate or reclaim land. They built a village on high ground along the river, and canals near the marshes, which were safe from the flooding, but some of them began to suffer illness. Khazaʿil, Jashʾam, Afaj, and Zubaid tribesmen were encouraged to settle on land granted in return for them paying the land's market price, while even cultivated tax farms, such as Nasiriya and Tahmasiya in the Middle Euphrates, were granted gratis to nomadic tribes and registered by their tribal sheikhs. In the north, the Hamawand and Jaf tribes began to settle in their farming places through the efforts of Midhat Pasha's successor,

62 Ibid., p. 131 (8 Şevval 1288); pp. 158–59 (28 Cemaziyelâhir 1289); *Zevrâ*, no. 38, 5 Zilhicce 1286.

Mehmet Rauf Pasha (1872–73).[63] Members of the Hamawand were given land in Bazian, on which they built houses, grew crops, and worked as police guards. The Jaf tribesmen in Shahrizor and Sulaymaniya, on the other hand, were separated from the authority of their chief, Muhammad Pasha, placed under the direct administration of the government, and granted land on which to settle, in return for a nominal fee. But some Hamawand and Jaf tribesmen left their settled lands after the departure of Rauf Pasha.

By 1876, agricultural land located in the Muntafiq tribal domain was being auctioned or transferred gratis to the tribal sheikhs, who constructed towns and villages and settled their tribesmen. Revenues obtained by selling state land were spent in resettling more tribesmen in the district, helping to increase the labour supply for cultivation and water-related public projects. At the same time, settlement exposed tribesmen to famine, natural disasters, and plagues, one of the most serious of which hit the marshlands in 1875.[64] While even remote lands in the districts of Erbil, Kirkuk, Baghdad, Dulaim, Karbala, Shamiya (Najaf), Samarra, and Hilla were sold to private investors at auction, tribal landholding also had become widespread outside the tribal districts of Sulaymaniya, Amara, and Muntafiq.

As growing investment in agricultural land improved productivity, Sultan Abdülhamid II became interested in the land. In 1881, he banned the new acquisition of *tapu* title on uncultivated vacant land and only allowed transaction by inheritance, sale, or partition on cultivated land in the province of Baghdad. Instead, he began to acquire the land for his privy purse (*hazîne-i hâss*). Repeatedly dismissing any local government proposals on agricultural issues and requests for a manual on the transfer of state land, he finally issued a decree provisionally to stop all transfers of state land. Nevertheless, the sultan did not state his reservation explicitly, in spite of several requests by the financial authorities, who pointed out that the decree deprived the treasury of a useful source of income. With the exception of a few grants to local sheikhs

---

63 The settlement of the Hamawand, the Jaf, and some other Arab tribesmen was due to the personality of the governor, Rauf Pasha, who had their respect and trust. Sheikh Mahmud in the Rawanduz district rebelled later, and the government subsequently confiscated his lands. TNA: FO 195/996, No. 19, 26 May 1873.

64 BOA, Ayniyât Defterleri 851, p. 234 (Gurre-i Safer 1293); 1012, p. 50 (3 Zilkâde 1292); 1014, p. 179 (Gurre-i Safer 1293); İ. Meclis-i Mahsus 2032, 21 Zilkâde 1290; TNA: FO 195/1076, From Surgeon Major Colvill, Civil Surgeon, Baghdad to Colonel J.P. Nixon, H.M's Political Agent, Turkish Arabia, 5 June 1875.

and other special cases, the local population could no longer purchase state land, and there was no further increase in tribal landholding.[65]

Through their land reform, the two powerful governors, Namık Pasha and Midhat Pasha, made agricultural resources more usable for production. They realized the need to overcome such harsh constraints as *uqr* share and unsecured land title to attract private investment in agricultural land and decisively implemented their reforms. Confident in his provincial administration in Baghdad, Namık Pasha first turned to the Land Code of 1858 as the fundamental land law to follow for a solution to the knotty problem of *uqr* land in the province. Although he slowly established the new principle of state land, his regulation impressed potential landholders to invest in agricultural land. Midhat Pasha, stabilizing the Ottoman rule in the province by the administrative reorganization by law, made functional the former governor's measures. The governor extended administrative tasks from the district to the village level and ended the tribal sheikhs' influence over tribal affairs by way of the reorganization. The resulting close interaction between officials and peasants in the field enabled officials to intervene in the practice of customary landholding and apply such key Ottoman land laws as the Land Code of 1858 and the Tapu Law of 1859. Consequently, private holdings of state land registered with a local land registry increased and expanded the cultivated area. Although the continued extension of private holding seemed to promise even further agricultural growth, the interest of Sultan Abdülhamid II in obtaining agricultural land as his private property brought it to a halt and once more reshaped the status of Ottoman state land.

---

65 Çetinsaya suggests that the sultan feared the land's acquisition by foreigners, especially the Persians and the British. Until 1890, he rejected all plans for reform offered by the provincial government, except for a proposal in 1887 to maintain the tithe tax at a fixed rate to ease the financial burden on the taxpayer and a request for 20,000 liras annually for public works. Gökan Çetinsaya, *The Ottoman Administration of Iraq, 1890–1908* (London: Routledge, 2006), p. 28.

CHAPTER 6

Modifications of the Land and Tax Systems

The land and tax policies that had changed the political status of the paramount tribal sheikhs began to benefit the sheikhs of smaller tribes after Midhat Pasha's departure from Baghdad in 1872. Both the private landholders and the government needed the lesser sheikhs' help to organize peasant tribesmen for cultivation and public water-control, irrigation, and land-reclamation projects, so the role of these sheikhs grew throughout the reign of Sultan Abdülhamid II (1876–1909). His prohibition against offering state land for sale in 1881 and mismanagement of the *tapu* system spurred the change, as he himself became a landholder and agriculturalist of large areas of productive state land, employing large numbers of peasant cultivators. He also was a consumer of water resources, which drove up the costs of agricultural production, especially for *tapu* holders and peasant cultivators on less productive lands, due to the limited availability of irrigation water.

Even when the Young Turk government took over the sultan's land as state domain (*mudawwala*) and resumed transfer of state land by *tapu*, it kept the same system of management. The peasant tribesmen sustained the steady agricultural growth, while their sheikhs gained political power and began to acquire land. Resuming *tapu*, however, was not an easy task for the Young Turks. On *tapu* land, land registration was deficient after many years of neglect under the former sultan and ineffective legislation meant to remedy the situation. As a result, on taking over the fertile lands of the former sultan's holdings as state domain, they attempted to promote agriculture through investment by landholders, pump owners, and tribal sheikhs who could provide capital, unlike the tax farmers, sheikhs of peasant tribesmen, and tribal peasants.

To understand the consequences of Namık and Midhat Pashas' land reform, this chapter examines why Sultan Abdülhamid stopped the transfer of possession right by sale and *tapu* registration, disregarding the efforts of the former Baghdad governors; and why and how the Young Turk government resumed *tapu* transfer and registration. Because of the increasing significance of foreign trade and agriculture, even in the remote province of Baghdad, this study puts some focus on the expanding economy, with its impacts on agriculture and land tenure, and searches for clues as to why, within a few decades after the land reform, absentee proprietors began to hold the land.

 | DOI:10.1163/9789004384347_008

1 Sultan Abdülhamid II's Land Acquisition

The reforms of the Tanzimat were suddenly curtailed after the Porte made Basra and Mosul separate provinces in 1875 and 1878 respectively. Basra was temporarily incorporated into Baghdad between 1880 and 1884 due to an uprising of the Muntafiq tribe but resumed independence with Basra, Amara, Muntafiq, and Nejd (al-Hasa) as its districts. It became strategically important when a large fort was constructed at Fao, which was hence converted from *nâhiye* to *kazâ*. Mosul was assigned the districts of Kirkuk and Sulaymaniya, which had long been under direct control of the Baghdad governor, and so the Baghdad province was reduced to the districts of Baghdad, Diwaniya, and Karbala. The governor's administrative authority was diminished as well, since the provincial departments for finance, education, the privy purse, justice, land registry, post and telegraphs, religious endowments, customs, public debt, tobacco régie, and sanitary service were made directly responsible to the corresponding ministries or departments in Istanbul. The Sixth Army continued to be stationed in Baghdad, but the governor had authority over only the gendarmerie (*zaptiye*) and the civil police. The gendarmerie, organized locally with the majority of its some 3,500 men recruited from the Kurds in the early 1900s, carried out general security duties in the countryside and assisted in the collection of tax revenues from the tribes.[1]

Under the centralized bureaucracy, the local administration was more closely linked to the fortunes of the Porte, whose debt and liabilities had never ceased to accumulate.[2] The Porte failed to make interest payments on some of its foreign loans in 1875, missed all payments due in the following year, and finally declared bankruptcy in 1878. After the default, it resumed domestic borrowing by issuing paper money (*kaime*), but when the value of the money plunged, the Porte had to negotiate with its foreign creditors for a repayment schedule. Forced to deal with this problem since the very beginning of his reign in 1876, Sultan Abdülhamid agreed in 1881 to the consolidation of internal and

1 Gökan Çetinsaya, *The Ottoman Administration of Iraq, 1890–1908* (London: Routledge, 2006), pp. 15–16.

2 The total debt was estimated at £36.5 million in 1860–61, including the exchange loss at 4.6 per cent of the total for 1860–62, and the budget deficits at 8.6 per cent for 1858–62. The foreign debt was 40 per cent of the total debt, while the internal debt in stock and bonds was 24.4 per cent of the total, the debt of the Ministry of Finance 12.2 per cent, and the sundry liabilities 10.2 per cent. TNA: FO 424/24, "Report on the Financial Condition of Turkey," Mr Foster and Lord Hobart to Earl Russell, Constantinople, 7 Dec. 1861, pp. 22–28.

foreign debt by enacting the Decree of Muharrem, which wrote off half the debt, and to pay for the interest on and redemption of the remaining debt. He allowed the commission for the public debt (the Council of Administration of the Ottoman Public Debt) to redirect the revenues from salt, tobacco products, stamp duties, spirits, fishery licences, and silk production to its own account.

Unprecedented in history, the drastic measures proved favourable to the economy in the long term. During this period, the interest rate in major European economies remained low. The Ottoman Empire attracted foreign direct investment and enjoyed relatively low interest rates on their bonds that stayed at 4 per cent in most years after 1886 until 1908. Along with the increase in foreign investment, which hit its peak between 1888 and 1896, the gross revenue of the Ottoman Public Debt Administration (OPDA) increased from about 13 per cent of total state revenue in 1881 to 17 per cent in 1911, while its total gross receipts increased by 160 per cent over those thirty years.[3] Its staff, who outnumbered that of the Ministry of Finance, were reputed to be more capable than local officials and so well paid that it drove up demand for both local and imported goods.

When the OPDA began operating in Baghdad and Basra in the early 1880s, the budgets of the local treasuries had to be scaled down because revenues from salt, tobacco products, stamp duties, spirits, fishery licences, and silk production were directly collected by the staff of OPDA and delivered to its account.[4] The total sum almost equalled one-third of the local revenue collected by 1916. For the regional economy, however, this was not disadvantageous, as the administration's large staff of well-paid consumers of imported and domestic products eventually did foster export-oriented marketing and the import of Western goods and new technologies.

Revenue collection for the repayment of public debt was not the sole outside element in the fiscal affairs of Baghdad, for the surge in foreign investment bolstered the revitalization of agriculture. In the Tanzimat period, the economic activities of foreigners in Baghdad had been limited to trade, small investments in telegraph lines, and the Lynch Brothers' river-navigating concern. Agriculture had seldom been one of their interests, except for exports of produce. Following the Anglo-Turkish Convention of 1878, the sultan restricted the commercial activities of the British even further and challenged their

3 Murat Birdal, *The Political Economy of Ottoman Public Debt* (London: I.B. Tauris, 2010), pp. 21, 106.

4 See e.g. *Sâlnâme-i Vilâyet-i Bağdad*, 1317 AH (1901/02 *Milâdî*), pp. 297–98; *Sâlnâme-i Vilâyet-i Basra*, 1318 AH (1902/03 *Milâdî*), p. 291.

influence in the region.[5] Yet, realizing that the interest rates had stabilized at a low level, he began to lure the investment of other foreign capital.

Among the vigorous competitors in applying for contracts and concessions, the Germans won the sultan's favour and started to establish businesses in Baghdad, Basra, and the Gulf region. According to Şevket Pamuk, direct foreign investment increased rapidly between 1888 and 1896, and most of it went into railway construction.[6] In 1899, the Ministry of Public Works gave a preliminary concession for constructing a railway between Istanbul and Baghdad to the Deutsche Bank, and in 1902, the Deutsche Bank and the Württembergische Vereinsbank won a contract for the Baghdad Railway from Konya to Baghdad, a distance of 2,000 kilometres, with a loan of 54 million francs granted by the Deutsche Bank. For the construction, the Société d'Étude du Chemin de Fer de Baghdad, formed by the Holzmann Company and several banks led by the Deutsche Bank, placed most of its orders with German industry.[7] In 1903, the Ottoman government revised the concession in order to extend the line to Aleppo and Khanaqin and gave the Germans financial and tax privileges, as well as the right to exploit mineral resources and to establish industries, river navigation, and piers at the terminal ports along the railway.[8]

As the railway construction in Baghdad encompassed the rivalry of foreign interests, Germany had begun to emerge as a strong rival to Great Britain in the 1890s, placing an imperial consulate in Basra in 1894 and a house of trade run by two young Germans there in the following year. By then, the Deutsche Orient Bank was about to open a branch in Baghdad, aiming to secure its foothold in the region, and regular sailings of the Hamburg-America Line to Basra also were expected to stimulate German commercial activity in the Basra and Baghdad markets. Although as late as 1906, Germans accounted for only 1.36 per cent of the total value of imports to Baghdad, while the British and Indians

5 The Ottoman navy had maintained a garrison at Doha since the expedition of Midhat Pasha in 1872, and in 1889 two additional gunboats were attached to the Basra flotilla. Between 1890 and 1894, small military guardhouses were built on the Shatt al-Arab, and in 1891 the Ottomans established an additional garrison at Udeid. They remained in occupation of Bubiyan, Safwan, and Umm Qasr, and in 1904 a large military expedition was sent to Nejd against Ibn Saud. Çetinsaya, *Ottoman Administration*, pp. 136–45; Frederick F. Anscombe, *The Ottoman Gulf: The Creation of Kuwait, Saudi Arabia, and Qatar* (New York: Columbia University Press, 1997), 144–53.

6 Şevket Pamuk, *The Ottoman Empire and European Capitalism, 1820–1913* (Cambridge: Cambridge University Press, 1987), p. 64.

7 Edward Mead Earle, *Turkey, the Great Powers, and the Baghdad Railway* (New York: Macmillan, 1923), pp. 29–52.

8 Ram N. Kumar, *Britain, India, and Iraq: A Study in British Diplomacy, 1898–1918* (Patna: Janaki Prakashan, 1992), pp. 69, 86.

controlled about 90 per cent, German traders were challenging British commercial supremacy with the support of their government.[9]

Noticing the merits of foreign investment, Sultan Abdülhamid himself also made investments in his estates from his privy purse (*hazîne-i hâss*). He had started land acquisition in 1877 and expanded it after banning the public sale of state land in 1881. At the same time, he restricted the transfer of the possession right on *tapu* land to inheritance, for which its transaction in the land market almost ceased. The provincial government in Baghdad repeatedly petitioned the sultan to lift the ban, observing that it retarded private investment in agriculture, but to no avail.[10]

Besides weakening the provincial governor's political authority, the sultan established a commission of *saniyya* (crown) land to manage his lands under direct supervision of the commander-in-chief of the Sixth Army in Baghdad and the lieutenant in Basra. The sultan's officials acquired land for him by purchase, gift, and the appropriation to the state permitted by law, as well as by confiscation from troublesome tribesmen on neighbouring lands. In addition, state land along new canals was acquired for the sultan, without compensation, under the pretext that it was wasteland, although it was almost always more fertile than other land.[11] This land was located in Hilla, Diwaniya, and Amara, on the left bank of the Tigris River from the town of Amara to Azair, and included irrigated lands on the Chahala Canal and on the right bank of the Tigris from the town of Kumait to Azair. The sultan also acquired large properties in the district of Nejd.

On his estates, the sultan collected the tithe, sheep tax, taxes on buffaloes and camels, and household fees. The largest of these, the tithe, was collected mainly by tax farming, lease, or directly from the tribal *serkâr* through crop sharing, and the revenue from each estate was used to pay its officials, irrigation and clerical staff, and an engineer. These managers prioritized the allocation of irrigation water and labour and explored innovations such as fishing ponds in Amara.[12] Peasant cultivators on the estates were exempt from military conscrip-

9 The British handled over 80 per cent of the value of the entire trade and an 85 per cent share of shipping in the Gulf before the 1910s. Kumar, *Britain, India, and Iraq*, p. 113.

10 Çetinsaya, *Ottoman Administration*, p. 28.

11 Albertine Jwaideh explains that twenty-one plots of reclaimed land, ranging from 2 dönüm to 167 dönüm, were acquired as wasteland. Albertine Jwaideh, "The *Sanniya* Lands of Sultan Abdul Hamid II in Iraq," in George Makdisi, ed., *Arabic and Islamic Studies in Honor of Hamilton A.R. Gibb* (Leiden: E.J. Brill, 1965), p. 331. BL: IOR/L/PS/20/250, *Reports of Administration for 1918 of Divisions and Districts of the Occupied Territories in Mesopotamia. Volume 1* (1919), p. 242.

12 Jwaideh, "*Sanniya* Lands of Sultan Abdul Hamid II in Iraq," pp. 326–36; BOA, Yıldız Mütenevvi Mârûzat Evrâkı (Y. MTV) 6–6, 9 Cemaziyelâhir 1298; TNA: FO 371/4150/187296,

tion and all forms of forced labour and were protected from tribal plundering and harassment by policemen. Expenses were easily recovered by charging high prices for leases and tax farming, and the peasant cultivators, lessening their subjugation to the paramount tribal sheikh, achieved greater productivity and enjoyed more prosperity than their counterparts on other lands.[13]

While making high returns from his investments in *saniyya* lands, the sultan vigorously engaged in other profit-making activities besides agriculture. As soon as he was made aware of the potential profits from the oilfields in Qaiyara and Tuz Khurmatu, identified in a geological survey in 1871, he immediately placed the fields under the control of the *saniyya* commission rather than the Imperial Treasury.[14] Also under that department, in 1904, he established the Hamidiye Steam Navigation Company with the purchase of the vessels of the Oman-Ottoman Company that had once belonged to the Ministry of the Navy. The new company was authorized to operate six steamers on the Tigris River between Baghdad and Basra by the end of 1905, while the Lynch Brothers' interests were allowed only two. In that year, the sultan's privy purse earned about 94,500 pounds sterling in total, equivalent to nearly a quarter of the combined annual revenues of the Baghdad and Basra provinces.[15]

The extensive operation of the *saniyya* commission contributed to peace and security in agricultural areas and raised the overall level of production. Exports of dates and barley increased to meet a growing demand in Europe, as did, to a lesser extent, the export of horses, hides and skins, wheat, and rice. Settlement of tribesmen followed, giving rise to new towns in Nasiriya, Amara, Kut, and Bughaila. Peasant workers attracted to the sultan's *saniyya* land for better pay drove up wages on private fields, over which the sheikhs of the peasant tribesmen gained bargaining power with government officials and private landholders. Domestic demand for grain and foreign goods increased along with population growth after 1850 due to the permanence of the government authority in tribal domains, the reduction of the overland journey

---

Administration Report, Revenue Board, Baghdad, 22 Mar.–31 Dec. 1917 (Baghdad: Printed at Government Press, 1918), p. 9.

13 The profitability of *saniyya* land drew interest from privileged investors such as Sassoon and Lynch to obtain special permission from the sultan to buy tracts of profitable land or date groves. BOA, Sadâret Resmî Mârûzat Evrâkı (Y.A. Res) 19–52, 27 Cemaziyelevvel 1300.

14 Stephen Hemsley Longrigg, *'Iraq, 1900 to 1950: A Political, Social, and Economic History* (London: Oxford University Press, 1953), p. 27.

15 Çetinsaya, *Ottoman Administration*, pp. 18, 129.

from Damascus across the desert to Baghdad from eighteen days to ten, and the availability of seven regular lines of steamers for trade.[16]

Private landholders near the sultan's lands, however, suffered both from the reduction in water flow caused by his estates' heavy water use and from a concurrent problem with the flow of the Euphrates River. Until 1880, the Hilla Branch of the river contained a larger water flow than its other branch, the Hindiya Canal, but after Midhat Pasha's flood-control project, the Hilla Branch received less and less water as silt pushed into it. French engineers called in to set up a masonry dam failed to prevent the Hilla Branch from drying up, and as more water flowed into the Hindiya Canal, the large volume of water during flood season made irrigation along the canal difficult. Maintenance of watercourses in the irrigated land consequently became expensive for the private landholder unless a sheikh could organize tribesmen for the work. When the Hindiya Barrage, rebuilt in 1891, collapsed in 1901, because the irrigation officials lacked the financial and technical capabilities to maintain it, the productivity of private land along the Euphrates River deteriorated even more rapidly. A great flood in Karbala at the end of Sultan Abdülhamid's reign, which severely damaged cultivated tracts of gardens belonging to the sultan's *saniyya* commission and the government itself, was triggered by the failure to repair a dyke belonging to lands held by *tapu* by Afzal Khan, an Indian, and another dyke belonging to lands in possession of Saiyid Dawud Effendi, Naqibzadah. Ordered to make repairs to prevent damage to nearby land, Afzal Khan replied that the construction of dykes for the land entrusted to him by *tapu* was not a condition of the land being so entrusted and that the rush of water from the Hindiya Canal could no longer be prevented by him or any private individual. Ultimately, the district government repaired the dykes.[17]

However, it could not prevent floodwater from flowing over the dykes and forming large marshes below the Husayniya Canal. Even after the Hindiya

16 The Porte began to publish a yearbook (*salname*) in 1847. Those for the province of Baghdad were published in 1872, 1875, 1882–86, and afterward, though still not yearly. According to the census of 1877, the population of Baghdad was 1,604,471, making it the largest among the main census districts of the empire. The number of buildings in Baghdad, 237,436, was also the largest among the census districts. The population and the number of buildings in Basra were 395,524 and 78,149 respectively. It is estimated that the population of both grew rapidly between 1831 and 1877, even when discounting the increase due only to the integration of the four provinces into Baghdad. For population movement in this period, see Kemal H. Karpat, *Ottoman Population, 1830–1914* (Madison: University of Wisconsin Press, 1985), pp. 117, 121, 128–29, 144–45, 152–53, 155–61, 164–69; Kerem Kayi, *Bagdad, 1831–1869: Untesuchungen zur Entwicklung einer osmanischen Provinzhauptstadt im 19. Jajrhundert* (Frankfurt am Main: Peter Lang, 2007), pp. 215–17.

17 TNA: FO 195/2367, Baghdad, 20 Mar. 1911, Enclosure III, dated 7 Feb. 1911.

Barrage enabled more water to be diverted into Hilla River, the marshes did not disappear, limiting land use along the Euphrates River and major canals. Major canals surveyed by Namık Pasha for crop sharing disappeared from the map in the Young Turks period. Even those canals recorded in the map edited by Captain Felix Jones in 1874 no longer had been in use. (See Maps 2.3 and 6.2.)

By the time Sultan Abdülhamid's rule effectively ended in 1908, his estates occupied no less than one-third of the whole cultivated area of Baghdad province. They included the greater part of the Samarra district; the Shadi and Bughaila estates on the Tigris; the estates of Aliawa in Khanaqin, the lower part of Mahrut, and the Uthmaniya and Waziriya estates in Baʿqūba on the Diyala; the Tash Canal in the Ramadi district; the Abu Ghraib estate in Fallujah; almost the whole of the Musaib district on the left bank of the Nil Canal; the Quss and Jurbuiya estates in the Hilla district; and the greater part of the Shamiya district on the Euphrates.[18] As the largest landowner in the province, the sultan looked to foreign investment as the key to economic growth, particularly foreign aid for water-control projects to harness the abundant waters of the rivers and canals. However, foreign capitalists were reluctant to commit to agricultural projects without access to landholding. Instead, they recognized that the construction of railways could open the way to substantial development and set their sights in that direction.

The sultan's land policies and the growing international presence had a mixed impact on the people of the Baghdad province. In a marsh area, for example, the anthropologist Shakir Mustafa Salim insightfully observes, in the late nineteenth century, peasant tribesmen who once had migrated from area to area still could maintain a certain level of income by making cash-bearing goods such as mat weaving. They could substitute the cultivation of land and supplement income from agricultural activities, probably owing to the expansion of regional trade and marketing.[19]

---

18 Jwaideh, "*Sanniya* Lands of Sultan Abdul Hamid II in Iraq," pp. 326–36.

19 Shakir Mustafa Salim, who lived in the village of Chibayish tribesmen in 1962, describes a change that followed Sultan Abdülhamid II's measures in the late nineteenth century:

"The history of Beni Isad in ech-Chibayish region shows that they had cultivated a large area of their enemies lands in il-Mijarra, Amara and il-Hwaiza districts for varying periods. However, towards the close of the last century and after the defeat of Shaikh Hasan Ahl Khayūn by the Ottoman army, they gave up the rich lands of Obū Ijaj, il-Abid, il-Hmaila, il-Awaidiya, etc., and utilized a much smaller area of hitherto uncultivated land in the vicinity of ech-Chibayish. In these new conditions, under which winter cultivation almost disappeared and summer cultivation could be carried out only occasionally, owing to successive flooding, mat-weaving was adopted as a means of livelihood, thus making cultivation less vital."

In the winter of 1904–5, the first feasible irrigation and land reclamation projects were designed by a British engineer, Sir William Willcocks, for the irrigated area between the Tigris and Euphrates Rivers in the vicinity of Baghdad. Submitted to the sultan through British Ambassador Sir Nicolas O'Conor, the proposal was virtually rejected by the sultan's request that the British set up a capital fund sufficient to carry out the plan. Some two years later, the sultan sent a French engineer named Cugnin to fix the Hindiya Barrage on the Euphrates River, but his repair lasted less than a year. Concerning a general reform of agriculture, when the sultan finally set out to implement it by establishing a reform commission, it soon ran into difficulties. According to the commission, because the system of state land had produced poor returns with little incentive to improve land productivity, the solution was the repeatedly proposed privatization of state land by sale and permanent settlement of tribesmen on the land.[20] In 1905, towards the end of his reign, Sultan Abdülhamid finally agreed to the planning of general reforms in three provinces by reform commissions but did not implement any of the commissions' proposals. In 1908 the Young Turks took over the government and began new land policies.

2 The Trade and Agricultural Policies of the Young Turk Government

While preserving the former sultan's land system, the Young Turks' government steadily increased foreign trade, particularly with the Germans. The Germans' commercial activities expanded for several years under the Young Turks, with practical effects on agriculture, manufacturing, infrastructure, and transportation, and trade grew in quantity and value as a result of increased German transactions in local markets. The German trading houses Berk, Püttmann & Co. and Robert Wönckhause and Company both had established operations in Basra to import sugar, spirits, wood, china, glass, machinery, iron, steel, coal, and hardware. Soon German interests increased their share in the Anglo-Turkish Commission for the navigation of the Shatt al-Arab, extended a cable to connect the Gulf with Europe, and undercut the rates charged by the British Lynch Brothers to ship freight on the Karun River from Muhammara to Ahwaz. In addition, by offering more generous credits than their rivals, the Germans bolstered demand for their manufactured goods. Having closely

Shakir Mustafa Salim, *Marsh Dwellers of the Euphrates Delta* (London: Athlone Press, University of London, 1962), pp. 83–84.

20 Longrigg, *ʿIraq, 1900 to 1950*, pp. 62–63; Çetinsaya, *Ottoman Administration*, pp. 38, 43, 46–47.

studied the local market, they knew how to maintain relations with the merchants by dealing in a diversity of articles and taking even small orders. Their elaborate showcases let them display more samples than the British, with prices quoted in local currency written in Arabic. In Basra, the German merchants' extensive trading network provided a variety of small articles and hardware that the British merchants did not supply. Credit was furnished by the Baghdad, Basra, and Mosul branches of the Ottoman Bank and the Baghdad branch of the Deutsche Orientbank.[21]

By the autumn of 1913, German operations, particularly in the trade of indigo and cotton, had penetrated into the other Persian and Arab ports on the Gulf, where the British had enjoyed commercial dominance, and so had taken away much of the Lynch Brothers' forwarding business from Ahwaz to Isfahan. Railway construction was expected to stimulate the Germans' trade and commerce even further, although the customs duty had been raised from 8 per cent to 11 per cent in 1906 and to 14 per cent in 1914. By 1916, the Hamburg-America Line was handling the largest imports of sugar and grains in the Gulf, and the German Robert Wönckhaus owned the dominant trading house in Basra.[22]

Meanwhile, diplomatic negotiations on the exploitation of oilfields also had raised German influence in the region. Negotiations between the Ottoman government and the Anglo-Persian Company that began in 1907 failed in the wake of the Young Turk Revolution. In 1912, Ernest Cassel, an English banker of German birth, formed the Turkish Petroleum Company in collaboration with the Deutsche Bank and Royal Dutch Shell in order to acquire oilfields throughout the Ottoman Empire. Since the Deutsche Bank group had already obtained the right to exploit minerals within twenty kilometres on both sides of the Baghdad Railway, which was then projected to extend to Basra or Kuwait, Germany was poised to expand its political influence and general position in the region through the exploitation of oilfields. In the end, however, a new Turkish Petroleum Consortium was formed by the Anglo-Persian Company, the Deutsche Bank, and the Turkish Petroleum Company with shares of 50, 25, and 25 per cent respectively.[23]

---

21 Çetinsaya, *Ottoman Administration*, pp. 46–47; Eugene Stanley, "Business and Politics in the Persian Gulf: The Story of the Wönckhaus Firm," *Political Science Quarterly* 48, no. 3 (1933), pp. 367–76.

22 Çetinsaya, *Ottoman Administration*, pp. 109–12; Stanley, "Business and Politics in the Persian Gulf," pp. 377–85.

23 Charles Issawi, *The Fertile Crescent, 1800–1914* (New York: Oxford University Press, 1988), pp. 367–72; Marian Kent, *Oil and Empire: British Policy and Mesopotamian Oil, 1900–1920* (London: Macmillan, 1976), pp. 33–94; Longrigg, *'Iraq, 1900 to 1950*, pp. 65–66, 174.

Increased interest in trade and commerce triggered further agricultural development by the public and private sectors after the end of Sultan Abdülhamid II's reign. Some six years after irrigation engineer Sir William Willcocks studied the old Hindiya Barrage and other irrigation facilities in 1902, he and a team from the Mesopotamia Irrigation Survey proposed repairing the barrages, reinforcing the embankments on the rivers, and installing escapes for floodwater, and the Ottoman government finally started rebuilding the Hindiya Barrage. Anticipating the project in 1907, the government had enacted a regulation requiring tribesmen living in the project areas either to serve as labourers on the public works or to build the facilities themselves. The tribal sheikhs of Najaf and Hindiya were summoned to the administrative headquarters of their districts to furnish lists of their tribesmen, whose labour the sheikhs were paid a lump sum for organizing.[24] Completed in 1912 under the Young Turks, the greatly improved Hindiya Barrage diverted a large volume of water down the Hilla Branch and opened more land to cultivation.[25]

On the Diyala River basin, where Reşit Pasha initiated a new policy of private landholding by *tapu* on state land during the Tanzimat period, numerous canals were pulled from the river for irrigating the lands of the private landholders (Map 6.1). There, varieties of cash crops, vegetables, and fruits were produced and sold in markets in Baghdad. Demand for their produce was high and brought large profits in this area, since Baghdad had developed as a provincial capital and accommodated a large urban population. Wheat had been the main locally grown crop, and dates continued to be the major product for export from Basra, Karbala, and Mandali. Barley now became a competitive crop for export because of its low prices and because of increased demand generated by military expansion and urbanization. Its production rapidly prevailed in the irrigated areas of the central and southern regions as the main crop, due to low production costs and peasant tribesmen as a cheap labour force for its cultivation.

The extension and improvement of agriculture following the successful reconstruction of the Hindiya Barrage in 1912 further strengthened the buying power of part of the population, while incomes generally increased thanks to the growth in trade and investment. Residential rents more than doubled, and the demand for building sites tripled the price of land in the city of Baghdad during the last two decades of Ottoman rule. Revenue from income and property taxes rose as well. At the same time, the influx of Europeans inspired local

---

24 TNA: FO 195/2367, Annexure B. Copy of a Decision Passed by the Commission of Public Works for the Sanjaq of Karbala, 11 July 1907.

25 Longrigg, *'Iraq, 1900 to 1950*, pp. 63–64.

residents to purchase imported apparel and wares of all descriptions as tastes and fashions began to follow the Continent, and Syrian and Turkish traders set up branches in Baghdad to handle German, Austrian, and French goods. New townships and police stations were established in rural areas, and despite turnover in the governorship, the tribal sheikhs became less resistant to the government amid the widening prosperity.

As the Young Turk government pursued additional efforts to revitalize uncultivated land, in 1911 it auctioned off scattered large parcels of 800 to 70,000 dönüm of state land in Mosul, Kirkuk, Baghdad, Hilla, and Basra, but mostly in Baghdad and Hilla along the Middle Euphrates.[26] It also encouraged the use of engine-driven pumps. After twenty-six of the pumps were installed on the Hilla Branch for the extension of water channels, improved production made the area one of the largest revenue-generating areas in the province. The selling price of the pump was reasonably set, based on the size of the pump, and instalment payments were arranged to the advantage of the buyer. The pre-war prices of Messrs. Blockey Cree & Co., who had sold many pumping sets, including the piping and erection but not the foundation bolts and foundation, are shown in Table 6.1.

TABLE 6.1 Prices of pumps

Size of pump (in inches)	Turkish lira
4	110
5	145
6	185
7	215
8	280
9	320
10	380
12	570

Note: The pump in the report was centrifugal with the size of its impeller diameter.
SOURCE: JOHN P. HEWETT, *REPORT FOR THE ARMY COUNCIL ON MESOPOTAMIA*, BL: IOR/L/PS/20/35, BAGHDAD, 1919, P. 20.

26 "Liste des Domaines du Trésor mis en vente aux enchères," *La Gazette Financiére*, quatriréme anne, no. 201, 5 Aug. 1913.

TABLE 6.2 Typical loan repayment schedule

	Surcharges (Interest)	Principal	Total payment
Year	Kuruş	Kuruş	Kuruş
1	2,625	3,625	6,250
2	2,250	4,000	6,250
3	1,875	4,375	6,250
4	1,500	4,750	6,250
5	1,125	5,125	6,250
6	750	5,500	6,250
7	375	5,875	6,250
8	0	6,250	6,250
Total	10,500	39,500	50,000

SOURCE: *BAGHDĀD VILĀYETI DĀKHILINDE ARĀḌININ̆ SŪRET-I IDĀRE VE TAṢARRUFUNA DĀʾIR TAʿLIMĀT <LĀʾIḤASI>DIR* [MEMORANDUM OF REGULATIONS CONCERNING LAND ADMINISTRATION AND LANDHOLDING IN THE PROVINCE OF BAGHDAD], PREPARED BY BAGHDAD TREASURER (*DEFTERDAR*) AHMED FAHMI (DATE UNKNOWN), ART. 88.

Although the purchaser of irrigation pumps had to accept certain restrictions, he could benefit from the favourable payment schedule of his loan. As an example, the repayment schedule by eight-year instalments for a ten-inch pump is assessed according to Table 6.2.

Considering the official rate of 1 Turkish lira to 100 kuruş, a purchaser of the ten-inch pump at 380 lira (38,000 kuruş) in Table 6.1 would have a loan of 39,500 kuruş, as the listed price excluded foundation bolts and other costs. The average rate of the annual surcharge (i.e., the interest rate) is estimated at 5.5 per cent in Table 6.2, which was considerably lower than borrowing from a private moneylender.[27] While repayment over eight years was standard, the purchaser could apply for a longer schedule at the same rate if he purchased infertile land.

For land on which large-scale irrigation was necessary, the purchaser was only required to make payment in the second year, when the produce was put on the market, and a repayment schedule covering between twelve and eighteen years was permitted. Because the deposit was only 5 per cent of the

27 The annual rate of surcharge (interest) is calculated by the equation: Principal = Total payment x $[1/(1+r) + 1/(1+r)^2 + \cdots + 1/(1+r)^8]$, where r is the rate of surcharge.

purchase price, and because the favourable annual rate of interest – as low as about 3 per cent – was better than the rate offered by private lenders, people without capital and tribal sheikhs could purchase the pumps. Both the pump owner and the *tapu* holder, moreover, were allowed a tax reduction of 18–20 per cent, which helped both to offset the high operating and maintenance costs of the pumps and to recruit peasant tribesmen to cultivate the reclaimed land. Since such loans were favourable to the borrower, even taking into consideration the weaker kuruş in Baghdad, irrigation pumps began to prevail along the major rivers and canals and furthered the progress of land reclamation in these areas.[28]

While irrigation agriculture was becoming the major objective of the government, the reorganization of land registration had become an immediate issue due to the former sultan's three decades of mismanagement. As more pumps were installed, the areas they irrigated extended over vacant land without registered landholders, spurring an interest in land acquisition, which had been banned for many years. Many laws were enacted accordingly, but without altering the foundation of *tapu* established by Midhat Pasha. They included the law on the delimitation and registration of immovable property of 5 February 1913, the law authorizing corporations to own land of 16 February 1913, the law on succession to real property with explanatory tableau of 6 March 1913, the law on mortgages of 10 March 1913, the law on the ownership of real property of 12 April 1913, and the law on the division of jointly owned real property of 1 December 1913.[29] In addition, regulations on landholding were enacted recurrently, based on the Land Code of 1858, Tapu Law, and amendments made by Namık and Midhat Pashas. Although these laws were effective on most state land, they were inapplicable to local practices regarding the reclaimed land that had expanded rapidly along with the introduction of pump irrigation and repairs to the Hindiya Barrage and other weirs.

3 Modification of the Land System

With increasing agricultural production a primary objective of development, the Young Turks paid more attention to land problems than former officials had. While the deficiencies of the land administration they had inherited prevented

28 "*Baghdād Vilāyeti Dākhilinde Arāḍiniñ Sūret-i Idāre ve Taṣarrufuna dā'ir Ta'limāt <Lā'iḥası>dir*," 15 *Mayıs* 1332 (15 May 1332 AH [1917]), Art. 88.

29 "Note on the Extent to Which Ottoman Law is in Force in Iraq," in TNA: CO 730/125/16, 28 Dec. 1927, 13 Feb. 1928, pp. 5–6.

them from dealing with the complicated issue of land rights, confusion grew out of a series of new land laws issued shortly before the war. According to the memorandum prepared by Baghdad treasurer (*defterdar*) Ahmed Fahmi, *Baghdād Vilāyeti Dākhilinde Arāḍiniñ Sūret-i Idāre ve Taṣarrufuna dā'ir Taʿlimāt* <*Lā'iḥası*>*dir* (Memorandum of Regulations concerning Land Administration and Landholding in the Province of Baghdad), the Young Turks continued the principles of *tapu* laid down by Namık and Midhat Pashas and put other lands under legislative controls while deregulating tribal holding.[30]

The memorandum is composed of three parts: general principles of land administration (Arts. 1–43); rules on lands (Arts. 44–185); and penalties (Arts. 186–204). It acknowledges nine categories of landholding, a clear distinction from the Land Code of 1858, and lists them in the second part: (1) land possessed by *tapu*; (2) state land cultivated by way of crop sharing; (3) land cultivated and irrigated by tribal sheikh (*serkâr*) and tribesmen; (4) land put under crop-sharing contract; (5) *uqr* land; (6) uncultivated vacant land; (7) land to be transferred to individuals in small pieces; (8) state land to be transferred by concession in large pieces; and (9) uncultivated vacant land to be cultivated by settling migrant workers and tribesmen. The government's aim was to put under legislative control agricultural landholding, customs of crop sharing, *uqr*, and tribal leaseholding, which the Land Code of 1858 and other state laws had been unable to do. It recognized the crucial role of the tribal sheikh and peasant tribesmen in advancing agricultural production along with the expansion of irrigation and land reclamation.

As a general principle, unlike the Ottoman Land Code of 1858 and other laws, the memorandum copes with new agricultural situations such as improved means of irrigation and the expansion of cultivated areas owing to it; increased demands for cultivating peasants, financial needs, resolution of land disputes; and preventive measures to avoid tribal breakdown. The government's institution of a water and land committee independent of the justice department dealt with the land issues, since the *tapu* office had been unable to deal with such complex procedures.

Combining new agricultural policies with the basic norm inherited from the Land Code of 1858, the memorandum divides the type of lands according

30 The title page states, "The copy is sent to the member of the administrative council of the province to scrutinize and the original one is submitted to the Ministry of Finance. [This memorandum is] written by Baghdad treasurer (*defterdar*) Ahmed Fahmi Bey." Although the exact date of issue is unclear, a handwritten note on the front page, "*Baghdād Vālī Muʿāvın ʿĀlīsi Saʿād Beğ Efendi Ḥaḍret Yede Taqdīm*," dated 15 *Mayıs* 1332 (15 May 1332 AH [1917]), suggests that the articles in the memorandum might have been written late in the Young Turks period.

to the means of irrigation, land use, and the size of the land, and it considers land irrigated by pump equally important to other land. To promote the cultivation of the pump-irrigated land and recruit peasant cultivators for it, the Young Turks enacted legislation intended to deregulate tribal landholding. Although the legislation granted the tribal sheikh, the tribal bailiff-*serkâr*, and the tribesmen a discount of one-fourth to one-third of the market value of the land if they purchased it jointly and exempted them from the registration fees if they reclaimed at least one-fourth of the land on their own, a household or family group in a village could claim the right of possession as an individual entity. That individual landholder could then cultivate the land by leasing it to the tribal sheikh or peasants in the village and reporting the leasing contract to the Committee of Land and Water Administration in Baghdad, which would examine the lease, request any needed amendments, and issue the permission. If the contract was made with a tribal bailiff-*serkâr* and unsettled peasant tribesmen, the committee also supervised the contract.

The maximum allowable area of landholding doubled from 500 müşâra to 1,000 müşâra and increased to 3,500 müşâra if the land had been uncultivated.[31] However, because the tribal custom of *niren* (fallow) was accepted, a tribal sheikh could register up to 2,000 müşâra of cultivated land and 7,000 müşâra of uncultivated land. Upon the transfer, the land committee recorded the method of crop sharing, the land's productivity, the size of the canal, and the power of the irrigation machine. To facilitate the transfer of uncultivated land for pump irrigation, the pump owner and the peasants were entitled to bid first, and the purchase price was the value of the land (i.e., the official price) plus the registration fee. For registered land whose area exceeded the maximum area of 1,000 müşâra, the landholder had to offer the peasants any of the land in excess of 1,000 müşâra for the market price. A person who resided outside the fields was allowed to purchase the land but was not allowed to resell it for five years, mortgage it, or give it to a religious endowment, except as the government permitted.[32]

The deregulation of tribal landholding certainly helped the pump owner arrange for tribal workers to cultivate the land after he purchased it. Due to the worsening labour shortage, however, the contract he made with the tribal sheikh was often to the advantage of the tribesmen, usually for a half-and-half division of the produce. In addition, it granted the tribesmen a prescriptive

31 The müşâra was measured by a unit called *zirâ'i*, approximately 0.5 metres, and one müşâra was 2,500 square metres, equal to one dönüm. An area of 1,000 müşâra or more was called *arâzi-i cesime* (i.e., large land). Fahmi Bey, Memorandum, Arts. 15, 16.

32 Fahmi Bey, Memorandum, Arts. 76, 77.

right to claim the possession right to a part of the land, typically half, for from twenty to ninety years of cultivation, much longer than the period for the prescriptive right under the Land Code. In fact, because the tribal sheikh bore the entire expense of planting and cultivation, he took half the produce and all the vegetables unless there were conditions to the contrary. After the term of the contract expired, he also had the right to register half the property as his own with the province's department of land registry, which the sheikh more frequently exercised where peasant tribesmen were in short supply, especially in the vicinity of Baghdad.[33]

Under the Young Turks, the procedure for land registration was as strict and complex as before, as British political officials later observed in their administrative report:

> After the purchase, the buyer obtained a certificate from the village headman describing the right that he held in the land and certifying that the land was unburdened except for his right. He then took this certificate to the Department of Land Registry, which referred the certificate to the administrative council of the subdistrict or district. The council considered the validity of the certificate and reported on it to the Department of Land Registry which then made sure there was no claim over the land as *vakıf*, state land, etc. The case was then referred to the Islamic court, which called two witnesses as to the title to the land, inscribed its conclusions in the certificate, and returned the certificate to the Department of Land Registry.[34]

But for a transfer by inheritance, the certificate that the village headman issued to the heir was accepted as sufficient for the title deed, unless the right was contested at the time of the request. The Department of Land Registry then sent the certificate back to the administrative council of the province to be formally and finally admitted as correct. After that, it was returned to the Department of Land Registry, which surveyed the land, recorded it, and issued the title deed.[35]

---

33 Charles Issawi, *The Economic History of the Middle East, 1800–1914* (Chicago: University of Chicago Press, 1966), pp. 171–78, quoted in Saleh Haider, "Land Problems of Iraq," Ph.D. diss., London University, 1942, pp. 556–660.

34 Great Britain, Office of the Civil Commissioner, "Review of the Civil Administration of the Occupied Territories of al 'Iraq 1914–1918," compiled in the Office of the Civil Commissioner, Baghdad, Nov.1918 (Baghdad: Government Press, 1918), p. 41.

35 In assessing the land value, the local land committee estimated the total production over twenty-five years of the land in each müşâra, as well as the market value of the land, trees, stream, and gardens, evaluating each tree in a feddân, if necessary. In order to estimate

In the tribal area below Baghdad, where there was no village headman, the administrative council in the district or sub-district processed the initial land registration application.

The convoluted registration procedure was intended partly to retain the government's power to prevent the transfer of land to objectionable persons or unqualified tribal sheikhs and partly to prevent complications of title by secret mortgages and the like. Every transfer of land or immovable property by inheritance, sale, gift, exchange, or mortgage, and every partition of it, had to be registered to obtain the title deed. The price at transfer, the area of transferred property, and the boundaries were set forth, and the courts were prohibited from recognizing any transaction not supported by a title deed. In the end, the procedure protected the interests of the government, the purchaser of the land, the qualified tribal sheikh, and the tribesmen against fraud.

A reliable title deed made cultivable land a marketable commodity in high demand, particularly in urban areas and along the projected line of the Baghdad Railway, and that demand was lessened neither by the higher purchasing costs of land nor by decreases in grain prices. There were numerous pieces of *tapu* land in the districts of Erbil, Kirkuk, Baghdad, Dulaim, Karbala, Shamiya (Najaf), Samarra, and Hilla, but there were few in the tribal districts of Sulaymaniya, Amara, and Muntafiq, except for the sub-district of Suq al-Shuyukh, because the government did not transfer the possession right in those districts. Although Sheikh Mahmud of the Hamawand had been granted the possession right on the tribal land, his holding was seized by the government after his rebellion. There were reportedly only two *tapu* lands in Shamiya, where the sheikh and *sayyid*s had feared that the registration of their lands for *tapu* would make them liable for military service. In contrast, the district of Hilla contained more *tapu* land than any other district, along with large areas of *mudawwala* land and private land, but the right of *uqr* established on all kinds of uncultivated private land caused endemic disputes over the shares.[36]

The Young Turk government could alter neither the *uqr* share nor the complicated procedure for placing a mortgage on *tapu* land. Upon foreclosure, the province's *tapu* (land title) department could sell mortgaged land without resort to the courts, because to mortgage his land, the landholder (or the landowner)

the land productivity, they calculated the quantity of the produce for a year, its average price in a period from ten to twenty years, and the total value during the period. TNA: FO 371/4150/187296, Administration Report, p. 13.

36 Reports of administration in the districts of Sulaymaniya, Erbil, Rawanduz, Kirkuk, Baghdad, Hilla, Dulaim, Diwaniya, Shamiya, and Basra in BL: IOR/L/PS/20/250, *Reports of Administration for 1918 of Divisions and Districts of the Occupied Territories in Mesopotamia. Volume 1* (1919).

had made over his title deeds to the mortgage broker. The landholder then obtained from the *tapu* office a printed form (*ilmühaber*) describing the location, boundaries, and value of the property to be mortgaged. This *ilmühaber* was signed by the village headman (*muhtar*) and imam of the district in which the property was situated and returned to the *tapu* office together with the title deeds (*hüccet*). After the *tapu* office endorsed the *ilmühaber*, the landholder, mortgage issuer, and broker appeared before a council consisting of the *tapu* office director (*müdîr*), the chief clerk of *tapu*, and the head clerk of the court with jurisdiction over any outstanding liabilities such as for taxation. If the council's inquiry was satisfactory, the formalities were completed on payment of the fees: 0.25 per cent of the mortgage value, 10 kuruş for the acquittal form, and various stamp duties. Interest on the mortgage was from 7 to 12 per cent, depending on the financial reputation of the client. In theory, the issuer of a mortgage could be a foreigner, but the *tapu* authorities were to raise all possible obstacles to such a transaction.[37] As the land market was commercialized, the rigid regulation of mortgages constrained the expansion of credit, because neither the purchaser of land nor the mortgage issuer wanted to risk having a faulty title, so both insisted on getting a title deed. On the other hand, enquiries and surveys did bring to light cases of illegal encroachment or occupation, enabling the government to recover fees due or to evict occupiers without title.

4 Agricultural Taxation and Revenues

Demonstrating the government's command over agricultural resources, in the province of Baghdad the tithe revenue from grain production continued to be the largest in total and steadily increased. The government's taxation scheme was based on the type of landholding: *mudawwala* land, *tapu* land, other state land, or *mülk* (private) land. For the *saniyya* land of the former sultan, as well as for *tapu* and *mülk* land, the methods of tax collection remained mostly unchanged from the previous periods, namely, direct collecting by officials, tax farming, and leasing. For the remaining areas in which crop sharing had been practised, the land was now designated as state domain, and the tribesmen cultivating the land were nominally considered lessees of the state land. Crop sharing was applied in the same way, but because the government share was

37 Halil Cin, *Osmanlı Toprak Düzeni Ve Bu Düzenin Bozulması* (Istanbul: Boğaziçi Yyınları, 1985), pp. 259–64; Great Britain, *Report by His Britannic Majesty's Government to the Council of the League of Nations on the Administration of 'Iraq for the year 1925* (London: HMSO, 1926), pp. 98–99.

now considered a tax, rent, or leasing fee, the tribal sheikh, or *serkâr*, of the cultivating tribes made a contract to determine their amount, and the state domains were listed in chapter VI of the state budget. (For a list of the chapters in the Ottoman budget, see Table 7.4.)

British officials who surveyed taxation in the late Ottoman period in search of a model for their own system found it was complicated but reasonably conformed to previous customs. On land irrigated by a lift and pumps, the tax was a fixed assessment according to the number of lift buckets or the size of the pump engine and paid by each owner of the lift either in cash or in kind. Crop inspection was unnecessary except when remission was claimed due to failure of a crop. In other areas, the rate of tax was determined customarily. One form of the assessment based on produce involved measurement by the irrigation department or by the political officer of the crops in each holding. Later the crops were classified as first class (good), second class (average) or third class (bad) just before harvest by an inspection committee, and the tax was set for each class of produce. Alternatively, relatively large croplands of no less than two müşâra (an acre and a quarter) were estimated by eye, rather than measured, and the whole operation of harvesting was supervised by the political officer and his assistant to ascertain the weights of the unthreshed crop, threshed grain, and straw in order to determine the rate of tax.[38] Yet another familiar method, *kharas* or *takhmin*, combined the estimation of area and quality. In it, the standard yield per dönüm was assumed to be 500 kilos for both wheat and barley, and from these amounts, a deduction (*tajbir*) was made according to the quality and quantity of crops estimated by eye for each area of 100 dönüm: (1) *Ala* (very good, 1/6 deduction); (2) *Ausat* (good, 1/5); (3) *Adna* (average, 1/4); (4) *Adna al-Adna* (average, 1/3); (5) 1/2 *Aid* (poor, 1/2), 1/3 *Aid* (2/3), 1/4 *Aid* (3/4), 1/5 *Aid* (4/5), 1/10 *Aid*, (9/10); (6) *Adim* and *Bor* (vacant; no revenue). Because these Ottoman tax customs were formulas that the people understood, and so were easier to use than other methods, British officials documented them as feasible measures to be followed.[39]

In practice, however, the Young Turks' efforts to formalize taxation caused problems that were worse than those under tax farming. In Hilla, where the cultivating peasant tribesmen saw their tax, rent, owner's share, and other fees greatly increase, their lease was usually disadvantageous to them since a *tapu* holder retained the right to evict his tenants, and a tax farmer could charge fraudulently higher taxes after the rapid break-up of the tribal system without

---

38 TNA: FO 371/4150/187296, Administration Report, pp. 14–18.

39 Iraq, Department of Agriculture, *Report on the Mesopotamian Spring Harvest, 1919* (Baghdad: Government Press, 1919), pp. 1–2.

provision of an effective substitute. Meanwhile, heavier taxes did not diminish the popularity of land acquisition, for the taxes on the purchased land were passed on to the cultivating peasants, even on the land of tribal sheikhs, which fuelled the discontent of the peasant tribesmen against their sheikh.

Even more serious examples of the deteriorated relations between peasant cultivators and landholders could be found in Suq al-Shuyukh, where the Sadun tribe acquired the possession right over land from the border of Nasiriya downward along the Akaika and Mazliq Canals as far as Hammar Lake in the former Muntafiq tribal domain. Now established as regular landowners, the Sadun took a one-half share of the dates and a one-third share of the grains, far larger owner's shares that the Muntafiq tribesmen ever fully accepted, spurring their constant struggle against the imposition of the Sadun and the government.[40]

For the government, higher taxes did not always yield larger revenues. Despite the priority placed on agricultural production in irrigated areas, it continued to be curtailed by the customary practice locally called *niren* (fallow), in which about half the irrigated land was left uncultivated each year. Net revenues were further decreased by the reduction of seed stocks for the next year's cultivation, various fees, damage to the crops, flooding, and other factors. Taking into account the fallow land and these reductions, according to a feature article in *La Gazette Financiére* on Iraqi agriculture, in 1911 net revenue was only about one-fourth of the average total, and the government's tithe revenue, reduced by the input paid by the government, averaged less than 9 per cent of the revenues in the irrigated areas where fallow was practised (Tables 6.3 and 6.4).

Considering the cost of irrigation funded by the government's agency for public works and the cost of agriculture furnished by individuals in the private sector engaged in cultivation, such as the landholder, tax farmer, tribal sheikh, and peasant tribesmen, agricultural costs were shared by the government and the private sector, with the government always providing at least half. Although these agricultural costs were high, the estimated value of land also was very high, more than enough to cover the costs of agriculture for the private investor. The sale of state land yielded large revenues to the government at a time when net tithe revenue was only between 11.9 per cent and 3.3 per cent, far below the cost of irrigation, as shown in Table 6.4.

In 1919, by contrast, according to the estimated expenditures on the production of wheat and barley for the harvest, the government still financed the cost of irrigation, £681,267 pounds including £66,667 pounds for construction

40 Çetinsaya, *Ottoman Administration of Iraq*, pp. 88–92.

TABLE 6.3 Net revenue of selected areas, 1911 (in Kuruş)

	Cost of irrigation	Cost of agriculture	Total	Net revenue & its % of total		Land value
Falluja	5,084,580	5,500,000	10,584,580	3,080,000	30	42,900,000
Hai	2,757,980	2,500,000	5,257,980	1,400,000	26.7	19,500,000
Basra	1,996,960	900,000	2,896,960	504,000	17.4	7,020,000
Euphrates	425,000	250,000	675,000	280,000	41.4	3,900,000
Beled	2,118,240	1,700,000	3,818,240	952,000	24.9	13,260,000
Nahrwan	1,817,120	2,000,000	3,817,120	480,000	12.5	6,600,000
Tigris East	1,006,760	1,000,000	2,006,760	560,000	28	7,800,000
(Navigation)	(48,380)		(48,380)			
Total	15,255,020	13,850,000	29,105,020	7,256,000	24.9	100,980,000

SOURCE: *LA GAZETTE FINANCIÉRE*, NO. 110, 7 NOV. 1911, P. 8.

TABLE 6.4 Tithe revenue of selected areas, 1911 (in Kuruş)

	Cost of irrigation	Tithe	Input	Net tithe & % of irrigation cost	
Falluja	5,084,580	770,000	165,000	605,000	11.9
Hai	2,757,980	350,000	75,000	275,000	10
Basra	1,996,960	126,000	27,000	99,000	5
Euphrates*	425,000	70,000	30,000	40,000	9.4
Beled	2,118,240	238,000	51,000	187,000	8.8
Nahrwan	1,817,120	120,000	60,000	60,000	3.3
Tigris East	1,006,760	140,000	30,000	110,000	10.9
(Navigation)	(48,380)		(5,000)		
Total	15,255,020	1,814,000	443,000	1,371,000	9

*Marsh area irrigated by floodwater

Note: Input is estimated at 21.4 per cent of tithe for Falluja, Hai, Basra, Beled, and Tigris East, 42.8 per cent for Euphrates, and 50 per cent for Nahrwan.

SOURCE: *LA GAZETTE FINANCIÉRE*, NO. 110, 7 NOV. 1911, P. 8.

and repair of roads and buildings. The agricultural costs paid by the private landholder, or the advance in cash, seed, cattle, pumping sets, and ploughs, amounted to £1,066,040 pounds.[41] So, clearly, the Young Turk government contributed to agricultural development on a large scale, for the substantial public spending on the irrigation cost and the relatively small tithe tax encouraged private individuals to purchase agricultural land and make improvements. The estimated land value reported for the irrigated areas was about 7.3 times the total cost of agriculture and 13.92 times the total net revenue, possibly suggesting a high demand for agricultural land (calculated from Table 6.3). In light of the contemporary situation of low interest rates, stagnant international trade, and a downturn in the domestic market, as Şevket Pamuk has explained, land represented a secure investment asset for merchants, traders, and urban notables.[42]

A declining share of tithe revenues in the total also suggests a diminishing significance of state land as a source of government revenues. In 1911, for example, the tithe there amounted to 52,717,500 kuruş (34 per cent of the total) and was followed as a revenue source by the customs revenue, 38,062,500 kuruş (25 per cent); the lease of state property, 18,045,000 kuruş (12 per cent); and taxes on animals, 17,947,500 kuruş (12 per cent). Compared with revenue in the Tanzimat era, the tithe had increased in amount, but its share in the total receipts had shrunk considerably, due to a drastic increase in customs revenue. While leasing continued to be applicable to the management of *mudawwala* land, land tax under direct official collection was only 2,062,500 kuruş (1.3 per cent), which suggests that tax farming still predominated.[43] As observed in the structure of the budget, however, large portions of indirect taxes were collected by the OPDA to repay public debts.

The variation in revenue sources caused by the expansion of trade was another noteworthy sign of agricultural progress. The value of date exports from Basra rose from £67,000 in 1868 to £328,000 in 1888, £386,000 in 1908, and £582,000 in 1913. Even more impressive, the value of wheat and barley exports reached £16,000 in 1868, £72,000 in 1888, and £612,000 in 1908, although it

41 John P. Hewett, *Report for the Army Council on Mesopotamia*, BL: IOR/L/PS/20/35 (Baghdad, 1919), p. 21.

42 Pamuk, *Ottoman Empire and European Capitalism*, p. 88.

43 The government's control over tax resources did not, however, extend to agricultural trade. The Ottoman Bank estimated the government's share of the receipts from grain exports in 1911 to be 30 per cent, while the agriculturalists received 54 per cent, and 16 per cent went to the costs of internal transport and storage and the dealers' profits. TNA: CO 696/5, "Note on the Administration of the Public Finance of 'Iraq, 1 April 1924 to 31 March 1925" (Baghdad: Government Press, 1926), pp. 18–23.

decreased to £373,000 in 1913 because of drought.[44] Wheat and barley were assumed to bear cash incomes for the landholder, tax farmer, tribal sheikh, and peasant tribesmen, thus cropland could yield large profits for them and its land value had increased, as observed in Table 6.3. Having become a tradable commodity, the possession right that Midhat Pasha intended to transfer to private individuals who would cultivate the land and pay taxes had become obsolete by the time of the Young Turks. Yet, in some cases, the purchase of state land was done without proper registration of the title, due to the deficiency of local land registries, which led to serious land disputes after the collapse of the Ottoman regime.

After the First World War broke out in 1914 and the Ottoman Empire joined the Central Powers, the Iraqi region became a battlefield in the conflict with Great Britain. The Ottoman government, therefore, took hasty measures to win the support of the tribal sheikhs, sowing the seeds of future trouble in Baghdad. As the British found upon occupation, titles to land were transferred by special decree to pro-Ottoman tribal sheikhs, official favourites, and merchants who invested in the purchase of pumps and other irrigation facilities. Although the registration records of these hurried transfers were incomplete, and thus not accurate, some recipients resold the land falsely. Still worse, during battles, the government destroyed the registers and files that did exist, exacerbating the land disputes that erupted after the war.[45] As agricultural land had attracted private investment because of its higher value, the security of the land registration procedure had not improved since Sultan Abdülhamid II intervened in it. Consequently, provision of a reliable land registration system built on the *tapu* that Namık and Midhat Pashas had established became an

---

44 The net profits of local traders from the export of agricultural produce increased because of a reduction in the export tariff that actually had taken place decades earlier. Under the Anglo-Ottoman commercial treaty of 1861, the export duty had declined from 12 to 8 per cent and annually thereafter by 1 per cent until it became fixed at 1 per cent *ad valorem*. With the consequent expansion of trade and exemption of foreign nationals from the *temettü vergisi* (Ottoman income tax), introduced in the 1890s at the rate of 5 per cent and increased after 1907 to a maximum of 50 Turkish lira, the Imperial Ottoman Bank opened branches in Baghdad, Mosul, and Basra in the 1890s, and the Eastern Bank opened a branch in Baghdad in 1912. Issawi, *Fertile Crescent*, pp. 173–75, 199–200.

45 The emergence of large landholding under the Land Code of 1858 in the Middle East has been an important subject of research for historians. See Frederic M. Goadby and Moses J. Doukhan, *The Land Law of Palestine* (Holmes Beach, FL: Gaunt, 1998); Haim Gerber, *The Social Origins of the Modern Middle East* (Boulder, CO: L. Rienner, 1987), pp. 67–185; Marion Farouk-Sluglett and Peter Sluglett, "The Transformation of Land Tenure and Rural Social Structure in Central and Southern Iraq, c. 1870–1958," *International Journal of Middle East Studies* 15, no. 4 (1983), pp. 491–505.

urgent task for the British administration and made the British mandate period a crucial transition from the Ottoman province of Baghdad to modern Iraq.

The modification of the land system after Tanzimat engendered an unprecedented change in society from the standpoint of land and agricultural history. During the long reign of Sultan Abdülhamid, his own acquisition of agricultural land, the prohibition against the privatization of state land by *tapu*, and his agricultural development measures mobilized large tribal populations for agricultural production on his lands and drew them into expanded works in urban areas. The Young Turk government that succeeded him took over his *saniyya* land and administered it as state (*mudawwala*) land, believing that was the most competent way to sustain land use and productivity. The Young Turks also maintained leasing and crop sharing in other state domains that the sultan had claimed in order to collect taxes and fees as rent, and they continued to recognize the *tapu* deed as the valid title to land, protecting the right of the landholder. While thus preserving the land system of the former sultan, the Young Turks' government steadily trudged forwards in agriculture and trade by encouraging pump irrigation and increasing the transaction of foreign trade by the Germans. Their administration is noteworthy as British officials later followed most systems innovated during this short period.

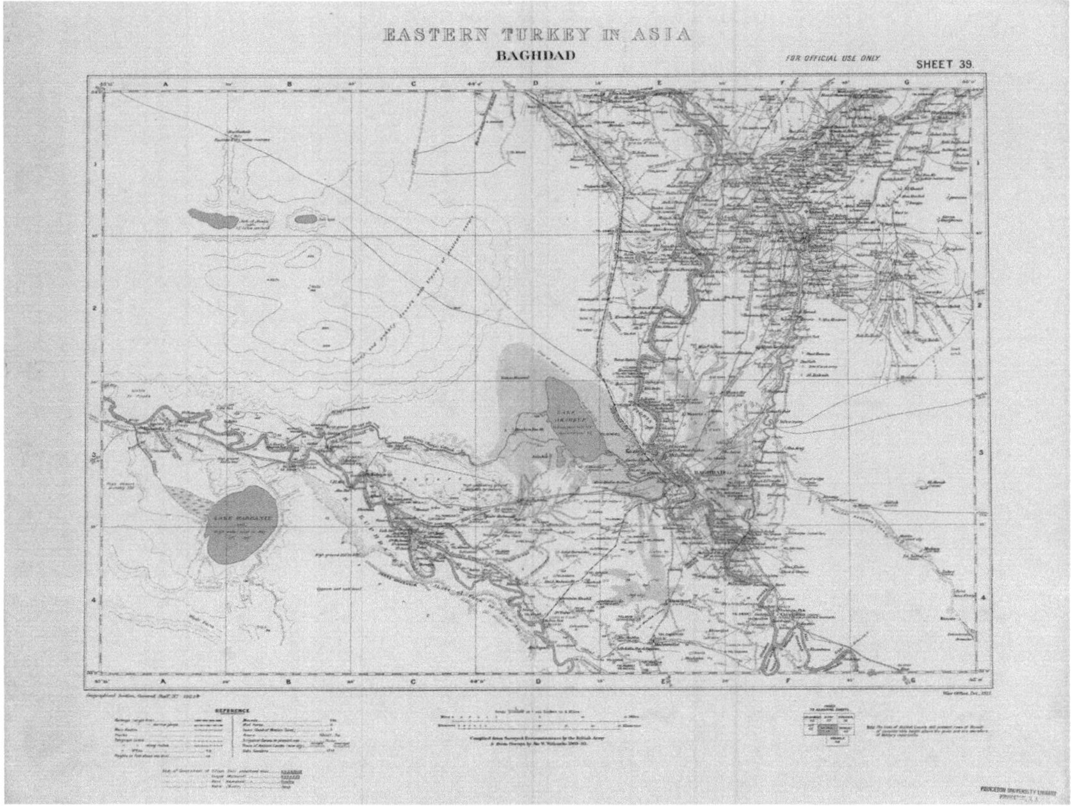

MAP 6.1 Eastern Turkey in Asia, Baghdad in 1917

SOURCE: EASTERN TURKEY IN ASIA, BAGHDAD, SHEET 39, SERIES I.D.W.O. NO. 1522 A, 1: 250,000 ([S.I.]: WAR OFFICE, 1917)

MAP SOURCE: PRINCETON UNIVERSITY LIBRARY: HTTPS://CATALOG.PRINCETON.EDU/CATALOG/6866234

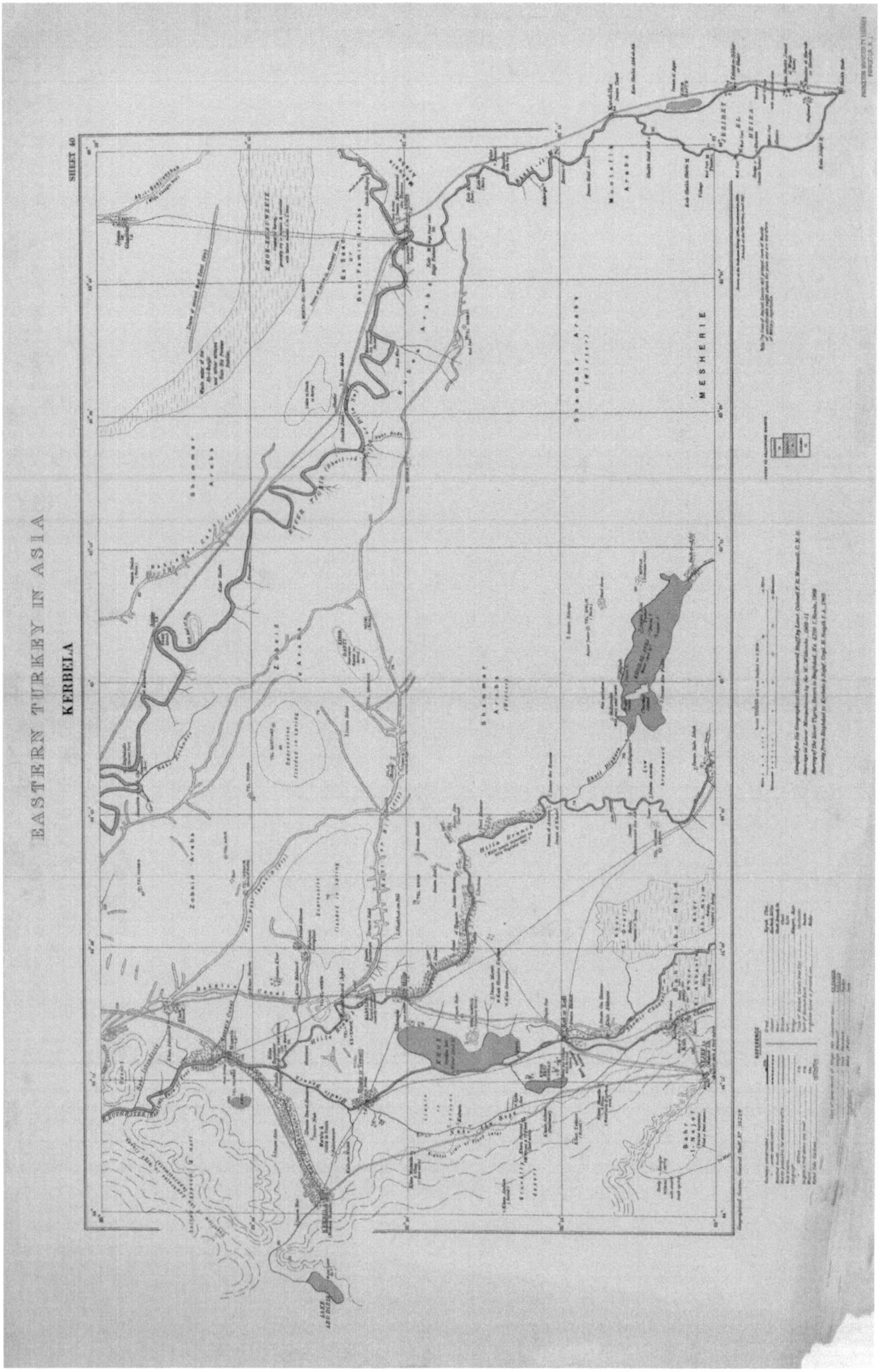

MAP 6.2 Eastern Turkey in Asia, Karbala in 1917

SOURCE: EASTERN TURKEY IN ASIA, KERBELA, SHEET 40, SERIES G.S.G.S. NO. 1522 A, 1: 250,000 ([LONDON]: [S.N.], 1915)

MAP SOURCE: PRINCETON UNIVERSITY LIBRARY: HTTPS://CATALOG.PRINCETON.EDU/CATALOG/6866235

CHAPTER 7

Land and Tax Systems during the British Occupation and Mandate Period

Following World War I, the provinces of Basra, Baghdad, and Mosul were, one by one, consolidated under the administration of the British forces. The integrated provinces began to recover from the war, and the British mandate government established in 1921 systematically set on agricultural taxation and land settlement based on the original Ottomans. The British by then adopted the Young Turk government's fiscal, tax, and land systems and revival of *tapu* for agricultural development. They restored the tax-collecting capacity of the government and expanded revenue sources. More land was being used not only to grow commercial crops, for both domestic consumption and exports, but also to accommodate irrigation canals, railways, roads, buildings, and housing, pushing up the value of land nearby. British officials, therefore, upheld the general principles of the Ottoman fiscal and tax systems, with just some modifications necessary for the expanded economy. Regarding land tenure, the British continued *tapu* tenure and tried to settle the numerous land disputes rooted in the Young Turk period. This chapter aims to give an overall picture of agriculture and the amended Ottoman systems, discussing first the rapid increases in expenditures, the reorganization of fiscal administration to cope with complicated fiscal affairs, followed by the revision of the Ottoman income tax, and the progress in settlement of the land disputes over *tapu* title and land registration.

1 Recovery of Administration and Agriculture

During the British occupation, the transfer of government from the military to a civil administration occurred quickly. Indian Expeditionary Force D landed in Fao in November 1914 and temporarily took charge of administration after the Basra province fell to it in April 1915. The force was transferred to the War Office in February 1916, becoming the Mesopotamia Expeditionary Force. It occupied Baghdad in March 1917, Kirkuk in late summer 1918, and after the Armistice of Mudros in October 1918, all places previously under control of the Ottoman Sixth Army. The civil administration of the Expeditionary Force soon was separated from the British India Office and reorganized into the Civil

 | DOI:10.1163/9789004384347_009

Administration of Mesopotamia under the Colonial Office in early 1919, and it established a provisional government centred on a core executive Council of Ministers in November 1920. What is known as the mandate government was formed in 1921, and on 23 August 1921, Faisal was enthroned as the king of Iraq (1921–33) under the British mandate. In March 1924, Iraq's Constitutional Assembly ratified the Treaty of Lausanne and passed the Organic Law and the Electoral Law, and in January 1926, the newly established government accepted a new Anglo-Iraqi Treaty, under which the mandate would be in force for twenty-five years unless Iraq was admitted to the League of Nations earlier as a fully independent state. In July 1926, the Iraqi parliament ratified the tripartite Anglo-Turkish-Iraqi Treaty, settling the status of Mosul, which led to both the early termination of the British mandate in 1932 and the admission of Iraq to the League of Nations.[1]

Upon gaining full control over the occupied territories in October 1918, the British occupation government began its state administration without causing a fundamental rupture from the previous Ottoman system. All former Turkish officials present in Baghdad were registered and re-employed.[2] Drawing on their knowledge of the existing Ottoman system and local customs, the government restored the districts and sub-districts with the appointment of political and financial officials as the chief administrators. It also repaired damaged infrastructure and facilities, secured safe roads and transport, and resumed operation of the port of Basra facilities, customs administration, communications, and railways that had been established by the Ottoman government.[3] Their recovery and concurrent improvement nurtured a boom in trade and raised constant revenues for the occupation government. The banks established during the Ottoman period – the Eastern Bank, the Imperial Bank of Persia, and the Imperial Ottoman Bank – continued in operation, stabilizing the boom and financing imports and exports without interruption. For currency for internal use, Expeditionary Force D paid for its local purchases and its payments to the Civil Administration of Mesopotamia in Indian rupees (silver and notes), which made the rupee in due course the medium of exchange. Turkish paper money was forbidden under a proclamation of December 1916,

1 Charles Tripp, *A History of Iraq* (Cambridge: Cambridge University Press, 2000), pp. 52–60.

2 TNA: FO 371/4150/187296, Administration Report, Revenue Board, Baghdad, 22 Mar.–31 Dec. 1917 (Baghdad: Printed at Government Press, 1918), p. 1.

3 Tripp, *History of Iraq*, p. 45; Peter Sluglett, *Britain in Iraq: Contriving King and Country* (London: I.B. Tauris, 2007), pp. 8–9; Philip Willard Ireland, *'Iraq: A Study in Political Development* (London: Jonathan Cape, 1937), pp. 112–19. For the British vision of Ottoman Iraq, see Toby Dodge, *Inventing Iraq: The Failure of Nation Building and a History Denied* (New York: Columbia University Press, 2003), pp. 43–61.

while the gold lira was continuously used for local purchases such as livestock, wool, houses, and land, and in intertribal transactions.[4]

Recovery of agriculture had taken place in the occupied areas during the war, owing to the Agricultural Development Scheme that the civil administration of the Expeditionary Force had designated. Its main function was to increase the production of cereals within the occupied areas, and after the armistice, the agricultural department of the civil administration replaced its tasks. As observed in the official report, they immediately began to repair damaged irrigation facilities, provide lost necessities, mobilize agricultural labour, and introduce technology. In response to an urgent need for grain crops for the military troops and people, British officers made elaborate surveys of local practice and custom and took measures suited to occasion demands.[5] In the north, as an example, producing wheat for most domestic consumption, they supplied plow animals and seeds that the escaping Turks had carried off. In the Erbil district, the richest wheat-producing area providing large quantities of grain to Baghdad and for export, the Revenue and Agricultural Departments hastily delivered some 302 bullocks for ploughing as a substitute for about two thousand mules that had been taken as pack animals during the war.[6]

In the irrigated areas, particularly along the Euphrates River, peasant tribesmen had used to work for organized government projects as forced levies or as a part of tribal duties, and British political officers inherited their customs and tradition. The Irrigation Department repaired damaged irrigation facilities, cleared silt, and constructed protective flood banks with the help of tribesmen organized by their sheikh or *serkâr* according to the customary levy on them. Their restoration was rather quick because irrigation systems had been preserved during the war.

Along the Euphrates, waterwheels (*karûd*) continued to operate from Ramadi to Nasiriya, and from Hit upwards, large waterwheels. In Nasiriya,

4 BL: IOR/L/PS/10/368/2, *Report on the Conditions for Trade in Mesopotamia, prepared in the Office of the Civil Commissioner in Baghdad* (Baghdad: Superintendent Government Press, 1920), pp. 9–10.

5 The main lines of work undertaken were: (1) an enquiry into the agricultural practices and cultivation in vogue; (2) experimental work with different varieties of cotton and wheat to discover those best suited to the country; (3) demonstration of the uses of labour-saving machinery in cooperation with the Mesopotamia agents for the manufacturers; (4) soil survey of the part of the area irrigated by canals taking off from the River Diyala; (5) study of insect pests and diseases of plants; and (6) advice to cultivators on general matters pertaining to agriculture. BL: IOR, MSS, Eur, F 235/5, *Administration Report of the Department of Agriculture in Mesopotamia for the Year 1920* (Baghdad: Government Press, 1921), p. 1.

6 Iraq, Office of the Civil Commissioner, *Administration Report of the Arbil Division for the Year 1919* (Baghdad: Government Press, 1920), p. 11.

where large marshes still appeared in the flooding season, a noria (*nāʿūra*, Persian waterwheel) had been used and maintained by the tribesmen. The reconstruction of the Hindiya Barrage by the Young Turks had already put under control floodwater and enabled pump irrigation in the Middle Euphrates. As observed from Diwaniya to Falluja, centrifugal pumps of oil engines made by British makers began to prevail with a delivery of six or eight inches in size.[7] Many canals in the Middle Euphrates rapidly recovered from the damage, and unused canals such as the Georgiya and Bani Hasan Canals on the Hindiya River reopened. These projects revitalized agriculture in the region, as noted by the new head of the Mahmudiya Canal, which reclaimed some 15,000 acres. The scattered tribesmen began to return to their former homes, even attracting nearby tribesmen, whose total numbers were estimated to be three times as many as the year before.[8]

The Hilla district, which had dried up years earlier, drew the attention of the British administration immediately after occupation for agricultural development. They planned to auction 200 acres near Hilla to produce green fodder for a government dairy farm. Owing to the armistice, the original scheme scaled down. Eventually 67 acres were cultivated and sown as oats; 22 acres, as Indian wheat; 32 acres, as local wheat; 5 acres, potatoes; 2 acres, lucerne and hemp; 2 acres, cotton; 3 acres, and groundnuts; 1 acres. This smaller project, however, produced larger yields of crops than before, leaving a favourable impression of the British on the peasants. Oats yielded 42 tons of green fodder for transport animals between the adjourning military camps. The productivity of wheat also was high, the imported seed of Punjab-15 wheat produced 596 pounds per acre, and wheat of Punjab-11, 824 pounds, compared to local wheat producing 428 pounds per acre that was still high, as the seeds provided were 80 pounds per acre. The local durum wheat was recorded 1,134 pounds per acre.[9]

Although the harvest was to be consumed by the military troops, its success attracted the interest of private investors in agricultural land in Hilla. The Young Turk government's attempt to introduce pump irrigation and import modern harvesting machine resumed. Two pumps were installed to supply water to the military dairy farm. The only major problems in those days was that the soil varied from heavy loam to stiff clay and that it tended to be deficient in producing vegetables and was inclined to be salty. The Lynch Brothers

---

7 BL: IOR, MSS, Eur, F 235/3, *Administration Report of the Agricultural Directorate for the Year 1919* (Baghdad: Government Press, 1920), p. 17.

8 BL: IOR, MSS, Eur, F 235/5, *Administration Report of the Department of Agriculture*, pp. 5–6, for Samawa, pp. 177, 180–81, for Hindiya.

9 BL: IOR, MSS, Eur, F 235/5, *Administration Report of the Department of Agriculture*, pp. 17–18.

imported twelve reapers but struggled initially to find a purchaser for them. Once a person named Rahman Effendi bought six of them, the reminder were quietly sold. Under the British occupation administration, after weeding and cultivating machines were demonstrated, over twenty orders were booked. In 1918, about ten portable threshing machines were brought into Mesopotamia.[10] Consequently, agricultural land along the Euphrates River that had begun to expand during the Young Turk period became productive, making the district a flourishing agricultural district.

Irrigation canals on the Diyala River continued to keep a high level of water discharge, as observed in Table 7.1, particularly after the Irrigation Department took control of the irrigation work in March and June 1918, on the left and right banks respectively, in place of the Political Department. As an example, it was customary each June to dam the Khalis Canal, whose bed lay above the water level, to raise the water level. But the first flooding often washed away the dam, so that water supply into the canal ceased. The construction of a new head to the Canal made large areas cultivable, irrigating the largest land in the Diyala region.[11] On the Euphrates River, as the district towns prospered, the numbers of irrigation canals rapidly increased. Even in Nasiriya, which Midhat Pasha established as the district centre, relocated from Suq al-Shuyukh, about fifty big and small canals had served for flow irrigation since the Ottoman era. They used *nāʿūra* (waterwheels), *karûd* (bucket lifts), *daki*, and even pumps to pull water into grain fields, and lifts for gardens. The tribal sheikhs by then had begun to install pumping engines, and desired more under the British administration.[12]

Cultivators on areas brought under cultivation were mainly peasant tribesmen who used to work as hired labour in irrigated areas. For the newly reclaimed areas along the Yusufiya Canal and the eastern borders of Hilla district, the sheikh of the Bani Ajil tribe reclaimed land with his tribesmen for cultivation. Those tribesmen, who had already worked as hired labourers under the custom of crop sharing during the Ottoman period, moved on a large scale to the Yusufiya lands, due to excessive rents in the Musaib districts. In other areas, the recruitment of peasant tribesmen followed the customary way of crop sharing and agreement known as *mugarisa*. The shortage of agricultural labour was not always favourable to the migrating peasant tribesmen

10 Ibid., pp. 21, 25.

11 Iraq, Office of the Civil Commissioner, *Administration Report of the Baʿqubah Division for the Year 1918* (Baghdad: Government Press), pp. 18–19.

12 BL: IOR/L/PS/20/250, *Reports of Administration for 1918 of Divisions and Districts of the Occupied Territories in Mesopotamia. Volume 1* (1919), p. 406. The method of *daki* is unclear in the document.

TABLE 7.1 Water discharge of major irrigation canals

River	Canals	Average discharge (cusec)	Area cultivated (acre)	Water duty (cusec)
Diyala	Khalis	540	13,814	26
	Ruz	295	6,716	23
	Haruniya	66	1,576	24
	Shahraban	39	1,674	43
	Mahrut	455	5,574	12
	Khorasan	341	10,922	32
Euphrates	Musaib	127	1,117	9
	Iskandariya	151	1,906	13
	Nasiriya	138	2,132	15
	Yusufiya	540	9,251	17
	Bani Hasan	487	6,161	12
	Husayniya	511	2,028	4*
	Georgiya	390	4,687	12
	Hilla (area)	3,500	70,000	20

*Water used for drinking purposes and tanks at Karbala.
Note: Discharge and duty are measured by cubic foot per second (cusec), and area by acre. Omitting the Husayniya Canal, the average duty for summer 1919 works out to 20 acres per cusec.
SOURCE: BL: IOR, MSS, EUR, F 235/3, *ADMINISTRATION REPORT OF THE AGRICULTURAL DIRECTORATE FOR THE YEAR 1919* (BAGHDAD: PRINTED AT THE GOVERNMENT PRESS, 1920), P. 8.

and soon caused numerous disputes among the landholder, tribal sheikh, and tribesmen, becoming a pressing issue for the British to solve for agricultural development.[13] Particularly in the Muntafiq tribal district, the disputes over land were frequent and, as agricultural production fully recovered, they became irresolvable.

As the British administration revitalized agricultural production to pre-war levels, it resumed tax collection as practised before. Involved in large managerial works, the local officials in charge were laden with heavy responsibility of collecting revenues from agricultural production. Alongside the agricultural improvement, the provincial treasury inherited from the Ottomans assumed a new aspect of fiscal administration as the revenue department. The details

13 Iraq, Office of the Civil Commissioner, *Administration Report of the Hilla Division for the Year 1919* (Baghdad: Government Press, 1920), pp. 1–3.

of fiscal problems and the British policies need to be examined, because agricultural taxation was a major task of the mandate government to increase the revenue under the principle of the balanced budget.

2 Problems of Fiscal Deficits

Although the British administration benefitted from the established Ottoman infrastructure, facilities, and institutions, it began to distinguish itself from them in how it financed the civil administration and its military operations. Comparing the structure of revenues in 1924 with 1911, as summarized in Tables 7.3 and 7.4, the revenue greatly increased under the British mandate. It resulted from customs and excise revenues that were about 3.85 times higher than those of the Ottomans by the mid-1920s, after the port of Basra had expanded and after its capacity had been improved with British aid to accommodate British steamships.[14] Its Revenue Department superintended the collection of the taxes for local spending – including the stamp tax and those on fish, salt, fishing and shooting licences, the skins of wild animals, silk, and liquor – that the Ottomans had earmarked for repayment of the public debt. Increased expenditures for postwar economic rehabilitation, defence, expanding the administration, and development, however, raised fiscal deficits so far above the Ottoman level that even the higher revenues from the postwar boom and expanding trade were insufficient to cover them. Between 1921 and 1923, when the mandate government had to finance military spending to suppress tribal uprisings and increased charges for levies, the deficits expanded rapidly. The revenues, still heavily reliant on agricultural taxes and customs duties, were slow to increase and fluctuated seasonally, for which their initial large increases were hardly sustainable.

As Figure 7.1 indicates, revenues increased steadily during the military control of Basra, Baghdad, and Mosul, between 1915 and 1918, then rapidly until 1921, as the civil administration's capacity for revenue collection improved and the agricultural development scheme became effective. In 1921–22, however, revenues dropped sharply, partly because the government granted politically motivated tax remissions on agricultural produce early in the financial year and partly because prices fell below the fixed conversion rates.[15] Ceaseless internal disturbance obstructed domestic commerce, and transit trade slowed

14 TNA: CO 696/5, Note on the Administration of the Public Finance of 'Iraq, 1 Apr. 1924–31 Mar. 1925 (Baghdad: Government Press, 1926), pp. 18–23.

15 TNA: CO 696/5, "Administration Reports, 1922–1924," p. 26.

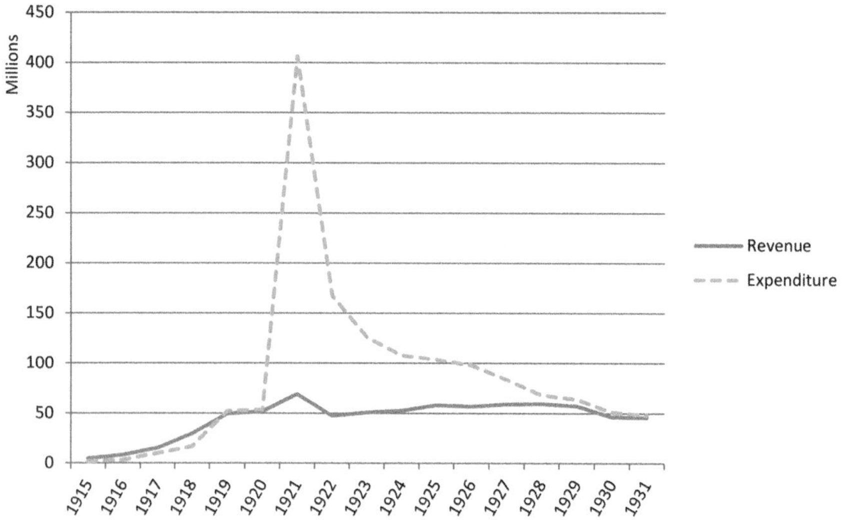

FIGURE 7.1 Revenues and expenditures of Iraq, 1915–1931 (in Rupees) (including the expenditures for the Iraqi army, the Royal Air Force, levies; administration of the high commission, and "miscellaneous")
SOURCE: TABLES 7.7 AND 7.8

after the land route to Persia was closed for two months. Because of previous over-importing, local market prices for goods had sunk from 20 per cent to 40 per cent below the invoice value in 1920. Especially grain prices had dropped as much as 100 per cent in some areas because of the rapid reduction in the size of the British garrison, and the purchasing power of individuals had diminished rapidly.[16] As a result, taxes on natural produce were down by nearly 10 lakhs rupees, while revenue from customs and excise was up by nearly 22 lakhs rupees because of the principal increases in import duties and tobacco excise in 1923.[17] Subsequently, due to increased customs revenues, the revenues recovered until 1925, but not to the previous level, and they dropped again after 1929 as the worldwide Depression set in.

Tackling the fiscal deficit had been the mandate government's major task. Particularly, military expenditures soon burdened the administration so heavily that they had to be checked, and revenue collection designated for military

16 TNA: CO 696/4, Colonial Office: Iraq Sessional Papers, "Administration Reports, 1921," p. 30.

17 The government made a settlement of its net liability to India, Rs 21.13 lakhs received from India for the period 1914–22, by direct cash remittance. TNA: CO 696/5, "Administration Reports, 1922–1924," pp. 8, 11.

use had to be closely monitored. In contrast to the Ottoman arrangement, under which taxes collected in kind were earmarked for military expenditures, the British applied strict procedures of accounting and revenue collecting.[18] The deficit, however, worsened as expenditures on the railways and the port of Basra were charged on the budget of 1920–21, and as the levies and the operation costs of the new army were added in 1922. Afterwards, expenditures continuously surpassed revenues, and the government incurred large accumulated deficits (Figure 7.1).

The deficits in the early years were financed by drawing first on the account of Expeditionary Force D in India, then on that of the Mesopotamia Expeditionary Force in 1916, and finally on the account of the Civil Administration of Mesopotamia after 1919.[19] The problem was partially solved by a compromise between the British Army, under the War Office, and the Civil Administration, under the Colonial Office, but that financial settlement was not sufficient to maintain a balanced budget.[20] During the fiscal years 1923 and 1924, the settlement of accounts between the British and Iraqi governments progressed, including the accounts received from India for the period 1914–22 under the general settlement devised at the Cairo Conference in 1921. In October 1924, the final statements of the current account were submitted by the accountant general, showing the debit and credit position of the Iraqi government vis-à-vis its principal foreign creditors and debtors – the British government, India, and the Mesopotamian Railways (previously the Baghdad Railway), which had been managed by the British until 31 March 1923.

After Iraq ratified the Treaty of Lausanne in 1924 and the new Anglo-Iraq Treaty in 1926, the British started pulling out of all state matters except foreign and military affairs. Thereafter the Iraqis were heavily burdened by requirements to pay for increased military expenditures and to repay the Ottoman public debt, but under a balanced budget, the revenues did not increase sufficiently to meet those requirements. The secretary of state for the colonies appointed a financial mission to report to the British and Iraqi governments

---

18 TNA: CO 696/1, Colonial Office: Iraq Sessional Papers, Administration Reports, 1917–1918, p. 9.

19 Ibid.

20 The War Office paid the Colonial Office £860,000 in February 1922. Of this sum, the Colonial Office credited to the Civil Administration the sum of Rs 10,441,116 (using decimal system), thus partly financing the net expenditure of Rs 17,717,030 for the military during 1919–20 and 1920–21 and leaving the civil deficit Rs 9,255,831.14.3 at the end of the fiscal year, 31 March 1921. The special deposit account was opened in this year for the adjustment of belated charges, mostly from India, and credits in the period from 1914 to 31 March 1919 with a credit of 10 lakhs. TNA: CO 696/5, Colonial Office: Iraq Sessional Papers, "Administration Reports, 1922–1924," p. 8.

how the budget could be balanced during the treaty period and still fulfill the requirements to pay for defence, administration, development, and the Ottoman public debt. When the resulting report of 1925 recommended transferring to Iraq the railway and electric power companies and the port of Basra, the transfer of the latter two took place without delay and that of the railway in 1936. As to expenditures, the report proposed suspending public works and irrigation and agriculture services, but the new repayment burdens required far more than even these budget cuts.[21] Parts of the deficit were solved by a series of British-Iraqi financial agreements under which the former arranged to repay some previous military and administrative expenses, but the government continued to run the budget in deficit throughout the mandate period, except in 1927.

3 Modification of the Ottoman Fiscal Administration

To deal with the deficit, the mandate government reorganized fiscal administration. One early, but little-noticed, change was to Ottoman accounting, which had been carried out by different financial officials without a supervisory office to coordinate their practices, so that an exchange between two departments was not satisfactorily transacted. In January 1921 an Accountant General's Office was formed with an accountant general, a British secretary, and an Iraqi assistant accountant general to coordinate all government accounting operations, such as the accounting, custody, and movement of funds and audit. Beginning in the fiscal year 1921–22, for expenditure, the main heading of the state budget was changed to chapter; the sub-heading, to section and vote; and the detailed heading, to article. For the votes, the sanction of the legislative body was required, and any excess over the votes or transfer between the votes required confirmation by the Representative Assembly of a proposal from the Council of State. The Ministry of Finance controlled the transfer between articles of the same vote. Expenditures on the accounts of Major Resource Operations and the Middle Eastern Expenditure made by the

21 TNA: CO 696/5, "Administration Reports, 1922–1924," p. 8; Great Britain, Colonial Office, *'Iraq: Report of the Financial Mission appointed by the Secretary of State for the Colonies to enquire into the Financial Position and Prospects of the Government of 'Iraq, 1925, presented by the Secretary of State for the Colonies to Parliament by Command of His Majesty, June, 1925* (London: HMSO, 1925), p. 55.

British military occupation administration were transferred to the high commissioner's office from the 1922 fiscal year on.[22]

Exercising more control over fiscal affairs and public finance than the Ottomans, the accountant general also drew up a set of accounting regulations for approval by the Council of Ministers. In April 1924 the auditor general's department was separated from the Ministry of Finance, responsible only to the legislative body, the Council of Ministers, and the Parliament. The auditor general issued the statement of public accounts regularly, and the accountant general's department of the ministry assumed responsibility for accounting and even such minor works as procuring, keeping, and issuing stamps, which were transferred from the controller of the government press in 1923. By 1925, the auditor general's office became an independent department, separate from that of the inspector general of accounts.[23]

Regarding revenues, the mandate government followed a system similar to that of the Ottoman budget until the fiscal year 1923–24, but it implemented a new principle of vote on account in the 1924–25 budget, and, in the fiscal year 1926–27, to gain more control over taxation, the Iraqi parliamentary government restored income tax (Table 7.3). The Directorate of Revenue, which had belonged to the Treasury's Department of State Domains, became an independent Department of Revenue that specialized in agricultural taxes and income tax. Its work extended over the categories known as votes one to five (agricultural taxes and revenues from government properties) in chapter I and as vote six (property tax) in chapter II of the Iraqi budget.

Stephen H. Longrigg, who authored the classic study *Four Centuries of Modern Iraq*, was appointed the first secretary of revenue in April 1926 and, concurrently, inspector general from June to January 1927. The director of the Revenue Department was appointed from among the Iraqi officials, as the closest liaison with Longrigg. After the first Iraqi revenue director was transferred, Longrigg took over the duties until Ahmed Fahmi, who had made a survey report on agricultural taxation in the Shamiya district that still is a highly regarded primary source on the subject, was appointed in May 1927. Fahmi was promoted later to accountant general, and Longrigg became the assistant adviser to the Revenue Department, which had gained the status of a ministry.[24]

22 TNA: CO 813/1, *Iraq Government Gazettes*, 1921–1925, p. 11; TNA: CO 696/4, "Administration Reports, 1921," pp. 28–29.

23 TNA: CO 696/4, "Administration Reports, 1921," p. 28; TNA: CO 696/5, "Administration Reports, 1922–24," pp. 2–3, 5.

24 The report for 1926–27 of the Revenue Department, under Director S.H. Longrigg, was comprehensive and highly regarded by contemporary British officials. Ahmed Fahmi

Under those two capable officials, the fiscal system was reorganized, collection of income tax began, the focus of agricultural taxation was changed from produce to land, and the assessment of land for taxation progressed rapidly.

The immediate and most impactful consequence of the reform of the fiscal system took place at the district level, where the Ottoman accounting system had prevailed without a clear distinction between civil and fiscal administration. Now, the director and accounting officials of the Revenue Department supervised revenue collection, and expenditure was under the control of the financial officials of the Ministry of Finance. In the district, the district governor (*mutasarrıf*) supervised both an accountant (*muhâsebe*) for revenue and an accountant for expenditures, whose functions had been combined since 1922 but were separated in 1928. All expenditure matters were put under direct supervision of the accountant general in Baghdad. In the type of sub-district known as *kazâ*, the *müdîr-i mâl* (district inspector) of the *kazâ* performed finance and revenue duties under supervision of the sub-district governor (*kâimmakâm*). In all other sub-districts (*nâhiye*), the sub-district administrator *müdîr*, under the Ministry of Interior, carried out financial and administrative duties, and for preparation of the 1928 budget, the Ministry of Finance provided the *nâhiye*s of Khanaqin, Daltawa, Falluja, Afak, Suq al-Shuyukh, Khurasan, and Hashimiya with a financial official (*memûr-u mâl*). At seven other *nâhiye* headquarters, the Ministry of Finance appointed a revenue clerk to secure at least a proper accounting of revenues. At the district level, the accountant had more clearly defined responsibilities, as well as more time to master the subject of revenue administration, with its latest developments, and to tour and inspect outstations, so he was better qualified to act as an expert adviser to his district governor and the administrative council.[25]

The systematic reorganization of the revenue department revitalized a centralized fiscal administration similar to the one that the Ottoman government had implemented in its province of Baghdad. The Ottoman system had secured revenues to fund its military operations and civil administration, and the people's incomes by way of tax farming and crop sharing. But it was insufficient to finance increasing expenditures, and it began to be modified under the mandate government.

---

made a survey report on agricultural taxation in Shamiya for the period between June 1926 and February 1927 and published the official report on the same district. Even today, the notes and reports of both Longrigg and Fahmi are valuable primary sources for the study of the agricultural tax system during the mandate period.

25 TNA: CO 696/7, Colonial Office, "Report on the Operations of the Revenue Department for the Financial Year 1928–29," pp. 1–2; TNA: 730/125/6, "Notes on the Extent to Which Ottoman Law is in Force in Iraq," 28 Dec, 1927, signed by C.A. Hooper.

Using some noteworthy customs, for example, was recorded in an administrative report for 1917–18 of the British Colonial Office, including the direct collection (*emânet*) of grains applied to the spending for the military troops in the province:

> Each *serkar* was told at what granary (*ambar*) he had to deliver the revenue share of his grain. At each granary there was a *Mamur Ambar* [*sic*] (granary official) and a clerk from the *Mamur Shubah* [*sic*] (district official), the one being a check on the other. The *Mamur Ambar* received and weighed the grain and then gave the tenderer a receipt. This receipt was then taken by the tenderer to the *Shubah*'s clerk, who compared the amount received with the receipt granted by the *Mamur Ambar*. The grain was then kept in the granary until it was taken over by a representative of the Department of Local Resources on behalf of the Army. For this grain, payment had to be made by the Military to the Civil Administration. In 1917 the rates were Rs 168 per ton for wheat and Rs 107 for barley, conventional rates based on the following three factors: (1) the pre-war prices of grain in Baghdad; (2) an addition for increased costs of collection taken as 12 1/2% of difference between the pre-war prices of grain in Baghdad and the prices prevailing in Baghdad at the time the calculation was made; (3) an addition of 10% for the margin. The prices to be paid by the Army for the 1918 grain were provisionally fixed at the same figure.[26]

By utilizing this Ottoman method of collecting revenue for military troops, the British were able to meet an immediate need for their own operations until 1921, when grain prices began to decline while the assigned amounts of crops remained unchanged, reducing the revenue. Military expenditure continued to increase, and the government had to modify the Ottoman method of tax collecting or implement tax reform.

Reviving Ottoman income tax was discussed as a solution to the fiscal deficit. The capabilities of the financial officials under British leadership enabled the government to resume collecting income tax, which had been suspended due to disagreement between British officials and local administrators. Under Ottoman law, persons liable to a specific tax were divided into groups according to the nature of their trade, profession, and so forth, and were ranged

26 TNA: CO 696/1, Colonial Office: Iraq Sessional Papers, "Administration Reports, 1917–1918," p. 9.

within those groups in three grades according to their tax-paying capacity.[27] The minimum amount of tax was set very low, so that even domestic servants and porters were included, and taxes of as little as ten piasters (less than 1.5 rupees [Rs 1.5]) per annum (p.a.) were collected, while the maximum payable by any individual was £T 50 (Rs 675) p.a.

In early 1919, the high commissioner of the Civil Administration of Mesopotamia agreed to a new income tax law based on Ottoman law, and in October tentative proposals were sent to all divisional and district officers for their opinion and for consideration by representatives of the local population. These proposals differed from Ottoman tax law in several respects. The British, for example, proposed to disregard the tax groups, except for the convenience of assessment; to exempt persons with incomes of less than Rs 3,000 p.a. from the tax; and to classify all persons with incomes from Rs 3,000 up to Rs 75,000 p.a. into grades, each grade having a maximum and minimum limit. Taxation was to be a levy of a fixed sum on all persons in any given grade. Those with incomes from Rs 75,000 up to Rs 100,000 p.a. were charged a uniform tax of 3,000 p.a., and those with incomes of Rs 100,000 and greater were charged more. Consequently, the proposals appeared to be more apparently favourable to the lower-income groups but much more disadvantageous to higher-earning merchants, traders, politicians, landholders, and farm owners.[28]

Considering the proposals carefully, the divisional and district officers and their administrative councils offered little criticism of the details of the scheme, making only two or three suggestions for a lower minimum than Rs 3,000. Still, some questioned whether an income tax should be introduced at all:

> The most strenuous opposition came from the municipal councils on which the commercial element is strongly represented. This is, though not unexpected, disappointing, for the commercial classes in this country, far from suffering hardship during the war, have actually become more prosperous, owing to the granting of large government contracts, the presence of large bodies of troops paid out of other treasuries, the

27 Nadir Özbek points out that the collection of income tax in the province of Baghdad assigned to gendarmerie in 1875 enhanced the government authority and increasingly became oppressive after Kurdish tribesmen were recruited for it during Sultan Abdülhamid II's reign. Özbek, *İmparatorluğun Bedeli: Osmanlı'da Vergi, Siyaset ve Toplumsal Adalet (1839–1908)* (Istanbul: Boğaziçi Üniversitesi Yayınevi, 2015), pp. 113–53.

28 TNA: CO 696/2, Colonial Office: Iraq Sessional Papers, "Administration Reports, 1919," p. 16.

TABLE 7.2 Income tax laws (summary)

Ottoman Turkish Law	British proposal
Persons liable to specific tax divided into groups according to nature of trade, profession etc., and ranged, within those groups, in three grades according to taxable capacity	Groups disregarded, except for convenience of assessment, and all persons with incomes of Rs 3,000 or more classified in grades, each grade having a maximum and minimum limit, with levy of a fixed sum on all persons in any given grade
Minimum very low, even domestic servants, wood cutters and porters included, and amounts as little as ten piasters (less than Rs 1 and 8 annas) p.a. collected	Incomes under Rs 3,000 exempt
Minimum payable by any individual £T 50 (Rs 675) p.a., proportional tax possibly higher, but unlikely, as most profitable professions all subject to the fixed rate	Incomes of from Rs 75,000 to Rs 100,000 p.a. to pay Rs 3,000 p.a, any incomes above Rs 100,000 p.a. to pay more

Note: Indian numbering of lakh is changed to a decimal system by using a thousand separator.
SOURCE: TNA: CO 696/2, COLONIAL OFFICE, IRAQ SESSIONAL PAPERS, "ADMINISTRATION REPORTS, 1919," P. 16.

> rise in the rupee exchange, the diversion of much of the Persian trade from the Caucasus to the Mesopotamian route, etc.[29]

Opposition was neither so strong nor so general as to make the revenue secretary change his opinion that the "income tax was in principle a fair tax and that postponing its imposition [would] throw an unduly heavy share of the cost of government on the shoulders of the agricultural community, allowing many to escape direct taxation who had profited most by the occupation."[30] In 1927, the Income Tax Law, based on the British proposal, was enacted, and collection began. Under this law, incomes under Rs 4,000 were tax exempt, and all persons, including British officials and residents, and all corporations with incomes above that amount, were taxed. But the exemption was applied to

29 Ibid.
30 Ibid.

most of the population, and the rest were taxed at such a low rate that revenue fell far below the estimated amount.[31]

Along with rehabilitating income tax, revenue officials set their sights on another tax reform: replacing the tithe that the Ottoman government had collected for centuries with a land tax, which Longrigg considered a fair, sustainable tax base. This reform required changing the method of tax assessment, settling boundary disputes, and registering landholders as taxpayers. Attempts to implement it progressed rapidly as British political officials in the districts and sub-districts gained intimate knowledge of local agriculture and land systems, but it provoked more tribal complaints and disputes.

4 Modification of the Ottoman Agricultural Tax System

According to a revenue circular issued in early 1918 by the Mesopotamia Expeditionary Force, its method of agricultural taxation would not differ from that of the Ottomans and would be carried out through the three steps of assessment, collection, and payment in different areas of production according to their methods of irrigation, types of produce, or forms of landholding. The tax assessment would be either fixed on the tax unit or proportional to the produce, depending on the type of land and local custom.

For tax collection, except regarding grains for military use, the government continued to use the Ottoman methods of direct collecting (*emânet*), leasing, crop sharing, and tax farming (*iltizam*). Trouble could be prevented and friction reduced if the local sheikh and *serkâr* were the tax farmers, and the tax was generally taken as a government share of the gross produce, whose assessment varied from area to area. In grain fields, as was the practice in irrigated tribal areas under the Ottoman regime, the crops were divided on the threshing floor, and the government share was collected by the tax farmer or delivered to the granary by the peasant for military use. For most summer crops, which were not required by the army, taxes were paid in cash according to a cash equivalent, or a conversion rate was fixed for each ton of the government share.

As the British recognized the government share as a tax, they surveyed the share area by area. On the previous *saniyya* and *mudawwala* land, the government's higher share became affordable for most peasant cultivators because of better land productivity. Such land, for instance that on the Yusufiya Canal, was leased out to a *serkâr* in a single block (*mukâtaa*), renewable annually or

31 TNA: CO 813/2, *Iraq Government Gazettes*, 1926–27, pp. 195–207, Income Tax Law, *Al-Waqāʾiʿ al-ʿIrāqīyah*, No. 551, 8 June 1927.

for a guaranteed term. The lease put all obligations on the *serkâr*, including maintenance of order, protection of telegraph lines and bridges, prevention of over-flooding, clearing of canals, proper cultivation, and collection and payment of revenue. In addition, he was to divide the land into fields of standard size and see to his customary responsibilities of sowing clean seeds, weeding, maintaining boundary roads between the various holdings, and planting certain numbers of trees other than date palms with permission. In return for his satisfactory service, he received a commission. The British policy on *saniyya* properties, however, was not uniform because the distinction between state land (*arâzi-i miriye*) and *mudawwala* land had principally disappeared before the occupation. The government share in particular varied from region to region. Nowhere did it take more than 36 per cent of the produce, allowing the customary rebate to revenue-paying sheikhs and *serkârs*. In the north-west, all the best estates that had a good water supply and were capable of growing rice belonged to the sultan, at rates above 40 per cent, but loans were granted generously all around.[32]

Outside the tribal areas, tax farming also resembled that of the Ottomans. The right to tax farming in a given area was let to an individual at auction, and he undertook collection by actual division on the threshing floor for crops divided by shares. The government share of produce customarily brought to town for sale was collected in cash on the sale price at markets set aside for the purpose. Articles of Iltizam Regulation No. 16 of 1929 show the continuity with the Ottoman practices in their details. For example, the minister of finance, instead of a finance official, entrusted the collection of the government share to a tax farmer. At the request of the district governor (*mutasarrıf*), their official defined the area of the tax farm if it was not larger than a whole sub-district (*kazâ*), and directed the auction held at the headquarters of the district concerned for twenty days. The tax-collecting right was granted to the highest bidder for less than three years, and the local financial authorities were not authorized to grant a right longer than one year without the sanction of the minister of finance.[33]

Meanwhile, at least one week before the auction the administrative council approved the beginning and end dates of the auction period, the produce to be collected by the tax farmer, the rate of the government share, the rate of deduction from the price of produce if allowed, the number of instalments, and the

32 TNA: CO 696/4, "Administration Reports, 1921," pp. 30–31.

33 Iltizam Regulations "No. 16 of 1929," Arts. 2–5. TNA: CO 813/3, *Iraq Government Gazettes*, 1928–1929, pp. 371–75.

payment dates. Any person desiring to bid for tax farming was required to put up security in the form of cash or property owned by him or his guarantor.[34]

When cash payment was required, however, the conversion rate from kind to cash fluctuated from time to time and place to place. Owing to the steady progress of military operations and the development of resources by the Agricultural Development Scheme, commodity prices declined, and after the armistice of 1919 they dropped sharply by more than 50 per cent. Grain prices, in particular, were influenced by the international market and by the exchange rate of rupees, which fluctuated after the war. Furthermore, in many places, it was unclear who was to carry the tax in cash to the government treasury. In villages without crop sharing, the amount due was assessed on the village as a whole, but under the prevailing system of agricultural partnership, the lists of nominal tithe payers changed frequently. A problem also arose when villagers contracted for the payment of their own tithes in tribal areas, making inquiries into individual holdings almost impracticable.[35]

Although the civil administration changed from the military occupation government to the Civil Administration of Mesopotamia in 1919, the Department of Revenue continued to take responsibility for fiscal and financial matters. By reorganizing the Ministry of Finance and appointing capable financial officials throughout the region, the mandate government became more and more reform oriented. Focusing on the inefficient way of taxation, as noted earlier, it decided to implement a fixed assessment on the area of land but to retain a body of Ottoman law and local customs familiar to the inhabitants. The various methods it used for assessing the rate of tax or rent to be collected are summarized in the British administration's report to the League of Nations for 1926:

34 Ibid., Arts. 7, 9.

35 According to Ahmed Fahmi, in Shamiya and Abu Sukhair, a committee of officials at the rank of *nazîr* (director), *kâimmakâm* (*qaymaqam*) or *müdîr-i mâl* (district inspector) was formed to supervise the measurement of rice crops so that the work was carried out fairly. *Sirkal*s whose lands were being measured and the owners of the produce watched the work. The *ra'is*, or the *shuba memûru*, showed the land and boundaries; the land official who was to measure the latitude of the cultivated land, known as the *umdat ardh* (chief land official), decided the latitude of the land to be measured, and a clerk recorded the latitude measurements in the proper register. In this way, the government began to collect the correct proportion of taxes in these vast districts, but since the committee of about one hundred officials took nearly two months to complete the measurement as far as the *qadhas* (*kazâ*) of Diwaniyah, Shamiyah, and Abu Sikhair and Hindiya, tribesmen of the Shammar and the Anezah sometimes bought rice at the centres of Shamiya, Hindiya, and Najaf while the government was still assessing the price and therefore paid varying prices. TNA: CO 730/121/1, "Report on Iraq" by Ahmed Fahmi, pp. 22, 31.

(1) Estimation of the crops by eye, standing or on threshing floors, by the assessment committee.
(2) [Tax] Farming (*iltizam*).
(3) Collection in the towns to which produce is brought.
(4) Fixed sum in cash, or cash and kind, per unit of lift, horse power of pumps, leather bucket, or waterwheel.
(5) Lump-sum assessment per number of bearing tree, fruit and date unit of area cultivated, irrespective of what is grown on land.
(6) Lump-sum assessment per unit of area cultivated, irrespective of what is grown on land.
(7) Calculation of area cultivated with average production, applied to rice crop.[36]

The new policy of a fixed assessment based on land area triggered an extension of cultivated area on lands whose title was unsettled. In the fiscal year 1926–27, the government applied the area-based assessment more widely in order to prevent the prearrangement of a knock-down price and corruption in the revenue assessment.[37] Now the tax basis was the average expected amount of the government's share of the crops, taking into account the productivity of the soil, the area and means of irrigation, the existing degree of development, proximity to markets, and the revenue derived in the past.[38] As the tax was paid in cash and its rate was fixed for a certain period, the reform eliminated the need for annual reassessment and diminished arbitrary assessments, fraud, and the inevitable delays of assessment caused by damage from insects, theft, and fire.[39] Revenue officials described and commented upon both the old and the new methods in their annual report for 1928–29, summarized in Table 7.6, in which tax farming was not listed.

36 Great Britain, *Report by His Britannic Majesty's Government to the Council of the League of Nations on the Administration of 'Iraq for the year 1926* (London: HMSO, 1927), pp. 80–81.

37 According to Ahmed Fahmi, criticism of the British misuse of tax farming limited its practice in parts of the country. TNA: CO 730/121/1, Iraq Original Correspondence, "Report on Iraq" by Ahmed Fahmi, Accountant General, Baghdad, 30 June 1926–10 Feb. 1927.

38 TNA: CO 696/6, Colonial Office: Iraq Sessional Papers, "Administration Reports, 1925–27," p. 7.

39 In addition to the income tax paid by professional, business, and salaried individuals, revenues from houses tax and stamp duties accounted for about 6 per cent of the total. The income tax was based on the former Ottoman *temettü vegisi* and consisted of a 5 per cent tax on the earnings of a public utility, a 3 per cent tax on salaries and wages, and a tax on the profits of a trade that was assessed on the rent of the place of business and the number of employees as indicator of wealth. TNA: CO 696/4, "Administration Reports, 1921," p. 9.

By implementing the land tax as a lump sum of cash per unit of area, the government could share the peasants' tax burden with that of the pump owners and landholders, who stood to make large capital gains from large increases in land value. It could also lighten the burden by setting a high minimum level of income subject to taxation or by granting incentives for investment in agriculture. Implementation, however, first required a laborious process of identifying the landholders and defining the boundaries of their land. Consequently, before the Anglo-Iraqi Treaty of January 1926, British land policies focused on ascertaining the boundaries, landholders, areas, and approximate tax values of lands.[40]

5 Modification of Ottoman Land Tenure

During the military occupation, in urgent need of producing crops for food, British officials had paid less attention to land problems than to agricultural development.[41] The deficiencies of the land administration they had inherited also prevented them from dealing with the complicated issue of land rights, which courts sometimes would recognize without title deeds or other hard evidence. Confusion grew over a series of new land laws the Ottoman government had issued shortly before the war in 1913. They included the law on the delimitation and registration of immovable property, the law authorizing corporations to own land, the law on succession to real property, the law on mortgages, the law on the ownership of real property, and the law on the division of jointly owned real property.[42] As a result, an increasing number of land disputes were brought to British officials and courts, which forced British officials to tackle the issue of land tenure.

The British maintained and strengthened the authority of the tribal sheikh where the tribal system remained the basis of district administration aiming at maintaining peace and order and paying his revenues. This policy, continuing from the Ottoman period, motivated tribesmen to accept British rule, and

40 TNA: CO 696/6, "Administration Reports, 1925–27," p. 7.

41 For British agricultural policies, see Keiko Kiyotaki, "The Legacy of Ottoman Land and Tax Systems in Iraq during the British Mandate Period," *International Journal of Turkish Studies* 19, nos. 1 & 2 (2013), pp. 38–41.

42 "Note on the Extent to Which Ottoman Law is in Force in Iraq," in Great Britain, Office of the Civil Commissioner, "Review of the Civil Administration of the Occupied Territories of al ʿIraq 1914–1918" compiled in the Office of the Civil Commissioner, Baghdad, Nov. 1918 (Baghdad: Government Press, 1918), pp. 5–6.

British officers acknowledged this merit in taking over the government. It was, however, ineffective in areas where land disputes arose between the *tapu* landholder, now called the *mallâk* (owner), and the sheikh of peasant tribesmen (*serkâr*), or between peasant tribesmen and the *mallâk* (owner). The general policy stood between the owner and cultivating peasant tribesmen and to prevent the sheikh of tribesmen *serkâr* to remove from their holding without due cause. The prolonged settlement of disputes involving merchants, traders, politicians, urban notables, and privileged tribal sheikhs, who mostly lived in Baghdad, impeded agricultural progress.

At the same time, the boom in the local economy and trade due to the war had driven up commodity prices, bringing wealth to merchants, traders, and urban notables, who sought to purchase not only urban properties but also agricultural lands as secure assets. The latter had gained value as the British undertook irrigation and land reclamation projects, offered seeds and capital stock for their development, and granted tax exemptions, but to facilitate their purchase, British officials needed to restore a system of transaction by mortgage, transfer by sale, and registration with the court.

The land policy that the British administration proclaimed officially in a revenue circular was a continuation of Ottoman land tenure and land registration. For example, officials acknowledged "*uqr*" land, *waqf* land, and four types of land classified according to the extent to which private rights had been recognized: (1) *sirf mulk* (*arâzi-i mülkiye*; private land), (2) *saniyya* or *mudawwala* (state land of the former sultan), (3) *arazi amiriyah* (*arâzi-i miriye*; state land held by private persons by *tapu* title deed), and (4) *arazi amiriyah* (*arâzi-i miriye*; state land).

In addition, British officials declared the object of their land policy was to obtain an adequate and trustworthy record of the rights in land, and specifically in the case of state land alienated by deed (*tapu*), and in the case of other state land (*arâzi-i miriye*), to ascertain what rights existed concerning lease, fees, cultivators, period of lease, the existence of trees and houses, and provision of credits. When British officials began registering the right of *tapu* on the basis of Ottoman Turkish law, however, they immediately discovered fraudulent registrations of *tapu* and a lack of evidence on the survey maps resulting from the loss of registry books and tax records during the war.[43] Particularly serious were the cases in which tribal sheikhs based their right to land on certificates they previously had received, for the role of the sheikhs was crucial to tribal contentment and peace and, therefore, to agricultural development

43 "Note on Land Policy," in Revenue Circular No. 15 (Baghdad, 29 May 1919).

and collecting agricultural taxes.[44] Some officials believed that replacing tribal landholding with private landholding would indirectly weaken tribal unity and so curtail tribal disturbances, but it actually led to prolonged conflicts of interest accompanied by fierce disturbances.

Still worse, a bewildering variety of regional practices had delayed execution of Ottoman land policies. In small towns such as Qurna, few transactions of land had taken place under the Ottomans, and in the tribal district of Amara, no one had applied for the individual right of land possession. Where numerous occupancy certificates had been issued to applicants without a proper survey and title search during the war, British officials were too uncertain to judge claims or enforce land registration.[45] There, land disputes often provoked tribal disturbances, as they did in Suq al-Shuyukh and Hilla, where great tracts of the land were held by *tapu*, but the state of the Ottoman records made identifying properties impossible.[46]

To settle the problems regarding *tapu* land, the British initially applied Ottoman land laws and local customs familiar to the inhabitants, which relieved the civil courts of considerable work and preserved the value of land as security for mortgage.[47] They reopened the *tapu* office in Basra in May 1916 and that in Baghdad in April 1918, to restore the registration of properties in urban areas.[48] These *tapu* offices dealt only with urban and garden properties and were forbidden from registering transactions in agricultural lands in Basra through 1918; in Baghdad, where the records had been removed by the Turks and only the redemption of mortgaged urban properties could be registered, the restriction lasted until April 1918. In that month the British assigned Captain G.F. Royds to the *tapu* office as a director in Baghdad supported by a staff of former *tapu* employees, including the former head clerk of the Ottoman *tapu* office in Baghdad, and some probationers. By the end of 1918, just 1,680 sales and 1,186 mortgages of landed properties in the city of Baghdad had been recorded, with total fees of Rs 56,876, but under the new officer, registration of urban properties progressed rapidly.[49]

---

44 Great Britain, Office of the Civil Commissioner, "Military Government of Baghdad, 17 March 1918," in *Administration Report of the Baghdad Wilayat, 1917, Mesopotamia* (Calcutta: Superintendent Government Printing, India, 1918), p. 171; Great Britain, Colonial Office, *Special Report on the Progress of 'Iraq during the Period 1920–1931* (London: HMSO, 1931), p. 83.

45 Office of the Civil Commissioner, "Review of the Civil Administration," pp. 16–17.

46 Ibid., pp. 42, 81; Colonial Office, *Progress of 'Iraq*, p. 83.

47 TNA: CO 696/1, "Administration Reports, 1917–1918," pp. 14, 40; CO696/5, "Note on the Administration of the Public Finance of 'Iraq," pp. 24–25.

48 Office of the Civil Commissioner, "Review of the Civil Administration," p. 40.

49 TNA: CO 696/1, "Administration Reports, 1917–1918," p. 14.

The British method of registration for urban properties was decisive in restoring the reliability of land as an asset. The land official first prepared a complete list of properties compiled into separate volumes for each quarter (*mahalle*), or other well-known equivalent of a quarter. Each property was given a number, so that all subsequent transactions could readily be traced in the index to the volume. This was a vast improvement on the Ottoman system, in which identifying properties was impossible without a preserved record of the date of some former transaction. Except for numbering the lots in the record, however, the Ottoman registration procedure, forms, and nomenclature were used. By the beginning of August 1919, deeds for nearly 16,000 of the 25,000 known properties in the city had been registered and duplicate copies of them made. The office then accepted transactions involving these registered properties, but until the end of the year, it limited such transactions to properties for which Ottoman title deeds were forthcoming as proof, and it issued no new deeds, only replacements for old title deeds that could be produced.[50]

When Mosul was occupied towards the end of 1918, a nearly complete set of registers of landed properties in Baghdad city and many volumes of records belonging to other towns were recovered. The central office of *tapu* in Baghdad had kept records of transactions sent from every district (*kazâ*) in the province, but the entries were unnumbered, and those from several different districts were sometimes recorded in the same book. Of the missing registers, only those for ten years prior to the war had been sent to the Record Office in Istanbul, and so would have been insufficient to trace the past record, if obtained.[51]

In 1919, the British administration asserted a need to focus on the tenure and ownership of agricultural land in order to resolve land questions systematically and also find a "less irksome method for the realization of state dues upon the land."[52] The measures it proposed were setting up divisions for land settlement and land claims, appointing land settlement officers with suitable staff in each division, properly mapping the country with the aid of a survey department, settling land disputes through the courts, and registering the rights determined by the courts. Initially, the Revenue Department was put in charge, aided by the Survey Department and the courts.[53] Once the political division was set as the unit of land settlement, systematic enquiry began in May 1919, applying the Ottoman Land Code until more knowledge could

50 Ibid.

51 TNA: CO 696/1, "Administration Reports, 1917–1918," pp. 14–15.

52 TNA: CO 696/2, "Administration Reports, 1919," p. 21.

53 Ibid., pp. 21–22.

be acquired.[54] By the end of 1919, the land officials under Captain Royds had used enlarged aerial photographs taken by the Royal Air Force to map Baghdad city at a scale of six feet to a mile, sufficient to identify each house and garden.[55] The register file numbers then were marked on each property on the map, as were the municipal house numbers. This method of map making for land registry was extended to other areas where maps were available. Although the new method was a dramatic improvement, few claims were put forward by people occupying state land (*arâzi-i miriye*) until those in the Hindiya district of the Hilla division began to register the land.

After the principle of land settlement was set, the British administration issued Land Settlement Proclamation No. 1 of 1920, organizing the two divisions of Hilla and Baghdad. The land officials were one British assistant land settlement officer, one Arab *mufattish* (*müfettiş*), one Indian *mudir* (*müdîr*), one assistant *mudir* (*müdîr*) to help with preliminary maps, 1 *tapu* clerk to examine documents, and 2 *katib*s (*kâtip*, vernacular clerks).[56] The Tapu Department was transferred to the newly formed Ministry of Justice at the end of 1920, and by early 1921, it had reopened all the local *tapu* offices. Complete surveys and registration then began without delay on agricultural land, but for the *tapu* land, still unresolved was the basic question of to whom a title deed should be issued. Under the Ottoman regime, the *tapu* official responsible for registration in all cases affecting *tapu* lands was only responsible for dividing the land among the heirs stated in the deed. The Islamic courts could not apply their laws to *tapu* land, so the Ministry of Justice now decided that the Islamic courts should issue deeds to the Muslims; and the civil courts, to the members of other religious groups.[57]

Under the settlement procedure, each area of operations was divided into blocks of land. Inside these blocks, the land was further divided into pieces (*qitʿa*) held by a *serkâr* (*serkal* or *sirkal* in the British documents). The piece of the land usually contained a number of individual holdings (*wusla*, or parcel) given to peasant cultivators by the *serkâr*. In the registry, the names of these cultivators of the individual holdings and their shares to the produce were to be recorded. Each land settlement official had provisional maps on a scale of 1:20,000, made by enlarging half-inch topographical maps already in existence, and all occupants of the land were called on to demarcate the boundaries of

54 Revenue Secretary E.B. Howell announced the promotion of land-claim settlement in his "Note on Land Policy" in Revenue Circular No. 15 (Baghdad, 29 May 1919).

55 Ibid., p. 81; Colonial Office, *Progress of ʿIraq*, p. 83.

56 TNA: CO 696/2, "Administration Reports, 1919," pp. 22–23.

57 TNA: CO 696/3, Colonial Office: Iraq Sessional Papers, Administration Reports, 1920, "Report on the *Tapu* Department for the year 1920–21," pp. 1–2.

their land except where the boundaries were disputed. Each holding within a block was then given a provisional number for reference.[58]

All claimants had to produce copies of their supporting documents, usually not a title deed but a copy of a *hujja shariya* (*hüccet-i şeriye*, an Islamic court decree), a *waqfiya*, or an *uqr* deed. Even the Ottoman Department of Awqaf never had taken out *tapu* title deeds for the vast properties of *waqf*, because the law of inheritance was not followed on *tapu* land as it was different from the Sharia law that the bulk of the population obeyed.

Although the new procedure of land settlement was formalized, it was slow to prevail because of the high registration fees and the insecurity of the deed. In particular, disputes over agricultural land between tribesmen and *tapu* holders or among tribesmen continued, for tribal occupants of lands on the Euphrates River had been in the habit of bequeathing, mortgaging, and selling their interest in the lands they occupied. Theoretically invalid according to Ottoman laws, such transactions still had been approved by Ottoman officials, so disputed lands were often registered by tribal sheikhs, merchants, and moneylenders who had no qualified interest in them.[59]

Another pressing issue for British officials involved the *tapu* land that had been alienated to private landholders by Ottoman authorities, as well as the land of the state domains, previously *saniyya* and *mudawwala* land, and other cultivated and uncultivated lands without title. Those lands, which were collectively described as *miri* (state) land in British documents, had been leased to the sheikhs of peasant tribesmen or to the highest bidders at public auction or were cultivated by crop sharing. The tax rate on such lands sometimes amounted to 40 per cent of the produce, and the methods of tax assessment, collection, and payment varied from area to area. In tribal areas cultivated by peasant tribesmen according to their own customs, the problems were too complex for the land official to handle, especially in regions of pump irrigation, where they had been complicated by endless disputes with the pump owner.[60]

In the area of the Diyala River and in the suburbs of Baghdad and major towns, agricultural land had been held largely by city residents who now, as the land settlement for claims over agricultural lands proceeded, registered and secured their titles. Representing a new type of landholder that the British expected to become an efficient land user, such wealthy townspeople had for many years sent their sons to be educated in India, Europe, or Syria, where

58 The Hindiya area was photographed, but planes were not available for Baghdad. For the progress of land registration, Kiyotaki, "Legacy of Ottoman Land and Tax Systems in Iraq," pp. 47–49.

59 TNA: CO 696/3, "Report on the *Tapu* Department for the year 1920–21," pp. 23–4, 26.

60 Sir Ernest Dowson, *An Inquiry into Land Tenure and Related Questions* (Letchworth, UK: Garden City Press, 1931), pp. 27–32.

they had become acquainted with modern methods of agriculture. Now the British anticipated that the increased security for life and property afforded by a stable government would lead townspeople who were landed proprietors to develop their estates to the utmost capacity.[61] Those expectations, however, ran up against a labour shortage created by the demands of the Arab Army, the British Army, the Civil Administration, and commercial firms, and by the return to India of some thirty thousand men in the Indian Labour Corps. Most affected were the summer crops, which required intensive cultivation along the canals. Landholders consequently turned to labour-saving agricultural machinery, such as lightweight threshing machines, corn mowers, lightweight iron ploughs for bullock or mule draft, and plough tractors. Samples of this machinery had been imported from British farms and demonstrated on government experimental farms, drawing public attention.[62]

While the merit of private landholding was becoming obvious in the Diyala region, the settlement of land claims lagged in areas occupied and cultivated by tribal sheikhs and peasants. Nevertheless, in order to change the basis of tax assessment from produce to land, the Revenue Department had to establish a quasi-property right of possession on the land for the taxpaying landholders, by settling the claims tribal sheikhs derived from their prescriptive right of occupation and cultivation. In contrast to Ottoman land reform, in which the *tapu* right had been established on the same principle, the British reform aimed to collect the tax from the landholder, regardless of the customary practices of crop sharing and tax farming. Consequently, the settlement of land claims was carried out differently on *tapu* land, the previous *saniyya* and *mudawwala* lands, and other state lands.[63]

Initially the British administration believed that the Ottoman *tapu* system provided the continuity of tenure necessary to permit the settlement of land claims, taxation, and agricultural improvements. In reality, as the costs of agriculture rose with inflation under the British occupation, the Ottoman system could not provide the necessary stimulus to agricultural production because the penalty for neglect never had been enforced, and absentee landlords had been allowed to proliferate. In addition, the system itself was inapplicable to tribal areas, where insecure property rights discouraged progressive settlers. Yet the government alone could afford the capital outlay necessary to complete the irrigation system, and then only if it could recover that outlay through tax revenues. The Ministry of Finance, therefore, recommended that

61 Iraq, Department of Agriculture, *Administration Report of the Department of Agriculture in Mesopotamia for the Year 1920* (Baghdad: Government Press, 1921), p. 3.

62 Ibid., p. 13.

63 TNA: CO 696/5, "Administration Reports, 1922–1924," pp. 32, 24–26.

> tithe should be definitely regarded as the government tax on cultivated land, and the right to use water by lift be covered by the tithe. (i) Any right to demand more than tithe should be based on its position as a landlord entitled to rent, its claim to repayment of the value of services rendered to the land. (ii) Government rent should be calculated on the capital value of the land, as ascertained from records of sales and other similar evidence of at approximately 20 years' purchase. (iii) Further demand should be assessed with reference to the cost of the services including interest and amortization charges on works and maintenance charges. (iv) Final assessment of land should not be made until the area concerned has been surveyed and information has been collected as to the land value and costs of services.[64]

To collect revenue on state land, the government had to establish tax units by registering all *tapu* land and by establishing private landholding on unregistered state land. However, by the end of 1925, the financial situation had changed rapidly. Spending on agricultural development, including irrigation and land reclamation projects, was drastically reduced, leaving agricultural improvements dependent on private investment in modern machinery, land improvement, and pump irrigation. The settlement of land claims then became an even more urgent priority in order to secure landholders who would make these investments as well as pay taxes.

As the British worked to complete the post-war reconstruction, they found collecting tithe by way of tax farming, lease, and crop sharing too inefficient and costly. Consequently, to abolish tithe and replace it with a land tax, their government began to lay down tax laws and regulations, and made great efforts to assess the fair value of land and to put in order the land registration that had stopped during the war. In this process, the principle of Ottoman state land continued and became the basis for the whole Iraqi land system. The British reopened the land registry, recovered lost records, and resumed registration efforts, which defined the land title and boundaries in large areas of disputed lands, but both the British officials and the Iraqi government had grave doubts about the *tapu* land system. New acquisition of *tapu* had been suspended after the decree of Sultan Abdülhamid II in 1881, and presumably during this suspended period, its registration and title deeds became deficient, while its holding became fragmented by inheritance. In other places, the Iraqi government failed to incorporate into its policies and reforms the wide variations in land use, different origins of peasant cultivators, and changing methods of agriculture. The reasons for continuing the existing taxation and land tenure shed

64 Ibid., pp. 24–26.

light on the enduring Ottoman influence on this unprecedented change in society. Examination of this issue continues in Chapter 8, as it resulted in new land legislation that favoured the landholders and rooted problems in tribal society.

TABLE 7.3 Changes in revenue chapters of budget, 1911–1929

Chapter	1911 (Ottoman)		1921/22–1923/24 (British)		1924/25 (British)		1928/29 (British)
I	Direct Taxes	I	Taxes on Natural Produce	I	Taxes on Land and Natural Produce and Revenues from Government Properties	I	Taxation on Agricultural and Natural Produce, Animals, Minerals and Government Properties
II	Stamp Taxes	II	Stamps, Fees and Registration	II	Property and Stamp Taxes	II	Property, Income Tax and Stamp Tax
III	Indirect Taxes	III	Customs and Excise	III	Miscellaneous Revenues	III	Miscellaneous Revenues
IV	Monopolies	IV	Commercial Departments	IV	Customs and Excise	IV	Customs and Excise
V	State Enterprises	V	Government Institutions	V	Posts and Telegraphs	V	Posts and Telegraphs
VI	State Domains	VI	Proceeds of Government Properties	VI	Other Government Services and Institutions	VI	Other Government Services and Institutions
VII	Tributes	VII	Interest, Commission, Etc.				
VIII	Miscellaneous	VIII	Miscellaneous Receipts				
IX	Recoveries						
X	Pensions						

SOURCE: TNA: CO 696/5, NOTE ON THE ADMINISTRATION OF THE PUBLIC FINANCE OF ʿIRAQ, 1 APR. 1924–31 MAR. 1925 (BAGHDAD: PRINTED AT THE GOVERNMENT PRESS, 1926), P. 18; CO 696/7, ANNUAL REPORT ON THE OPERATION OF THE REVENUE DEPARTMENT OF THE MINISTRY OF FINANCE FOR THE FINANCIAL YEAR 1928–29 (BAGHDAD: PRINTED AT THE GOVERNMENT PRESS, 1929), PP. 23–27.

TABLE 7.4 Chapters in the Ottoman budget for the provinces of Baghdad, Basra, and Mosul, 1911

Chapter		Articles	
I	Direct Taxes	i	Taxes on land and house property
		ii	*Temettü* or tax on professional and trade income
		iii	Military service exempting payments
		iv	Road tax
		v	Taxes on animals
		vi	Agricultural tithes
		vii	Tobacco and silk tithes
		viii	Taxes on private forests
		ix	Taxes on minerals and quarries
		x	Taxes on receipts against payment of taxes
II	Stamp Taxes	i	Stamp duties
		ii	Court and notarial fees
		iii	Fees on registration of land titles
III	Indirect Taxes	i	Liquor excise
		ii	Tobacco vending licenses
		iii	Customs
		iv	Ports and navigation and lighthouse dues
		v	Fees for veterinary services
		vi	Shooting and fishing licenses
IV	Monopolies	i	Salt
		ii	Tobacco excise
		iii	Gunpowder
		iv	Mint receipts
		v	Post, telegraph, and telephones
V	State Enterprises	i	Tigris and Euphrates Steamship Services
		ii	Mines worked by government
VI	State Domains	i	Sales and leases of state immovable and movable property
		ii	Produce of state forests
VII	Tributes		Nil

TABLE 7.4 Chapters in the Ottoman budget for the provinces of Baghdad (*cont.*)

Chapter		**Articles**	
VIII	Miscellaneous	i	Interest and commission on resource operations
		ii	Receipts of Agricultural Bank
		iii	Fines
		iv	Miscellaneous
		v	School fees
IX	Recoveries	i	Recoveries of advances by Treasury
X	Pensions	i	Pension deductions

SOURCE: TNA: CO 696/5, NOTE ON THE ADMINISTRATION OF THE PUBLIC FINANCE OF ʿIRAQ, 1 APR. 1924–31 MAR. 1925 (BAGHDAD: PRINTED AT THE GOVERNMENT PRESS, 1926), PP. 18–19.

TABLE 7.5 Revenue chapters and votes of budget, 1924/1925

Chapter		**Vote**	
I	Taxes on Land and Natural Produce and Revenue of Government Property	1	Agricultural produce
		2	Other natural produce
		3	Animals
		4	Minerals
		5	Rents and tolls
II	Property and Stamp Taxes	6	Property tax
		7	Stamp duties
III	Miscellaneous Revenues	8	Pension contribution
		9	Interest
		10	Resource and Treasury operations
		11	Sale of land and buildings
		12	Refunds of legal expenses
		13	Miscellaneous
IV	Customs and Excises	14	Import duties
		15	Export
		16	Transit

TABLE 7.5 Revenue chapters and votes of budget, 1924/1925 (*cont.*)

Chapter		Vote	
		17	General
		18	Miscellaneous
		19	Liquor excise
		20	Salt excise
		21	Tobacco excise
		22	Opium
		23	Miscellaneous
V	Post and Telegraph	24	Postage and message revenue
		25	Miscellaneous
VI	Other Government Services and Institutions	26	Court fees and fines
		27	Tapu
		28	Health Services
		29	Schools
		30	Police
		31	Army
		32	Jails
		33	Publications
		34	Public Works Department
		35	Irrigation Department
		36	Survey Department
		37	Chief Navigation Authority
		38	Government Press
		39	Stationery Department
		40	Agricultural Department
		41	Veterinary

Note: The above information is taken from the *Bulletin Annuel de Statistique*. It actually appeared in the annual budgets as in the table.

SOURCE: TNA: CO 696/5, NOTE ON THE ADMINISTRATION OF THE PUBLIC FINANCE OF ʿIRAQ, 1 APR. 1924–31 MAR. 1925 (BAGHDAD: GOVERNMENT PRESS, 1926), PP. 18–23.

TABLE 7.6 Methods of assessment of agricultural and natural produces

Method	Assessment process	Produce or land	Remarks
Place of consumption	Percent of sale price of produce in markets	Natural produce and vegetables	Useful for taxing minor products
Place of customs	Imposition of fixed sum in cash per unit of weight	Any produce exported; liquorice	Useful
Government headquarters	Imposition of fixed sum in cash at an excise office	Produce subject to excise duty; tobacco	Useful
Assessment by estimation	Estimation of quantity of produce on threshing floors	All produce except dates, fruit, vegetables, and tobacco	Actively superseding this method in favor of others
Assessment by measurement	Measurement of area of growing crops by ropes	Any grain crops; winter grains, rice, and cotton	Valuable for rice
Assessment by count	Count of trees	Date and fruits	Widely used
Lump sum in cash per plough	Annual count of all plough	Winter grains grown on land of rain and flow irrigation	Standard method for winter crop in the north
Leasing of land by public auction	Selection of tenant by auction	Miri lands with no recognized tax payer	Practiced on *saniyya* and *mudawwala* lands
Lump sum in cash per area	Classification of land according to quantity and value of produce	All surveyed lands	Highly approved and being extended
Lump sum in cash per unit of lift	Annual count of units of power of water lifting device	Any produce grown by lift irrigation except gardens	Broadly applied on river banks

TABLE 7.6 Methods of assessment of agricultural and natural produces (*cont.*)

Method	Assessment process	Produce or land	Remarks
Tathlith or *Takhmis*	Lump-sum demand calculated as average of previous 3, 4, or 5 years	Any produce of lands where tax payer agrees	Useful to avoid necessity of direct assessment; Instituted in 1926

SOURCE: TNA: CO 696/7, COLONIAL OFFICE: IRAQ SESSIONAL PAPERS, "REPORT ON THE OPERATIONS OF THE REVENUE DEPARTMENT FOR THE FISCAL YEAR 1928–1929," PP. 51–52.

TABLE 7.7 Revenues of Iraq, 1915–1931 (in Rupees)

	1915–16	1916–17	1917–18	1918–19	1919–20	1920–21	1921–22	1922–23
	Rs	Rs	Rs	Rs	Rs	Rs	Rs	Rs
Land and natural produce taxation and revenues from government properties	2,555,976	2,186,555	7,934,295	21,747,430	19,827,290	14,886,733	17,245,168	14,032,046
Property and stamp taxes	118,528	105,820	157,720	346,500	500,000	738,500	3,415,208	3,805,154
Miscellaneous revenues	59,641	44,545	226,524	74,800	78,000	2,202,992	4,296,181	4,321,356
Customs and excise	1,834,497	5,764,400	6,738,000	6,500,000	22,024,000	27,665,412	21,250,420	21,377,193
Post and telegraph					5,350,150		5,444,092	2,816,502
Other government services and institution		6,930	195,509	644,450	1,757,070	3,868,207	1,173,894	1,114,826
Total	4,568,642	8,108,250	15,252,048	29,313,180	49,536,510	49,361,844	52,824,963	47,467,077
Recoverable loans and advances by British government								
Ottoman debt revenues						2,409,558		
Non-recoverable grants by British government								
Defense (grant-in-aid)								
Grant-in-aid of civil deficit							16,264,849	
Grand Total	4,568,642	8,108,250	15,252,048	29,313,180	49,536,510	51,771,402	69,089,812	47,467,077

Note: The format of a thousand separator is used instead of Indian numbering.

SOURCE: FOR THE YEARS BETWEEN 1915–16 AND 1919–20, *REVIEW OF THE CIVIL ADMINISTRATION OF MESOPOTAMIA*, PP. 118–19, CITED IN *IRAQ ADMINISTRATION REPORTS*, 1914–1932, V, PP. 120–21; FOR THE YEAR 1920–21, *ʿIRAQ, REPORT ON ʿIRAQ ADMINISTRATION, OCTOBER 1920–MARCH 1922*, PP. 36–37, CITED IN *IRAQ ADMINISTRATION REPORT, 1914–1932*, VII, PP. 228–29; FOR THE YEARS BETWEEN 1921–22 AND 1926–27, *REPORT BY H.M.'S HIGH COMMISSIONER ON THE FINANCES, ADMINISTRATION AND CONDITION OF THE ʿIRAQ* (BAGHDAD, 1928), PP. 115–19; FOR THE YEARS BETWEEN 1925–26 AND 1930–31, *IRAQ ADMINISTRATION REPORT, 1914–1932*, VII, "THE YEAR 1931," PP. 50–51; FOR THE YEAR 1931–32, IBID., "THE YEAR 1932," PP. 22–23. SEE ALSO GREAT BRITAIN, *REPORT BY HIS BRITANNIC MAJESTY'S GOVERNMENT TO THE COUNCIL OF THE LEAGUE OF NATIONS ON THE ADMINISTRATION OF ʿIRAQ FOR THE YEAR 1925; THE YEAR 1927; THE YEAR 1928; THE YEAR 1929*.

	1923–24	1924–25	1925–26	1926–27	1927–28	1928–29	1929–30	1930–31	1931–32
	Rs	Rs	Rs	Rs	Rs	Rs	Rs	Rs	Rs
	14,468,789	15,292,318	18,312,438	17,537,493	17,900,835	18,751,302	16,804,706	10,473,478	8,350,782
	4,385,020	3,207,734	4,097,184	3,455,391	3,256,963	3,481,449	3,716,692	3,552,355	4,164,224
	3,932,259	1,988,756	2,226,444	2,294,131	2,394,934	1,923,885	1,762,995	1,606,728	2,658,953
	24,181,838	24,900,629	25,377,514	25,271,711	27,506,717	27,508,794	27,463,859	23,535,103	24,778,460
	3,317,365	3,273,810	2,995,270	2,721,521	2,726,269	2,704,038	2,673,060	2,858,519	2,705,167
	655,376	4,069,348	3,993,084	3,670,227	3,511,279	4,099,735	3,956,167	3,630,598	3,344,425
	50,940,647	52,732,595	57,001,934	54,950,474	57,296,997	58,469,203	56,377,479	45,656,781	46,002,014
			1,100,000	1,750,000	1,800,000	975,000	900,000	800,000	
	50,940,647	52,732,595	58,101,934	56,700,474	59,096,997	59,444,203	57,277,497	46,456,781	46,002,014

TABLE 7.8 Expenditures of Iraq, 1915–1931 (in Rupees)

	1915–16	1916–17	1917–18	1918–19	1919–20	1920–21	1921–22	1922–23
	Rs	Rs	Rs	Rs	Rs	Rs	Rs	Rs
Public debt and pensions						10,651	1,880,978	1,664,31[illegible]
Civil list							799,514	1,008,72[illegible]
Parliament								
Comptroller and Auditor General								
Council of Ministers							306,949	126,84[illegible]
Ministry of Foreign Affairs								
Ministry of Finance	555,392	919,085	5,189,233	9,321,690	7,817,470	1,360,694	4,737,786	4,426,04[illegible]
Customs and excise	111,898	385,800	580,350	675,000	1,740,550	6,009,621	1,943,625	2,177,50[illegible]
Ministry of Interior							7,569,841	4,441,28[illegible]
Jails	20,126	44,460	98,517	167,400	747,830	687,169		
Iraq Police	199,146	286,975	890,163	1,204,080	1,936,940	5,183,115	7,824,484	7,684,95[illegible]
Health Services	61,345	87,180	139,887	463,750	2,875,600	3,342,696	3,401,109	2,745,91[illegible]
Ministry of Irrigation and Agriculture								
Veterinary Department						906,277	558,368	223,53[illegible]
Department of Agriculture					716,270	674,607	804,221	679,84[illegible]
Survey Department					144,230	381,488		
Special Capital Works								
Ministry of Defense							5,527,233	7,633,43[illegible]
Ministry of Justice	120,207	127,295	214,983	373,000	892,320	1,069,431	1,506,529	1,495,04[illegible]
Tapu Department					100,460	357,405	579,762	493,05[illegible]
Ministry of Education		23,530	35,500	180,000	989,250	1,246,853	1,906,448	1,967,38[illegible]
Ministry of Communication and Works					5,062,280	38,098	10,821,274	400,73[illegible]
Public Works Department		105,450	461,400	874,700	6,611,720	9,935,059		3,500,07[illegible]

1923–24	1924–25	1925–26	1926–27	1927–28	1928–29	1929–30	1930–31	1931–32
Rs	Rs	Rs	Rs	Rs	Rs	Rs	Rs	Rs
1,711,421	1,709,551	1,734,186	1,920,178	1,775,418	1,721,294	1,774,122	3,115,861	3,917,095
975,662	963,057	955,386	1,057,843	940,188	880,026	868,712	860,850	775,305
16,579	372,818	906,203	883,868	811,641	1,044,149	885,595	686,841	723,801
	40,138	57,779	66,809	73,968	93,476	108,638	113,989	106,856
136,809	127,648	167,295	183,829	615,304	134,100	122,972	136,415	189,864
					125,390	165,396	223,485	327,594
4,578,669	4,344,363	4,454,784	4,166,196	4,224,823	4,335,665	4,146,226	4,063,923	3,581,317
1,923,536	1,859,976	2,271,256	2,032,557	2,043,986	2,419,883	2,562,845	2,227,756	2,198,354
4,088,989	4,267,620	3,956,954	3,940,258	3,708,100	4,123,060	4,698,204	3,663,985	3,755,143
6,597,346	7,043,100	7,671,537	7,984,298	7,723,365	8,342,669	8,091,149	7,897,091	7,306,189
2,083,546	1,936,292	1,948,983	2,292,023	2,405,097	2,558,901	2,823,974	2,598,791	2,535,474
				822,233	279,416	325,707	46,081	
219,386	283,521	295,982	282,191	311,360	366,331	384,647	324,424	
541,965	608,223	586,207	1,095,575	1,734,432	1,199,574	762,522	732,425	576,019
					598,934	583,832	510,311	
				1,670,877	1,284,044	1,153,788		
6,483,854	9,774,120	13,108,931	11,838,637	12,920,802	14,042,452	12,035,427	10,426,985	9,937,195
1,380,735	1,359,207	1,299,161	1,403,764	1,348,888	1,347,927	1,382,049	1,357,695	1,338,696
438,431	427,175	451,094	485,829	447,841	467,151	476,600	469,025	380,066
1,784,267	2,132,839	2,274,525	2,693,250	2,742,007	3,201,734	3,716,400	3,841,379	3,851,418
431,287	579,500	823,804	772,276	156,040	122,743	134,267	123,574	998,394
2,862,580	3,221,738	2,301,734	3,740,073	3,282,036	5,313,317	4,494,561	3,062,188	1,981,871

TABLE 7.8 Expenditures of Iraq, 1915–1931 (in Rupees) (*cont.*)

	1915–16	1916–17	1917–18	1918–19	1919–20	1920–21	1921–22	1922–23
	Rs	Rs	Rs	Rs	Rs	Rs	Rs	Rs
Irrigation					5,225,000			3,549,51
Post and Telegraph Services					4,572,950		7,044,484	4,363,69
Sulaymaniya Province (temporary)								
Total							57,212,605	48,581,92
Defense								
Iraq Army (grant-in-aid)						1,132,862		
Royal Air Force							300,584,641	100,732,25
Levies					3,202,890	3,053,008	9,022,465	8,733,79
H.Q. & divisional revenue	554,230	1,183,425	2,418,235	3,390,100	8,350,770	1,991,665		
Administration						10,695,070	1,803,510	803,25
Miscellaneous						4,046,626	37,798,348	8,676,36
Land acquisition					1,201,250	30,269		
Non-effective charge						1,578,205		
Total							349,208,964	118,945,66
Grand Total	1,622,344	3,163,200	10,028,286	16,649,720	52,187,780	53,730,869	406,421,569	167,527,59

Note: Miscellaneous expenditures include capital expenditure on Mesopotamian Railways and its maintenance; settlement of refugees, civil deficits (grant-in-aid), loss by exchange on funds supplied by India, Samarra antiquities, Iraq native levies, and compensation to Iraqi and British officials. The format of a thousand separator is used instead of Indian numbering.

SOURCE: FOR THE YEARS BETWEEN 1915–16 AND 1919–20, *REVIEW OF THE CIVIL ADMINISTRATION OF MESOPOTAMIA*, PP. 118–19, CITED IN *IRAQ ADMINISTRATION REPORTS*, 1914–1932, V, PP. 120–21; FOR THE YEAR 1920–21, ʿIRAQ, REPORT ON *ʿIRAQ ADMINISTRATION, OCTOBER 1920–MARCH 1922*, PP. 36–37, CITED IN *IRAQ ADMINISTRATION REPORTS, 1914–1932*, VII, PP. 228–29; FOR THE YEARS BETWEEN 1921–22 AND 1926–27, *REPORT BY H.M.'S HIGH COMMISSIONER ON THE FINANCES, ADMINISTRATION AND CONDITION OF THE ʿIRAQ* (BAGHDAD, 1928), PP. 115–19; FOR THE YEARS BETWEEN 1925–26 AND 1930–31, *IRAQ ADMINISTRATION REPORTS, 1914–1932*, VII, "THE YEAR 1931," PP. 50–51; FOR THE YEAR 1931–32, IBID., "THE YEAR 1932," PP. 22–23. SEE ALSO GREAT BRITAIN, *REPORT BY HIS BRITANNIC MAJESTY'S GOVERNMENT TO THE COUNCIL OF THE LEAGUE OF NATIONS ON THE ADMINISTRATION OF ʿIRAQ FOR THE YEAR 1925; THE YEAR 1927; THE YEAR 1928; THE YEAR 1929.*

1923–24	1924–25	1925–26	1926–27	1927–28	1928–29	1929–30	1930–31	1931–32
Rs	Rs	Rs	Rs	Rs	Rs	Rs	Rs	Rs
3,311,266	2,376,553	1,591,303	2,533,284	2,819,693	2,998,990	2,882,444	2,114,345	1,280,671
2,860,342	3,058,263	2,573,944	2,548,976	2,615,239	2,899,916	2,739,913	2,560,102	2,412,330
		806,797						
42,426,670	46,485,702	50,237,845	51,921,714	55,193,338	59,901,142	57,319,391	51,157,521	48,173,660
		1,100,000	1,750,000	1,800,000	975,000	900,000		
73,218,763	52,856,315	43,741,862	36,717,000	21,973,840	3,983,338	3,050,305		
9,764,488	8,152,652	8,226,683	7,126,569	4,304,788	2,843,751	2,488,188		
495,182	366,007	311,312	312,653	328,278	329,221	333,360		
13,553	171,575	32,465	83,671	33,432	95,721	2,434		
83,491,986	61,546,549	53,412,322	45,989,893	28,440,338	8,227,031	6,774,287		
125,918,656	108,032,251	103,650,167	97,911,607	83,633,676	68,128,173	64,093,678	51,157,521	48,173,660

CHAPTER 8

The Decline of the Ottoman Legacy

Embarking on the journey towards independence after the Anglo-Iraqi Treaty of 1926, the government of Iraq began by introducing legislation that consolidated its authority over agriculture, taxation, and land tenure.[1] British influence gradually diminished, as the parliament and the Council of Ministers became the major policymakers. The clearest indication of this shift in power was the income tax law that the Iraqi parliament passed in 1927, which turned many British officials and foreign companies into taxpayers, exempting most of the local population. In agriculture, replacement of the tithe by a land tax began – along with the settlement of disputes on land tenure – addressing irregularities and the complications of current legislation. These modifications of the Ottoman land and tax systems by the government brought different consequences than had the changes during the British mandate period. Detailing them, this chapter discusses how the decline of the Ottoman legacy occurred and concludes the story of Ottoman land reform in the province of Baghdad. Particularly examined are problematic agricultural situations, the rapid expansion of cultivated state land owing to irrigation pumps, and Iraqi land policies. These new factors, intentionally or not, altered the customary ways of agricultural production and revenue distribution, widening income inequality between landholders and the cultivating tribal sheikhs and tribesmen. Consequently, they may explain why, as Hanna Batatu has described, a landed class emerged and peasant tribesmen became impoverished tenants after Iraqi independence in 1932.[2] To complete my inquiry into the Ottoman land reform, I end with British officials' warnings about this unprecedented change in Iraqi society from the standpoint of land and agricultural history.

1 Deteriorating Agricultural Situations

Although the government of Iraq gained authority under the British mandate after 1926, the insecure political environment continued, requiring it to spend

1 For more detail on Anglo-Iraqi relations and treaties, see Peter Sluglett, *Britain in Iraq: Contriving King and Country* (London: I.B. Tauris, 2007), pp. 49–64, 123–24.

2 Hanna Batatu, *The Old Social Classes and the Revolutionary Movements of Iraq* (Princeton, NJ: Princeton University Press, 1978), pp. 63–152.

 | DOI:10.1163/9789004384347_010

much more on military forces and much less on agricultural development. The frontiers of the country remained undetermined to the north of Mosul and on the borders with Syria, Saudi Arabia, and Persia. Internally, discontent with the new authority revived the incessant tribal disturbances of past centuries. As a result, defence of the country required air and ground forces far larger than its own, and large increases in revenues were needed to avoid budget cuts in areas other than defence.

Towards the end of the mandate, however, exports declined sharply as the worldwide Depression set in. The currency in circulation was still the rupee imported from India, formerly linked to the pound sterling but now controlled by the British by the law of 1927. Issue of an Iraqi dinar linked to the pound sterling, which the government repeatedly proposed, had been delayed by complications from the pound sterling's return to the gold standard in 1925. All these uncertainties deterred long-term capital investment, except for foreign investment in the exploitation of oil, the dredging of Basra's ports by the Port Authority, and public projects on indispensable infrastructure.

The worsening economic situation, influenced by uncertainty, moreover, severely impacted the government, which relied on customs and excise and agricultural taxation as the main sources of state revenues. Because these revenue sources depended on international markets and domestic harvests, they were irregular and, once deflation began, the prices decreased, which in turn caused decreases in the government's revenues, becoming insufficient to pay for needy expenditures. For example, in 1926 export prices for barley increased due to a decrease in supply from Russia, while wheat prices were somewhat below normal. Accordingly, exports of barley soared from 1,339 tons, between July 1925 and June 1926, to 125,887 tons, for the year 1926–27; in the same period, wheat exports increased, though less spectacularly, from 188 tons to 1,644 tons. However, the larger grain exports failed to bring an increase in revenue. At the same time, date exports fell from 151,020 tons to 79,624 tons because of an outbreak of cholera and consequent restrictions on export.[3] In 1929, revenue from agriculture and customs decreased, more sharply in the case of agriculture, without recovering during the mandate period (Figure 8.1). The reduced share of agriculture in total government revenue after 1928 was especially concerning as it was the main source of income for the large peasant population.

3 Great Britain, *Report by His Britannic Majesty's Government to the Council of the League of Nations on the Administration of 'Iraq for the year 1927* (London: HMSO, 1928), pp. 165–66.

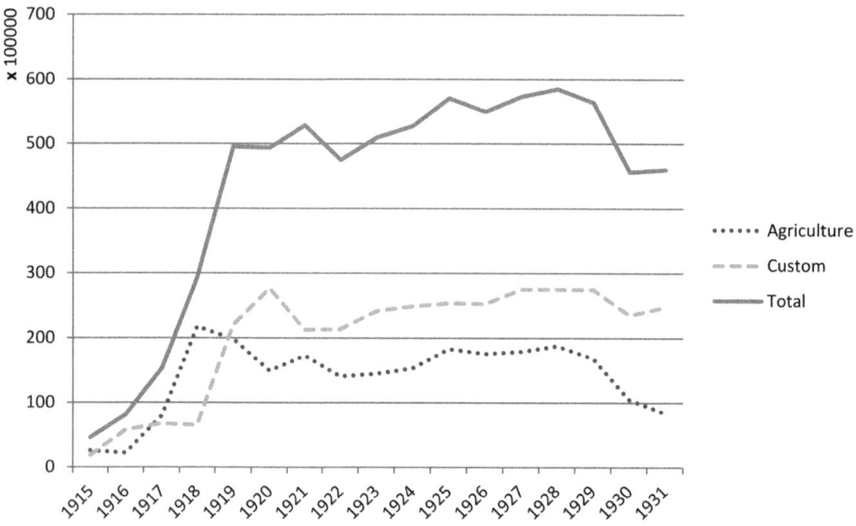

FIGURE 8.1 Agriculture and customs revenues in Iraq, 1915–1931 (in Rupees)
NOTE: TOTAL IS THE TOTAL REVENUES INCLUDING AGRICULTURE, CUSTOMS, AND OTHER GOVERNMENT REVENUES.
SOURCE: TABLE 7.7.

Under the Ottomans, agriculture had been the largest sector – in 1911, it still provided 63 per cent of total government revenue.[4] But once it fell below customs revenues, in 1919–20, it never again surpassed them. The reasons for the reversal include a change in how customs duties were calculated (from an *ad valorem* basis to a fixed basis), and a widening and more diverse customs revenue stream, due to the concessions for oil and cotton and the resumption of Persian pilgrim traffic after the war. In response, the Department of Revenue prioritized reforming inefficient tax collection in agriculture, drawing on a body of Ottoman laws and local customs that were familiar to local inhabitants. It commenced replacing the tithe with a land tax, at a fixed rate on the area of landholding, which lessened the government's reliance on the tax farmer, village headman, and tribal sheikh as intermediaries in tax collection. In spite of the reforms, crop prices, which had begun to fall in 1921, dropped steeply in 1929–30, severely lowering agricultural revenue.

As another solution to revenue decreases, the Department of Revenue was commissioned to focus on tax matters independently of the Ministry of Finance and increase tax revenues. To ensure a stable source of tax revenue, income tax

4 TNA: CO 696/5, Note on the Administration of the Public Finance of ʿIraq, 1 Apr. 1924–31 Mar. 1925 (Baghdad: Government Press, 1926), pp. 18–23.

collection, which had stopped during the war, was revived. While income tax was gradually accepted by the populace, it could not prevent revenue from agricultural and other direct taxes from declining rapidly. In this movement, indirect revenue, such as excise and the customs duties from the port of Basra, continued to be a significant source of government revenue, even though such duties were easily influenced by external conditions and so at risk of rapid decline. Consequently, the government sought to expand its stable resources, such as the state monopolies and services, which already supplied about one-fifth of its total revenue. The port in Basra was transferred to the Port Authority, and electricity companies were operated by the government. However, their complete transfer, such as that of the railway, from the British to Iraqi government was still progressing, which deterred inflow of their revenues.

Besides transferring public utilities, the government also secured steady revenue sources previously assigned to the Ottoman Public Debt Administration (OPDA). Under the Ottoman regime, two tax collecting agencies were beyond the control of the provincial government treasurer (*defterdar*) – the OPDA and the Department of Mudawwala (previously, the *saniyya* administration). British officials during the mandate period collected their revenues, including those assigned for the repayment of public debt, salt, tobacco products, stamp duties, spirits, fishery licenses, and silk production. Their revenues were spent for local expenditures until the government separated a portion of the revenue in the budget for the annuity payment. The OPDA claimed for loss of their revenues collected by British officials, but the government settled the disputes and began negotiations for determining Iraq's liability after the Treaty of Lausanne ratified by Turkey in 1923.

The agricultural sector's decreased significance in government revenues after the Ottoman period is clearly observed by the remarkable difference in the shares of direct and indirect taxes, as shown in Figure 8.2. According to the Ottoman budget system applied in the province of Baghdad in 1911, chapters of the budget were reclassified into direct taxes, including taxes from agricultural production, land, and natural produce; indirect taxes, including customs and excise; and others, being property and stamp taxes and income from post, telegraph, and other government services and institutions (Table 7.4). Applying the classification of direct taxes, indirect taxes, and other revenues from the state institutions in the Ottoman budget, observation of their shares in the total revenues shows a change in the fiscal structure from the Ottoman period.

During the period of occupation and civil administration until 1921, the respective shares of indirect and direct taxes fluctuated considerably because revenues from customs and excise duties were curtailed during the reconstruction of the port facilities. But the damaged infrastructure and facilities

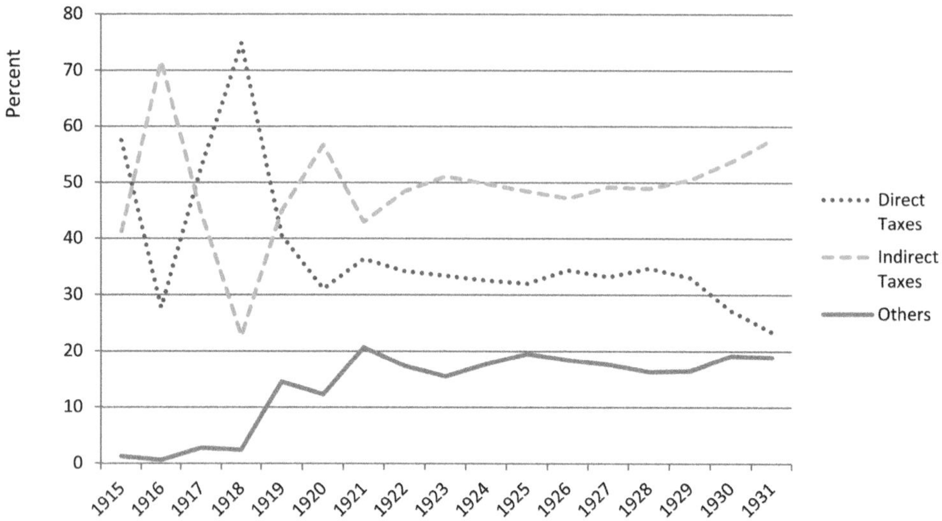

FIGURE 8.2 Percentage shares of direct and indirect taxes in government revenues, 1915–1931
NOTE: DIRECT TAXES INCLUDE TAX REVENUES FROM LAND AND NATURAL PRODUCE; INDIRECT TAXES FROM CUSTOMS AND EXCISE; AND OTHERS FROM PROPERTY AND STAMP TAXES, POST AND TELEGRAPH, AND OTHERS FROM GOVERNMENT SERVICES AND INSTITUTIONS.
SOURCE: TABLE 7.7.

were quickly restored to meet the immediate need for revenue, and imports increased rapidly, as did exports of agricultural produce. Then, with customs furnishing the largest portions of state revenues, agriculture's share, or the direct tax, fell to just above 30 per cent and declined to only a quarter of the total after 1929. With the decrease in agriculture's share, that of revenues from customs duties and excises, categorized as indirect taxes, rose to 50 per cent or more, and that of the other revenues, mainly from government services and institutions, steadily increased to about 20 per cent, where it remained relatively constant during the mandate period (Figure 8.2).

The worldwide Depression's impact on agriculture certainly played a role, but as will be discussed more thoroughly below, the most important reason for the decline in the share of agricultural revenues was serious deflation caused by pegging the exchange rate of the rupee to the pound sterling. The reduced share of agriculture in state revenues limited public investment in agriculture. Expecting more private investment, the government decreased the budget for agriculture and irrigation-related projects. Deteriorating situations worsened its consequences, particularly, price deflation so severely affected peasant tribesmen and their sheikh that a detailed examination is necessary.

2 Problems Associated with the Indian Rupee

Under the Ottoman regime, the Turkish lira (gold) was the legal tender, and the piaster (kuruş) in coins and paper money had been widely used in the province of Baghdad. Thus, when the British occupation troops began their administration, using Indian rupees, and started withdrawing Turkish currencies from circulation, they caused confusion among the people and instability on the exchange market. For about two and a half years after the beginning of the military occupation in Basra in 1914, some £T250,000 of Turkish lira (gold) were still in circulation, but neither Turkish silver coin nor paper money was in use. The exchange rate between the Turkish lira and the rupee was nominally fixed in December 1914 but dropped because the government was incapable of controlling the local exchange market. Demands for payments from the government that already had been fixed in piasters were made payable at 7 piasters per rupee and 102.6 piasters per lira (Rs 14.66 per lira).[5]

But many people were anxious to clear debt and mortgages in Turkish liras (gold) and thus accepted the inflated value of Rs 15 and slightly over per lira, although an official rate of Rs 14 or Rs 14.0.4 (14 rupees and 4 pice) per lira prevailed in Basra. Eventually the money market was stabilized by a proclamation in August 1917 under which all contracts made in Turkish lira, as well as debts, rent agreements, and *compialas* (a local form of promissory note) concluded prior to 1 April 1917, could be legally discharged in Indian rupees at the official rate of Rs 14.4 (14 rupees and 4 anna) per lira.[6] In May 1920, Turkish paper money was declared not to be legal tender, and thus not acceptable for payment of any debt. Although Iraq did little business with India and a great proportion with Great Britain, the rupee remained the sole official currency throughout the British mandate period. Nevertheless, considerable amounts of gold currency, mainly Turkish lira, circulated in Iraq through 1927, as much as £T1.5 million of it in towns.[7] The Persian keran and Maria Theresa thaler, silver coins that had circulated during the Ottoman period, also were in use for regional trade, but because of their limited circulation, they had little impact on the local economy and commerce except on transit trade with neighbouring countries.

5 TNA: CO 732/2, War Office, 16 May 1917, "Currency Situation, Basra," G.O.C., Force 'D' to War Office, 13 May 1917.

6 TNA: T 1/16244, Political Department, India Office, From Sir Percy Cox (Baghdad), 5 May 1917; BL: IOR/L/PS/10/846, P4369, 1919, "Mesopotamia: Currency Position," pt. 2.

7 TNA: CO 730/115/2, "Iraq's Currency in Financial News," by R.V. Vernon, Financial Advisor to the Government of Iraq, cutting from the issue dated 28 July 1927.

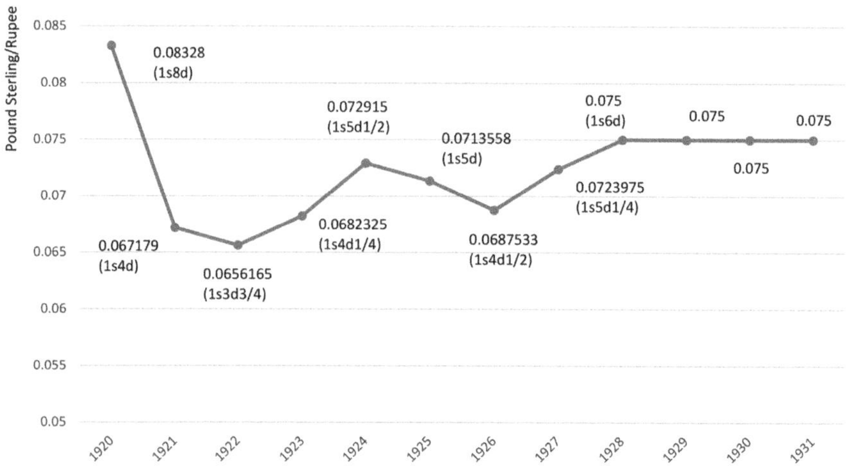

FIGURE 8.3 Exchange rates of Indian Rupee in terms of Pound Sterling, 1920–1931 (monthly average)

NOTE: 1 POUND STERLING = 20 SHILLING (S); 1 SHILLING = 12 PENCE (D); 1 PENNY = 4 FARTHINGS; 1 FARTHING = 1/4 (D).

SOURCE: BL: IOR/R/20/A/4315, RATE OF EXCHANGE OF INDIAN RUPEE, FROM L.S. AMERY TO RESIDENT AT ADEN, 18 JAN. 1928.

Although the British claimed that the rupee was not legal tender, its official use for revenue collection and expenditures in Indian rupees such as payments of military forces, government officials, and state expenditures made this imported rupees circulate as the local currency. Without delay, the weakening exchange rate of the Indian rupee in terms of the pound sterling became another irresolvable problem for Iraq's mandate government. The pound sterling itself had been troublesome, as it had ceased to be pegged to the gold standard at the outbreak of war in 1914. It was pegged again to the standard only at the end of 1925. Between 1914 and 1925, this policy reduced the value of the pound sterling and caused high inflation. By linking it to the gold standard at th pre-war rate in 1925, the British government deliberately triggered deflation but, suffering from the Great Depression, once more abandoned the peg in 1931.

Between 1898 and 1915, the Indian rupee was generally devaluated against pound sterling, though the exchange rate was stable at 1 shilling 4 pence. It rose to 2 shillings 6 pence during the war, and had been stable at around 2 shillings in 1919. As Figure 8.3 shows, it fell in 1920 to 1 shilling 8 pence, while pound sterling itself was being transacted at a discount in terms of dollar in that year. In 1922, however, the exchange rate of the rupee against the pound sterling drew a keen concern of the government because of its rapid fluctuation. The rate fell to 1 shilling 3 pence and, after pound sterling returned to the gold standard, rose to 1 shilling 5 pence by 1925 and 1 shilling 4 1/2 pence in 1926.

Meanwhile, in December 1927 enactment of a law proposed by Sir E. Hilton Young fixed the Indian rupee's rate of exchange at 1 shilling 6 pence, an intentionally overvalued rate, for the real rate was estimated at 1 shilling 4 pence (Figure 8.3). This was harmful for Iraq and other countries using the Indian rupee, including India, where the economy was plunged into severe deflation, and the peasants into extreme poverty. Although the Indian government complained repeatedly against this unfair manipulation of the exchange rate, not until 1935 was it able to establish Reserve Bank of India and implement monetary policies to control the outflow of gold.[8] The British mandate government's use of the Indian rupee in Iraq was troublesome after the rate also was fixed at the overvalued 1 shilling and 6 pence in December 1927. Without the capacity to implement monetary policies, the government struggled to cope with deflation and recession. Because of the overvaluation of the Indian rupee, the price of Iraqi export goods became artificially higher than that of their competitors in the international market, which depressed Iraqi exports and income. The government thus had to compensate for the decline in revenue in various ways, for example – as British officials suggested – by increasing railway fares and awarding subsidies. However, its measures had limited effects on the prices of daily necessities such as salt that the government rigidly regulated against the price movement. While the price of other goods decreased, the price of these regulated goods did not. This situation was particularly harmful to peasant tribesmen purchasing them in rupees.[9]

As the rupee was fixed at its higher value, it initially favoured producers of export grains because they could be marketed at higher local prices, thus making larger profits. However, global prices for agricultural products stagnated in the 1920s and accelerated the fall at the outset of Great Depression. Taking 1925 as a base of the index of the commodity prices in the world market, it declined to 87.4 in 1926, 87.2 in 1927, and 83.0 in 1928, before plummeting to 76.6 in December 1928, 74.6 in June 1929, and 65.1 in December 1929.[10] Particularly, world grain prices fell significantly in 1928–29, which put considerable downward pressure on agricultural prices in Iraq. Because the rupee was linked to

---

8 BL: IOR/L/F/7/895, "The Rupee Ratio," in Memorandum by the Secretary of State for India, 25 Nov. 1930; Parekunnel J. Thomas, "Indian Currency in the Depression," *The Economic Journal* 48, no. 190 (1938), pp. 237–47.

9 TNA: CO 730/115/2.

10 TNA: DO 35/218/8, "Empire Co-operation and the Gold Problem," in E.M.H. Lloyd, Empire Marketing Board to Sir E.J. Harding, Dominion Office, 27 Feb. 1930 (memorandum read at a meeting at Sir Basil Blackett's house on Monday, Feb. 24), p. 3.

the gold exchange standard at the fixed rate, the price of export grains in general fell with world prices.

Domestically, producers of grains or peasant cultivators suffered badly from the fall in grain prices, particularly when they owed debt. The landholders paying land tax also were hurt from the loss of revenue, because the land tax did not fluctuate as much with agricultural production as with the tithe. Moreover, declining international commodity prices aggravated government revenues because customs and agriculture so dominated total revenues. This deflationary pressure continued until the British government gave up the gold standard permanently in 1931. As a countermeasure, the Iraqi officials repeatedly petitioned the British government to stop the use of the Indian rupee and circulate the Iraqi dinar as the official currency. Because their proposals always were rejected, the Iraqi economy faced decreasing prices and stagnating exports. After independence, in 1933 Iraq finally introduced its own currency, the dinar, under supervision of the Board of Currency, although it still was linked to the pound sterling. The currency issues, along with deflation and recession, provocatively affected agriculture in the irrigated area using imported pumps and producing exports grains. Particularly, as examined below, many pump owners, who imported pumps and their parts from Britain, were indebted to their suppliers, and were in serious danger of default.

3 The Problems of Pump Owners

Under the Ottomans, the narrow tracts of land on the banks of the Twin Rivers had been irrigated by direct lift from the rivers by artificial means. Lift irrigation by pumps with oil engines had been used as the government had recognized the importance of irrigation pumps, which could carry water deep into uncultivated land, thus designating the expanded land as *karûd*, and had set a regulation on their landholding. During the war, however, many pumps fell into disuse, their essential parts stolen, and only when the British set up mechanics' shops did they re-enter use, proving once again their worth in agricultural production.

Both during and after the post-war recovery, then, British administrators saw land and crop prices increase as a result of improvements to agriculture and land use and thus encouraged expanded pump irrigation. Intending purchasers could receive advice from the director of agriculture and his officers as to the correct strength of engine and size of pump for their needs. Upon purchase, they could obtain credit for the trade and a rebate of customs duty payable on oil engines and pumps, with a certificate from the local assistant political officer for their use in agriculture.[11] Still more, British officials attempted to promote land reclamation by means of pumps imported from Great Britain. A supply of kerosene and fuel oil, obtained from Persia by an agent of the Anglo-Persian Oil Company, Messrs. Strick, Scott, and Company, increased in 1918 after the establishment of new depots to meet the demands of pump irrigation and river transportation. Accordingly, the charge for inland water transport was reduced, cutting the selling price of oil to the public from 15 to 13 annas per gallon.[12]

This protective measure continued to the favour of the pump owners under deflation and fluctuating rate of rupees. The government's continuing flood-control initiatives on the major rivers and canals also provided an incentive for private investment in pump irrigation. In particular, a law enacted in 1926 to encourage the installation of powerful mechanical pumps to increase the area under cultivation triggered the purchase of pumps by townsmen, who expanded their interests into the countryside.[13]

In addition, the credit market favoured borrowing to purchase pumps – low interest rates meant that lenders were more likely to be repaid. In 1926, as an example, agricultural loans amounted to Rs 990,690, and the sum of Rs 1,169,918 was recovered during the same year. Interest was charged at 5 per cent, except on some seed loans and on all loans granted in the north-eastern area, which still was suffering from the war. In some cases, when payment was made on the due date, the interest was remitted, if not charged on the whole period of the loan. The rate of 5 per cent was very low, since the official rate of interest according to Turkish Law, as recorded in the report of the Tapu Department for 1919, was 9 per cent, and some mortgages were charged even more.[14]

Meanwhile, district administration improved over fiscal matters, carried out by *mufattish* (*müfettiş*, divisional inspector), *mudir mal* ([*müdîr-i mâl*] district inspector), *mamur shubah* (Indian *tahsîldar*, tax gatherer), assistant *mamur* ([*nâib*] deputy official), and *katib* ([*kâtip*] clerk of first and second grade). Along with the opening of *tapu* offices in all divisions of Baghdad province,

11 Revenue Circular, No. 33, Baghdad, 18 May 1920; John P. Hewett, *Report for the Army Council on Mesopotamia*, BL: IOR/L/PS/20/35 (Baghdad, 1919), p. 20.

12 TNA: CO 696/1, Revenue Department, "Administration Report, 1918," p. 5.

13 Keiko Kiyotaki, "The Legacy of Ottoman Land and Tax Systems in Iraq during the British Mandate Period," *International Journal of Turkish Studies* 19, nos. 1 & 2 (2013), p. 50.

14 Great Britain, Board of Trade, Department of Overseas Trade, *Economic Conditions in Iraq*, reported by C. Empson, Commercial Secretary to His Majesty's Embassy at Baghdad, August 1933 (London: HMSO, 1933), p. 26.

they provided security for the rights of the proprietors of the pump and the land, as well as for the pump.[15]

After irrigable land thus became a more secure investment, by 1926, the British encouragement of private investment in irrigation pumps finally began to achieve its goal. Post-war inflation and a slump in trade had stopped by then, and in Basra and Baghdad, prices had fallen as much as 30 per cent below war levels, except in Mosul, where prices had already been very low.[16] With the consequent decline in prices for land and pumps, numerous applications were received from merchants and traders for advice on opening up estates, especially on riverine tracts irrigable directly by pump.[17] The government promoted imports of irrigation pumps and agricultural machines from Britain and other countries, which became more affordable through government aid and cheaper oil prices. A number of prominent Iraqi politicians, including Prime Minister Yasin al-Hashimi (1924–25 and 1935–36), became interested in purchasing a pump for large-scale land irrigiation, and a law enacted in 1926 provided a substantial tax concession for pump users. Favourable loans were offered to pump purchasers, often on a basis of 25 per cent in cash down, 25 per cent in two 18-month instalments, and the balance in 24 or even 30 months; in the event of bad harvests, extensions were given at the prevailing rates of interest.[18] As a result, large profits were made by means of pump irrigation in the three years before the Depression, and townsmen with little capital and no knowledge of farming hastened to acquire land and install pumps. By the end of 1930, over 2,500 pumps were in operation, and the area under cultivation had been increased by approximately a million acres.[19]

During 1927, moreover, oil production impacted on prevailing pump irrigation practices and on the economy. A subsidiary of the Anglo-Persian Oil Company, Khanaqin Oil Company, had established a refinery at Alwand for the oil produced at Naht Khana, which supplied sufficient oil for local consumption. The construction of a pipeline to the Mediterranean also had become a promising project because of expected large demand in the West. Until then,

---

15 "Report by the Director of *Tapu*," Iraq, Department of Agriculture, *Administration Report of the Department of Agriculture in Mesopotamia for the Year 1920* (Baghdad: Government Press, 1921), pp. 2–3. J.F. Webster officiated as deputy director of research in addition to his duties as agricultural chemist during the period that Roger Thomas was director of agriculture.

16 TNA: CO 696/3, "Report on the *Tapu* Department for the year 1920–21," p. 2.

17 TNA: CO 696/5, "Administration Reports, 1922–1924," p. 15.

18 Great Britain, Board of Trade, Department of Overseas Trade, *Economic Conditions in Iraq*, reported by C. Empson, p. 26.

19 Sir Ernest N. Dowson, *An Enquiry into Land Tenure and Related Questions* (Letchworth, UK: Garden City Press, 1931), p. 29.

the local sale of oil could increase revenue from excise duty. With agriculture, trade, and now oil production as principal economic interests for the government, pump irrigation drew greater attention because of the cheap local oil and low transport costs, and politicians, parliament members, and merchants acquired the imported pumps, increasing the cultivated areas and grain production.[20]

Towards the end of the British mandate, however, in the transition to a new Iraqi government from the late 1920s to the mid-1930s, the government's role as the chief promoter of pump irrigation instigated prolonged trouble over irrigated areas occupied by tribesmen. Under the Ottomans, the land irrigated by pump had been cultivated either by the tribesmen who already occupied the land or by tribesmen recruited by their sheikh or the pump owner through leasing, crop sharing, or partition of the land. In that era, the pump owner did not claim the *tapu* right, because land legislation had not guaranteed his claim, but as new legislation gradually did so during the mandate period, conflicts developed between pump owners and tribesmen who had a prescriptive right to the land based on their occupation and cultivation of the reclaimed land. Those clashes were especially serious on land that had risen in value. It disturbed the harmonized practices of agriculture, land tenure, and taxation that the British were unwilling to modify, even though it caused serious conflicts of interest between them.[21]

When both the export of agricultural produce and prices dropped sharply after the worldwide Depression began, affecting Iraqi trade in early 1930, many pump owners, including a number of political figures, could not pay British manufacturers for their pumps. The fixed rate of rupees against the pound sterling made their debt heavier, while falling grain prices brought far less revenues for them. Unable to get out of recession, the government, which had encouraged the importation of pumps, resorted to another protective measure for them. Those pump owners and landholders had already gained political power, as the British officials had turned to advisory roles, and attempted to protect their own agricultural investments. Thus, the government implemented new land and agricultural policies, despite their detrimental effects on the peasant tribesmen and their sheikhs.

---

20 Great Britain, *Report by His Britannic Majesty's Government to the Council of the League of Nations on the Administration of 'Iraq for the year 1928* (London: HMSO, 1929), pp. 111–13.

21 For tax policies in this period, see Kiyotaki, "Legacy of Ottoman Land and Tax Systems in Iraq," pp. 41–46.

4 New Land Legislation

Previously, after promulgation of the first constitution in 1925 and ratification of the new Anglo-Iraqi Treaty in 1926, the British administration had begun pulling out of state affairs, and the Iraqi parliamentary government had commenced to focus on land policies, with rapid progress in the cadastral survey and land settlement.[22] The Anglo-Iraqi-Turkish Treaty, ratified in July 1926, had given the Iraqi government access to *tapu* records in the former Ottoman provinces of Baghdad, Basra, and Mosul, enabling it to settle land claims over large areas of *tapu* land. Its aim was to impose the land tax concurrently with the settlement of land claims, thereby increasing revenue to reduce fiscal deficits, but it also attempted to create as many small independent landholders as possible by ending grants of large blocks of land to individuals and the free alienation of state (*arâzi-i miriye*) land.

Some seven years after the new constitution was promulgated, the government enacted Land Settlement Law No. 50 of 1932 for the settlement of land claims under the new principle. The customary rights of *uqr*, possession (*tasarruf* in the Ottoman period), *lazma*, and *mugharisa* (plantation) were recognized as rights. Qualified applicants were granted *tapu*; others, *lazma*; and unclaimed land was classified as state land (*miri sirf*, Art. 1). On *muwat* (*arâzi-i mevât*, vacant) land, the relevant provision of the Ottoman Land Code ceased to apply, and it was included in the category of *miri sirf* (Art. 6). Article 11 defined *lazma* land tenure for the first time, requiring the settlement officer to grant *lazma* according to Lazma Law No. 51 of 1932 on land used in a productive manner for fifteen years prior to the date of the land settlement. The same article specified that the pump owner was entitled to claim the *lazma* land tenure unless the land irrigated by his pump was cultivated before the installation of the pump and within fifteen years prior to the law's promulgation. In the latter case, the settlement officer could "take cognizance of any agreement concerning this land and also the area actually cultivated by those with interests therein" (Art. 11).

The customary right of usufruct, *lazma*, was officially recognized in Article 1 of Lazma Law No. 51 of 1932 as "the rights awarded in land of the category '*miri* not granted in *tapu*' in pursuance of Article 11 of Land Settlement Law No. 50 of 1932." The obligation to cultivate the land was extended to four years, compared to three years for *tapu* land, but the agricultural practice of fallow was not deemed a failure to cultivate (Art. 8). In addition, the provisions of the (Ottoman) Land Code were to be applied unless modified by this law (Art. 10), and the Ministry of Finance was charged with the execution of the law

22 TNA: CO 696/6, "Administration Reports, 1925–27," p. 4.

(Art. 12). In the early 1930s, the Land Settlement and Lazma Laws immediately prompted the settlement of claims to land in this category, as settlement officials scrutinized the claim to *tapu* more strictly. *Lazma* land registered in this way continued and is the origin of present *lazma* tenure in Iraq.

Due to the Iraqi government's growing political authority and the financial crisis of the Depression years, the Land Settlement and Lazma Laws became fundamental to protecting pump owners' interests, both in the land and in securing peasant tribesmen to cultivate their land. Specifically, the Iraqi government created a new form of land tenure called *lazma*, which gave a prescriptive right of possession on state land on the same principle as *tapu*. Accordingly, it modified tenancy on tribal lands, regardless of the claims of cultivating peasant tribesmen and their sheikhs, legitimizing this new tenure through land legislation that was distinct from the Ottoman land laws.[23] Because this Lazma Law entitled the pump owner to claim the *lazma* right, although the cultivating tribesmen also had a right in the land, in 1929 the government already had prepared a new land law. In it, the pump owner was listed as the farm owner, and after the mandate regime ended, the Iraqi parliament enacted it in 1933 as the Law Governing the Rights and Duties of Cultivators. The resulting rapid spread of *lazma* land tenure over unalienated state land, supported by the Land Settlement Law of 1932 and the Lazma Law of the same year, drew the serious concern of British officials from its outset, as has been observed by many historians of mandate period Iraq.[24]

5 The Problems of the Serkâr and Peasant Tribesmen

To complete the history of land tenure, the fate of the *serkâr*, or the sheikh of lesser peasant tribes and tribesmen, needs to be examined, as it is key to understanding the modification of the Ottoman state land system in Iraq. Crucial to this investigation is the Law Governing the Rights and Duties of Cultivators

23 Dowson, *Enquiry into Land Tenure*, pp. 25–26.

24 The Law Governing the Rights and Duties of Cultivators of 1933 has been discussed by the major historians of this period. See Gabriel Baer, "The Agrarian Problem in Iraq," *Middle Eastern Affairs* 3, no. 12 (1952), p. 382; Sluglett, *Britain in Iraq*, pp. 180–81; ʿImād Aḥmad al-Jawāhirī, *Taʾrīkh Mushkilat al-Arāḍī fī al-ʿIrāq, 1914–1932* (Baghdad: Al-Jumhūrīyah al-ʿIrāqīyah: Manshūrāt Wizārat al-Thaqāfah wa al-Funun, 1978), pp. 340–56; Joseph Sassoon, *Economic Policy in Iraq, 1932–1950* (London: Frank Cass, 1987), pp. 169–70; Samira Haj, *The Making of Iraq, 1900–1963: Capital, Power, and Ideology* (Albany: State University of New York Press, 1997), p. 50; Charles Tripp, *A History of Iraq* (Cambridge: Cambridge University Press, 2000), p. 85; Doreen Warriner, *Land Reform and Development in the Middle East: A Study of Egypt, Syria, and Iraq* (London: Royal Institute of International Affairs, 1957), pp. 136–37.

of 1933, examined below. As Peter Sluglett explains in his authoritative work on the British mandate period, "the application of this law, particularly at a time of severe agricultural depression, explains much of the considerable movement of the population from the rural to the urban areas in search of employment." Its provisions "were so extreme," he continues, "even some members of the Iraqi cabinet wondered if they might not be contravening some of the clauses of the International Anti-Slavery Convention."[25] The law, moreover, imposed serious effects on the tribal society and tax-farming practices that the Ottoman provincial government, local people, tribal sheikhs, and tribesmen had long known.[26]

In contrast to the Ottoman period, first, the new law defined ownership not only as a right to ownership in the land but also as an entitlement to various privileges. Now, those who farmed alienated *miri* land (held by *tapu* or *lazma* deed) that was irrigated by flow, rain, pumps, or any other means of irrigation, were under the landholder's authority. A pump owner legally became the farm owner, permitted by government to develop agriculture on unalienated *miri* land (*arâzi-i miriye*). Under the empowered pump owner, anyone who leased such lands from him or any agent hired to manage the pump owner's land for cultivation was also classified as the farm owner. The *serkâr*, or the sheikh of the cultivating peasant tribesmen, who had played a major role in agricultural production and crop sharing, was considered merely an employee of the farm owner. Accordingly, the *serkâr* (now called *sirkal*) no longer had to be the sheikh of the peasant tribesmen but could be any person who managed the cultivation by the peasants in exchange for a share in the crops. In a more important change affecting the peasant tribesman themselves, Article 1 of the law defined them as persons who cultivated the land for a share in the crops or fixed wages.

In the tribal areas during the Ottoman period, the *serkâr* usually had worked together with the government officials, tax farmer, peasant tribesmen, and local service providers, but the duties of *sirkal* were greatly reduced in Article 6 of the new law. Now he was to manage cultivation on the number of feddâns stipulated by the farm owner. He supervised the work of the *fellāh* (*fallāḥ*, peasant), but had to execute all arrangements decided by the owner. Even though the *serkâr* had been the sheikh of peasant tribesmen, he was deprived of the prestigious chieftainship. He had to inform the owner, without delay, of

25 Sluglett, *Britain in Iraq*, p. 180.

26 The Law Governing the Rights and Duties of Cultivators, No. 28 of 1933 (From Iraq Government Gazette, No. 31, 30 July, 1933; Published in *al-Waqā'i' al-'Irāqīyah*, no. 1267 of 1–7–33) is included in TNA: FO 624/1/428/1, Iraq, Correspondence, "Laws Relating to Agriculture," Minute Sheet, a memorandum to the High Commission of 27 Jan. 1930.

every instance of negligence that he could not prevent; and had to protect the crops against natural and other calamities and any harmful encroachments on cultivation.

The duties of the *fellāh* also were defined in Article 9 of the law. He was to grow the crops decided for the land and endeavour to tend their growth; protect, stack, and remove the crops to the places assigned. He had to execute the arrangements, orders, and necessary work issued by the farm owner or *sirkal*, according to their powers as laid down in the law. He had to endeavour to fend off, at once, natural and other calamities or encroachments in any way harmful to the crops, and inform the *sirkal* or owner of the occurrence of such calamities and encroachments without delay.

Defining the roles and obligations of the *sirkal* and *fellāh* by law caused serious problems for them. They drew serious concerns of the British officials and administrators who had become acquainted with agricultural conditions through their survey works. Among them was J.F. Webster, a British official who had worked for the Department of Agriculture as a researcher during the mandate period and had become inspector general of agriculture by the time the law was being considered in 1930. His famous memorandum presents the depth of the peasant's problems and clue to understanding the decline of the Ottoman legacy in this period.

According to Webster, once the farm owner became the agricultural authority, protected by law, the *sirkal* and *fellāh* were obliged to carry out his orders under threat of severe legal penalties. As a consequence, they were tied to the land by debts they had incurred to the owner for seed, livestock, and agricultural implements or loans in cash. If they refused to carry out their duties, the farm owner could employ another *sirkal* or *fellāh* to carry out such duties and debit the cost of doing so against the defaulting *sirkal* or *fellāh*.[27]

Supplies necessary for cultivation had never been considered debt in the Ottoman custom of crop sharing, Webster continued; rather, the supplies were connected to the entitlement to the share of the produce, and thus part of risk sharing. Referring to the sheikh of peasant tribesmen as the "*Lazmah*" holder

27 The cover letter to Webster's note read, in part:

"I have the honor to transmit to you herewith a copy of a note by the late British Inspector-General of Agriculture.... This note was handed to me by Mr. Webster shortly before his final departure from Iraq and represents the view he himself originally laid before the Iraqi authorities in 1930 at the time when the first draft of the Law was under consideration."

Copy of the note of J.F. Webster (E. 191/191/93) in No. 807 (428/7/33) of the Baghdad Embassy, 22 Dec. 1933; TNA: FO 371/17858, Political Departments: General Correspondence, Political (Eastern) Iraq, 1934; TNA: FO 624/1/428/7; BL: IOR/R/15/5/163, "File 2/10 Iraq Law Governing the Rights and Duties of Cultivators."

(who had a prescriptive right to the land), instead of as the *sirkal*, Webster criticized the proponents of the new law:

> There is no doubt that the non-success of a great many new agricultural ventures in recent years has been due, in past, to the difficulties experienced by the "Farm owner" in establishing control over the "*Lazmah*" holders and their *fellaheen*.
>
> For better or worse, the greater parts of these new comers into agriculture have been active politicians, and it was inevitable that they should seek some legal remedy for their trouble.[28]
>
> They have been granted very extensive tracts of valuable government land, not only without payment, but also with revenue privileges, provided only that they undertook to exploit such lands. The terms "development and exploitation" have been universally interpreted as meaning only, the erection of a pump and engine for irrigation purposes, and a subsequent attempt to farm the lands using the "*Lazmah*" holder and his *fellaheen* as the basis of their labour supply, and following the customary share-system of farming as almost universally practiced by existing "*Tapu*" holders.
>
> Naturally friction followed, for the "*Lazmah*" holders regarded the new pump owner as a mere outsider who supplied water against payment (by crop-share), and themselves as the proprietors of the land and the sole agricultural authority.
>
> Conversely, the pump-owner regarded himself as the proprietor and farmer, and the "*Lazmah*" holder as his employee. This latter position has been legalized.[29]

Webster considered the pump owners as the new landholders, granted extensive tracts of state land, without payment and with revenue privileges for land reclamation and irrigation for agricultural production. However, they relied on the peasant tribesmen, now called *fellaheen*, and their sheikh, or the "*lazmah*" holder, to cultivate the lands. The customary crop sharing had been practised by them since the Ottoman period and predominated on existing *tapu* lands. He thus predicted grave conflicts between the *sirkal*, or tribal sheikh, and the pump owner.

Under the law, a *sirkal* or *fellāh* who had unpaid debt could neither move to another farm nor obtain employment in government departments, municipalities, or registered companies. If he did so and was found indebted, he had

28 Ibid.

29 Ibid.

to repay to the owner one-third of the pay or wages or one-third of the benefits assigned to him during the whole period of his stay in the owner's employment (Art. 15). Such a restriction and obligation had rarely been seen in the irrigated areas under the Ottomans. By registering agricultural *sanad*s and agreements with a notary public, *qaimmaqam* (*kâimmakâm*), or *mudir nahiya* (*müdîr-i nâhiye*) delegated by the minister of justice (Art. 26), an owner could punish severely a defaulting sheikh and peasant cultivator, exercising an authoritative power that in the Ottoman period had been reserved to the paramount sheikh or the government. In short, the law brought an end to local customs and tribal traditions, and thus the principles of state land that the Ottoman land system had harmonized in agricultural production throughout a long history. Whereas the British administration had not wanted to change the concept of state land ownership, the newly empowered parliamentary government, whose members were pump and land owners, did.

The law drew harsh criticism from British officials while it was being drafted, and even anger from those who were well aware of the indigenous practices of agriculture, tax collecting, and land tenure. The adviser to the Iraqi Ministry of Interior, Sir Kinahan Cornwallis, charged that "it would impose on the *fellaheen* a relationship with their employers not far removed from serfdom" and would apply to the whole of Iraq "an organization inspired by experience of pump cultivation in the Baghdad and Kut provinces (*liwas*)."[30] To no avail, Cornwallis produced an alternative draft that would regularize the position and rights of pump owners without depressing the status of the *fellaheen* and incurring the risk of agrarian unrest. In a note he handed to the British ambassador in Baghdad shortly before his final departure from Iraq after the end of the mandate, J.F. Webster predicted trouble among the *fellaheen* if the law should ever be put into general operation.[31]

Webster apparently warned against hasty reforms that disadvantaged the holders of prescriptive right. As he pointed out, the peasants had been badly affected by the sudden slump in agricultural prices during the Great Depression, the uncertainty of development under the mandate government, and the use of the Indian rupee as an official currency.[32]

The rupee in Baghdad was at a discount of 1 per cent on the rupee in Bombay, and the discount rate was rising as the rupee depreciated against the pound sterling. The Iraqi government could not control fluctuations of the exchange

30 TNA: FO 624/1/428/1, Iraq, Correspondence, "Laws Relating to Agriculture."

31 Copy of the note of J.F. Webster (E. 191/191/93); No. 807 (428/7/33) of the Baghdad Embassy, 22 Dec. 1933; TNA: FO 371/17858, Political Departments: General Correspondence, Political (Eastern) Iraq, 1934; TNA: FO 624/1/428/7; BL: IOR/R/15/5/163.

32 TNA: CO 696/7, Colonial Office: Iraq Sessional Papers, "Administration Reports, 1928–1931," pp. 7–9.

rate, which since 1927 had been fixed by law at an overvalued rate of Rs 1,600 per £100. Likewise, the Iraqi government could do little about the overvalued rupee and the consequent declines in exports and prices of agricultural produce, even after Great Britain went off the gold standard in 1931. Still worse, in the early 1930s, the worldwide Depression also began to affect the Iraqi economy, lowering further the price of grain. The tonnage of the grain exported in 1930, for example, was 60 per cent greater than for the previous year, but the relative increase in the total value of the export was only 10 per cent. During the last five months of 1930, when the price of imported manufactured articles dropped by about 15 per cent, the average price of export products fell nearly 40 per cent.[33]

Amid the problems with the rupee and the impact of the Depression, Webster perceived the peasants' need for the Ottoman practice of crop sharing, which had ceased to function under the new law. Consequently, upon leaving Iraq, he cautioned the British ambassador:

> The share of the *fellah* is such that unless he has his "customary" perquisites, such as free grazing for a goat or two, free firewood, and a certain amount of free vegetables, and a certain amount of stolen produce, it is doubtful if he could exist. The old type "farm owner" accepted this, cursed his *fellaheen* for a set of rascally thieves, but winked at their stealing in "reason."
>
> The new type of agriculturalist, whilst doing nothing to ameliorate the conditions of the *fellah*, refuses to tolerate these "customs," and has provided (article 49) dire pains and penalties....
>
> ... In times of agricultural depression, or in the hands of an unskillful farmer, the *fellah* under the provisions of the present law is doomed to perpetual indebtedness, and since he cannot leave the land, he is, in reality, reduced to the status of a slave. Such a state of affairs is almost inevitabl[y] followed, sooner or later, by revolution.[34]

Nevertheless, the Iraqi cabinet's persistent attempts to bring the draft of the law before the parliament were only delayed, not thwarted, by a communication from the high commissioner to the Ministry of the Interior. The commissioner objected to the proposed law on the grounds that (1) it would prejudice the recommendation on land tenure forthcoming from a special enquiry by

33 TNA: CO 696/7, "Administration Reports, 1928–1931, Customs and Excise," pp. 7–9.

34 Copy of the note of J.F. Webster (E. 191/191/93); No. 807 (428/7/33) of the Baghdad Embassy, TNA: FO 371/17858; FO 624/1/428/7; BL: IOR/R/15/5/163.

Sir Ernest Dowson; (2) one of its articles appeared to constitute a breach of the International Anti-Slavery Convention to which Iraq had adhered; and (3) the local authorities in the *liwas* (districts) had not been consulted in drafting it.[35]

Despite the high commissioner's objections, Dowson, who surveyed Iraq for just three months after lengthy negotiations with the Iraqi government, presented recommendations that were rather supportive of the law. He concluded that the Ottoman government had granted the *tapu* right without properly investigating prescriptive rights and the settlement of conflicting claims. Because the transfer of land by *tapu* title, therefore, caused violent complaints from tribesmen, giving *tapu* tenure was not to be recommended so long as tribal solidarity and other communal divisions remained strong. In its place, a standard leasehold agreement was appropriate for holding state land and could be made with enterprising townsmen, as well as with others who had tribal affiliations.[36]

When the mandate regime ended, a new and even more comprehensive Law Governing the Rights and Duties of Cultivators passed swiftly through the Iraqi parliament for enactment in 1933. With the Land Settlement Law and Lazma Laws of 1932, it promoted registration of *lazma* title on *miri* land, and the spread of *lazma* land in irrigated areas, benefitting pump owners.

As of 1932, the previous government had created only two land settlement committees, staffed by senior officials who wanted to avoid complicated troubles, but the new government increased the number of these committees to nine in 1936 and appointed competent officials to them. Wallace Lyon, one of three British land-settlement officers, described his work between 1932 and 1941 in a memoir. He would summon all claimants to the land's *lazma* title, either peasant sheikhs or peasant tribesmen, and would grant the title according to their claims. But they were soon forced to sell it in order to purchase seed and other necessities, or to mortgage it, apparently because of the depression of agricultural prices. He also transferred the *tapu* right to those who proved their prescriptive right on the land, legally admitted the customary prescriptive right of *lazma* as the land title based on the Lazma Law of 1932, and settled disputes among claimants accordingly. In a memoir, he elaborated on his work in

35 TNA: FO 624/1/428, "Law Relating to Agriculture," Minute Sheet.

36 The pump owner wished to participate in agricultural improvements by simply searching for a suitable stretch of *miri* land (*arâzi-i miriye*), entering into an agreement with some group of claimants to prescriptive rights over it, and then applying to the governor of the province for permission to install the pumps with a permit from the Irrigation Department and the approval of the State Domain Department. Dowson, *Enquiry into Land Tenure*, pp. 31–32.

the tribal domain of the Shammar Toga in the Kut district, which happened to be where British Consul in Baghdad Henry Creswicke Rawlinson had recorded in his diary a conversation with the *zabit* from a notable family in Baghdad about ninety years earlier. As Lyon recalled,

> after hearing all the evidence I allocated to each who had anything approaching a bona fide claim about five times as much as he was capable of cultivating in any one year, situated on the right bank approximately where they had previously cultivated. Where this fell in an area now under power pump I rewarded the pump owner with an extra amount of equivalent area at the tails of his holding. The remainder I registered in the name of the government. This enabled the Shammar Toga to continue with their primitive methods with reasonable room for expansion if they so desired, though I was pretty certain that in spite of my warning they would sell their birth rights for a mess of pottage after I had passed on.
>
> I gave all judgements on the spot and offered to advise and help any who wished to appeal. Strange to relate, however, they all took it well – from the wealthy Mayor of Baghdad, who had a big holding, down to the poorest pair of brothers who had established a claim.... When the first of these brothers made his application, claiming for himself and his brother, I told him to go and fetch his brother so that both could put their thumb marks on the document. He replied that he was unable to bring him. When I asked why he said, "We have only one 'dish dash' [an ankle – length shirt] between us and I am now wearing it. But I will go and give it to him and he will then come and put his mark."[37]

The tribal domain of the Shammar Toga had been farmed out to a tax farmer chosen from the established families of the officials and notables in the city of Baghdad, and the land system had been put in order under the cultivating tribal customs. As observed in Table 8.1, in the district of Kut in 1936, landholding under the tenure of *mulk* (*arâzi-i mülkiye*, private land) or *matruk* (*arâzi-i metrûke*, common land) and *tapu* land were limited to only 29, 1,843, and 89,065 dönüm respectively – small areas compared with the other districts. By contrast, in Kut, the new tenure of *lazma* was established in large areas, amounting to 465,444 dönüm, and more than twice this area was unregistered as *miri sirf* (state land).

---

37 David K. Fieldhouse, ed., *Kurds, Arabs and Britons: The Memoir of Wallace Lyon in Iraq, 1918–44* (London: I.B. Tauris, 2002), p. 197.

TABLE 8.1 Areas of land-claim settlement (in dönüm) as of October, 1936

	Baghdad	Kut	Kirkuk	Dulaim	Hilla	Total
Mulk	47,095	29	–	4	–	47,128
Matruk	20,328	1,843	6,254	13,948	313	42,686
Waqf	76,199	–	18,232	–	–	94,431
Tapu	293,232	89,065	275,825	109,517	4	767,643
Lazma	617,201	465,444	19,849	186,845	5,006	1,294,345
Miri Sirf	496,664	975,742	32,870	407,068	25,661	1,938,005
Total	1,550,733	1,532,127	353,072	717,386	30,986	4,184,304

SOURCE: TNA: FO 624/7/623, EMBASSY, HIGH COMMISSION AND CONSULATE, IRAQ: CORRESPONDENCE, LAND SETTLEMENT, 1936.

These numbers, estimated as percentages in Table 8.2, show some regional characteristics of the new land policies. While in Kut, over twice the area remained unregistered versus registered, in Kirkuk, peasants and other landholder could claim *tapu* title in large areas.[38]

TABLE 8.2 Areas of land-claim settlement (in percent) as of October, 1936

	Baghdad	Kut	Kirkuk	Dulaim	Hilla	Total
Mulk	3	–	–	–	–	1.1
Matruk	2	0.1	1.8	1.9	1	1
Waqf	4.9	–	5.2	–	–	2.3
Tapu	18.9	5.8	78.1	15.3	–	18.3
Lazma	30.9	30.4	5.6	26	16.2	30.9
Miri Sirf	32	63.7	9.3	56.7	82.8	46.3
Total	100	100	100	100	100	100

SOURCE: TNA: FO 624/7/623, EMBASSY, HIGH COMMISSION AND CONSULATE, IRAQ: CORRESPONDENCE, LAND SETTLEMENT, 1936.

38 For the progress of land settlement and large landholding after the survey, see Sassoon, *Economic Policy in Iraq*, pp. 155–74; Marion Farouk-Sluglett and Peter Sluglett, "The Transformation of Land Tenure and Rural Social Structure in Central and Southern Iraq, c. 1870–1958," *International Journal of Middle East Studies* 15, no. 4 (1983), p. 498.

Tables 8.1 and 8.2 show that in some districts large numbers of *lazma* titles were granted in a short period as a result of land-claim settlement. In Kirkuk, approximately 78 per cent of the settlement (by area) was made for *tapu* title, but in Baghdad and Dulaim, it was 19 per cent and 15 per cent respectively. *Lazma* title accounted for only 5 per cent of the area registered in Kirkuk but 31 per cent and 26 per cent in Baghdad and Dulaim respectively. In Kut, where Lyon was a settlement officer, 30 per cent was registered for *lazma*, and about 64 per cent was left as state land (*miri sirf*). In Hilla, where land settlement was slow, only 16.2 per cent was registered for *lazma*; almost all the rest remained state land.[39]

With the rapid spread of *lazma* land, what J.F. Webster had predicted in 1930 came to pass. As a result, in 1938, the government amended the Land Settlement Law to reduce the amount of *lazma* land granted and to increase the *miri sirf* available for distribution to small tenants or peasants in the future. The amendment also addressed the problems created when a person with no previous connection to the land was granted a title deed (*shart-name*) within just a few days, without the notification of the settlement, and so could establish a claim to *lazma* with a view to subsequent sale. In order to prevent such prejudice to the rights of the original cultivators by influential persons, the whole

39 The total area, in which the land settlement operation had been carried out up to 17 Jan. 1938 amounted to 5,461,753 dönüm situated in the *Liwa*s of Kirkuk, Baghdad, Kut, Diyala, Dulaim, and Hilla, or a little over one-seventh of the total cultivable area, which was estimated at 1,844,000 feddân or 36,880,000 dönüm. TNA: FO 624/10/171. The land settlement committee was said to have made a very valuable contribution to stability and security in the country. The table below, on the number of applications for title, shows large numbers of small *lazma* land holders had been given the tenure, which they had never before enjoyed, but it does not show the occupation and place of residence of the applicants.

Place	1–50 dönüms	51–100 dönüms	101–500 dönüms	Over 500 dönüms
Falluja 2	330	13	5	1
Yusufiya 2	70	8	6	6
Tarmiya 3	35	25	16	3
Tarmiya 4	28	15	11	4
Garma 2	80	22	11	1
Kadhimiya 4	245	38	24	1

TNA: FO 624/7/623, Embassy, High Commission and Consulate, Iraq: Correspondence, Land Settlement, 1936.

of the second paragraph of Article 11 (a) of the Lazma Law, which privileged pump owners, was cancelled.

In summary, the principle of Ottoman state land continued and became the basis for the whole Iraqi land system. Registration efforts carried out by British officials defined the land title and boundaries in large areas of disputed lands, but both those officials and the Iraqi government had grave doubts about the *tapu* land system. Land legislation on the new land title of *lazma* and the cultivation rights favoured farm owners. By legislating the duties of the peasant cultivators, it tied the peasants to work for those owners. The peasant tribesmen, who had moved to another field whenever a dispute occurred over the tax, or difficulty over grazing or irrigation arose, were no longer allowed to move. Hastily enacted with little consideration for the principles of state land, the worldwide Depression, and currency matters, these changes aggravated the problems of the land system and impoverished the peasant cultivators by fettering them to one farm owner's land.

Seeking reasons for the departure from the Ottoman system, this chapter first examined the declining share of agricultural revenues in total revenues. Because these revenues consistently fell short of customs revenues and were unable to keep pace with increasing expenditure, agriculture lost its significance vis-à-vis trade, commerce, and oil production. The government then adopted a policy of protecting pump owners and landholders against the interests of cultivating peasant tribesmen and their sheikhs but actually made the problem of the agricultural sector worse by using the Indian rupee as its official currency. When the rupee was fixed in 1927 at an overvalued rate against the pound sterling, Iraqi politicians and parliament members who imported irrigation pumps from the United Kingdom were affected. Still, with the progress of flood control, the irrigated areas expanded, and under the secured registration system of land title, those pump owners began to register their irrigated land. Because the legacy of the Ottoman tax and land systems remained an obstacle to development, in order to remove them for reforms in favour of pump owners, the government enacted legislation modifying tenancy on tribal lands, disregarding the claims of cultivating peasant tribesmen and their sheikhs.[40] This led the disintegration of tribal society and reduced numerous peasant tribesmen to the status of tenants-at-will. Nevertheless, this explains only in part the fundamental changes that the Iraqi government made in

---

40 Stephen Hemsley Longrigg, *'Iraq, 1900 to 1950: A Political, Social, and Economic History* (Oxford: Oxford University Press, 1953), pp. 176–220.

altering the Ottoman legacy. Hit hard by the worldwide Depression, government officials claimed they had to initiate a lengthy sequence of modernization to overcome its impact, but they favoured investors from their own ranks, to the detriment of the tribesmen. The high cost of their first, hasty measures suggests that tribal tradition and local custom were intangible assets that society had inherited from the Ottoman Tanzimat era.

Conclusion

The province of Baghdad, on the Fertile Crescent, was blessed with the Euphrates and Tigris Rivers and a large peasant population. In contrast to the image of oppressive Ottoman rulers in the Arab region, the Baghdad governors in the Tanzimat period capably consolidated the province and implemented modernizing reforms. Agricultural progress, one of their most important accomplishments, which led to ameliorated economic conditions, can be observed in how cultivated land was expanded through public water control, irrigation, and land reclamation projects, and in how the tribal labour force was increased through conciliation with the tribal sheikhs. The governors' efforts to introduce commercial agriculture and expand foreign trade, moreover, stimulated people's interest in agricultural investment. Supplementing these tangible supports were sweeping reforms of tax farming and land tenure aimed at providing private individuals with economic incentives to cultivate abandoned agricultural land or uncultivated land, which likewise encouraged investment in land.

This book has revealed these tax farming and land tenure reforms to be key ingredients of agricultural progress, alongside provincial administration, tribal policies, and other modernizing reforms during the Tanzimat period. The book has also explored the role of local custom and tribal tradition in tax farming and *tapu* landholding and the impact of the Ottoman reforms on their relations. In this regard, it has been seen that the custom of crop sharing was crucial to how tax farming and *tapu* landholding operated and promoted agricultural production activities. The reason for this may lie in the fact that the Ottoman governors, appreciating the benefits of crop sharing practised for tax collecting, continued it while expanding the tax farming area. On the land newly transferred by *tapu* title, they also applied tax farming as a method of tax collection with the custom of crop sharing. In case the official collected the tax directly, he also relied on the custom of crop sharing by which the tax was collected as the government share. On infertile land where the government could not implement tax farming or land sale for *tapu* landholding, it carried out irrigation and land reclamation, co-operating with the tribal sheikhs and tribesmen without rescinding their custom and tradition. Such practice, recognized as institutional complementarity in economics, improved the production of crops on the fields and consequently increased tax revenues for the government.

The governors' achievements, however, have largely gone unnoticed by researchers. This book has traced the history of their reforms and modification

 | DOI:10.1163/9789004384347_011

on tax farming and land tenure in the province of Baghdad from Ali Rıza Pasha's reconquest of Baghdad in 1831 until the end of the British mandate period. Looking at their arrangement with the indigenous custom of crop sharing has provided a tool of observing agricultural improvements, which has also explained why Ottoman tax farming, landholding, and the custom of crop sharing continued through the British mandate period. After the modification by the Iraqi government, however, their characteristic combination broke down, and a grave consequence on peasants and tribal society occurred. For understanding the reason, Ottoman land reform needs to be evaluated, together with a glimpse into the continuity of the basic principle on *tapu* landholding through the mandate period.

The book first examined the practice of tax farming from the early Ali Rıza Pasha period, during which his government exercised little authority. While tax farming provided the governor with a tool for revenue collecting and tribal policy in the early Tanzimat period, it also served as a political tool for exercising his authority over the paramount tribal sheikhs. The government replaced lifetime tax farming permanently for short-term tax farming during the Tanzimat period, transferring lifetime farms to new farmers at public auction for a fixed term. This change was critical in putting tax farming under the government's strict control. It also benefitted tribal administration, promoted irrigation and land reclamation, and brought increases in agricultural production and tax revenues.

During the governorship of Necip Pasha (1842–49), the new method of tax farming came into wider use, providing support for agricultural production. Organizing projects to promote agricultural development, Necip Pasha repaired, at public expense, the Hindiya Barrage, irrigation canals, bridges, roads, and granaries. To raise revenues from the revitalized land, he divided it into tax farms and put them up for auction at prices that, although higher than they had been, still allowed farmers a handsome profit due to increased production. With a shortage of other investment opportunities, tax farming became a lucrative business, attracting the private investment of the governor himself and his relatives, officials, notables, military officials, ulema, merchants, traders, and tribal sheikhs. The sheikhs initially rejected the imposition of tax farming, instead of tribute, but upon realizing its profitability, they accepted it and soon tended to abuse their position. They offered bribes to the governors and officials concerned, charging oppressive taxes on their tribesmen. Because Necip Pasha overlooked the sheikhs' oppressive collection, large tribal uprisings broke out, causing his removal and more centralized government.

Between 1849 and 1852, under governors Abdi Pasha, Vecihi Pasha, and Namık Pasha in the first term, agricultural production regressed owing to destructive battles with the tribesmen. After a ceasefire was agreed, and during the term of Reşit Pasha (1852–57), tribal tax farming resumed, and the agricultural economy began to improve. Discerning the strategic importance of Baghdad as a frontier province during the Crimean War, Reşit Pasha prioritized the integration of the tribal domains. He auctioned off among the tribal sheikhs the district governorships, with the right to tax collecting, and appointed the highest bidder as the paramount sheikh, district governor, and tax farmer of his tribal district. Making short-term appointments, of between one to three years, moreover, the governor gained the upper hand over the sheikhs. Combining the tax farm and district into a single unit for tribal administration prevailed as a political tool of effective tribal administration, establishing peace and order in the agricultural areas. It also set a trend of the powerful tribal sheikhs' holding high posts in government.

During Reşit Pasha's relatively long term in office, commerce, foreign trade, transportation, and infrastructure all improved greatly as the urban entrepreneurs and tribal sheikhs to whom he granted the tax farms initiated irrigation and water-control projects. In addition, he discounted the auction price on infertile land and offered tax privileges and incentives to the sheikhs for engagement on them. Owing to these measures, the tribal sheikhs attempted to improve land productivity and extended the area of crop fields, organized their peasant tribesmen as field workers, provided them with seed, and engaged in commercial agriculture for profit.

The consistent procedures for auctioning and contract drew more private investors to tax farming, and the local custom of crop sharing ensured their collection of the government's share. Nevertheless, the spread of tax farming raised a new problem of patchy land use on the farms of business-oriented tax farmers, who avoided the costly maintenance of marginal areas. To address this issue, Reşit Pasha held a public sale of uncultivated lands under new land legislation. The purchaser was to maintain watercourses in his fields and take responsibility for farming according to the local practice. In return, the pasha gave the landholder various kinds of financial support, such as grants-in-aid for cleaning irrigation canals and constructing farmhouses for the settlement of the peasant tribesmen cultivating the fields. The land sale, which took place in limited areas in the Diyala River basin where the cost of irrigation was less, stimulated agricultural activities and raised the general income level of peasants in the area.

In solid congruity with peasant and tribal societies, the reformed practice of tax farming successfully raised agricultural revenues by way of crop sharing. However, the tax farmer's unwillingness to cultivate infertile land, because of the high cost of irrigating the land for reclamation, increasingly troubled the government, which needed more tax revenues. Consequent to Reşit Pasha's governorship, the Land Code of 1858 and Tapu Law of 1859 were applied, instituting the registration of transferred state land by *tapu* title. The Land Code particularly had an enduring impact on agriculture in irrigated areas, because of the governor's promotion of land sales and the complementing role of *tapu* with tax farming and customary private landholding for improving land use under the practice of crop sharing. How the Code was applied and why it should have contributed to agricultural production has been little understood. My examination has presented the unique combination of tax farming, landholding, and crop sharing as being a reason for agricultural improvement since Namık Pasha's governorship.

The book next explored the land tenure on agricultural land that evolved after the Land Code of 1858. By the early 1860s, the rigidity of land use and uncertainty in the land market became critical problems for the provincial government, which sought to exploit new tax resources and off-budget revenues. Specifically, in order to sell uncultivated land, the government launched the tenure of *tapu* land, based on the Ottoman Land Code of 1858, and initiated the idea of a private property right in land. Namık Pasha, having already become an important Porte figure, returned as Baghdad governor in 1861. He established a centralized government by putting districts and sub-districts under his direct command, and because he appointed the major officials, his authority became more dictatorial than that of previous governors over fiscal affairs and more powerful than ever over the tribal sheikhs. Although unyielding against the tribal rebellions, he took a more flexible approach to agriculture and land problems. On land tenure, he defined the tradition of *uqr* as a new entitlement of the owner to a share in the land's produce. This helped to diminish friction on the land transaction in the market. Now, uncultivated private land could be sold to a new landholder who would cultivate it. As the land consequently rose in value, however, the original private owners of the *uqr* land raised legal disputes in the Islamic court and stalled the use of the land. Where the cost of irrigation was high, or where the tax farmer was politically influential, the transfer of vacant land also was sluggish because the large government share reduced the net profit to the land purchaser.

The system of land registration by *tapu* came into effect when Midhat Pasha (1869–72) found a procedural solution to the *uqr* problem. Known for his various achievements in modernization, he established a local land registry office in Baghdad and issued the title deed locally to reduce registration time. In this way, he could supervise the application of strict rules on land tenure and more effectively protect the right of the new landholder against the original landowner's claim of *uqr*. He confirmed state ownership of the tribal lands and conferred the possession right on individual tribesmen who could cultivate the arable, barren land or uncultivated land and pay the tax from the produce, intending to settle them on their land and have them work permanently as agricultural labourers. Interest in landholding increased dramatically under his measures, though only the wealthy could afford the purchase, and raised larger revenues than before.

The land sale Midhat Pasha promoted for agricultural improvement eventually came to a halt, though the land registry of *tapu* continued. Assured by the custom of crop sharing for profiting, in 1881 Sultan Abdülhamid II (1876–1909) prohibited land sales to individuals. Instead, he began acquiring land under his own management, called *saniyya*, and his officials applied tax farming, leasing, crop sharing, and tribal custom to collect the owner's share from his estates. With increases in domestic demand and exports of agricultural products, his venture yielded high returns. In 1908, the Young Turk government took over the *saniyya* land, as state land called *mudawwala*, with no fundamental change in management. Since agriculture also continued to be a primary issue in the Young Turks' policies, the extension of cultivation beyond the existing croplands became a matter of particular concern, and the government promoted pump irrigation along the major canals. As the tribesmen again took on importance as labourers on the reclaimed lands and irrigation works, the government deregulated the system of land transfer involving the tribesmen. This change affected the contract between the pump owner and the cultivating sheikh and peasants, the tribal acquisition of *tapu*, and the registration of communal land cultivated by way of crop sharing, and it revitalized private investment in the purchase of pumps and settlement of the tribesmen on land.

After World War I and during the British mandate period (1921–32), without effective alternatives, *mudawwala* land was maintained as the state domain; under the same type of management as before, tax farming, leasing, crop sharing, and tribal ways continued. British officials reopened the land registry, recovered lost records, and resumed registration. Although agriculture's proportion of gross domestic product decreased, the volume of its production increased as a result of flood control, irrigation, and drainage works and the use of fertilizers, better seed, locust control, and engine-driven pumps. Because of this continuity, this book has shed light on the land and tax policies of the British mandate government and analyzed their amendments of the Ottoman practice of tax farming and land tenure.

During the British mandate period, the British, while working to complete the post-war reconstruction, found collecting tithe by way of tax farming, leasing, and crop sharing too inefficient and costly. Consequently, to abolish tithe and replace it with a land tax, their government began to lay down tax laws and regulations and made great efforts to assess the fair value of the land and put in order the land registration that had stopped during the war. On cultivated land extended by pump owners, the government no longer guaranteed gains as a new perception of the farm owner emerged under law. Now the cultivating peasant's share was inclusive of agricultural costs and borrowing, to his disadvantage, which considerably decreased his earnings, as the repayment of debt weighed heavily on him.

Towards the end of the British mandate period, the local custom that endorsed agricultural progress and consequent modernization began to disintegrate. The traditional share contracts for tax farming and crop sharing that had prevailed in the Ottoman period became obsolete. To replace them, the government resorted to hasty measures that permitted tenant farming and debt contracts, disregarding both the traditional tribal and local customs that coordinated agriculture, landholding, and tribal affairs. Implemented against the advice of some British officials to preserve that Ottoman legacy, it led to the hasty penetration of the market economy into tribal areas and impoverished cultivating peasants. Peasant tribesmen were now tenant farmers of landholders, and obliged to pay their rent in cash, but many of them defaulted. Doreen Warriner has pointed out this outcome in *Land Reform and Development in the Middle East*. This book has presented its historical background, dating from the Ottoman period a century earlier. Namık and Midhat Pashas could never have foreseen that the land reforms they crafted in the Ottoman context would eventually be reshaped by others to reduce the peasant tribesmen to impoverished tenants-at-will of tribal sheikhs and landowners.

APPENDIX

Lifetime and Short-Term Tax Farming

The restructuring of tax farming, from lifetime to short-term, requires scrutinizing because of its crucial effects on the fiscal system, tribal administration, agriculture, and economy in the province of Baghdad. During the governorship of Ali Rıza Pasha (1831–42), lifetime farms were confiscated and sold at auction, or if the tax farmer was deceased, the contract was not renewed for his heirs. Reşit Pasha (1852–57) used state laws to institute short-term tax farming throughout the province. The work of Mehmet Genç reveals the gravity of the change from lifetime to short-term tax farming in terms of the initial payment, tax, and years of contract. In doing so, it further indicates why the Baghdad governors actively undertook irrigation and land reclamation and encouraged tax farmers to clean the small branch canals running through their farms and improve agricultural activities in the field.

> The lifetime farmer paid the auction price of the tax farm at the beginning, usually between two to ten times the annual profits of the tax farm, which the treasury estimated by subtracting the tax payment to the government from the estimated annual revenue of the tax farm. The amount of the tax was fixed at the time of contract, either in cash or in kind, or both.... For example, for the collection of an export tax on cotton and cotton thread in Istanbul in 1792, the value of the tax was 14,357 akçe (120 akçe = 1 kuruş in 1788). Revenues collected by the tax farmer were estimated at 62,290 akçe. The profit of the tax farmer estimated by the Treasury was 47,932 akçe, and the payment in advance was settled at 280,500 akçe, about 5.85 times the yearly profit.[1]

Based on Genç's study, the systems of lifetime and short-term tax farming are summarized in Tables A.1 and A.2.

1 Mehmet Genç, "Osmanlı Maliyesinde Malikâne Sistemi," in Osman Okyar and Ünal Nalbantuoğlu, eds., *Türkiye İktisat Semineri* (Ankara: Hacettepe Üniversitesi, 1975), pp. 238, 260.

 | DOI:10.1163/9789004384347_012

TABLE A.1 Revenues of lifetime tax farming

	year 0	year 1	year 2	year 3	year n ...
Government	a (Ye–T)	T	T	T	T ...
Tax farmer	–a (Ye–T)	Y_1–T	Y_2–T	Y_3–T	Yn ...–T

a: multiplier from two to eight (Genç's estimate)
Y1: produce market price x share of the government at year 1
Ye: estimated value of produce x market price x share of the government
T: tax

TABLE A.2 Revenues of short-term tax farming (two-year contract)

	Period I (1–2)		Period II (3–4)		Period III (5–6)		Period IV (7–8)	
	year 1	year 2	year 1	year 2	year 1	year 2	year 1	year 2
Government	D_I+T_1	T_2	$D_{II}+T_1$	T_2	$D_{III}+T_1$	T_2	$D_{IV}+T_1$	T_2
Tax farmer	$-D_I+(Y_1-T_1)$	Y_2-T_2	$-D_{II}+(Y_1-T_1)$	Y_2-T_2	$-D_{III}+(Y_1-T_1)$	Y_2-T_2	$-D_{IV}+(Y_1-T_1)$	Y_2-T_2

Y1: produce market price x share of the government at year 1
T1: tax at year 1
D_I: deposit at period I

To illustrate the difference between lifetime and short-term tax farming, Table A.3 provides numerical examples of production, tax, and tax farmer's revenue, including the shares of peasants and other costs for eight years. In this example the multiplier a=4, and Ye=80. In lifetime farming, the production fluctuates, but the government tax is fixed, therefore the tax farmer's revenue fluctuates with the production. The tax farmer's total profit depends on the amount of initial payment and both the quantity of yearly production and its market prices.

TABLE A.3 Lifetime tax farming

	Deposit	Year 1	Year 2	Year 3	Year 4	Year 5	Year 6	Year 7	Year 8
Production	0	100	120	110	70	80	130	100	110
Government (tax)	320	20	20	20	20	20	20	20	20
Tax farmer	−320	80	100	90	50	60	110	80	90

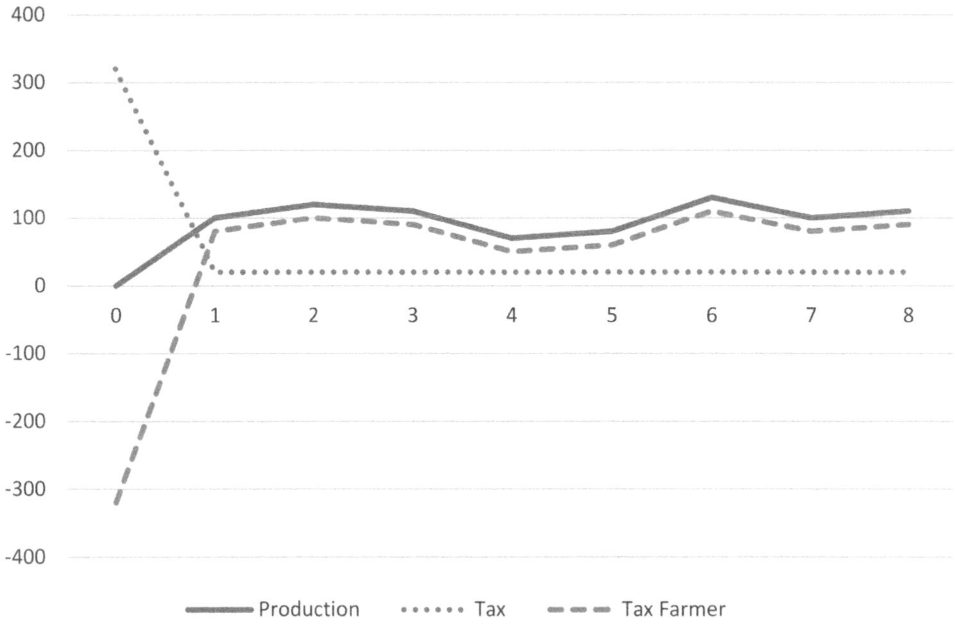

FIGURE A.1 Distribution of tax and tax farmer's profit in lifetime tax farming

Because of the fixed tax and deposit, maximizing the production could be a good incentive for the tax farmer to make investment in increasing production, assuming the market prices are steady. For this reason, he usually was a high-ranking official, wealthy urban notable, merchant, trader, or money changer who could afford both the initial payment and subsequent capital investment in the land.

To understand short-term tax farming, Table A.4 applies the same concept of Genç, using the same number for production, the same amount of initial tax, a two-year term of contract, and the reduced deposit. The amounts of the deposit and the tax depend on the production of the last period of tax farming, and the tax fluctuates more than the deposit because it is put up at auction.

TABLE A.4 Short-term tax farming

	Period I (Years 1–2)			Period II (Years 3–4)			Period III (Years 5–6)			Period IV (Years 7–8)		
	Deposit	Year		Deposit	Year		Deposit	Year		Deposit	Year	
		1	2		1	2		1	2		1	2
Production		100	120		110	70		80	130		100	110
Government (tax)		20	20		30	30		15	15		20	20
Tax and deposit	130	150	20	140	170	30	130	145	15	140	160	20
Tax farmer		−50	100		−60	40		−65	115		−60	90

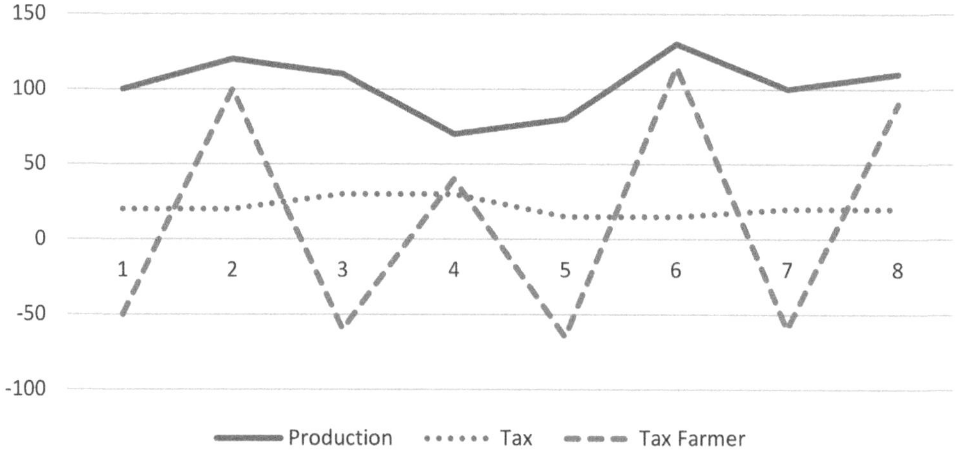

Note: To simplify, the tax farmer's revenue is linear, but the tax farm is assumed to be put up at auction for the term of two years.

FIGURE A.2 Distribution of tax and tax farmer's profit in short-term tax farming

The above two examples suggest a few noteworthy impacts from the shift from lifetime to short-term tax farming:

(1) The government's revenues continue to be the initial payment and the tax, but the initial payment becomes smaller and the tax larger than in lifetime tax farming.

(2) In short-term tax farming, the amounts of both the tax and the initial payment depend on the total production in each period because larger production in a

period is assumed to increase the amount of the tax and the initial payment in the next period.

(3) The government's revenue from the tax and the initial payment fluctuates according to the total production.

(4) The tax farmer's revenue fluctuates more than the government's revenue because the initial payment is small and the tax is affected by the production.

(5) Thus, increasing their revenues becomes an incentive for both the government and the tax farmer to increase the total production.

Glossary

ağnâm rüsûmı	tax on sheep and cattle
akd-i şirket	agricultural partnership
alây	regiment of troops
alây-ı piyâde	regiment of infantry
alây-ı süvâri	regiment of cavalry
amele rüsûmı	fees given to various workers in cultivated fields
arâzi memûru	land official
arâzi-i metrûke	public land
arâzi-i mevât	wasteland
arâzi-i miriye	state land
arâzi-i mülkiye	private land
aşîret-i aklâm-ı selse	tribe administered by government officials
aşîret bedevî	camel-and-horse breeding tribe
ayân	notable
batman	unit of weight equal to 12.82 kilograms (= 10 okka)
bedel-i misl	land price assessed by the land's market value
bekçi	watchman of a dyke
berât	imperial edict
berâtîl	commission of a tax farmer in tribal areas
berber	barber
bîle	unit of area for vegetable garden
binbaş-ı bozuk	irregular troops
büstân	unit of area for vegetable garden
cerîb	unit of area for date-palm grove equivalent to the area covered by one hundred palm trees
çertik	rice field watered by small runnel
Cezâ-yı Kanûn-nâme	Penal Code
çifthâne vergisi	household dues
çiftlik	quasi-private land established on state land
dâhiliye	domestic affairs
dâim-i mezra'a	rain-fed field
davâ-yı meclis	minor court in a district or sub-district
defterdar	treasurer
Defterhâne	Office of Land Registry
Defter-i Hâkanî	Office of Land Registry established under the *Defterhâne*
değirmân rüsûmı	tax charged on a watermill
demirbaş	stock reserved for farming

demirci	blacksmith
der-uhdeci	tax-collecting agent
devvâş	thresher
dirâ	tribal domain
dîvân-ı temâyîz	judicial court
dönüm	unit of area equal to 0.25 hectare
ekrâm	additional portion of free land given to a *serkâr* as a reward
emânet	direct collection of tax by government officials
emlâk-ı kayd	property record book
emlâk-ı mazbûta	private property
emr-i âlî	imperial decree
Erkân-ı Harbiye	Department of General Staff
ers	unit of length equal to 0.65 metres
eshâb-ı zemîn	landholder
eshâb-ı zirâi	peasant cultivator
evkaf-ı müdîr	*vakıf* official
Evkaf Hümayûn Nezâreti	Ministry of Religious Endowment
Evkaf Odası	Islamic Office of Religious Foundations
feddân	unit of area equal to 0.25 hectare. The area in the irrigated zone was determined according to the quantity of seeds sown
fellâh	tribesman specialized in farming
hafr rüsûmı	dues on a runnel in marsh areas
hakk-ı karâr	prescriptive right
hakk-ı müzâra'a	right to claim a share in the peasant's produce
hâne	household
***harâç* (land)**	private (land) established in the Islamic period
harâc-ı ferâğ	registration dues on the transfer of the possession right in state land
harâc-ı intikâl	registration dues of legitimate heirs to the possession right in state land
harâc-ı mukâseme	tax on *harâç* land assessed on the produce
harâc-ı muvazzaf	tax on *harâç* land assessed by the area of cultivation
hâriciye	foreign affairs
hâss	revenues of more than 100,000 akçe allocated to the sultan's household members and other high officials
hedâvî	gift
hums	land tax equivalent to one-fifth of the produce
hüccet-i şeriye	ownership deed
icâre-i muaccele	immediate payment; land value

icâre-i müeccele	deferred payment; tax
icâre-i zemîn	rent
ilmühaber	memorandum
ilmühaber-i muvakkat	(temporary) application form for land registration
iltizam	tax farming
irâde	imperial decree
kadı	judge
kadılık	office of the Islamic court
kâimmakâm	sub-district governor
kâimmakâmlık	district governed by a *kâimmakâm*
kanûn-nâme	code of laws
kârıh	hydraulic engineer
karûd	field irrigated by water lifts
kâtip	scribe
kazâ	sub-district of a province
kese	unit of currency equal to 500 kuruş (= kîse)
keyyâl	measurer
kibî	field in marsh areas
kışlak	mountain pasture
Komisyon-ı Umûr-ı Nâfia	Commission of Public Works
kuruş	unit of currency equivalent to 2.18 pence (110 kuruş = £1); equivalent to 1.92 pence (125 kuruş = £1)
lâyıha	memorandum
lazma	land deed registered in the Land Register which confers the possession right in state land to an individual
maârif	education
Mahkeme-i Istînâf	Superior Court of Appeal
mahlûl (land)	escheated or vacant; state (land) in which the possession right has reverted to the state
mâl kâtibi	financial clerk
mâl memûru	financial official
mâl-i miri	fixed tributes paid by the tribal sheikh
mallâk	landholder
mamlûk	military slaves bought in Georgia (*Gürcistan*)
mazbata	official report
meclis-i idâre	administrative council
Meclis-i Mahsûs-ı Vükelâ	Special Council of Ministers
Meclis-i Tanzimât	Council of Reformation
Meclis-i Vâlâ-yı Ahkâm-ı Adliye	Supreme Council of Judicial Ordinances

mevât **(land)**	waste (land)
mevleviyyet	chief judge
miri **(land)**	state (land)
muâvin	assistant
mudawwala **(land)**	state (land)
muhâsebeci	local treasurer
mukâtaa	unit of area irrigated by a major irrigation canal; unit of tax farm
mukayyid rüsûmı	household dues collected from migrating tribesmen
mutasarrıf	district governor
mutlak	free land given to a *serkâr* for tribal uses
mübâzirci	seed owner
müdîr	sub-district administrator; government official (director)
müdîrlik	sub-district administered by a *müdîr*
müfettiş	judicial inspector
mülâk **(land)**	private (land)
mülkiyet senedi	ownership deed
mültezim	tax farmer
müşâra	unit of area equal to 42.25 square metres (= 100 square erş)
mütevellî	administrator of a *vakıf* nominated in its *vakfiye*
müzâra'a	local practice of crop sharing
naccâr	carpenter
nâfia	public work
nâhiye	sub-district of a province administered by a deputy of the district governor
nâib	vice-judge
nakldâr	transporter
Nazîr-i Mukataât	Minister of State Estates
nehir icârı	fee for using water from a stream
niren	tribal custom of fallow
ocaklık	state land reserved for military expenses
okka	unit of weight equal to 1.282 kilograms
öşür	tithe
öşür **(land)**	private (land) established in the Islamic period
otlak	grassland
para	unit of currency equal to 0.096 penny (= 0.05 kruş)
piyâde	infantry
qirân	local unit of currency equal to 9.6 pence (= 5 kruş)
rakaba	ownership right
rüçhân **(*hakkı*)**	preference right

saih	field perennially irrigated by canal
sâkî	irrigation specialist of tribal origin
sancak	district of the province
***saniyya* (land)**	crown (land)
sarrâf	money changer or moneylender
sedd ağası	government official in charge of irrigation
serkâr	supervisor of farming, traditionally a village headman or tribal sheikh; bailiff
sipahi	cavalryman
sirkal	supervisor of farming or *serkâr*
sû bedeli	fee for water use
sû memûru	government official in charge of irrigation
sûlı mezra'a	irrigated field
süvâri	cavalry
şâhit ikâmesi	witness of birthplace
şahne	police guards
şâmî	local unit of currency equal to 8.5 kuruş
şerîk	agricultural partner
şeriye	juridical and legal affairs
şikâret	reward given to a *serkâr* or seed owner as a right to sow a certain quantity of seeds for his use
şikâret-i muâf	*şikâret* free of tax charges
şitvî	field along canal cultivated for winter crops
şuf'a (hakkı)	pre-emption right
tabûr	battalion of troops
tagar	unit of weight equal to 1,025.6 kilograms (= 800 okka)
tahrîr-i nüfûs-i kâtip	clerk of population census
tahrîrât	official letter
takrîr	official report
Takvîm-i Vakâyi	government newspaper
talimât	governmental instruction
Tanzimat	Reformation
tapu	land deed registered in the Land Register which confers the possession right in state land to an individual
tapu misli	land price estimated by the land's cultivation value
tapu senedi	title deed
tasarruf	possession right; the right of using and cultivating the state land
telegraf memûru	telegraph official
***temlîk* (land)**	privately-owned (land) conferred by the sultan

temlîk-nâme	patent which acknowledges a private holding of state land
ticâret	trade and commerce
Ticâret-i Kanûn-nâme	Commercial Code
timar	fief on which annual revenue is less than 20,000 akçe
***ukr* (Ar. *uqr*)**	share of the produce from private (*harâç* or *öşür*) land taken by the landowner as a rent or lien
ulema	legal specialist
vakfiye	act of an owner turning his property into a *vakıf*
***vakf-ı gayr-i sahîh* (land)**	*vakıf* (land) established on state land
***vakf-ı sahîh* (land)**	*vakıf* (land) established on private land
vakıf	religious endowment
vâlî	provincial governor
vasıta	commission of a tax farmer
vasle	local unit of area equal to 1,690 square metres (= 40 müşâra)
vecih	local unit of area equal to 2 feddân
vezne	unit of weight equal to 51.28 kilograms (= 40 okka)
vilâyet	province
yaylak	mountain pasture
yurtlık	state land reserved for military expenses
zabit	government official in a village
zeamet	fief on which annual revenue is from 20,000 akçe to 100,000 akçe
Zevrâ	government newspaper published in Baghdad
zirâ	unit of length equal to 0.65 metres

Bibliography

Archival Documents

Republic of Turkey, Prime Ministry, General Directorate of State Archives, Directorate of Ottoman Archives, Istanbul, Turkey.

İrâdeler:

Dahiliye, Hariciye, Meclis-i Vâlâ, Meclis-i Mahsus, Mesâil-i Mühimme, Şûrâ-yı Devlet

Bâb-ı Âlî Evrâk Odası Sadâret Eevrâkı:

Mektûbî Kalemi, Mektûbî Kalemi – Umum Vilâyet

Muallim Cevdet Tasnifi:

Evkâf, İktisat, Maliye

Yıldız Belgeleri:

Sadâret Resmî Mârûzat Evrâkı, Mütenevvî Mârûzat Evrâkı

Bâb-ı Âsafî ve Bâb-ı Âlî Defterleri:

Ayniyât Defterleri, Buyruldu ve İlmühaber Defterleri

Bâb-ı Defterî Defterleri:

Başmuhâsebe Kalemi

Dîvân-ı Hümâyûn Defterleri:

Mukâtaʿa Defterleri, Mukteza̧ Defterleri, Mühimme Defterleri

Maliyeden Müdevver Defterler

Maliye Nezâreti Defterleri:

Maliye Kalemi Defterleri, Mesârifât Defterleri, Vâridât Muhâsebesesi Defterleri

Istanbul University, Istanbul Turkey.

MS. TY 748, *Tanzîmât Hayriyeden İtibâren 1278 Tarihine Kadar Nesr Olunan Kavânîn ve Nizâmât.*

The National Archives, London, UK.

Colonial Office

Foreign Office

Public Record Office

HM Treasury

The British Library, London, UK.

India Office Records

Royal Geographical Society Archives, London, UK.

Newspapers

Takvîm-i Vakâyi (İstanbul [Istanbul], 1247–95 AH).
Zevrâ (Bağdad [Baghdad], 1286 AH).
La gazette financiére: organe financier, commercial et industriel des intérêts de l'empire Ottoman (Constantinople, 1909/10–1914).

Maps

Eastern Turkey in Asia, Baghdad, Sheet 39, Series I.D.W.O. No. 1522 a, 1: 250,000 ([S.I.]: War Office, 1917).
Eastern Turkey in Asia, Kerbela, Sheet 40, Series G.S.G.S. No. 1522 a, 1: 250,000 ([London]: [S.N.], 1915).
Bağdad ve Bağdad'tan Hille'ye kadar Harîtası [ms. map], (İstanbul Üniversitesi Kütüphanesi, TY 9486–8, n.d.).
Collingwood, W., *Trigonometrical Survey of a Part of Mesopotamia from Hilla to the Ruins of Niffer with the Rivers Euphrates and Tigris in 1861–62* [map] 1.2 cm = 2,000 yards (London, n.d.).
Jones, James Felix, *A Plan of the Ruin of Babylon and of the Surrounding Country* [map] drawn from the surveys of Commr. Selby I.N., Lieuts. Bewsher & Collingwood I.N., ed. Captn. Felix Jones, I.N. (London: John Murray, 1874), scale: 1:253,440, in *Dr. William Smith's Ancient Atlas*, ed. William Smith (London: John Murray, 1872–74).
Lynch, Blosse H., *The Tigris between Baghdad and Mósul*, 1 cm = 5 mile (published for the Journal of Royal Geographical Society by John Murray, 1839), in Blosse H. Lynch, "Note on a Part of the River Tigris, between Bagdád and Sámarrah," *The Journal of the Royal Geographical Society of London*, 9 (London, 1839).
Selby, W.B., and J.B. Bewsher, *Trigonometrical Survey of a Part of Mesopotamia from Sheriat el-Beytha (on the Tigris) to Tel Ibrahim with the Rivers Euphrates and Tigris in 1862–65* [map] 6 mm = 1,000 yards (London, n.d.), to accompany the paper by Liet. J.B. Bewsher/ [engraved by] Edwd. Weller, in Liutenant J.B. Bewsher, "On Part of Mesopotamia, from Sheriat El-Beytha, on the Tigris, and Tel Ibrahim," *The Journal of the Royal Geographical Society* 37 (London, 1867).
Selby, W.B., W. Collingwood, and J.B. Bewsher, *Surveys of Ancient Babylon and the Surrounding Ruins with Part of the Rivers Tigris and Euphrates in 1860 to 1865* [map] 1 cm = 1 mile (London, 1885).
Turkey, Başbakanlık Osmanlı Arşivi, Harîta 511, OD 5/2, *Osmanlı Devleti Zamanında Bağdad Vilâyet* [ms. map], 1:250,000 (n.d.).
Wyld, James, *Map of the Ottoman Dominions in Asia: with the Adjacent Frontiers of the Russian and Persian Empires* [map], 1 mile = 2.2 inches (London, 1835).

Government Publications

Great Britain

Great Britain, Admiralty War Staff, Intelligence Division, *A Handbook of Mesopotamia* (London: The Division, 1916–17).

Great Britain, Board of Trade, Department of Overseas Trade, *Economic Conditions in Iraq*, reported by C. Empson, Commercial Secretary to His Majesty's Embassy at Baghdad, August 1933 (London: HMSO, 1933).

Great Britain, Colonial Office, *ʿIraq: Report of the Financial Mission appointed by the Secretary of State for the Colonies to enquire into the Financial Position and Prospects of the Government of ʿIraq, 1925, presented by the Secretary of State for the Colonies to Parliament by Command of His Majesty, June, 1925* (London: HMSO, 1925).

Great Britain, Colonial Office, *Special Report on the Progress of ʿIraq during the Period 1920–1931* (London: HMSO, 1931).

Great Britain, the Directorate General of Public Security, Baghdad, *Reports of Administration of the Various Divisions and Districts of Mesopotamia for the years 1917–21* (Baghdad, n.d.).

Great Britain, House of Commons, "Reports from Her Majesty's Representatives respecting the Tenure of Land in the Several Countries of Europe: 1869–70, Presented to both Houses of Parliament by Command of Her Majesty, Part II," in *Accounts and Papers*, vol. 67 (London: Harrison and Sons, 1870), Enclosure 2 in No. 15, Trebizond, Consul Palgrave (signed W. Gifford Palgrave).

Great Britain, Naval Intelligence Division, *Iraq and the Persian Gulf* ([London]: Naval Intelligence Division, 1944).

Great Britain, Office of the Civil Commissioner, "Administration Report, Hilla District, 1917," in *Administration Report of the Baghdad Wilayat 1917, Mesopotamia* (Calcutta: Superintendent Government Printing, India, 1918).

Great Britain, Colonial Office, *Reports of Administration in the Districts of Sulaymaniyah, Erbil, Rawanduz, Kirkuk, Baghdad, Hilla, Dulaym, Diwaniya, Shamiya, and Basra* (Calcutta: Superintendent Government Printing, India, 1919).

Great Britain, Colonial Office, *Report by His Britannic Majesty's Government to the Council of the League of Nations on the Administration of ʿIraq for the year 1925* (London: HMSO, 1926).

Great Britain, Colonial Office, *Report by His Britannic Majesty's Government to the Council of the League of Nations on the Administration of ʿIraq for the year 1926* (London: HMSO, 1927).

Great Britain, Colonial Office, *Report by His Britannic Majesty's Government to the Council of the League of Nations on the Administration of ʿIraq for the year 1927* (London: HMSO, 1928).

Great Britain, Colonial Office, *Report by His Britannic Majesty's Government to the Council of the League of Nations on the Administration of 'Iraq for the year 1928* (London: HMSO, 1929).

Great Britain, Colonial Office, *Report by His Britannic Majesty's Government to the Council of the League of Nations on the Administration of 'Iraq for the year 1929* (London: HMSO, 1930).

Iraq, Department of Agriculture, *Cultivation for Winter or Shitwi Crops in Iraq* (Baghdad: Government Press, 1919).

Iraq, Department of Agriculture, *Report on the Mesopotamian Spring Harvest, 1919* (Baghdad: Government Press, 1919).

Iraq, Department of Agriculture, "Report by the Director of *Tapu*," *Administration Report of the Department of Agriculture in Mesopotamia for the Year 1920* (Baghdad: Government Press, 1921).

Iraq, Office of Civil Commissioner, *Administration Report of the Arbil Division for the Year 1919* (Baghdad: Government Press, 1920).

Iraq, Office of Civil Commissioner, *Administration Report of the Ba'qubah Division for the Year 1918* (Baghdad: Government Press, 1920).

Iraq, Office of Civil Commissioner, *Administration Report of the Hilla Division for the Year 1919* (Baghdad: Government Press, 1920).

Iraq, Office of Civil Commissioner, *Administration Report of the Baghdad Wilayat, 1917, Mesopotamia* (Calcutta: Superintendent Government Printing, India, 1918).

Iraq, Office of Civil Commissioner, *Review of the Civil Administration of Mesopotamia* (London: HMSO, 1920).

Iraq, Office of the Civil Commissioner, "Review of the Civil Administration of the Occupied Territories of al 'Iraq 1914–1918," compiled in the Office of the Civil Commissioner, Baghdad, Nov. 1918 (Baghdad: Government Press, 1918).

Iraq

Ahmed Fahmi, *Baghdād Vilāyeti Dākhilinde Arāḍiniñ Sūret-i Idāre ve Taṣarrufuna dā'ir Ta'limāt <Lā'iḥası>dir* (Baghdad, n.d.).

Republic of Iraq, Ministry of Economics, Principal Bureau of Statistics, *Statistical Abstract 1950* (Baghdad: The Bureau, 1952).

Turkey

Düstur, First Series (Dâr-i Saadet (İstanbul): Matbaa-i Âmire, 1289–1335 AH).

Mecelle (*Mecelle-i Ahkâmı Adliye*), prep. Himmet A. Berki (Ankara: Banka ve Ticaret Hukuku Araştirma Enstitüsü, 1959).

Sâlnâme-i Vilâyet-i Bağdad, 1317 AH (1901/02 *Milâdî*).

Sâlnâme-i Vilâyet-i Basra, 1318 AH (1902/03 *Milâdî*).

Sâlnâme-i Vilâyet-i Musul, 1310 AH (1894/95 *Milâdî*).

Books and Articles

ʿAbdul Raḥmān, ʿAbdul Raḥīm and Yuzo Nagata, "The Iltizām System in Egypt and Turkey," *Journal of Asian and African Studies* 14 (1977).

Abdullah, Thabit A.J., *Merchants, Mamluks, and Murder: The Political Economy of Trade in Eighteenth-Century Basra* (Albany: State University of New York Press, 2001).

Ahmed Lûtfî Efendi, *Vaka'anüvîs Ahmed Lûtfî Efendi Tarihi*, translit. Yüncel Demirel (Istanbul: Türkiye Ekonomik ve Toplumsal Tarih Vakfı, 1999), vol. 7.

Akgündüz, Ahmet, *Islâm Hukukunda ve Osmanlı Tatbikatında Vakıf Müessesesi* (Ankara: Türk Tarihi Kurumu Basımevi, 1988).

Akyıldız, Ali, *Tanzimat Dönemi Osmanlı Merkez Teşkilatında Reform (1836–1856)* (Istanbul: Eren Yaıncılık, 1993).

Akyıldız, Ali, *Osmanlı Finans Sisteminde Dönüm Noktası: Kâğıt Para ve Sosyo-ekonomik Etkileri* (Istanbul: Eren Yayıncılık, 1996).

Alchian, Armen A., and Harold Demsetz, "The Property Right Paradigm," *Journal of Economic History* 33, no. 1 (1973).

Al-Allāf, Abd al-Karīm, *Baghdād al-Qadīma* (Baghdad: Maṭbaʿat al-Maʿārif, 1960).

Al-Anṣārī, Aḥmad Ibn Nūr, *al-Nuṣrah fī Akhbār al-Baṣrah*, ed. Yūsuf ʿIzz al-Dīn (Baghdad: Maṭbaʿat al-Majmaʿ al-ʿIlmī al-ʿIrāqī, 1969).

Al-Ansari, Nadhir A., "Water Resources in Iraq," *Journal of the Geographical Society of Iraq* 14, no. 1 (1981).

Anscombe, Frederick F., *The Ottoman Gulf: The Creation of Kuwait, Saudi Arabia, and Qatar* (New York: Columbia University Press, 1997).

Ateş, Sabri, *The Ottoman Iranian Borderlands* (Cambridge: Cambridge University Press, 2013).

Âtıf, Kuyucaklızade Mehmet, *Arâzi Kânûnnâme-i Hümayün-i Şerhi* (Istanbul: Mahmut Bey Matbaası, 1319 AH [1900 or 1901]).

ʿAzzāwī, ʿAbbās, *Ta'rīkh al-ʿIrāq baina Iḥtilālayn* (Baghdad: Maṭbaʿat Baghdād, 1935–56), vols. 7–8.

Baali, Fuad, "Social Factors in Iraqi Rural-Urban Migration," *Americal Journal of Economics and Sociology* 40 (1966).

Baer, Gabriel, "The Agrarian Problem in Iraq," *Middle Eastern Affairs* 3, no. 12 (1952).

Barazi, Nuri, *The Geography of Agriculture in Irrigated Areas of the Middle Euphrates Valley* (Baghdad: Al-Ani Press, 1961).

Barkan, Ömer L., "Türk Toprak Hukuku Tarihinde Tanzimat ve 1274 (1858) Tarihli Arazi Kanunnamesi," *Türkiye'de Toprak Meselesi* (Istanbul: Gözlem Yayınları, 1980).

Barkan, Ömer L., "Türk-İslâm Toprak Hukuku Tatbikatının Osmanlı İmparatorluğu'nda Aldığı Şekiller: Malikâne-Dîvânî Sistemi," *Türkiye'de Toprak Meselesi* (Istanbul: Gözlem Yayınları, 1980).

Barkey, Karen, *Bandits and Bureaucrats: The Ottoman Route to State Centralization* (Ithaca: Cornell University Press, 1994).

Barnes, John R., *An Introduction to Religious Foundations in the Ottoman Empire* (Leiden: Brill, 1986).

Barth, Fredrik, *Principles of Social Organization in Southern Kurdistan* (Oslo: Bødrene Jørgensen, 1953).

Batatu, Hanna, *The Old Social Classes and the Revolutionary Movements of Iraq* (Princeton, NJ: Princeton University Press, 1978).

Belin, M., "Étude sur la propriété foncière," *Journal Asiatique* 5, no. 18 (1861) and 19 (1862).

Bewsher, J.B., "On Part of Mesopotamia Contained between Sheriat-el-Beytha, on the Tigris, and Tel Ibrahim," *Journal of the Royal Geographical Society of London* 37 (1867).

Birdal, Murat, *The Political Economy of Ottoman Public Debt* (London: I. B. Tauris, 2010).

Blaisdell, Donald C., *European Financial Control in the Ottoman Empire* (New York: Columbia University Press, 1929).

Blunt, Anne, *Bedouin Tribes of the Euphrates* (London: Harper & Brothers, 1879).

Boesch, Hans Heinrich, *Wasser oder Oel: Ein Buch uber den Nahen Osten* (Bern: Kummerly & Frey, 1944).

Buckingham, James S., *Travels in Mesopotamia* (London: H. Colburn, 1827).

Bussow, Johann, *Hamidian Palestine: Politics and Society in the District of Jerusalem, 1872–1908* (Leiden: Brill, 2011).

Al-Bustani, Mehdi J.H., "Bağdad'daki Kölemen Hâkimiyetinin Te'sisi ve Kaldırılması ile Ali Rıza Paşanın Vâliliği (1749–1842)" (Ph.D. diss., Istanbul University, 1979).

Çakır, Baki, *Osmanlı Mukataa Sistemi (XVI–XVIII. Yüzyıl)* (Istanbul: Kitabevi, 2003).

Çetinsaya, Gökan, *The Ottoman Administration of Iraq, 1890–1908* (London: Routledge, 2006).

Ceylan, Ebubekir, *The Ottoman Origins of Modern Iraq: Political Reform, Modernization and Development in the Nineteenth-Century Middle East* (London: I. B. Tauris, 2011).

Cezar, Yavuz, *Osmanlı Maliyesinde Bunalım ve Değişim Dönemi: XVII.yy dan Tanzimat'a Mali Tarih* (Istanbul: Alan Yayıncılık, 1986).

Chalcraft, John T., *The Striking Cabbies of Cairo and Other Stories: Crafts and Guilds in Egypt, 1863–1914* (Albany: State University of New York Press, 2004).

Chesney, Francis R., *The Expedition for the Survey of the Rivers Euphrates and Tigris* (London: Longman, Brown, Green, and Longmans, 1850), vol. 1.

Chiha, Habib K., *La province de Baghdad: Son passé, son présent, son avenir* (Cairo: Al-Maarif, 1908).

Cin, Halil, *Osmanlı Toprak Düzeni ve Bu Düzenin Bozulması* (Istanbul: Boğaziçi Yayınları, 1985).

Cin, Halil, *Mirî Arazi ve Bu Arazinin Özel Mülkiyete Dünüsümü* (Konya: Selçuk Üniversitesi, 1987).

Çizakça, Murat, *A Comparative Evolution of Business Partnership: The Islamic World and Europe, with Specific Reference to the Ottoman Archives* (Leiden: E. J. Brill, 1996).

Çizakça, Murat, "The Economy," in *The Cambridge History of Turkey*, ii: *The Ottoman Empire as a World Power, 1453–1603*, ed. Suraiya Faroqhi and Kate Fleet (Cambridge: Cambridge University Press, 2013).

Cole, Juan R. I., and Moojan Momen, "Mafia, Mob and Shiism in Iraq: The Rebellion of Ottoman Karbala 1824–1843," *Past and Present* 112, no. 1 (1986).

Cooper, Andrew F., *British Agricultural Policy, 1912–36* (Manchester: Manchester University Press, 1989).

Coşgel, Metin M., and Thomas J. Miceli, "Risk, Transaction Costs, and Tax Assignment: Government Finance in the Ottoman Empire," *Journal of Economic History* 65, no. 3 (2005).

Cuinet, Vital, *La Turquie d'Asie* (Paris: E. Leroux, 1892–1900), vol. 3.

Al-Dāhirī, ʿAbdul Wahhāb Maṭar, *Iqtiṣadiyāt al-Iṣlāḥ al-Zirāʿī* (Baghdad: Maṭbaʿat al-ʿĀnī, 1976).

Darling, Linda T., *Revenue-Raising and Legitimacy: Tax Collection and Finance Administration in the Ottoman Empire, 1560–1660* (New York: E. J. Brill, 1996).

Davies, Hywel D., "Observations on Land Use in Iraq," *Economic Geography* 33, no. 2 (1957).

Davison, Roderic H., *Reform in the Ottoman Empire, 1856–1876* (Princeton, NJ: Princeton University Press, 1963).

Dodge, Toby, *Inventing Iraq: The Failure of Nation Building and a History Denied* (New York: Columbia University Press, 2003).

Dowson, Ernest N. *An Inquiry into Land Tenure and Related Questions* (Letchworth, UK: Garden City Press, 1931).

Dūrī, ʿAbd al-ʿAzīz, "Baghdad," in *The Encyclopaedia of Islam* (Leiden: E. J. Brill, 1960).

Earle, Edward Mead, *Turkey, the Great Powers, and the Baghdad Railway* (New York: Macmillan, 1923).

Erol, Mine, *Osmanlı İmparatorluğunda Kâğıt Para* (*Kaime*) (Ankara: Türk Tarih Kurumu Basımevi, 1970).

Fahmy, Khaled, *All the Pasha's Men: Mehmed Ali, His Army and the Making of Modern Egypt* (Cambridge: Cambridge University Press, 1997).

Faroqhi, Suraiya, *Towns and Townsmen of Ottoman Anatolia: Trade, Crafts and Food Production in an Urban Setting, 1520–1650* (Cambridge: Cambridge University Press, 1984).

Faroqhi, Suraiya, *Pilgrims and Sultans: The Hajj under the Ottomans, 1517–1683* (London: I.B. Tauris, 1994).

Faroqhi, Suraiya, "Crisis and Change" in Halil Inalcik (ed.) with Donald Quataert, *An Economic and Social History* (Cambridge: Cambridge University Press, 1994).

Fattah, Hala M., "The Politics of Regional Trade in Iraq, c. 1840–1917," *New Perspectives on Turkey* 6 (Fall, 1991).

Fattah, Hala M., *The Politics of Regional Trade in Iraq, Arabia and the Gulf, 1745–1900* (Albany: State University of New York Press, 1997).

Fernea, Robert A., *Shaykh and Effendi* (Cambridge, MA: Harvard University Press, 1970).

Fieldhouse, David K. (ed.), *Kurds, Arabs and Britons: The Memoir of Wallace Lyon in Iraq, 1918–44* (London: I. B. Tauris, 2002).

Floor, Willem, "The Rise and Fall of the Banū Kaʿb: A Border State in Southern Kuzestan," *Iran: Journal of the British Institute of Persian Studies* 44 (2006).

Fox, William C., "Baghdad: A City in Transition," *The East Lake Geographer* 5 (1969).

Fraser, James Baillie, *Travels in Koordistan, Mesopotamia, & C.* (London: Richard Bentley, 1840).

Gabbay, Rony, *Communism and Agrarian Reform in Iraq* (London: Croom Helm, 1978).

Genç, Mehmet, "Osmanlı Maliyesinde Malikâne Sistemi," in Osman Okyar and Ünal Nalbantuoğlu (eds.), *Türkiye İktisat Semineri* (Ankara: Hacettepe Üniversitesi, 1975).

Genç, Mehmet, "Esham," in *Islam Ansiklopedisi* (Istanbul: Türkiye Diyanet Vakfı İslâm Ansiklopedisi Genel Müdürlüğü, 1988–), vol. 11 (1995).

Gerber, Haim, *The Social Origins of the Modern Middle East* (Boulder, CO: L. Rienner, 1987).

Goadby, Frederic M., and Moses J. Doukhan, *The Land Law of Palestine* (Holmes Beach, FL: Gaunt, 1998).

Granott, Abraham, *The Land System in Palestine: History and Structure* (London: Eyre & Spottiswoode, 1952).

Grove, Anthony N., *Journal of a Residence at Baghdad* (London: James Nisbet, 1832).

Gulick, Kahtan John, "Baghdad: Portrait of a City in Physical and Cultural Change," *Journal of the American Institute of Planners* 33, no. 4 (1967).

Güran, Tevfik, *Tanzimat Döneminde Osmanlı Maliyesi: Bütçeler ve Hazine Hesapları, 1841–1861* (Ankara: Türk Tarih Kurumu Basımevi, 1988).

Haider, Saleh, "Land Problems of Iraq" (Ph.D. diss., the London School of Economics and Political Science, 1942).

Haider, Saleh, "Land Problems of Iraq," in Charles Issawi (ed.), *The Economic History of the Middle East 1800–1914* (Chicago: The University of Chicago Press, 1966).

Haider, Shākir Nasir, *Aḥkām al-Arāḍī wa-l-Amwāl Ghair al-Manqūla* (Baghdad: Maṭbaʿat al-Iʿtimād, 1941–42).

Haj, Samira, *The Making of Iraq, 1900–1963: Capital, Power, and Ideology* (Albany: State University of New York Press, 1997).

Hasan, Muhammad Salman, "The Role of Foreign Trade in the Economic Development of Iraq, 1864–1964: A Study in the Growth of a Dependent Economy" in M. A. Cook (ed.), *Studies in the Economic History of the Middle East* (London: Oxford University Press, 1970).

Hathaway, Jane, *The Politics of Households in Ottoman Egypt: The Rise of the Qazdağlıs* (Cambridge: Cambridge University Press, 1997).

Herzog, Christoph, *Osmanische Herrschaft und Modernisierung im Irak: Die Provinz Bagad, 1817–1917* (Bamberg: University of Bamberg Press, 2012).

Hurşid Pasha, Mehmed, *Seyâhatnâme-i Hudûd* (Istanbul: Takvimhâne-i Âmire, 1277 AH [1860]), translit. into Turkish in Alâattin Eser, *Seyâhatnâme-i Hudûd* (Istanbul: Simurg Kitapcılık ve Yayıncılık, 1997).

Hüsnü, Hüseyin, *Arâzi Kânûnnâmesi Şerhi* (Istanbul: Kanaat Kitaphanesi 1324 AH [1908–09]).

İnalcık, Halil, "The Emergence of Big Farms, Çiftliks: State, Landlords, and Tenants," in Çağlar Keyder and Faruk Tabak (eds.), *Landholding and Commercial Agriculture in the Middle East* (Albany: State University of New York Press, 1991).

İnalcık, Halil (ed.), with Donald Quataert, *An Economic and Social History* (Cambridge: Cambridge University Press, 1994), vol. 2.

Ionodes, Michael George, *The Régime of the Rivers Euphrates and Tigris* (London: E. & F. N. Spon, 1937).

Ireland, Philip Willard, *'Iraq: A Study in Political Development* (London: Jonathan Cape, 1937).

İslamoğlu-İnan, Huri, *State and Peasant in the Ottoman Empire* (Leiden: E. J. Brill, 1994).

İslamoğlu-İnan, Huri, "Property as a Contested Domain: A Reevaluation of the Ottoman Land Code of 1858," in Roger Owen (ed.), *New Perspectives on Property and Land in the Middle East* (Cambridge, MA: Harvard University Press, 2000).

Issawi, Charles, *The Economic History of Turkey 1800–1914* (Chicago: The University of Chicago Press, 1980).

Issawi, Charles, *The Fertile Crescent, 1800–1914: A Documentary Economic History* (New York: Oxford University Press, 1988).

Jawād, Muṣṭafá, Aḥmad Sūsah, Muḥammad Makīyah, and Maʿrūf Nājī, *Baghdād* (Baghdad: Niqābat al-Muhandisīn al-ʿIrāqīyah, 1969).

Jastrow, Morris Jr., *The War and the Baghdad Railway* (London: J. B. Lippincott, 1917 and 1918).

Al-Jawāhirī, ʿImād Aḥmad, *Taʾrīkh Mushkilat al-Arāḍī fī al-ʿIrāq: wa Dirāsah fi al-Taṭawwurāt al-ʿĀmmah, 1914–1932* (Baghdad: Al-Jumhūrīyah al-ʿIrāqīyah, Manshūrāt Wizārat al-Thaqāfah wa al-Funūn, 1978).

Johl, S.S. (ed.), *Irrigation and Agricultural Development: Based on International Expert Consultation, Baghdad, Iraq, 24 February–1 March 1979* (Oxford: Pergamon Press, 1980).

Jones, James Felix, "Province of Baghdad," in *Selections from the Records of the Bombay Government*, no. 43 (Bombay: Bombay Education Society's Press, 1857).

Jwaideh, Albertine, "Midhat Pasha and the Land System of Lower Iraq," *St. Antony's Papers*, no. 16 (Oxford: Oxford University Press, 1963).

Jwaideh, Albertine, "The Saniyya Lands of Sultan Abdul Hamid II in Iraq," in George Makdisi (ed.), *Arabic and Islamic Studies in Honor of Hamilton A. R. Gibb* (Leiden: E. J. Brill, 1965).

Jwaideh, Albertine, "Aspects of Land Tenure and Social Change in Lower Iraq during the Late Ottoman Times," in Tarif Khalidi (ed.), *Land Tenure and Social Transformation in the Middle East* (Beirut: American University of Beirut, 1984).

Kaçar, Mustafa, "Osmanlı Telegraf İşletmesi," in Ekmeleddin İhsanoğlu and Mustafa Kaçar (eds.), *Çağını Yakalayan Osmanlı!* (Istanbul: İslâm Tarih, Sanat, ve Kültür Araştırma Merkezi, 1995).

Karakoç, Serkiz, *Tahsiyeli Arâzi Kânûnı ve Tapu Nizamnamesi* (Istanbul: Kitaphane-yi Cihan, 1340 AH [1924]).

Karpat, Kemal H., "Land Regime, Social Structure and Modernization in the Ottoman Empire," in William R. Polk and Richard L. Chambers (eds.), *Beginnings of Modernization in the Middle East* (Chicago: University of Chicago Press, 1968).

Karpat, Kemal H., *Ottoman Population, 1830–1914: Demographic and Social Characteristics* (Madison: The University of Wisconsin Press, 1985).

Kayi, Kerem, *Bagdad, 1831–1869: Untersuchungen zur Entwicklung einer osmanischen Provinzhauptstadt im 19. Jahrhundert* (Frankfurt am Main: Peter Lang, 2007).

Kent, Marian, *Oil and Empire: British Policy and Mesopotamian Oil 1900–1920* (London: MacMillan, 1976).

Al-Khālid, Khalīl Ibrāhīm, *Ta'rīkh Aḥkām al-Arāḍī fī l-ʿIrāq* (Baghdad: Al-Jumhūrīyah al-ʿIrāqīyah, Wizārat al-Thaqāfah wa-l-Iʿlām, Dār al-Rashīd, 1980).

Khoury, Dina Rizk, *State and Provincial Society in the Ottoman Empire: Mosul, 1540–1834* (Cambridge: Cambridge University Press, 1997).

Kiyotaki, Keiko, "Ottoman Land Policies in the Province of Baghdad, 1831–1881" (Ph.D. diss., University of Wisconsin-Madison, 1997).

Kiyotaki, Keiko, "The Implementation of the Administrative Law of 1864 in the Province of Baghdad," in Markus Köhbach, Gisela Procházka-Eisl, and Claudia Römer (eds.), *Acta Viennensia Ottomanica* (Vienna: Selbstverlag des Instituts für Orientalistik, 1999).

Kiyotaki, Keiko, "The Practice of Tax Farming in the Province of Baghdad," in Colin Imber and Keiko Kiyotaki (eds.), *Frontier of Ottoman Studies* (London: I.B. Tauris, 2005), vol. 1.

Kiyotaki, Keiko, "Ottoman State Finance: A Study of Fiscal Deficits and Internal Debt in 1859–63," Working Paper No. 90/05, Department of Economic History, London School of Economics, September 2005, published in Kaan Durukan, Robert W. Zens, and Akile Zorlu-Durkan (eds.), *Hoca, 'Allame, Puits de Science: Essays in Honor of Kemal H. Karpat* (Istanbul: The Isis Press, 2010).

Kiyotaki, Keiko, "The Legacy of Ottoman Land and Tax Systems in Iraq during the British Mandate Period," *International Journal of Turkish Studies* 19, nos. 1 & 2 (2013).

Koetschet, Josef (Dr. K), *Erinnerungen aus dem Leben des Serdar Ekrem Omer Pascha* (Sarajevo: D. A. Kajon, 1885).

Kuehn, Thomas, *Empire, Islam, and Politics of Difference: Ottoman Rule in Yemen, 1849–1919* (Leiden: Brill, 2011).

Kumar, Ram N., *Britain, India, and Iraq: A Study in British Diplomacy, 1898–1918* (Patna: Janaki Prakashan, 1992).

Kuran, Timur, "Separation of Powers and the Medieval Roots of Institutional Divergence between Europe and the Islamic Middle East," in Masahiko Aoki, Timur Kuran, and Gérard Roland (eds.), *Institutions and Comparative Economic Development* (New York: Palgrave Macmillan, 2012).

Kütükoğlu, Mübahat S., *Osmanlı Belgelerinin Dili* (*Diplomatik*) (Istanbul: Kubbealtı Akademisi Kültür ve San'at Vakfı, 1994).

Lambton, Ann K.S., *Landlord and Peasant in Persia* (London: Oxford University Press, 1969).

Lewis, Bernard, "Ottoman Land Tenure and Taxation in Syria," *Studia Islamica* 50 (1979).

Lier, Thomas, *Haushalte und Haushaltpolitik in Bagdad*, 1704–1831 (Würzburg: Ergon Verlag, 2004).

Litvak, Meir, *Shiʿi Scholars of Nineteenth-Century Iraq* (Cambridge: Cambridge University Press, 1998).

Longrigg, Stephen Hemsley, *Four Centuries of Modern Iraq* (Oxford: Clarendon Press, 1925).

Longrigg, Stephen Hemsley, *ʿIraq, 1900 to 1950: A Political, Social, and Economic History* (London: Oxford University Press, 1953).

Lorimer, John G., *Gazetteer of the Persian Gulf, Oman, and Central Arabia* (Calcutta: Superintendent of Government Printing, 1908–1915), vol. 2.

Low, Charles Rathbone, *History of the Indian Navy (1613–1863)* (London: Richard Bentley and Son, 1877).

Lynch, Henry Blosse, "Notes on a Part of the River Tigris, between Baghdad and Samarra," *Journal of Royal Geographic Society of London* 9, no. 3 (1839).

Al-Madfai, Kahtan A. J., "Baghdad," in Morroe Berger (ed.), *The New Metropolis in the Arab World* (New Delhi: Allied Publishers, 1963).

Mahdi, Kamil A., *State and Agriculture in Iraq: Modern Development, Stagnation and the Impact of Oil* (Reading, UK: Ithaca Press, 2000).

Malenbaum, Wilfred, *The World Wheat Economy, 1885–1939* (Cambridge, MA: Harvard University Press, 1953).

Mardin, Ebül'ulâ, *Toprak Hukuku Dersleri* (Istanbul: Stad Matbaası, 1947).

Markham, Clements A., *A Memoir of Indian Surveys*, 2nd ed. (London, 1878).

Marufoğlu, Sinan, *Osmanlı Döneminde Kuzey Irak* (Istanbul: Eren Yayıncılık, 1998).

McCarthy, Justin, *The Ottoman Turks: An Introductory History to 1923* (London: Longman, 1997).

Mikhail, Alan, *Nature and Empire in Ottoman Egypt: An Environmental History* (New York: Cambridge University Press, 2011).

Mikhail, Alan, *The Animal in Ottoman Egypt* (New York: Oxford University Press, 2014).

Moutafchieva, Vera P., *Agrarian Relations in the Ottoman Empire in the 15th and 16th Centuries* (New York: Columbia University Press, 1988).

Murphy, Rhoads, "The Ottoman Centuries in Iraq: Legacy or Aftermath? A Survey Study of Mesopotamian Hydrology and Ottoman Irrigation Projects," *Journal of Turkish Studies* 11 (1987).

Nājī, Ibrāhīm, *Kitāb Ḥuqūq al-Taṣarruf wa Sharḥ Qānūn al-Arāḍī* (Baghdad: Dār al-Islām, 1923).

Al-Najjār, Jamīl Mūsā, *Al-Idārah al-ʿUthmānīyah fī Wilāyāt Baghdād* (Cairo: Maktabat Madbūlī, 1991).

Nakash, Yitzhak, *The Shiʿis of Iraq* (Princeton, NJ: Princeton University Press, 1994).

Al-Nawwār, ʿAbd al-ʿAzīz Sulaymān, *Taʾrīkh al-ʿIrāq al-Ḥadīth min Nihāyat Ḥukm Dāwūd Bāshā ila Nihāyat Ḥukm Midḥat Bāshā* (Cairo: Dār al-Kātib al-ʿArabī, 1968).

Newman, Andrew, *Safavid Iran: Rebirth of a Persian Empire* (London: I. B. Tauris, 2006).

Nieuwenhuis, Tom, *Politics and Society in Early Modern Iraq* (The Hague: Martinus Nijhoff, 1981).

North, Douglass C., and Robert P. Thomas, *The Rise of the Western World: A New Economic History* (Cambridge: Cambridge University Press, 1973).

North, Douglass C., *Institutions, Institutional Change, and Economic Performance* (Cambridge: Cambridge University Press, 1990).

Ongley, Frederich (trans.), *The Ottoman Land Code* (London: W. Clowes and Sons, 1892).

Orhonlu, Cengiz, "Dicle ve Fırat Nehirlerinde Nakliyat," in Orhonlu, *Osmanlı İmparatorluğunda Şehircilik ve Ulaşım Üzerine Araştırmalar*, ed. Salih Özbaran (Izmir: Ege Üniversitesi Edebiyat Fakültesi Yayınları, 1984).

Ortaylı, İlber, *Tanzimattan Sonra Mahalli Idâreler, 1840–1878* (Ankara: Sevinç Matbaası, 1974).

Özbek, Nadir, *İmparatorluğun Bedeli: Osmanlı'da Vergi, Siyaset ve Toplumsal Adalet (1839–1908)* (Istanbul: Boğaziçi Üniversitesi Yayınevi, 2015).

Pamuk, Şevket, *The Ottoman Empire and European Capitalism, 1820–1913* (Cambridge: Cambridge University Press, 1987).

Pamuk, Şevket, *A Monetary History of the Ottoman Empire* (Cambridge: Cambridge University Press, 2000).

Pamuk, Şevket, "The Evolution of Financial Institutions in the Ottoman Empire, 1600–1914," *Financial History Review* 11, no. 1 (2004).

Pamuk, Şevket, "Institutional Change and the Longevity of the Ottoman Empire, 1500–1800," *Journal of Interdisciplinary History* 35, no. 2 (2004).

Pamuk, Şevket, "From Debasement to External Borrowing: Changing Forms of Deficit Finance in the Ottoman Empire, 1750–1914," in Ş. Pamuk and R. Avramov (eds.), *Monetary and Fiscal Policies in South-East Europe: Historical and Comparative Perspective* (*Conference Proceeding*) (Sofia: Bulgarian National Bank, 2006).

Pamuk, Şevket, *The Ottoman Economy and Its Institutions*, Variorum Collected Studies Series (Farnham, UK: Ashgate, 2009).

Penrose, E.T., and E.F. Penrose, *Iraq: International Relations and National Development* (London: Ernest Benn, 1978).

Petermann, Heinrich, *Reisen im Orient 1852–55* (Leipzig: Veit, 1860–61).

Pistor-Hatam, Anja, "Pilger, Pest und Cholera: Die Wallfahrt zu den Heiligen Stätten im Irak Als Gesundheitspolitisches Problem im 19. Jahrhundert," *Die Welt des Islams* 31, no. 2 (1991).

Pollard, Sidney, *The Development of the British Economy, 1914–1950* (London: Edward Arnold, 1962).

Poyck, A.P.G., "Farm Studies in Iraq," *Mededelingen van de Landbouwhogeschool te Wageningen, Nederland* 62, no. 1 (1962).

Quataert, Donald, *The Ottoman Empire, 1700–1922* (Cambridge: Cambridge University Press, 2000).

Rawlinson, Henry C., "Notes on a March from Zoháb at the foot of Zagros, along the Mountains to Khúzistán, and from Thence through the Province of Luristan to Kirmánsháh, in the year 1836," *Journal of Royal Geographical Society of London* 9, no. 2 (1839).

Rich, Claudius James, *Narrative of a Residence in Koordistan during the years 1830 and 1831* (London: Duncan and Malcom, 1839).

Rousseau, Jean Baptiste, *Description du Pachalik de Bagdad* (Paris: Treuttel et Würtz, 1809).

Sâbit (Süleyman Fâik), *Bağdad'da Kölemen Hükûmetinin Teşekkül ile İnkırâzına dâir Risâledir* (Istanbul, 1292 AH [1875]).

Sahillioğlu, Halil, "Sıvış Year Crises in the Ottoman Empire," in M. A. Cook (ed.), *Studies in the Economic History of the Middle East* (London: Oxford University Press, 1970).

Sahillioğlu, Halil, "Osmanlı Döneminde Irak'ın İdarî Taksimatı," *Belleten* 54, no. 211 (1990).

Salim, Shakir Mustafa, *Marsh Dwellers of the Euphrates Delta* (London: Athlone Press, University of London, 1962).

Salzmann, Ariel, "An Ancien Régime Revisited: 'Privatization' and Political Economy in the Eighteenth-Century Ottoman Empire," *Politics & Society* 21, no. 4 (1993).

Salzmann, Ariel, *Tocqueville in the Ottoman Empire: Rival Paths to the Modern State* (Leiden: Brill, 2004).

Sassoon, Joseph, *Economic Policy in Iraq, 1932–1950* (London: Frank Cass, 1987).

Şener, Abdüllatif, *Tanzimat Dönemi Osmanlı Vergi Sistemi* (Istanbul: İşaret Yayınları, 1990).

Seyitdanlıoğlu, Mehmet, *Tanzimat Devrinde Meclis-i Vâlâ (1838–1868)* (Ankara: Türk Tarih Kurumu Basımevi, 1994).

Shaw, Stanford J., "The Origins of Representative Government in the Ottoman Empire: The Provincial Representative Councils, 1839–1876," in Bayley R. Winder (ed.), *Near Eastern Round Table, 1967–1968* (New York: Near East Center and the Center for International Studies, New York University, 1969).

Shaw, Stanford J., "The Nineteenth-Century Ottoman Tax Reforms and Revenue System," *International Journal of Middle East Studies* 6, no. 4 (1975).

Shaw, Stanford J., and Ezel Kural Shaw, *History of the Ottoman Empire and Modern Turkey*, ii: *Reform, Revolution, and Republic: The Rise of Modern Turkey, 1808–1975* (Cambridge: Cambridge University Press, 1977).

Shields, Sarah D., *Mosul before Iraq: Like Bees Making Five-Sided Cells* (Albany: State University of New York Press, 2000).

Sinapli, Ahmet N., *Mehmet Namık Paşa* (Istanbul: Yenilik Basımevi, 1987).

Sluglett, Peter, *Britain in Iraq, 1914–1932* (London: Ithaca Press, 1976).

Sluglett, Peter, *Britain in Iraq: Contriving King and Country* (London: I.B. Tauris, 2007).

Sluglett, Marion Farouk-, and Peter Sluglett, "The Transformation of Land Tenure and Rural Social Structure in Central and Southern Iraq, c. 1870–1958," *International Journal of Middle East Studies* 15, no. 4 (1983).

Sousa, Ahmed, *Irrigation in Iraq: Its History and Development* (Baghdad: New Publishers, 1945).

Stanley, Eugene, "Business and Politics in the Persian Gulf: The Story of the Wönckhaus Firm," *Political Science Quarterly* 48, no. 3 (1933).

Stella, Peter, "Tax Farming: A Radical Solution for Developing Country Tax Problem?," IMF Working Paper 92/70, September 1992.

Tabakoğlu, Ahmet, *Gerileme Dönemine Girerken Osmanlı Maliyesi* (Istanbul: Dergâh Yayınları, 1985).

Tacan, Necati, "Tanzimat ve Ordu," in Turkey, Ministry of Education, *Tanzimat: Yüzüncü Yıl Dönümü Münasebetile* (Istanbul: Maarif Matbaası, 1940).

T.C. Başbakanlık Devlet Arşivleri Genel Müdürlüğü, *Başbakanlık Osmanlı Arşivi Rehberi* (Ankara, 2010).

Thomas, Parekunnel J., "Indian Currency in the Depression," *The Economic Journal* 48, no. 190 (1938).

Toprak, Zafer, "Osmanlı Devleti'nde Para ve Bankacılık," *Türkiye Ansiklopedisi* 3 (1991).

Tripp, Charles, *A History of Iraq* (Cambridge: Cambridge University Press, 2000).

Tuchscherer, Michael, "Some Reflections on the Place of the Camel in the Economy and Society of Ottoman Egypt," trans. S. Faroqhi, in Suraiya Faroqhi (ed.), *Animals and People in the Ottoman Empire* (Istanbul: Eren Yayıncılık, 2010).

Vaumas, L'abbé É. de, "Introduction Géographique à l'Étude de Baġdād," *Arabica* 9 (October 1962).

Vefik, Abudurrahman, *Tekâlif Kavâidi* (Istanbul: Matbaa-yı Kader: Kanaat Matbaası 1328–30 AH [1910–12]).

Venzke, Margaret L., "Aleppo's *Mālikāne-Dīvānī* System," *Journal of the American Oriental Society* 106, no. 3 (1986).

Venzke, Margaret L., "Special Use of the Tithe as a Revenue-Raising Measure in the Sixteenth-Century *Sanjaq* of Aleppo," *Journal of the Economic and Social History of the Orient* 29, no. 3 (1986).

Warriner, Doreen, *Land and Poverty in the Middle East* (London: Royal Institute of International Affairs, 1948).

Warriner, Doreen, *Land Reform and Development in the Middle East: A Study of Egypt, Syria, and Iraq* (London: Oxford University Press, 1962).

Wellsted, James Raymond, *Travels to the City of the Caliphs, along the Shores of the Persian Gulf and the Mediterranean*, 2 vols. (London: Henry Colburn, 1840).

Willcocks, William, *The Irrigation of Mesopotamia* (London: E. & F. N. Spon, 1911).

Willcocks, William, "Two and a Half Years in Mesopotamia," *Blackwook's Magazine* 199 (March 1916).

Wirth, Eugen, *Agrargeographie des Irak*, Hamburger Geographische Studien Im Selbstverlag des Institut für Geographie und Wirtschaftsgeographie der Universität Hamburg (Hamburg, 1962).

Yaycıoğlu, Ali, *Partners of the Empire: Crisis of the Ottoman Order in the Age of Revolutions* (Stanford, CA: Stanford University Press, 2016).

Yediyıldız, Bahaeddin, *Institution du Vaqf au XVIIIe Siecle en Turquie* (Ankara: Société d'Histoire Turque, 1985).

Index

If you have any questions regarding this title, please contact:

Koninklijke Brill BV
Plantijnstraat 2
2321 JC Leiden
Email: info@brill.com

Batch number: 10703823